PRAISE FOR *STORMING THE COURT*

"Guantánamo, Episode I . . . [a] brisk and thoughtful account."
—*San Francisco Chronicle*

"A page-turner . . . [Goldstein has] a journalist's eye and a lawyer's keen deconstruction ability."
—*The Hartford Courant*

"A compelling story with contemporary significance."
—*Booklist*

"A nonfiction book with the drama and pacing of a novel. *Storming the Court* presents the most vivid account of the life of law students since the 1970s-era novel and film *The Paper Chase*."
—*Connecticut Post*

"A breathless narrative . . . interesting both as a backdrop to today's situation at Guantánamo and because he gives a near-perfect portrait of Harold Koh."
—*Legal Times*

"Beautifully told . . . profoundly moving."
—William Sloane Coffin, former chaplain of Yale University

"*Storming the Court* movingly captures the emotional highs and despairing lows of the victims and their lawyers. . . . It reads like a mystery thriller that grips you from the first page to the last."
—Gerald Stern, author of *The Buffalo Creek Disaster: How the Survivors of One of the Worst Disasters in Coal-mining History Brought Suit Against the Coal Company—and Won*

STORMING THE COURT

HOW A BAND OF LAW STUDENTS
FOUGHT THE PRESIDENT—AND WON

Brandt Goldstein

SCRIBNER
New York London Toronto Sydney

♨

SCRIBNER
1230 Avenue of the Americas
New York, NY 10020

First Scribner trade paperback edition 2006

SCRIBNER and design are trademarks of
Macmillan Library Reference USA, Inc., used under license
by Simon & Schuster, the publisher of this work.

For information about special discounts for bulk purchases,
please contact Simon & Schuster Special Sales:
1-800-456-6798 or business@simonandschuster.com.

DESIGNED BY LAUREN SIMONETTI
Set in Simoncini Garamond

Manufactured in the United States of America

1   3   5   7   9   10   8   6   4   2

Library of Congress Cataloging-in-Publication Data
Goldstein, Brandt.
Storming the court: how a band of Yale law students fought the President and
won/Brandt Goldstein.
p. cm.
Includes bibliographical references and index.
1. United States—Trials, litigation, etc. 2. Refugees—Law and legislation—United
States. 3. Detention of persons—United States. 4. Haitians—Cuba—Guantánamo Bay
Naval Base.
I. Title.

KF228.U5G65 2005
342.7308'dc22   2005047768

ISBN-13: 978-0-7432-3001-8
ISBN-10:   0-7432-3001-9
ISBN-13: 978-1-4165-3515-7 (Pbk)
ISBN-10:   1-4165-3515-2 (Pbk)

The names of some individuals in this book have been changed.

For my parents,
Jone Rymer
and
Irwin J. Goldstein

Contents

One

THE COUP

Port-au-Prince, September 28, 1991.

A NTENOR JOSEPH SWEPT into KID headquarters, several men flanking him. The building's courtyard was packed, his wife and fellow democracy activist, Yvonne Pascal, wedged in among the nervous crowd. It was late afternoon, hot and still, with heavy clouds interrupting the sunshine.

"*Tande! Tande!*" he yelled. "Listen up! We think there's going to be a coup tonight! Everybody's got to leave!"

Yvonne's heart jumped. There was an explosion of protest in Creole.

"How do you know?" someone called out.

"Evans got the word," Antenor replied, his voice echoing off the walls. "There's no way to stop it now. *Go home!*"

The shouting continued, but people began streaming out. Rumors had been flying through the city for weeks: President Jean-Bertrand Aristide was in trouble. Antenor's warning only confirmed what everyone had feared.

Yvonne fought her way through the crowd to her husband. He pulled her aside.

"Tonight, tomorrow," he said. "No one knows for sure. But it's coming."

Her chest felt tight. She had to get home, find the children.

"Don't go outside," he said. "Whatever you do."

"What about you? Where will you be?"

"I may not see you for a while," he whispered, holding her close. Everyone at the meeting was in danger, but as a key figure in KID—the

Confederation for Democratic Unity—Antenor would now be a hunted man.

He hurried Yvonne outside, his arm around her. Downtown Port-au-Prince was a circus of hawkers and hustlers, the street choked with dented pickup trucks and *tap-tap* buses in frantic colors. Horns blared and thick blue exhaust clouded the air. Antenor signaled for a taxi, something they could not really afford. Several motored by—beat-up Toyotas and Hondas jammed with passengers—and he finally broke into a run, flagging one down at a clogged intersection. Yvonne squeezed in, and as the car pulled away, she watched her husband stride back toward the courtyard.

The cab careened around open-air markets and abandoned construction projects, then descended into Cite Soleil, a labyrinth of tin shanties and open sewers. Yvonne paid the driver and scurried down a muddy pathway. Shriveled men were hunched over dominoes. Bare-chested children in rags kicked at an empty plastic jug. Dogs scavenged through garbage, their ribs straining against sagging flesh.

She reached her three-room shanty, breathless. Her mother, Thérèse, was cooking rice and beans over a charcoal fire. Her six-year-old son, Jacques, sat on the floor, copying his name on a scrap of paper. Yvonne gave the boy a relieved kiss, then ran out to retrieve her eleven-year-old, Daniel, who was playing soccer in the nearby dirt churchyard. He didn't want to leave, but she dragged him home.

With both kids inside, Yvonne ventured out to warn the neighborhood about the coup. There was little need. People already knew. She could feel it around her—a hard, dark fear. Young men were stockpiling machetes and rakes, shovels and old planks of wood, anything that might serve as a weapon. She grabbed someone's arm. You can't fight bullets with a stick, she argued. They had to resist, the man said. If enough people went to the palace, they could stop the military.

She shook her head. This was sheer stupidity. We have to stay alive for tomorrow! she cried. But they wouldn't listen. Resigned, she used the fading daylight to fill extra jars with water at the public stone fountain. It would be too dangerous to go out after dark.

Through the evening and all the next day, Yvonne and her family waited, tense, uncertain. Other local organizers rapped on the door, slipped in to talk with her. The *teledyòl*—rumor mill—was churning. But there were no soldiers around. It was strangely quiet.

And then, as darkness fell, gunfire erupted.

Yvonne raced into a bedroom with the boys and yanked them to the floor, shielding their bodies with her own. Bullets ricocheted off the corrugated metal roof with a loud *pang-pang-pang*. There was shouting, punctured by more gunshots. Screams and cries followed, and her children broke into sobs. She crouched over them, singing, raising her voice whenever the guns grew loud. It went on all night, the air laced with the acrid smell of burning tires from protest barricades. Well after sunrise, her children finally collapsed into sleep.

Later, the news crackled over her father's transistor radio on Radio Soleil: Aristide had been forced out of the country. She slumped in despair. Everything she and Antenor had worked for— Aristide's election, a new beginning, a country where her children could have hope—was gone. Yvonne lay low with her family for several days, worrying, brooding. Finally, with the gunfire growing sporadic and distant, she stole outside to investigate. Clumps of melted tires smoldered in the alleys. Bodies lay in pools of blood, flies buzzing around them, dogs tugging at their limbs. A heavy truck rumbled by on the main road. Her neighbor passed on the rumor: the coup leaders had ordered the dead dumped in Titanyen, the paupers' graveyard north of the capital.

Darting through the shadows, shanty to shanty, Yvonne made her way to the nearby pawnshop. She gave the owner a gourde, about twenty cents, to use the telephone. There was no answer at the KID office. She dialed the number again and again with no luck. Fearing the worst, she finally risked a visit to another KID member in a neighboring slum. Antenor, he reassured her, was safe. He'd gone into hiding in the Carrefour-Feuilles section of town, a poor hillside quarter overlooking the Port-au-Prince Bay. But KID's headquarters had been ransacked and the group's leader, Port-au-Prince mayor Evans Paul, had been arrested and beaten at the airport.

Yvonne steeled herself. While she did not have her husband's public profile, she was a known activist in Cite Soleil, which put her in serious danger. Graver still, authorities would see her as a means to track down Antenor. She got home as fast as she could, and with soldiers prowling the streets, she kept to the shanty, her children beside her.

Several weeks later, her husband remained in hiding; Aristide was still out of the country; and Cite Soleil had plunged into a state of constant terror. Every day now, people in Yvonne's neighborhood were slipping away. She knew some were bound for the countryside, seeking refuge with friends or relatives. But others were headed for the coastal areas— the beaches near Cap-Haïtien; the island of La Gonâve—where the boats lay waiting.

New Haven, September 4, 1991.

A sturdy Asian man shuffled into class with an overstuffed leather brief-case and a Lands' End canvas bag bursting with papers. He wore a navy blue blazer, and his stick-straight hair framed an open, fleshy face. He broke into a big grin.

"Hi, hi. I'm Harold Koh," he said in a guttural buzz. "Welcome to Yale Law School."

Koh greeted several students by name. They glanced around, wondering how he knew who they were.

"You've all got four classes this semester: constitutional law, torts, contracts—and the one that really matters." Koh thrust his index finger in the air and his eyes lit up.

"This one! Procedure!"

Tory Clawson, a lanky first year in Birkenstocks, laughed along with everyone else. Nothing seemed to have gone right during her first day, but she'd heard that Koh's class was something special.

"Civil procedure is the ball game!" Koh shouted. "The ball game. Everything comes down to procedure. Does everyone understand this?" He paused as if he expected the students to answer.

"If you don't know procedure, nothing else matters. Contracts. You can have the most airtight contract claim in the world. You don't know how to file a complaint, you're out of luck. Torts. Someone can run over you with a tractor while a TV news crew films it. You don't understand how to take discovery, you'll never get the videotape!"

More laughter. Koh took off his coat and paced back and forth, limping slightly on his right leg.

"Procedure. Procedure. Everything," he said in a self-mocking tone, "comes down to procedure."

Koh went to the blackboard. Papers rustled on the desks as Tory and the other students reached for their pens.

In small capital letters, in the upper right-hand corner of the board, he wrote: 1. BIPOLAR & ADVERSARIAL.

"What's the essence of a lawsuit in our system?" he asked, eyebrows raised. No one answered.

"In a civil system like they have in France, everyone cooperates in a search for truth. The parties work together to figure out what happened and how to make sure justice is done. But what do we do here in America? What do we do?"

He made a fist and shook it.

"Fight?" someone offered.

"Right! We fight. We fight. Our system is bipolar: two parties. And it's adversarial. *Roe versus Wade. Brown versus Board. Marbury versus Madison.*"

Tory scribbled quickly.

Koh clenched both fists and held them out. "Let's say there's a disagreement between two parties. They start here." He set his fists a few inches apart, indicating the extent of the dispute.

"But when they go to court, they don't cooperate. They each take a harder line. They stake out positions here"—he moved one fist far to his right—"and over here"—and the other fist far to his left.

"Then pow!" He slammed his fists together. "They collide! And through this adversarial system, through this fight, what do we expect to happen?"

He paused for a moment, waiting for an answer.

"We expect the truth to emerge, right? Justice to be done. Right?"

Tory had come to Yale hoping to get involved in human rights work, though she wasn't quite sure what lawyers in that area actually did. The idea had seized her during a stint volunteering in Nepal, where she'd witnessed the country's 1990 democratic revolution firsthand. After marching with hundreds of thousands through Kathmandu's dusty streets, she dashed for cover as the soldiers opened fire. Terrified, she watched as the crowds sprinted off barefoot, leaving behind crumpled bodies amid a sea of flip-flops. But the momentum shifted that day. The king soon lifted the ban on political parties, and jubilant throngs flooded the city squares. Surrounded by bright flags and chanting activists, Tory felt an overwhelming exhilaration. These people had changed the world.

Many Americans had been talking about going home, but that was the last thing on Tory's mind. Despite continued violence—and the worries of her parents back in Bernardsville, New Jersey—she was now more determined than ever to stay and help the country as much as she could.

She'd been driven by that impulse since the age of twelve, when she saw a Save the Children ad featuring a little Nepalese girl. The flickering images of a destitute child among the craggy mountains captured her imagination, gave her a purpose. She took up babysitting so she could sponsor a child herself, mailing off checks to the organization every month. By age twenty-two, she had spent a year and a half in Nepal, working as a volunteer in literacy programs and fighting the sale of children into sexual slavery. But in the wake of the revolution, she wanted to do something bigger, more political. Then she learned that American attorneys had come to Kathmandu to draft the country's new constitution. A human rights lawyer, she thought. That's what I'll be.

But now that she'd arrived in New Haven with her batik print shirts and Nepalese bedspread, law school seemed to have been an awful plan. The Sterling Law Quadrangle, a run-down Gothic warren, teemed with superachievers who wore their ambitions like designer labels. There were published authors, national champion debaters, people who'd triple-majored in college. Some students already had Ph.D.'s. Political arguments raged in the dimly lit hallways and the cramped courtyard. Everyone seemed to know so much about the law already—the names of the big firms in New York and Washington, the important judges. She felt she'd never catch up.

"Each of you thinks you're the mistake," Dean Guido Calabresi had sighed at his September welcome speech. "You believe you're the one student who shouldn't be here. The one who'll be exposed as a fraud. Well, I assure you, none of you is that person." Tory didn't buy it. I *am* the mistake, she thought, eyeing the other members of her 160-person class. Though she'd excelled at Trinity College, getting nearly all A's, she couldn't shake the feeling that she'd been swimming in a very small pond. She was never going to make it at Yale.

Normally outspoken, she turned mute in class, scared of sounding stupid. The dense course material disappointed and befuddled her. There was nothing about human rights. Instead, she was puzzling over an ancient contract case about the late delivery of a crankshaft for a mill. And while she'd had high hopes for constitutional law, it turned out to be a quagmire of irrelevance. Who *cared* whether a farmer had to obey a wheat production quota? Within days she hated opening her casebooks.

Civil procedure, the least intuitive of Tory's four required courses, should have been the biggest problem of all. It covered the technical rules of the system—how to file and litigate a case in court—and was chock-full of quirky, intricate concepts. But Professor Koh blew away the Socratic confusion of her other classes. With a patter of corny jokes and references from Michael Jackson to Marlon Brando, he reduced the most incomprehensible case to a simple idea, introduced every new concept in a way she could readily understand.

"Forum shopping! Forum shopping!" Koh repeated. "Does everyone understand what this means?"

Tory scrawled the words in her notebook.

"Parties looking for a jurisdiction with law that's more favorable or a judge more likely to rule for them. How's it work? How's it work? My daughter. Emily. Just six years old! She wants soda. So what's she do? 'Mommy, can I have some Sprite?'"

Here Koh's speech mimicked his daughter's—high-pitched, pleading—to much laughter. Then he was back to his own voice, earnest, intense.

"My wife says, 'No.' So what's Emily do? She's smart! She comes to me! *A different judge!* 'Daddy, can I have some Sprite?' 'Sure!' What's just happened? My daughter is a party who has gone from a less favorable forum to a more favorable one to secure the ruling she wanted! That's forum shopping!"

No matter how complicated a topic first seemed to Tory, Koh made it accessible with a divide-and-conquer strategy. He cut every issue into tiny parts, then numbered every one, delivering each part to the class as a discrete nugget of crucial information. "There are four (or six, or three) things you need to know . . ." prefaced his analysis of any doctrine, criticism of any theory. The legal opinions Tory read went on for pages and pages, a mass of foreign jargon that she would highlight, underline, and reread—all to no avail. But at the end of class, when Koh was done with a case, he'd tied it up in a neat, numbered bundle.

Dispensing with the meandering philosophical style of Tory's other courses, Koh controlled his students as much as he did the material. They were absorbed into his lectures, literally assigned parts to play. With each topic he introduced, he would designate a person as the keeper of that snippet of learning.

Whenever he returned to the topic, he'd cue the student: "Because federal judges are what kind of judges?"

"Article III!" came the answer.

"Article III judges. Article III of the Constitution!" Koh shouted. "Appointed for how long?"

"For life."

"For life! Why does that matter?"

"They don't have to worry about political pressure."

"Right! That was the first day of class. Remember? The seven parts of our traditional bipolar model of adjudication! Number five: a neutral, competent decision maker. In the federal courts, a judge who is appointed for life. A decision made by the framers of the Constitution to ensure that judges are impartial and will not try to appease the political branches of our government!"

At times, Koh conducted class almost as if it were an orchestra, gesturing and pointing to students as he turned the pages of his casebook. It all happened at a dizzying pace and Tory had to write as fast as she could to keep up. There were days when she felt overwhelmed by the sheer amount of material, and Koh's intensity could be intimidating. But she left class optimistic and energized, the logic of the subject beginning to take hold in her mind, the cases starting to fit together in a grand pattern.

It wasn't just that she felt Koh helped her truly understand the law. It was his passion and conviction that the legal system could secure justice. Now and then, he would point out where an outcome was unfair, where critics had their concerns: "We don't *really* believe judges are neutral, do we? The tradition of legal realism, right? It's all politics?" But most of the time, he seemed to side with the reasoning of the case they were studying—explaining why it made sense and how the law had evolved over time to become a fair system.

Tory knew there were other celebrated teachers at Yale. She'd heard the students rave about them in the chandeliered dining hall: Bruce Ackerman, an eminent constitutional theorist, all waving arms and mad chalkboard slashes; Akhil Amar, a wispy, bearded prophet who specialized in the mind-bending subject of federal jurisdiction; Owen Fiss, a guru of 1960s Supreme Court jurisprudence who, according to legend, had once gleefully hurled the Federal Rules of Civil Procedure across the classroom to demonstrate their worthlessness.

But for Tory, Koh had a charismatic presence all his own, and many at Yale seemed to share her enthusiasm. While the average law school class had thirty to forty students, Koh's lecture courses ballooned to two hundred people or more. Students crowded around him in the halls and

jammed his office, repeated favorite lines from his courses like a cate-
chism, and sought his advice on everything from summer jobs to romantic interests. Tory still had doubts about her other classes and her own
intellectual talents. She also remained unsure where human rights fit into
the equation. But Koh made her hopeful that Yale was the right place for
her after all.

Lisa Daugaard had nothing but disdain for Harold Koh and pretty much
all of Yale Law School, for that matter. In her estimation, it was packed
with corporate careerists and liberal sellouts, and the institution itself was
too hidebound and self-satisfied to do much good in the world. Her first
semester, she lit into her contracts professor for teaching a case involving
a black lynching, nearly driving the woman to tears. Then she went after
her constitutional law instructor for giving short shrift to *Korematsu,* the
Supreme Court decision allowing internment of Japanese Americans during World War II. Outside of class, she ran with the Law and Liberation
crowd, who saw the legal system as a tool for rich, white men to maintain
their money and power. If there was a leftist cause at the law school, Lisa
Daugaard was inevitably protesting louder than anyone, and it wasn't
long before many at Yale were calling her "Lisa Do-Good."

Though she was still in her early twenties, Lisa's activism stretched
back two decades. When she was only four, she'd tugged her younger sister out to the backyard of their Seattle home, positioned her against one
of the family's two cottonwood trees, and tied her to the trunk with a
jump rope. Lisa then bound herself to the other tree. Their father soon
emerged to find Lisa glaring at him defiantly, her confused sister beside
her. He decided not to cut down the cottonwoods after all.

Lisa's activist drive was powered by a ferocious intellect. She skipped
kindergarten and then everything after seventh grade, enrolling at the
University of Washington at the age of twelve. Most every subject came
easily to her, but it was history that seized her imagination. She devoured
books about Europe's exploitation of Africa and the Caribbean during
the era of colonialism. The abuses committed by the Western powers infuriated her, and she fantasized about joining an indigenous rebellion
back in the nineteenth century.

Lisa finally found the fight she'd been itching for when, just seventeen
years old, she entered graduate school at Cornell. It was the mid-1980s,
and students across America were demanding that universities divest

their endowments of companies doing business in South Africa, then still under apartheid. Lisa became a leader in one of the bitterest divestment struggles in the nation, with protesters numbering in the thousands. Her clashes with campus police began with sit-ins, then escalated after she padlocked a building to prevent a board of trustees' meeting. She ended up with an arrest record longer than her transcript. Eventually, the officers all knew her by sight: a short, cute brunette in a cheerful T-shirt and jeans. After arguing her way through countless disciplinary proceedings, she took to representing other students against the administration. She won almost every case. Law, Lisa came to realize, could play a key role in her activism. She dropped out of her Ph.D. program in political science and headed off to Yale.

Lisa met Harold Koh in the spring of 1991, as a second-year student in his international business transactions class, known as IBT. She hated every minute of it. "It was the most intellectually bankrupt material I've ever dealt with," she complained to a classmate. "I have no fucking clue why I stayed in the class." What was the real meaning of all the lists he wrote on the board, the principles he plowed through each day? In Lisa's view, Koh was blindly endorsing "the repressive project of American capitalism"—and co-opting his students along the way. She found his teaching style as dubious as the coursework itself. Why should everyone just parrot Koh's words back to him? Wasn't anyone interested in challenging his ideas?

After the IBT class, she'd seen enough: Koh was of the system, by the system, and for the system. She would never have dealt with him again had it not been for a radical New York lawyer on campus named Michael Ratner. To Lisa, Ratner was the anti-Koh. Bearded, bald, and fond of quoting Che Guevara, he'd represented everyone from inmates in the 1971 Attica prison rebellion to Nicaraguan citizens attacked by U.S.-funded contras. Ratner had come of age at Columbia Law School during the Vietnam War, and he considered most politicians "corrupt assholes." Along with his colleagues at the Center for Constitutional Rights, he'd even sued to halt the president from sending U.S. troops into battle. Twice. "What's the purpose of going along with the status quo?" Ratner would ask. "The government has enough paid people to do their dirty work."

Lisa had first spoken to Ratner while at Cornell, seeking legal advice in her fight against the administration, and when she learned that he taught a human rights clinic at Yale, she couldn't wait to sign up. It would mean the chance to file real cases with a lawyer she considered a role model. But to Lisa's bewilderment, Ratner's co-teacher was, of all people, Harold Koh. She couldn't fathom what interest Koh might have in human rights—and how could he and *Ratner* be working together?

She joined the clinic anyway, and as the weeks passed, Lisa found herself even more puzzled by Koh. The students in the Lowenstein International Human Rights Clinic were generally like sixties activist Allard Lowenstein himself—idealists committed to social justice. Koh just didn't seem to fit. Yet he'd *founded* the clinic. And here he was, suing a Guatemalan general for torture, staying late to finish court filings himself.

But Lisa had more important things to do than figure out her professor's contradictions. She had her own torture case in Nicaragua to work on with Ratner, and a new issue, not connected to the clinic, had grabbed her attention. In early October, the newspapers were filled with images of dead bodies in Port-au-Prince. There'd been a violent military coup in Haiti's capital, forcing the nation's first democratically elected president to flee the country.

The news left Lisa deeply troubled. Given her fascination with the colonial era, she already knew plenty about Haiti's blood-soaked past. Almost two hundred years earlier, the former French colony's half-million slaves had revolted against their plantation masters, defeating Napoleon's army and creating the world's first black republic. But history had not been kind to Haiti since then. France demanded massive reparations as a condition of trading with its former colony, crippling Haiti's fledgling economy. The United States, with its own restless slave population, refused to recognize the new country for decades. During World War I, American Marines invaded Haiti to stem creeping German influence, and through much of the twentieth century, the United States supported brutal dictatorial rule in the name of regional stability.

The two constants in Haiti seemed to be terror and a massive divide in wealth. The point was driven home by a novel Lisa had read, *The Comedians* by Graham Greene, depicting life under the Duvalier regime in the 1960s. There was a sliver of the obscenely rich, known in Haitian Creole as the *boujwazi,* with their distended bank accounts and Hermès accessories. Then there were the rest of the people—impoverished, often illiterate, and hopeless. For years, the *boujwazi* had sided with any dictator willing to keep the starving masses in their place, a task carried out with the eager assistance of the Haitian Army.

But in December 1990, something Lisa considered almost miraculous had happened. Buoyed by popular will and backed by the United Nations, the country held its first democratic election. In a landslide that defied almost all expectations, the people brought to power a radical, charismatic priest named Jean-Bertrand Aristide. A child of the slums and a gifted orator, Aristide had preached for years about the rights of the poor, surviving ambushes and assassination attempts until followers declared that he was *mistik,* protected by special powers. We will *all* "sit around the table," Aristide promised his fellow Haitians, "instead of just a few, with the rest underneath, catching the crumbs."

He took office in February 1991, amid riotous celebration, and true to his word, his first act was to invite the poor to lunch on the lawn of the National Palace. Lisa was ecstatic. The new president's political movement, Lavalas, or The Flood, involved precisely the sort of popular activism she believed in most, uniting thousands of local organizers and democracy supporters in the name of self-government and economic justice. Yet all her study of history had convinced her that Lavalas could never succeed. Democracy rarely if ever prevailed in postcolonial developing countries. The poor and the weak almost never won—and certainly not in a system as corrupt as Haiti's.

As it turned out, Lisa's initial fears were realized in just a few short months. From the start, the country's *boujwazi* considered Aristide a grave threat to their wealth and position, and the new president was on equally precarious terms with the Haitian military. After he dismissed several generals and pressed for economic reform, rumors of a coup gathered like dark clouds. The gale hit on the night of September 29, 1991.

Depressed, Lisa sat in the dining hall and read the details. After nightfall, soldiers had charged the president's home north of the capital. Aristide fled to the National Palace, where crowds had converged from the slums to defend him, but he was captured and dragged to the headquarters of the Haitian military. Brigadier General Raoul Cedras, chosen by Aristide to lead the armed forces, was waiting for him. "I'm the president now," Cedras allegedly said to his troops. "What should I do with the priest?" They urged him to execute Aristide. But after hasty intervention by foreign diplomats, the ousted leader was shoved onto a plane bound for Venezuela.

In the weeks that followed, hundreds, perhaps thousands, of Aristide supporters were beaten, shot, and attacked with machetes, tortured and terrorized into silence. But as Lisa had expected, the international community did little in response. A trade embargo imposed by the Organization of American States was meant to force Cedras to the bargaining table, yet over time all it did was devastate Haiti's poor. She saw Washington's other diplomatic efforts as pathetic, empty gestures. Nor was she surprised. Haiti was poverty-stricken, black, and strategically insignificant—and Aristide's anticapitalist diatribes had earned him enemies at the Central Intelligence Agency and the State Department.

A month after the coup, with no end to the violence and no sign that Aristide would soon return, newspapers reported another development: Haitians were fleeing their country. Old fishing boats, rickety sailing vessels—people would rig any craft available, gather cornmeal and drums of water, and shove off in the dead of night. Around Halloween, the U.S. Coast Guard intercepted the first boats in the Windward Passage between Haiti and Cuba, taking everyone aboard and destroying their vessels as hazards to navigation. By mid-November, over one thousand Haitians were crammed onto Coast Guard cutter decks, sleeping on cardboard mats.

Still, the boats kept coming. Soon there were fifteen hundred refugees* in U.S. custody. Then two thousand. Reports of vessels lost at sea piled up, with hundreds of people missing, presumed drowned. The Coast Guard was now deploying fifteen cutters for the operation, among the largest efforts it had ever undertaken in the Caribbean, and while the Navy assisted with two more ships, even that wasn't enough.

Human rights groups and some members of Congress called on President George H. W. Bush to bring the Haitians to the United States and grant them "temporary protected status," as the federal government had done for refugees from Kuwait, Lebanon, and elsewhere. But the White House refused, and the cutters cruised in slow circles off the coast of Cuba, awaiting further orders. Coast Guard spokesmen made no effort to hide their distress when they talked to the media. "The numbers are building up," one official warned the *New York Times*. "The ships involved are building up, and this thing is coming to a boil."

Yvonne stopped typing to listen. More gunshots followed, but they were still in the distance.

*See List of Terms, p. 317.

She studied the leaflet in the secondhand typewriter and tried to ignore her hunger. She'd eaten only a piece of bread that evening, washed down with a cup of watery hot chocolate. A few days earlier, she'd had nothing.

She adjusted her flickering gas lamp and went back to typing.

Pa dekouraje. Don't be discouraged.

Pa kite Makout yo pran pouvwa. Don't let the Macoutes take over.

Titid ap tounen. Aristide will return.

She pulled the paper out and set it on the stack of finished leaflets. Every day, more people fled Cite Soleil. Soldiers had killed a member of KID in her neighborhood, and she only dared to visit Antenor, who was still in hiding, on rare occasions. But Yvonne refused to keep quiet. If people didn't speak out, the whole country was going to fall apart.

A muffled hum emerged from across the sewage canal, growing into the familiar rumble of a military truck. She paused. The truck drew closer, accompanied by staccato gunfire, then ground to a halt. There were angry voices and footsteps.

She checked the door, her breath coming in short gulps. The heavy, old-fashioned key rested in the iron lock; the handle was secure. Then she thought of the lamp. She hurried to cut off the flame.

Thud-thud-thud.

Yvonne froze. They were outside her shanty.

Crack! The door smashed against the wall. Soldiers bolted into the room. She screamed.

"Kouche atè a!" one of them commanded.

They threw her to the floor. A heel ground into her back.

Yvonne's mother, Thérèse, stumbled out of bed.

"Rete la!" Thérèse begged the men. *"Rete la!"*

One of them replied with a punch. She collapsed.

A soldier hovered over Yvonne, his boot now digging into her spine.

"I'm . . . pregnant," she gasped.

Two soldiers yanked her arms behind her and forced handcuffs around her wrists.

"Kote Evans Paul?!" Where is Evans Paul?!

"I . . . don't . . . know."

A soldier grabbed her leaflets, kicking over the table. The typewriter crashed to the floor.

"What about these?!" he yelled, shaking the papers.

Another soldier kicked her in the mouth before she could answer. The taste of blood bloomed on her tongue.

"Manman, manman, manman!" Daniel and Jacques were screaming from the other room. Yvonne struggled to stay conscious, to mumble something to them from her swollen lips.

The men dragged her outside and heaved her into their truck. Thérèse cried from the door, but the engine kicked over, drowning out her voice. The rest of the soldiers jumped in and they roared away.

The men kicked and spat on Yvonne as the truck bounced along the potholed road. Finally, they lurched to a halt. The soldiers forced her to her feet and marched her into a squat concrete building: Recherches Criminelles. She mouthed a prayer. Ostensibly the Criminal Research Bureau of the Port-au-Prince Police, it functioned more like a torture chamber.

The soldiers pushed her past several prisoners and shoved her into a dark cell. Sometime later, two men entered. They wore the light shirts and dark blue pants of Haitian policemen and the taller one had on sunglasses in classic Macoute style. He took a long drag on his cigarette, then exhaled in her face. She coughed hard.

They knew Antenor Joseph was in hiding, he told her. They knew he was somewhere in Port-au-Prince.

"Where?" he demanded.

She pursed her lips, eyelids heavy, and shook her head.

He rammed the cigarette into her shoulder, driving the burning ash through her skin. She jerked her arm back with a scream.

Then they began hitting her. There were rifle butts, fists, and boots. Her body snapped with the blows, heaving one way and then another. The pain turned to numbness and confusion. She felt something hot and wet on her legs. Blood was streaming out of her, soaking her jeans a deep crimson.

The baby was gone.

When Yvonne came to, she was lying on the cell's concrete floor. Her back burned and pus oozed from the cigarette wound. Her clothes were caked with blood.

Dazed, her throat parched, she drifted in and out of consciousness. She heard other cell doors creak open as prisoners were dragged off, pleading, groaning.

Then her own door opened. She knew what was about to happen. They would take her outside and put a gun to her head. There would be a single shot, and she would collapse. Then they would heave her body into a truck and drive off to Titanyen.

But instead, the guards took Yvonne to a military hospital. She spent three days handcuffed to a bed, wondering why they had spared her.

Doctors appeared, examined her, left. And then, with no explanation, a guard unlocked her handcuffs. He escorted her to the entrance and pushed her outside.

Yvonne squinted, numb, eyes adjusting to the harsh midday sun. She touched her forehead with a wince. It was badly bruised. A truckload of soldiers rattled past, and she shrank back into a shadow.

She couldn't go on like this. She'd told others not to flee, to stand firm, but Yvonne now realized it was impossible for her to stay. If she remained in Cite Soleil, sooner or later, they would kill her.

It was the week before Thanksgiving at Yale: cold, dark, and busy, with everyone now deep into the semester. Plenty of first-year students struggled in the early months before finding a rhythm to the coursework and a niche in the school's politically charged social world. For Tory, though, things had gone from bad to worse. Her "small group" constitutional law class was meant to provide guidance and support, but the atmosphere had turned poisonous. There were bitter arguments about feminism and abortion rights, and at a cocktail party at her professor's house, too much alcohol turned a debate into a full-blown fistfight. The class assignments, meanwhile, left her miserable. Despite hours of effort, Tory couldn't figure out how to write her first paper, a legal memorandum analyzing several court cases. "I'm not going to tell you your work is good," the professor told her, "because it's not."

Even more depressing, Tory found herself souring on Harold Koh. In September, the dean had stressed to Tory and all of her classmates that they were "off the treadmill." He meant they were free from the pressure of grades (the school ran on an Honors/Pass system) and job-hunting (a Yale law degree opened most any door). Follow your passion, Calabresi had implored. Don't mindlessly jump through hoops and collect gold stars on your way to graduation. And yet as the fall semester went on, Tory began to think that if anyone were still on the treadmill—and encouraging others to join him—it was Koh.

He often talked up the career path of clerking on an appellate court and then the Supreme Court, working at the Department of Justice, and ultimately becoming a law professor, all of which he had done. The students surrounding him were hypercompetitive Ivy Leaguers, the type who most intimidated Tory. They all seemed to be playing the system for advantage—

angling for research positions with professors, eyeing the prestigious private firms, and lining up recommendations for judicial clerkships. And when it came to the clerkship game, a letter from Koh was among the most valuable at Yale. He'd helped send over two dozen students to the Supreme Court, many of them to his mentor, Justice Harry Blackmun. Entire law schools couldn't match those numbers.

Tory knew she didn't want to be part of that world. As far as she could tell, Koh didn't value the sort of in-the-trenches public interest activity that had brought her to Yale in the first place. She'd heard that Koh ran some kind of international litigation clinic, but she assumed it was just another exercise in what she dismissively called "being high-powered." As the weather turned cooler and the leaves fell, she lost interest in his class, smirking at the eager students who flocked around him. Why care so much, she wondered, when the only goal was winning a fancy position, an important title? Increasingly convinced that Yale was no place to do human rights work, Tory began to think about leaving law school.

The Lowenstein Clinic's weekly meeting had just wrapped up, and Lisa Daugaard was stuffing her papers into her backpack when Michael Ratner made a last-minute announcement. Earlier that day, he'd spoken with a lawyer in Florida named Ira Kurzban, a longtime advocate for a cause few people cared about: the rights of Haitian refugees. On the phone from Miami, Kurzban had sounded a little frantic to Ratner. He was suing the U.S. government over some massive federal operation in the Caribbean and needed emergency help.

Lisa immediately volunteered along with two other students, and they were soon on a conference call to Florida. Kurzban, deluged with work, only had time to give them a quick summary. The Coast Guard had supposedly run out of space to hold Haitians on its cutters, he said. The administration had been trying to send the refugees to other Caribbean countries with little success. So, under orders from the White House, the Coast Guard had started to return the refugees to Port-au-Prince.

Convinced innocent people were about to be killed, Kurzban and other immigration lawyers in Miami had hastily filed a lawsuit against the Bush administration to halt the repatriations. The case, *Haitian Refugee Center v. Baker,* was named for the lead defendant, Secretary of State James Baker. A lower court had issued an emergency ruling in the refugees' favor, but Kurzban had to defend it the next day on a fast-track appeal. There was a lot of technical research to be done and not enough attorneys to help. Kurzban needed answers by the next morning.

As Lisa hurried through her assignment that night, she got a glimpse of the central issues in the case. It turned out that the Coast Guard was intercepting the Haitian vessels under a 1981 agreement between the Reagan administration and former Haitian dictator "Baby Doc" Duvalier. The Reagan-Duvalier deal gave the United States the unusual right to force Haitians back to their homeland if they were headed to America without permission. The United States had no such agreement with any other country in the world, but fleeing Haitians, President Reagan had said in an official proclamation, "threatened the welfare and safety" of the United States. Predictable enough, Lisa thought: the White House had promised to keep foreign aid flowing to a dictator to prevent an influx of poor, black immigrants.

But the deal had a critical exception. The United States had declared that it would not return anyone to Haiti who qualified as a bona fide political refugee, as opposed to an "economic migrant" simply looking for a better life. This was a legal duty, not an act of charity. Under both American and international law, people fearing persecution based on their political beliefs, race, or certain other factors could not be returned to their persecutors. The bedrock principle of non-return, or non-refoulement, as it was known in immigration law, dated back to a United Nations treaty drafted after the Holocaust. Over one hundred nations, including the United States, had adopted the treaty's principles.

To ensure that no political refugees were sent back to Haiti, the Immigration and Naturalization Service, or INS, had kept officials stationed on the Coast Guard cutters plying Caribbean waters. The screening procedure was brief. Whenever a Haitian vessel was intercepted, an official would ask each person a few questions and then make a snap decision: on to the United States to file a formal asylum claim, or back to Port-au-Prince.

The INS statistics on Haitian refugees were striking. Though Haiti had suffered under repressive dictators for most of the past decade, the INS had rejected 99.9 percent of the fleeing Haitians intercepted by the Coast Guard. Out of 23,000 people interviewed from 1981 to 1991, only 28 were taken to America. During the same time frame, the United States had welcomed hundreds of thousands of refugees from elsewhere around the world, including Cuba, the then–Soviet Union, Cambodia, Ethiopia, Vietnam, Afghanistan, and Iran.

In the view of people like Kurzban, the Haitian interdiction process reflected a virulent, entrenched racism. He knew the interviews tended to be mere formalities, conducted right after the Haitians had been plucked from the sea, exhausted and dehydrated. The INS simply declared everyone an economic migrant and sent them back—and the practice was continuing despite the coup. But with the Cedras regime terrorizing Haiti, the lawyers in Florida were demanding an end to the rushed interviews. They called for a more careful method of identifying people who had legitimate claims of persecution.

With a better understanding of the Kurzban team's objective in *Baker,* Lisa faxed off her research late in the evening and went to bed. To her disappointment, there was nothing more to do on the case the next day because the lawyers had left the country. After a lot of procedural wrangling, the Florida court had halted the repatriations and granted Kurzban's group access to the Coast Guard cutters in the Caribbean. They were now going to investigate the way the INS was conducting the interviews. Lisa kept tabs on things through the newspaper. Events were unfolding fast, and attention now focused on the American naval base in Cuba.

The court order preventing the Coast Guard from sending refugees back to Haiti created an instant crisis for the White House. Bush officials now had to find somewhere to hold five thousand tired and hungry people. The administration did not want to bring them to Miami for fear of encouraging more Haitians to flee. Nobody considered that a wise political move, especially with a U.S. presidential election looming. As the clock ticked, officials raced through other alternatives, including Caribbean islands like Vieques, off the coast of Puerto Rico. But they could find no place with the infrastructure to build a sufficiently large refugee camp. Finally, they turned to Guantánamo Bay.

The naval base at Guantánamo, on Cuba's southern tip, was America's oldest overseas military facility, a forty-five-square-mile windswept stretch of hills taken by U.S. forces in 1898 during the Spanish-American War. American control of the land around the bay was formalized in 1903. That year, President Theodore Roosevelt's administration leased it from the newly formed Republic of Cuba as a naval base and coaling station. Almost ninety years later, the federal government was still paying a yearly rent check of about four thousand dollars to a disgusted Fidel Castro, who refused to cash it. The troops at "Gitmo" had waited out the Bay of Pigs invasion and the Cuban missile crisis on high alert, but those dramatic days were gone. With the fall of the Soviet Union, the base had lost most of its strategic importance, and it wasn't the place an ambitious young officer wanted to be.

The government had little precedent for detaining people on Guantánamo, though in the late seventies, about one hundred Haitian refugees had been held there briefly after they had tried to sail for the United States. Now, though, officials from the Justice and State Departments embraced the Guantánamo option. The INS screening interviews would be much easier on land, and the base had the necessary infrastructure and an advantageous location. It was less than 125 miles from Haiti but well beyond U.S. borders, with severely limited access from the mainland. That gave the government effective control over the press and any other group that might seek contact with the refugees.

But the most important factor behind the decision was a legal one: Justice Department officials believed that American law didn't apply to foreigners on an overseas military base. Assuming that Justice was right, the INS could process the asylum seekers on Guantánamo without following all the requirements of domestic immigration law. And the government would have a strong argument for getting Kurzban's lawsuit thrown out of court.

Defense officials didn't like the Guantánamo plan one bit. They had no interest in playing caretaker for thousands of Haitians, particularly on an overseas base. Building a refugee camp would take money and manpower no matter where it was done, but Guantánamo presented special headaches. Castro had cut off the water in 1964, so the base depended on an expensive desalinization plant. Food and other supplies had to be delivered by barge or military transport planes. And while the oppressive heat didn't seem to bother the iguanas, sand flies, or banana rats, few human beings spent time on Guantánamo without complaining about it. In a last-ditch argument, the Pentagon insisted that the treaty with Cuba only permitted naval activities on the base, but Justice and State prevailed.

Two days before Thanksgiving, Marine brigadier general George Walls Jr. and a Joint Task Force made up of hundreds of GIs from all four branches of the military arrived at Guantánamo to carry out Operation Safe Harbor. Working under a blazing Caribbean sun, the troops pitched 135 twenty-person tents at an unused training site, providing accommodations for more than 2,500 refugees. The Haitians were directed off their Coast Guard cutters and funneled to the new camp in yellow school buses. Within days the camp was filled to capacity, and Walls received orders to expand the operation. He set up a massive facility on the inactive McCalla Airfield—hundreds more tents, along with showers and rows of portable latrines, all surrounded by razor wire. Soon, more than six thousand refugees were warehoused on the base under the guard of nearly two thousand soldiers.

With the cutters emptied, the Kurzban team's examination of the interview process took place on Guantánamo. The results made Kurzban seethe. After conducting several depositions, he concluded that the asylum officers responsible for screening the refugees didn't know basic facts about Haiti's political situation. Worse, he got the strong sense that they were under pressure from Washington to "screen in" as few people as possible, ignoring legitimate claims in order to keep the numbers down.

Kurzban and his team returned to Miami to convey their findings to the judge in the *Baker* case, a liberal-minded maverick named Clyde Atkins. Their efforts paid off, briefly, as Judge Atkins kept the ban on refugee returns in place. The media, meanwhile, latched on to the story of careless INS interviews—and the number of political refugees screened in to the United States shot up. But the government quickly appealed, and over the next several weeks, a series of contradictory rulings followed. In a game of judicial whack-a-mole, the conservative federal appellate court in Atlanta, Georgia, knocked down lower-court orders for the refugees as fast as they were issued.

The *Baker* litigation was now the talk of the Lowenstein Clinic. In class, in the hallways, Lisa would ponder each new ruling with the other students. *Baker* had a special excitement to it. The clinic's current torture cases against dictators and military figures sought "retrospective relief," meaning compensation for victims who'd been hurt long ago. But Kurzban and his colleagues were trying to stop injustice on the fly, forcing reform of an ongoing foreign policy operation. Adding to the sense of urgency, the crisis continued to play out in the papers, often on the front page, alongside reports on the harsh political situation in Haiti and the desperate circumstances of ordinary Haitians.

To the students' disappointment, the appellate court threw out the

Baker case for good in early February 1992. The court's decision came down to one principle: Haitians were outside the United States, so they had no protection under American law. In fact, the court implied, they had no rights at all. No matter how the INS might mishandle their asylum claims, no matter what fate they might face in Haiti, they had no recourse. The Coast Guard repatriation process resumed the day of the court's decision, and Kurzban and the other *Baker* lawyers were now down to one option: the U.S. Supreme Court.

———

Yvonne returned home to her shanty, bruised and hobbling, just long enough to see her children. Her mother bathed her and put coffee compresses on her head. Jacques was crying; Daniel, too frightened to speak. Yvonne reached for them and smiled weakly. Everything is okay, she promised. Everything is all right. She tucked them into bed, and at last managed to sing them to sleep.

Back in the kitchen, she whispered to her mother that she had to leave. They'd all be safer without her around. She didn't know where she'd go, she said, brushing away the tears. Somewhere far away. Perhaps Baradères. She asked Thérèse to tell the boys *manman* had gone on a little trip. When Yvonne had figured things out, she would call the pawnshop or send a letter.

Her mother nodded. It turned out that a local police officer had tipped off the military on Yvonne's whereabouts. He was prowling the neighborhood, his rifle slung over his shoulder, and he'd surely be looking for her again.

She woke early the next morning and stuffed a few things, including her KID papers, into an old backpack. It would still be hours before the women went to the open ditches to wash clothes, and the only sound was a crying rooster. She did not expect to see anyone from the police or military at this time of day, but just in case, she pulled a floppy straw hat down low over her face. Then she slipped out the back of the shanty and hurried along the sewage canal.

It was the same route she'd once taken to school. She'd been an excellent student—so promising, in fact, that the nuns had moved her to the morning classes, where French was spoken instead of Creole and all the other children wore better uniforms than Yvonne's parents could afford. They were just able to eke out tuition for her—her mother earning a dollar a day sewing baseballs while her father scraped for work as a handyman. But then Thérèse fell ill with tuberculosis and lost her job.

Crushed, Yvonne had to leave school. She began asking questions about the gaping divide between rich and poor, questions her nervous parents warned would only lead to trouble. Her sister and brother didn't cause such problems. What drove Yvonne to stick her nose where it didn't belong? But after she met Antenor Joseph, a hard-driving activist in a neighboring slum, she turned radical. An aide to KID leader Evans Paul, the future mayor of Port-au-Prince, Antenor was committed to democracy in Haiti as if his life depended on it. Yvonne threw herself into the cause with him, and after Aristide declared he would run for president, she gave every free moment to the election effort: organizing voters, teaching the illiterate how to mark the ballot. Following Aristide's stunning victory, she celebrated all night with Antenor and her neighbors in Cite Soleil, dancing to the music of Haitian singer Manno Charlemagne.

The sun was casting shadows on the puddle-filled streets when Yvonne reached the Carrefour-Feuilles neighborhood where Antenor was now hiding. She'd been told to go to a certain intersection and wait near a stall where someone sold coffee. A young man finally passed by, murmuring her name. He hurried her through a maze of alleys—left, right, then left again—to the safe house.

It was dark inside. As Yvonne's eyes adjusted to the gloom, her husband appeared to her, first in outline, then feature by feature—his high forehead, his bright eyes. Antenor gasped at the welts on her face, gathered her in his arms. But when he asked her about the baby, she could only shake her head. An hour later, anguished and afraid, Yvonne told him she was headed for the countryside. Before she went, her husband fished twenty gourdes out of his pocket, about four dollars. He pressed the money into her hand.

"*Kenbe fèm,*" Antenor choked. Be strong.

———

The students shook off the New England cold, shedding their Patagonia fleece jackets and long wool coats, pulling notepads out of backpacks. It was a month into the new semester, late February. The Lowenstein Clinic was on scheduled hiatus until the fall, and Michael Ratner would not be on campus for several months. Koh was now teaching a course about the president's foreign affairs powers.

A stack of photocopies made its way around the class. Koh held up the decision. It had sputtered out of his fax machine the morning before: one brief sentence announcing that the Supreme Court had refused to hear the *Baker* case. The ruling of the Eleventh Circuit Court of Appeals in Atlanta would stand. The Kurzban team was done.

Only one of the nine justices, Koh said, had voted to review the case—Harry Blackmun. Koh read Blackmun's dissent aloud: "'If indeed the Haitians are to be returned to an uncertain future in their strife-torn homeland, that ruling should come from this Court, after full and careful consideration of the merits of their claims.'"

Koh shook his head. "Does everyone understand how extreme the Eleventh Circuit decision is?" he asked. "The court said these people have no rights! *None!* They're down on Gitmo right now. They're in detention at the hands of our government. And they're going through interviews that are almost certain to send them back to Haiti and maybe a death sentence. But they don't get a lawyer. They don't get a lawyer. It's like *Gideon versus Wainwright,* right? Does everyone see this?"

Along with his students, Koh had been following *Baker,* and as a former Supreme Court clerk, he'd offered his views to Kurzban's colleagues about the odds that the high court would agree to review the case. Koh hadn't been optimistic, for the court rarely interfered with the president's decisions in foreign affairs. It was a hesitancy he considered both unwise and unfaithful to the Constitution. The court had to stay involved, Koh had argued in his recent book, to protect against presidents who were "evil, foolish, or inattentive." When judges kept a hands-off attitude toward foreign policy, he said, it could lead to disaster, from Nixon's bombing of Cambodia to the Iran-contra scandal. With *Baker,* Koh believed the justices had failed again.

He normally would have turned to other class materials by now, for he always had his performance meticulously laid out. But today he was too troubled to stop talking about Kurzban's suit.

"Does anyone know," he asked, "where the case was filed?"

"Florida?"

"Miami. Southern District of Florida. Very risky forum. Can anyone explain why?"

No one answered.

"The Eleventh Circuit! Appeals go to the Eleventh Circuit! You never want to be in front of a court that conservative. Not on a case like this.

Not if you're Haitian. You're guaranteed to lose on appeal. So what do you do instead?"

"File somewhere else?"

"You could file somewhere else! Where? Where?"

"Actually, can't you sue in any federal court in the country?"

"Right. There are fifty states this case could have been filed in. Why?"

"There's personal jurisdiction because the government's found in all of them."

"So why do you care? Why's that matter?"

"You can look at different courts and find the one with the judges who might rule for you."

"Right! Right! And you can look for a circuit with the most lenient standards for issuing a temporary restraining order. But think about it, think about it. These people are not just deprived of lawyers. They're at the total mercy of our government. You can't physically beat a death-row inmate. But you can beat a Haitian on Guantánamo, and according to the Eleventh Circuit, there's nothing the guy can do about it. Does everyone see this?"

Koh explained that a small group in Congress was still seeking temporary protected status for the refugees, which would allow them into the country for at least the short term. But he said it was unlikely to happen. Haitians, even pro-democracy activists running for their lives, were simply too unpopular. Nobody cared.

"So now what happens?"

Koh shrugged. "The government continues its repatriation program entirely unconstrained by law. The case is dead."

Koh liked to finish class on an upbeat note, but he had nothing else to say. Most of the class packed up and trudged out, though several students stuck around to ask questions. He recognized them as friends of the Lowenstein people who'd been following *Baker*.

"Where do you think the case should have been filed instead?" one asked.

"The Second or Ninth Circuit," Koh said, referring to federal courts in New York and California. There were a number of liberal judges in both places.

"What about political pressure?" someone else chimed in. "Like going after Bush and trying to convince him to change the policy?"

Koh shook his head. "Forget it," he said. "Super Tuesday's just three weeks away."

The Republican primaries in eight states were scheduled for the same day in mid-March. While President Bush was the clear leader, right-wing nationalist Pat Buchanan was pressuring him in the South. Bush was not about to weaken his support in Florida over the Haitians, especially given some voters' hostility to immigration.

Koh finally cut off the discussion. It was late. He had to pick up his two-year-old son, William, and get home.

His breath plumed in the chilly air as he walked to his dented silver Subaru. He had not been this troubled by a ruling from the Supreme Court for a long time, and he felt all the more stung because he'd actually worked on the case. A lawyer on the Kurzban team had called for help the night before the Supreme Court filing deadline. Koh had never been involved in litigation against the government, but he'd agreed to pitch in. He'd ended up drafting a brief until dawn—for nothing, it turned out. As he yanked a parking ticket off his windshield and dumped his notes on the passenger seat, Koh figured he was done with *Baker* and the Haitian refugees for good.

Two

FILING A NEW LAWSUIT

LISA DAUGAARD WAS ALMOST a month into her last semester of law school, and she was distraught. She'd never had a job in her life, and it seemed that everyone at Yale already had a position lined up after graduation except for her. She didn't know where she wanted to work and had a ton of debt to pay off. Hearing other students' success stories only increased her anxieties. She broke down in tears at a dinner party after learning a classmate was interviewing with a nonprofit organization that had rejected her own hasty application.

One of her friends took her outside. It was cold and dark, and she hugged herself as they stood on the sidewalk.

"I've really screwed everything up," Lisa sobbed. "I haven't taken the right classes, I haven't sucked up to the right professors, and now I don't know what I'm going to do."

"Those aren't the choices you've made," her friend said matter-of-factly. "If you gave a shit, you know you could get a clerkship or whatever else you wanted."

But Lisa's concerns weren't just about the future. She was woefully behind in her coursework, thanks to her involvement in an endless stream of political causes. While many of her classmates had one unfinished paper to complete from an earlier semester, she had four—and they were not assignments that could be churned out in a weekend with some extra coffee. Each required heavy research and was expected to cover fifty pages or more.

When Lisa regained her composure, she realized that at least for the short run, she had to change everything she was doing. Her last three months at Yale were going to be one frantic race to graduate and find a job. The next morning, she started off with a new plan, dutifully heading to the library to research an overdue constitutional law paper. She went to all her classes, did her required reading, and looked into public interest fellowships, though the deadlines for most were long past.

While her Lowenstein Clinic friends were still talking about the *Baker* case, Lisa tried to steer clear of the discussion. She had a gut sense that some sort of project might come out of it, and she knew she didn't have the time. For once, she thought, I'm not getting involved.

But her political habits were not so easily broken. Just days after the dinner party, she found her mind drifting back to Guantánamo. The next time she was in the dining hall, she plopped down at a table with some other Lowenstein types, including fellow third years Michael Barr and Graham Boyd, and was soon immersed in the conversation. As they discussed the Coast Guard repatriations, Lisa's academic concerns faded, and a familiar, energizing feeling began to take hold of her—the feeling of camaraderie and higher purpose in organizing a group around a common political goal.

Everyone believed something had to be done, though the motivations varied. For Michael, a politically ambitious third year with bushy hair and an easy grin, the interest in *Baker* and the refugees was personal. His grandmother had fled Poland just before World War II, later reaching the United States by stowing away with Michael's father, then a young boy, in a freighter compartment. Given his Jewish background, Michael was quick to connect the situation in the Caribbean with a dark episode from America's past. Months before Hitler's tanks rumbled into Poland, the steamship *St. Louis* had reached the waters off of Miami carrying hundreds of German Jews seeking asylum. The Roosevelt administration sent the ship back to Europe, and many aboard ultimately perished in Nazi concentration camps.

Graham Boyd had his own view of the Haitian refugee situation, based on a deep distrust of U.S. foreign policy. Growing up, he'd been a staunch believer in Ronald Reagan, and supported the U.S.-backed contras fighting the socialist government in Nicaragua. "Freedom fighters," the president had called them. But after months of debate with his liberal college friends, including Michael Barr, Graham had gone to Nicaragua as an aid worker to see the situation for himself. Driving a supply truck on roads littered with land mines, he'd witnessed deadly contra attacks on civilians—and returned to the United States a leftist. He looked the part now, too, wearing

John Lennon glasses and a ponytail. Graham had strong doubts about the Bush administration's spin on the Haitian refugees. The country was in chaos. People were getting killed. How could the White House call most everyone fleeing an "economic migrant"?

Running through the students' conversation was also the conviction that the Bush administration was engaging in a grand hypocrisy. In November 1989, the president had hailed the fall of the Berlin Wall and the rise of democracy in Eastern Europe, and a month later, the administration sharply criticized Hong Kong for sending boat people back to Vietnam. But now, a fledgling democracy in America's own backyard had collapsed. Haitians were fleeing for their lives, and the United States, land of immigrants and freedom, was doing everything it could to keep them out.

As the discussion grew more intense, Michael Barr threw out an idea—something he'd actually been pondering for a while. Why not file a new case for the Haitians? Michael conceded it sounded a bit crazy, especially after the Kurzban group's tough defeat in *Baker*. But he insisted there had to be a way to do it. While many at Yale, particularly conservatives, might have rolled their eyes, Barr was talking to some of the most idealistic and aggressive left-wing students in the school. Heads nodded, slowly, as they wrapped their minds around the idea. Even without any real research, most took it on faith that another case could be filed. As Graham Boyd put it, repeating an activist's mantra, "If there's an injustice, there's got to be a lawsuit."

Moreover, they all had at least modest experience with the real practice of law, through the Lowenstein Clinic or other Yale clinics that provided legal services to the poor, the homeless, prison inmates, and others who couldn't afford a lawyer. Everyone understood the basics of researching a legal claim, and some had experience dealing with clients and presenting a case to a judge. In addition to her Lowenstein efforts, Lisa had worked on several lawsuits for the homeless and had also spent months investigating and drafting papers for a suit involving a racially motivated attack against a minority business. Graham, under the guidance of his clinical professors, had even argued a case before the Connecticut Supreme Court.

Still, the students realized a new lawsuit for the refugees would be far more complex than anything they'd worked on before. There were endless legal and logistical issues to consider, starting with the fact that they could not possibly go it alone. No matter how talented or confident Lisa, Michael, Graham, and the others were, none had passed the bar yet. They could not even sign court papers. If they were serious about Guantánamo, they would need experienced attorneys to join them. Perhaps even a law firm.

Making all that happen was a task ideally suited to Michael Barr. The more cynical students in his class considered him a political insider, but the fact was that he excelled at working the system. Unlike Lisa, he was apt to see that big, established institutions could serve as allies rather than enemies. While she was blocking trustees' meetings at Cornell, Michael, only an undergraduate at Yale, had flown to South Africa on an apartheid fact-finding mission with university officials, including former secretary of state Cyrus Vance. Lisa Daugaard ended up in the back of a police cruiser; Michael Barr got a Rhodes scholarship.

Michael suggested they start by talking to Harold Koh. The students knew he was familiar with the *Baker* case and had worked on the Supreme Court papers. Even Lisa had gained a guarded respect for him after a semester in the Lowenstein Clinic. And everyone figured that if Koh signed on, Ratner would get involved as well, though he wouldn't officially be at Yale again until fall.

The question was how far Koh would be willing to go. Barr, sensitive to such things, realized it wouldn't be an easy sell. The new lawsuit was a politically stupid move for a young, ambitious professor. The risks were high; it would be easy to fail; plenty of people in Washington would be pissed off. And Koh had a lot to lose. At the age of thirty-six, he'd already been offered the deanship at Berkeley—and were a Democrat to become president in the upcoming election, Koh would likely be short-listed for a key political appointment. People on that kind of track didn't file lawsuits against the White House. In fact, very few attorneys even thought about doing such a thing. But Michael believed they should sound him out anyway, especially given another key fact: Koh was the son of a political refugee.

———

After years of dictatorship, South Korea enjoyed a brief moment of democratic rule in 1960. But the prime minister was ousted in a coup the following year, as the military seized control of the National Assembly and outlawed all political activity. Everything that Kwang Lim Koh, Harold's father, had been working toward most of his life—a free, democratic, unified Korea—was destroyed. Despite offers of high political rank, Kwang Lim refused to pledge loyalty to the new regime. Had he been in Korea at the time of the coup, he would likely have been jailed, or worse. As fortune had it, though, Kwang Lim was in Washington with his young family. He'd been serving as a diplomat for the fallen democratic government, and he sought asylum in the United States.

Exiled at age forty, Kwang Lim moved to New Haven, took a part-time position at Yale, and devoted himself to raising his six children. While Harold and four of the others were American-born, Kwang Lim saw them as he saw himself—Korean. To succeed in their new country, he believed they had to follow his own survival strategy while growing up in Japanese-occupied Korea: rely on effort and self-discipline to attain such extraordinary academic success that those who made the rules would have no choice but to accept them as equals. Kwang Lim's Japanese teachers had berated him for belonging to an inferior race, even beating him for speaking Korean instead of Japanese. But he'd gone on to become valedictorian at Seoul National University at a time when the Japanese were trying to purge the esteemed institution of Koreans. Decades later, his old Japanese classmates still reverently called him sensei—teacher. "Always work harder than everyone else," Kwang Lim instructed his children. "If it comes down to willpower, you will always win."

The lesson that determination and hard work could control almost any situation took hold of Harold with particular intensity. At age six, he was struck by polio. But with his father urging him on in the hospital hallway, he'd willed himself to walk again. Struggling through two operations, leg braces, and endless rehabilitation, he tried to understand why the disease had chosen him. Harold decided that fate had given him a trade-off—a weak, spindly leg but an agile mind. So he turned to his schoolwork with ferocity.

Koh proved himself to his father and his teachers again and again: summa cum laude at Harvard; a Marshall Scholarship to Oxford; honors at Harvard Law School and a post at the *Harvard Law Review;* then a Supreme Court clerkship, confirming him as one of the most promising law graduates in America. But after his year working for Justice Harry Blackmun, Koh discovered there was no obvious next rung to climb on the ladder. He was forced for the first time to decide what the purpose of all his hard work should be.

He started with the safest, most conservative option available, a prestigious private law firm in Washington, but found the drudgery of corporate litigation unbearable and soon left. It was a move his future wife, Mary-Christy Fisher, had recommended at the outset. "I thought you were going to *do* something," she'd said acidly when he first mentioned the firm.

On the strength of his credentials, Koh then took a post at the Justice Department's Office of Legal Counsel, working with an elite group of lawyers advising the Reagan White House. If prestige and power were his goals, he could not have done much better in the legal profession. But given his father's bitter experience, Koh was acutely sensitive to the dangers of a leader who overstepped the bounds of law, and he soon developed doubts about his job. He was directed to work on a brief contesting an international court's review of CIA operations in Nicaragua. He also worked on the legal justification of Reagan's invasion of Grenada, carried out without congressional approval. Both tasks left him queasy, and in time he came to see Attorney General Edwin Meese as a dangerous man, all too capable of abusing his power.

Two years into the job, Koh decided he'd had enough. After discovering that he was a natural in the classroom while serving as visiting lecturer, he became a professor at Yale—and began writing about the critical role the courts played in constraining presidential action in foreign affairs.

But Koh's time at the Justice Department had laid bare a deep conflict within him. Kwang Lim had taught Harold not only to work hard, but to keep a low profile and avoid controversy. He'd stressed that Koreans were by nature a conciliatory, conflict-averse people, that little good could come from activism as a way of life. Following the rules of the establishment was the wiser course—especially for outsiders struggling to earn their place in the community. And yet in his own life, Kwang Lim had been a man of uncompromising principle, banished from Korea precisely because he'd supported democracy so fiercely.

———

There was a knock on the door. Michael Barr poked his head inside. Lisa Daugaard was right behind him.

Did Koh have a few minutes? He waved them in. Koh was wary of Lisa, whom he considered very smart but lacking in judgment and common sense, and he felt Barr was something of a smooth talker, too comfortable in his own skin for someone in his mid-twenties.

After a few moments of chitchat, Michael turned the topic to *Baker*. He went over recent events on Guantánamo, then launched into an attack on White House policy: The government was sending the Haitians back without due process; the United States treated refugees from no other country so unfairly; the Supreme Court should have reversed the Eleventh Circuit; this was the *St. Louis* all over again.

Koh listened, a little impatient, waiting for Barr to get to the point.

"We've been talking to several other people and we're exploring what we might do," Michael said.

"What do you mean?"

"We're wondering about the possibility of filing another lawsuit."

Sure, Koh thought. Lisa the wild activist and Michael the amateur politico are going to sue the Bush administration. Koh was as disturbed as they were about the case. But criticizing a Supreme Court decision was one thing; filing suit with the fantasy of changing the outcome was another matter altogether.

"Who would bring the case?" he asked. His tone did not betray his reaction.

"Well, that's one of the things we've been talking about," Michael said. "We were wondering what kind of interest you might have."

Koh paused.

"Who else do you see working on this?"

"To start, probably Graham Boyd and Sarah Cleveland and Paul Sonn. And we've got some others who're interested, too."

Koh was not impressed. He knew the Boyd kid had argued a Connecticut Supreme Court case, but Boyd struck Koh as having an inflated sense of his abilities. While Sarah might have been a Rhodes scholar like Barr, Koh hadn't thought much of her comments in his IBT class. Paul Sonn was an enigma—very bright, as far as Koh could tell, but so lacking in self-confidence that he barely opened his mouth.

"What about other lawyers?" Koh asked.

Michael said he'd been looking into that.

Right, Koh thought.

"So, what would the guts of the complaint be?"

"We were thinking probably along the lines of *Baker*—the INA and other statutes, plus some constitutional claims," Michael said, referring to the Immigration and Nationality Act.

"Equal protection," Lisa interjected.

"So you've researched the issues?"

"Not in any formal way yet, beyond what we know about *Baker*, though we've been looking over some cases."

That was vintage Michael Barr, Koh thought: finding a diplomatic way of saying no, we really haven't done much of anything. Koh had heard enough. He had to prepare for class.

"Why don't you dig a bit into the legal theories," he said abruptly, more to get them out of his office than anything else. They promised to stop by again soon, and Koh gave them a noncommittal nod as they left.

Lisa and Michael headed down the hall believing they'd made some headway with him. And they had, but not in the direction they assumed. Koh considered the idea of a new suit almost ludicrous.

Up to that point, the cases filed by Koh and his students had been against individual defendants accused of torture in other countries. They were foreign dictators and military officers—people who often didn't show up in court, leaving the Lowenstein Clinic free to press the matter uncontested. The cases were hard work but manageable. The factual investigation required the documentation of harm to one, two, or perhaps a half-dozen plaintiffs. The legal work was generally limited to briefs on a single statute, known as the Alien Tort Claims Act. And the proceedings moved at a deliberate pace, usually heading toward a default judgment against the defendant.

The lawsuit Lisa and Michael were talking about could not have been more different. They wanted to pick a fight with the U.S. Department of Justice, a litigation machine with thousands of lawyers, endless resources, and a client—the Bush administration—that would never yield. The case would involve presidential foreign policy, a major Coast Guard operation in international waters, and a detention camp on a U.S. naval base fifteen hundred miles away. The potential plaintiffs numbered in the thousands. There was no way to communicate with them, and if that ever became possible, language and cultural barriers would surely complicate matters even more. Lawyers could go their entire careers and not see a suit of such complexity.

Adding to the delusional quality of the proposal was Lisa and Michael's suggestion that law students would be doing much of the work. Not only that, but all the people they'd mentioned to Koh were in their final year of school. Graduation day was just a couple of months away. What then?

No, Koh thought to himself. This was a fool's errand.

* * *

A day or two later, Graham Boyd dropped by the Stop & Shop super-market on Dixwell Avenue, a grimy street running through the slums northwest of the Yale campus. Along with several other students, he'd begun to do a little research on a new case for the Haitians and had spent his afternoon puzzling over the Immigration and Nationality Act. He was sorting through his grocery list when someone called out to him. He glanced up to find Harold Koh shuffling down the aisle.

Graham hung out with the Lowenstein crowd, but he hadn't been part of the clinic itself and wasn't that familiar with Koh. Graham's im-pression was that he was a very cautious man. A couple of years earlier, he'd asked Koh to sign a brief by another scholar in an abortion lawsuit and Koh, despite agreeing with the argument, had refused. "A person's reputation is the most valuable thing he has," Koh had said. "I've got to be careful what I put my name to, and I didn't help write this thing." Graham had left Koh's office shaking his head. It was hard enough to mobilize people for a cause without nitpicking over who chose every last word on a brief.

But now, to Graham's surprise, Koh started peppering him with ques-tions about the *Baker* case. He seemed especially curious to know whether Graham would commit to working on a new lawsuit.

"Yeah," Boyd assured Koh. "I want to be involved."

The gears in Koh's mind were whirring. There'd been another article in the paper about Guantánamo that morning, and it ate at him; re-minded him that he'd helped out on *Baker* and lost. He sized Graham up as he considered the other people Lisa Daugaard and Michael Barr had mentioned. They were only a start. But what if they could put together a really big team?

At 11:45 that night, the telephone rang in Sarah Cleveland's apart-ment. She pushed aside her homework and grabbed the receiver.

It was Harold Koh.

Sarah was shocked to hear from a professor at such a late hour, par-ticularly one she didn't know all that well.

He skipped the pleasantries. Several students seemed serious about filing a new lawsuit for the Haitian refugees on Guantánamo, he said. They'd all mentioned her name.

Despite what Koh had seen in class, Sarah, a reedy southerner who punctuated everything she said with a laugh, was a talented student. Her traditional liberal politics stemmed from her childhood in Birmingham, Alabama, where she'd attended an all-white public school that had ducked a desegregation order. Sarah was eleven or twelve years old when she finally grasped the situation, and had ended up in an ugly fight with her parents. Sensitive to civil rights issues ever since, she'd spent the summer after her second year of law school at the NAACP—and she was appalled by Bush's policy on the Haitians.

Sarah had heard the talk about filing a new case, but she hadn't expected anything to come of it. The evening Koh called, she'd been planning a trip to Cancún for spring break. After an exhausting two and a half years at Yale, she'd promised herself she would take it easy her last semester. She wanted to lie on a beach, drink margaritas, and think about something—anything—other than law.

Sarah knew well enough what Koh would expect if they filed a new lawsuit. Everyone would be working like hell.

"So if this thing goes ahead, would you be a part of it?" he asked.

"Yes," she said. "Absolutely."

Room B04A was perhaps the gloomiest spot in the entire law school, a cramped basement space with scuffed walls and ragged, squash-colored carpet. But when Koh entered the room, it was humming. Lisa, Michael, Sarah, Graham, and other third years were elbow to elbow around the dilapidated conference table, law books, memos, and legal pads at the ready. A pack of younger students sat on the floor, notebooks resting on their laps. Despite putting out a notice about the meeting, Koh hadn't expected so much interest. As he made his way through the thicket of legs and backpacks, he recognized several faces from his recent civil procedure class, including Tory Clawson's.

Koh had decided it was time for everyone to put up or shut up about Haiti. A few days earlier, he'd called the third years into his office and asked each student to research a key legal question in the case over the weekend. His expectations were low. If they all focused on the law in a disciplined way, he figured, they'd realize that a new suit would be next to impossible.

He turned first to Paul Sonn, a shy third year who may have been the most gifted legal thinker in the group. Though Paul supported the refugees, he was the one real doubter among the students, unsure that a new case had any chance. Over the last several days, he'd written a memo on one of the trickiest legal issues: could they get past the res judicata effect of *Baker*?

It was one of the key doctrines that Koh focused on in his civil procedure course. Res judicata, he would explain to his students, bars a case from being filed twice. "It's Latin for 'the thing is decided'!" he'd shout. "You get one bite at the apple!" Bush's screening policy on Guantánamo had already been challenged in the *Baker* case, so Koh's first question—and the issue that had nagged at Paul from the start—was whether they could even get into the courthouse.

In a halting voice, Paul explained that *Baker* had been a class action on behalf of all Haitians who were on Guantánamo at the time of the suit or who would reach the base in the future. By extension, they'd all had their bite at the apple. So the res judicata effect of *Baker* applied to any Haitian who ended up on Guantánamo even months later.

That meant a new case was impossible. Faces around the table fell and Michael Barr shot Paul a disappointed look. He'd been pushing his friend to find a way around *Baker*.

Koh paused, then shook his head. "There are a lot of other problems with this case, but it isn't barred."

Paul looked miserable. Had he screwed up that badly?

"There's no way the Supreme Court would duck the issues here," Koh said. "If they took this case, which they would if the government lost in the court below, they'd go straight to the merits. And they'd rule against us in a heartbeat."

The students traded uneasy looks with each other, wondering if Koh were about to kill the case.

But as Koh silently flipped through Paul's memo, he found himself more and more impressed. The work was outstanding. Koh disagreed with the bottom line, but he considered that a matter of Paul's inexperience.

"Listen," Koh said. "One way to help get us out of the woods on res judicata is if we have a new party involved in the suit, someone other than the Haitians themselves."

He turned to another student, Adam Gutride. "What'd you find on the First Amendment?"

"Well, if the government's barring lawyers from Guantánamo, that could violate their own free speech rights," Adam said. Lawyers had a right to communicate with their clients, and a 1972 Supreme Court case held that the First Amendment applied to military bases. Adam held up a bunch of circuit court decisions elaborating on the principle.

"Okay." Koh nodded. He was pretty sure of the point already, but once again, the preparation was good. "So that gives us a new party. We get a public interest group that wants to represent the refugees on Guantánamo—could even be us. Lawyers trying to counsel them about their situation. We make a claim based on our First Amendment right to speak with our clients."

"Wait," someone said. "The Florida lawyers already raised that issue."

"I think it was only for themselves," Koh said. "Not as a class of all lawyers who want to meet with the refugees. So even if the claim's the same, it's different people making it."

There were vigorous nods around the table.

But the First Amendment argument had its own weaknesses, and one of them quickly came to the fore. Guantánamo Bay was not a typical military installation. It was outside U.S. borders. Did the First Amendment apply there? What about the other parts of the Constitution? Or federal statutes like the Immigration and Nationality Act, the INA? Did *any* American law apply on Guantánamo?

With these and other murky legal questions to address, Koh went around the rest of the table. One by one, the students presented their work, citing cases, parsing footnotes, sketching out lines of reasoning. And to Koh's amazement, they all concluded that the suit could go forward.

Graham Boyd had come up with novel arguments under the INA. Sarah Cleveland had pulled together a mountain of research on the U.N. treaty banning the return of refugees to their homeland. Lisa, convinced it was "fucking racist" to put Haitians on a separate asylum track from every other nationality, had struggled with an equal protection claim, the basis of *Brown v. Board of Education.*

There were problems with all the work. But in some cases, it was that the reasoning had been *too* creative, departing from bad precedent in clever but implausible ways. Graham had twisted the INA into a pretzel, while Lisa was trying to shrug off decades of legal doctrine. She faced a seemingly impossible task with equal protection, since the Constitution gave Congress power to do virtually whatever it wanted in immigration. It could even target a racial group and limit the number allowed to come to the United States. She hadn't found a way around the precedents yet, but she'd spent four days at the computer and had a stack of cases and articles six inches thick to prove it.

Koh had entered the room ready to tell the students no case could be filed. Now, though, he was flirting in the most tentative way with the opposite idea. They'd shown him effort and imagination. They'd turned out in greater numbers than he'd expected. And they were pressing to take the next step, eager to see just how far they could go.

With their enthusiasm overpowering some of his reservations, he decided to see them through a more serious round of preparation. He told Sarah and Michael to begin work on a complaint—the key document for initiating a lawsuit, spelling out the facts at issue and the legal relief requested. The more complete a picture they could give the court, the better, Koh said. They needed the most up-to-date information on Coast Guard interdictions and INS interviews. He left them to figure out how to find it all.

He asked other students to dig deeper into two legal theories that seemed the most promising. One was the First Amendment claim that lawyers had a right to communicate with their clients, even on Guantánamo. The other theory was its mirror image: that the refugees had a constitutional right to consult a lawyer before being sent back to Haiti.

Koh liked the claims because they did not attack Bush's policy directly. Nobody was calling on the administration to shut down Guantánamo. The established screening process on the base could continue, the argument would go, but lawyers should be there to ensure that it was fair and accurate.

As the meeting drew to a close, he doled out more assignments in rapid succession. There were statutes to review, cases to analyze, legislative history to dig through, lawyers to call. On and on Koh went.

Tory Clawson, sitting in a daze against the wall, tried to keep up with it all. Having decided to try Yale for one more semester, she'd been thrilled when she heard about the Guantánamo meeting. Working for refugees was exactly the kind of project she was itching for, something that finally made law school relevant. But when she'd discovered that Koh was in charge, her heart sank. She was sure the project would boil down to the usual careerists currying favor with him instead of mounting a real effort to help the Haitians.

An hour into the meeting, though, she was rethinking things. Koh seemed genuinely worried about Guantánamo. Tory had never seen him so serious. He hadn't cracked a joke since he walked in. Nor did the third years sitting around the table seem to be the usual "Koh groupies." Lisa Daugaard certainly wasn't. Not only had she been talking back to Koh, she'd even called him *Harold*.

"Tory?"

Shocked to hear her name, she looked up to see everyone in the room gazing at her. Koh asked if she would help research the legal status of Guantánamo Bay. A third year would be responsible, he said, but extra hands were needed. The work had to be done right away.

"Well . . . sure."

"The issue is, we want to make it look as much like American territory as possible," Koh said rapidly. "More like New Mexico than New Guinea." For the first time that day, there were laughs. "There's a treaty on this. Start with the *Baker* papers and dig up anything else you can. There should be some law review articles that'll help."

Tory nodded, jotting the information down, her hand shaking. She still had yet to learn some of the basics of legal research, and when it came to international law, like treaties, she didn't know a thing. But she was in now.

As Koh wrapped up, he ticked off the team leaders: Lisa Daugaard, Michael Barr, Graham Boyd, Sarah Cleveland, Paul Sonn, and several others. "Everyone else," Koh ordered, "give your leader your phone number, your dorm or address, any other way to contact you. I want a working list of every person who's involved. We need to have the complaint drafted in its entirety and the memorandum of law has to be done within the week. It's got to cover absolutely every argument the Justice Department might raise in a motion to dismiss. We're not even *thinking* of filing something without our entire response to the government worked out."

Students were buzzing in the hallway, trading phone numbers, setting up meetings, planning for a quick pizza. Lisa introduced herself to Tory and patted her on the back. She knew it paid to make fresh volunteers feel needed.

Tory thanked her nervously. "I'm really not sure I know how to find all the stuff Professor Koh needs."

"Don't worry." Lisa grinned. "You'll be fine. Harold probably knows half of it already, and if you get confused, just get me or Graham. I'll be on Lexis all night," she added, referring to the legal database.

Heart pounding, Tory headed down to the international law library, a labyrinth of stacks below the school. She'd heard Lisa was incredibly smart, if a little crazy. But more than anything, she just seemed friendly, and Tory was glad for the reinforcement. She didn't feel like she had a lot to contribute compared with the third years, who all seemed more like junior professors than students. As for Koh, Tory wasn't sure just what to think anymore. But she was determined to help the refugees.

"TRO practice is brutal," said Michael Ratner, Koh's Lowenstein teaching partner, on the phone from New York. "I mean *brutal.*"

He was referring to a temporary restraining order: an emergency measure used by the courts only in extreme circumstances. In a typical lawsuit, lawyers might wait for months to appear before a judge. But an attorney seeking a TRO was often in court within a few hours of filing papers. A TRO application was how Koh and the students would have to jump-start the case if they decided to go ahead with it. The Coast Guard was sending Haitians back from Guantánamo so quickly that if they didn't move soon, there might be no one left to help.

"If you get the TRO," Ratner went on, "it's almost worse because then you're not controlling the pace anymore. The other side immediately tries to get the order stayed, and you have to play defense. It's extremely intense, and people get really worked up. You're filing pleadings left and right—it's just crazy, Harold. Crazy."

For more than an hour Koh and Ratner went over litigation strategy, legal claims, the government's defenses, the role the students would play. Ratner pointed out that if they went forward with such a huge case, they'd need more resources than the Lowenstein Clinic could offer. More space. More computers and printers. High-speed copiers. A messenger service. Money for plane tickets. Paralegals for photocopying and organizing documents. Secretaries. In short, they needed a large law firm.

"Actually," Koh said, "Michael Barr's been working on that. He says he can get some people from Simpson Thacher."

Ratner was amazed—and, like Koh, more than a little incredulous. Simpson Thacher & Bartlett was a major Wall Street law firm that represented investment banks and multinational corporations. Michael Barr had worked there the previous summer. It was hard for either Koh or Ratner to imagine that Simpson Thacher would get involved in such a controversial and time-consuming project.

"Would they really be willing to stick their necks out on this?"

"Barr claims they're interested." Koh shrugged.

He doubted Michael could come through, but he had other things on his mind. He eyed a memo on his desk from Lisa Daugaard. She was pushing for the equal protection claim.

"You know," he continued after a moment, "even if we get Simpson, even if everything else lines up the right way, if we do this, we're going to lose."

Ratner agreed, but suggested that wasn't the point. Over the last two decades he had honed the strategy of filing a case to keep the issue in the news and force it onto the political agenda. He used litigation like a spotlight, dragging government officials and what he considered to be their wrongheaded policies into the glare. He rarely expected to win.

"We'd still do a lot of good by filing the case," Ratner went on. He pointed out that the government had been much more careful in their handling of asylum claims during the *Baker* litigation. With the courts and the media watching, the screen-in rate had shot up from less than 3 percent to as high as 85 percent. But with *Baker* dead, the government was again sending most people back to Port-au-Prince. Were they all simply economic migrants? If so, why had almost none been fleeing a few months earlier, when Aristide was president?

Koh pondered the spotlight theory. When he'd founded the Lowenstein Clinic with Ratner, the older civil rights lawyer's thinking had come as a breath of fresh air to him. But Koh still didn't want to bring a case he was certain they would lose.

"I take this personally," Ratner said, relating how his father had fled the Jewish pogroms in Russia and, years later, in Cleveland, had hired Holocaust survivors to work in the family business. Ratner still remembered glimpsing the numbers tattooed on their arms.

Koh thought about the images he'd seen on television: repatriated people on the docks in the Haitian capital, waiting in long lines as the army fingerprinted them.

"My dad first came here on a boat forty-two years ago," Koh mused. "San Francisco. Thought America was the greatest country in the world. He had this incredibly strong belief that you've got to fight for the underdog because no one else will."

"Well, you know," Ratner said, "he's right."

"It's funny. He was a huge Red Sox fan. We used to go see them play a doubleheader against the Yankees every year. We'd take the train down to New York in August. I think they lost every game for about five years."

Koh chuckled and fell silent.

"Look, Harold," Ratner finally said after an hour of conversation. "I can't take the lead on this thing. I've done this too many times and I've got other things on my plate. But if you want to do it, I'll back you every step of the way."

About one hundred miles from Port-au-Prince, on the coast near the impoverished town of Baradères, Yvonne spent the last of her money for the ferry. It was little more than a rowboat with an old, coughing motor. She'd never been on the water before, and she huddled in fear as the vessel sloshed about in the waves toward La Gonâve, a sleepy island halfway between Haiti's northern and southern peninsulas. She was seasick the whole way and decided that she hated boats.

On La Gonâve, Yvonne set off with several other Port-au-Prince activists seeking sanctuary along the island's north shore. A rainstorm the night before had made the trail a mess, and she was soon spattered with mud. They trudged up and down over steep hills, passing poor farms with scrawny goats and chickens. The sun was intense and there was no breeze, leaving her soaked in sweat. As evening fell, they came upon a small village near the coastal fishing town of Les Etroits. She was hungry and tired.

At first, the village seemed to be nothing more than a few huts made of scrap wood and palm fronds. But hidden among the trees was an old white church, part commune, part fugitive camp, where to Yvonne's amazement the pastor was harboring Aristide supporters from the capital. She had no money, but the pastor dismissed her concern with a wave of his hand.

"Ou se pitit Bondye," he said. You are God's child.

She thought she'd finally found a safe place to wait out the violence in Port-au-Prince. But only a few days later, a band of soldiers attacked the village merchant. His wife's screams were the last straw for Yvonne. Until that moment, she'd had little interest in all the talk of boats leaving the country. Now, she wanted to know everything—when, where, how much. A sailing vessel was about to depart from Les Etroits, down the beach, but the captain wanted one hundred American dollars from each passenger. Then she learned that people were building a boat just outside the village where she was staying. She went to investigate and found a group of men hurriedly pounding away at the hull under some palm trees. The boat didn't look like it would be ready for weeks, but a teenager from Cite Soleil whispered that they'd be leaving any day now, possibly for Cuba.

Yvonne grabbed his arm.

"M ap vini avè w," she said. I'm coming with you.

He studied her face, then nodded. There was no talk of money.

Later that afternoon, she went inside the church to write her mother, an icy guilt flooding through her. She had no idea when she would next see her children. Yet what else was there to do? She halted herself mid-thought, wiped her eyes, and went in search of the pastor. He'd promised to help her get a letter to Port-au-Prince.

The next night, the boy from Cite Soleil shook her awake.

"Yvonne, Yvonne," he whispered. *"Annou ale."*

Drowsy and disoriented, she followed him through the trees and out to the sand. Waves lapped at the beach. A flashlight beam sliced through the darkness, guiding the way to a rowboat just offshore. Yvonne waded through the shallows with the boy and climbed in. It was cool and the breeze played with the back of her neck. She shivered.

As they rowed out, the bigger boat emerged, its mast rising into the night sky. The awful ferry trip crept back in her mind. What would she do if they capsized? She imagined herself slapping at the black water, gasping for air as she sank.

The rowboat pulled alongside the larger vessel. It smelled of freshly cut wood. There were candles and more flashlights, and she caught glimpses of heads and limbs.

There seemed to be a special list of passengers, and arguments ensued about who could get on.

"Listen!" she finally hissed. "We don't have time for this. Would you please just pull me up?"

Arms reached out for her, and she hit someone as she tugged herself aboard.

"Aw!"

"Fè atansyon!" Careful!

"That's my head!"

"Padon, padon," Yvonne whispered. Sorry.

Everywhere she put a foot or hand, she pressed against warm flesh. There was no room. She squeezed into a small space on the edge of the boat, packed so tightly between two others that she had to bury her elbows in her stomach. She could feel someone's breath on her legs; her feet were resting on another person's arm. Still more people climbed onto the boat, and the waterline was now nearly at the gunwale. All around her, people were praying to Bondye and the *vodou lwa,* or spirit, known as Agwe, who ruled the seas.

There was a rumble beneath her as the boat's small engine jumped to life. They slowly turned away from shore, rocking in the waves, and the first sensations of nausea gripped her. She gazed back at the strip of beach, the clumps of palm trees, the ghostly steeple of the church beyond. Ignoring the voice inside her, the one protesting that this was her home, Yvonne squared herself to face the ocean.

"I've been at this for a long, long time and the government has pulled just about everything you can imagine on me. But this case was as bad as it gets."

Lisa, Koh, and the others hunched over the telephone, listening to Ira Kurzban and his colleagues recount their war stories about *Baker.* The Justice Department had been nothing short of vicious, Kurzban warned. They'd broken basic rules of procedure, he said, and even manufactured evidence. One of the tricks was appointing a no-name bureaucrat as an assistant secretary of defense for one day. The "assistant secretary" had then signed a prefabricated affidavit warning that all of Haiti was sailing for Florida. But just days later, he'd admitted that he actually knew very little about the true situation.

The courts had been just as hostile. At one point, Kurzban's team had been directed to respond to a complex Justice Department motion in less than two hours, a transparent gambit, he said, to ensure the government won. Meanwhile, at every hearing in Miami, military and Coast Guard officials had piled into the courtroom to stare down Judge Atkins. It had all been a little unnerving, said Kurzban's colleague, attorney Cheryl Little.

"Anyway," Kurzban said, "tell us what you're thinking."

Koh cleared his throat. "Well, we've been researching the issues and we certainly want your input and advice. If we all think it makes sense to go ahead, I'd be taking the lead and Michael Ratner would have a role, and as we said, we've got a team of students here. We've faxed you some of their memos."

There was a long silence followed by a few coughs. As Lisa Daugaard read the situation, this was a question of turf. Public interest lawyers didn't work for the money. There wasn't any. Most did it because they were fiercely dedicated to a cause. The attorneys from Kurzban's team were top immigration specialists, and Lisa figured that after years of working on Haitian refugee issues, they had understandably begun to see certain cases as their own. But now Koh was suggesting that he, a professor with little expertise in the area, and a bunch of students might file a case that in some sense belonged to this other group.

"I don't know how far you're going to get after what happened in the Eleventh Circuit," said one of the *Baker* attorneys. "That was as negative a ruling as we're going to see."

The group at Yale waited, letting the discussion play out. There were a number of other immigration experts on the call from around the country, and few of them sounded supportive.

"I'm just not sure there's a good-faith basis for another case," one attorney chimed in.

"I think I have to second that."

"We've got just terrible precedent in the Eleventh Circuit now. Do we really need another circuit running against us on these issues?"

In this skeptical frame of mind, the *Baker* lawyers asked for a summary of Yale's research. The students faced intense, even hostile questioning, but would not back down. Several times, they surprised even themselves by answering sharp questions with a precise citation to a case footnote or a statutory provision. Graham, correct or not, felt the lawyers had become too familiar with the law and were no longer able to see it with fresh eyes. And Lisa believed the people at Yale had another advantage: energy. The Kurzban group, after almost three months of nonstop work, sounded exhausted and demoralized to her.

When the inquisition was over, the students received no warm pats on the back. But Kurzban agreed there was a fighting chance on the First Amendment argument that lawyers had a right to talk with their clients. The Eleventh Circuit, he pointed out, had entirely ignored a key case supporting that principle, and another court might look more favorably on it. Plus, the claim would not be barred by res judicata because—as Koh had said earlier—the Kurzban attorneys had only pressed the argument on behalf of themselves. Any lawyer who hadn't been involved in the *Baker* lawsuit would still be taking a first bite at the apple.

The discussion ended with the tacit understanding that if Koh and the students felt prepared to file, they would go ahead. But some of the lawyers on the call made it perfectly clear that in their view, the people from Yale were in way over their heads.

Thinking about the case more seriously now, Koh mulled over ways he could limit the risks. One major advantage Yale had over the *Baker* team was the chance to select a more sympathetic court. Like his daughter, Emily, Koh was looking for the right forum. Koh and the students had sifted through a lot of different jurisdictions and judges, but Ratner told them the choice was easy: the U.S. District Court for the Eastern District of New York, located in the heart of Brooklyn.

"Just to reach the courthouse," he pointed out, "you've got to walk through a part of town that's got about every ethnic background you can imagine." More than half black and Latino in 1992, Brooklyn was home to perhaps one hundred thousand Haitians—one of the greatest concentrations outside of Haiti. Ratner figured people who lived or worked in Brooklyn, including Eastern District judges, would be especially sensitive to the racial undercurrents of the case. He considered the liberal New York press another plus. Sympathetic articles about the lawsuit would force the Bush administration to defend its policy not only in court but also to the public.

The clincher was the Eastern District's proximity. A couple of the more supportive immigration experts had talked up the Northern District of California because of the number of liberal judges there, but that was 2,500 miles away. Brooklyn was just two hours from New Haven—a ride on the Metro North commuter railroad, then the 4 or 5 subway line from Grand Central Station to Borough Hall.

Koh finally agreed on Brooklyn, too, for another reason. It would take an ultraconfident judge to rule against the Bush administration in such a high-profile case, and after sifting through a great many candidates, Koh had fastened on one man: the Honorable Jack B. Weinstein. Famous for handling massive class actions involving victims of asbestos and Agent Orange, the bald, bushy-eyebrowed Weinstein had a formidable intellect and was intimidated by no one. Conservatives complained that he simply did whatever he thought justice required, sometimes bulldozing decades of precedent as he went. That, however, would suit Yale just fine. And by happy coincidence, Weinstein was in the Eastern District.

There was, however, a problem. As in every other federal court, judges in the Eastern District were chosen at random for each new case. In Brooklyn, they used an old, hand-cranked wooden wheel for the task. Koh didn't want to bend the rules, but he considered it pointless to go to the wheel and end up with a Reagan appointee who would bounce them out of court in an hour.

One of Koh's former students who'd gone on to clerk for Weinstein had the solution: Don't file a complaint, she said. That's what would trigger the wheel. If the Yale team went in with an application for a TRO but no complaint, the case might get sent to the rotating "Miscellaneous Judge," who handled certain emergency matters. It would be an odd procedural maneuver because filing a complaint was the standard way to initiate a case. But Weinstein was slated to be the Miscellaneous Judge on March 16, just a week away.

Koh told Ratner his plan.

"That's nuts," Ratner said. He was usually the gambler, the one willing to play fast and loose with the rules. But not this time. It seemed like judge shopping to him, pure and simple. "They used to pull this in the Southern District when I clerked for Judge Motley," he said. "But I'm telling you, it'll never work today. I've filed in the Eastern District for years and it's just not going to happen."

Koh persisted. "If it doesn't work out," he said, "we can always go to the wheel."

Against his better instincts, Ratner gave in.

Tory had performed in choirs for much of her life, including her years at Trinity, and all morning she'd been singing—old Beach Boys, a college tune, whatever came to her. She was in a good mood. She was on her way to Miami.

She jogged over to the dining hall from her dorm room, legal pad in hand, and found Lisa Daugaard sitting in the center of a group of first years. They would all be interviewing Haitians who'd been screened in to the United States from Guantánamo.

"We want you to find out whatever you can about the camp," Lisa was saying.

Everyone scribbled notes, nodding.

"How the refugees are treated. How the camp is organized. How they eat and sleep. Anything. We just need to know what's happening down there."

Lisa gulped the rest of her Coke and unwrapped a candy bar: break-fast.

"The biggest thing is the interviews. We have government contacts on Guantánamo sneaking us information, and they've told us some people are apparently getting interviewed twice. They get screened in, which means they're supposed to come to the United States. But then the INS makes them go through the interview all over again, meaning they could be sent back to Haiti. We're not sure why. Just find out whatever you can."

Tory bounded back to the dorm. Her earlier research on the legal status of Guantánamo had seemed important because Koh needed the information. Tory had done the best she could, reading and tabbing material for him most of the night. As far as she could tell, the key point was something Koh already knew. According to the treaty with Cuba, Guantánamo was under the "complete jurisdiction and control" of the United States. That made it seem a lot like American territory, and thus subject to U.S. law.

But wading through dense legal materials just didn't ignite her imagination, even when there were real-world consequences. She was amazed at the way Lisa could sit in front of the computer reading cases on the Lexis or Westlaw databases for hours, her eyes darting from line to line. The impending trip to Miami was what mattered to Tory. She was about to meet real people who'd been stuck on this mysterious piece of land in Cuba. Hearing their stories, learning about their country and their lives—now *that* was exciting. She was on the sort of adrenaline high she hadn't felt since Nepal.

It was nearly five a.m., and while Lisa and Michael refused to admit it, they were engaged in a game of chicken. Both were tapping away at computers, and neither one was willing to stop working on the court papers before the other. The main motivation was the knowledge that every passing day meant more refugees had been sent back to Port-au-Prince, but a culture was also developing among the students—an intense dedication to the team itself. No matter what the hour, people were researching, writing, or hashing out ideas by phone with one of the immigration experts in Florida or California. Every evening, Koh worked with a different student to shape one of the legal arguments. Every morning, he found a cluster of notes taped to his door and his voice mail full. Nobody was going to class. Meals were rushed or skipped in favor of huge cups of coffee and doughnut holes. All-nighters were becoming a badge of honor.

After little more than two weeks, the team was on the verge of filing the lawsuit. They had researched and honed the claims, chosen a court, and perhaps even a judge. And now they finally had plaintiffs as well. Michael Ratner had found two advocacy groups, including the Haitian Centers Council in Brooklyn, that wanted access to Guantánamo. But the big news was a secret message from the naval base received by a Haitian activist in New York. Several American priests had been allowed on Guantánamo to comfort the refugees, and one of them had used a military fax machine to send a note with the names of six Haitians who wanted help. The name at the top of the list was Dr. Frantz Guerrier. When the fax reached New Haven, the students were ecstatic. It was like a flare on the horizon, confirming that real, live human beings were out there, in need.

And yet for all the momentum at Yale, Koh remained deeply ambivalent about going ahead with the suit. Though he hadn't said a word to the students, in the back of his mind he'd held on to the option of calling everything off. It would still be a simple move at this point because there were no real consequences to all their work. They'd gone to no court, phoned no newspaper, contacted nobody in Washington.

If Yale were really going to file the case, though, Koh now had to act. Under the rule of "administrative exhaustion," federal agencies generally couldn't be sued until they had first rejected a plaintiff's demand for relief. Assuming the exhaustion rule applied, it meant that before going to court, Koh would have to call on Gene McNary, the INS commissioner, to halt the interview process on Guantánamo. But once Koh contacted McNary, he would be publicly committing himself to the suit and its political consequences. He still had grave doubts about the legal arguments, and felt Lisa, Michael, and the others had wildly unrealistic expectations. In fact, he was starting to resent their pushiness.

Yet a thought, repeated by the students, kept nagging at him: if they didn't do something, no one would. And Koh knew more than most about how brutally the Haitian military treated its own people. One of the first Lowenstein Clinic torture cases had been filed against a former Haitian dictator for the 1989 torture of several prominent political activists—including KID leader Evans Paul. After demanding democratic reforms well before Aristide was elected, Paul had been beaten nearly to death. Though Koh had never met him, he knew Paul had been in a wheelchair for a year and still walked with a limp.

Alone in his office, Koh thought things over until late into the evening. When he finally left, the streets were empty and silent except for the distant rumble of a garbage truck.

The conversation at home with his wife, Mary-Christy, was brief. She was a public interest attorney who'd litigated plenty of lawsuits herself, and she suspected the demands of this case were going to be extreme.

"What do you think?" he asked her.

"If you believe it's the right thing to do, then you should file it," she said. "You should file it, and you should see it all the way through."

The next morning, Wednesday, March 11, Koh signed the letter to the INS, demanding access to Guantánamo Bay and a response by the following Monday. Then he gave it to his secretary and asked her to send it by registered mail, fax, and Federal Express.

"All of those?" she asked.

"We need to be sure this guy McNary gets the letter."

———

Simpson Thacher & Bartlett occupied a dozen floors at the top of a gleaming steel-and-glass tower on Lexington Avenue, directly across from Grand Central Station. The firm offices, trimmed in soothing sea green, housed several hundred attorneys and a huge support staff. Simpson was a moneymaking machine, generating revenues in the hundreds of millions of dollars. Its lawyers spent sixty or more hours at work each week, and most of that time was devoted to the corporate clients who paid handsomely for Simpson's services. But some went to pro bono work, helping nonprofit organizations and low-income New Yorkers and immigrants with their legal problems.

It was this tradition that Michael Barr had in mind when he called Simpson about the Guantánamo case. During his summer at the firm, Michael had worked on a development project in Eastern Europe for its most famous partner, former secretary of state Cyrus Vance. And while many summer associates were collecting their hefty paychecks for tasks of little consequence, Michael had also been shrewd enough to line up a second project, this one with managing partner Conrad Harper, a former NAACP lawyer who was president of the New York City Bar Association. Eight months after his stint at the law firm, Michael pressed the

Haitian refugee cause with both Vance and Harper. He stressed the injustice of Bush's policy while avoiding the shrill, activist language that might have alienated them, and had soon won support for the lawsuit at the firm's highest level.

Michael then made a third call to Simpson, this one to a liberal young associate, Jennifer Klein, who had spent her last year of law school at Yale. Would Jen be interested in the case? And did she know a partner who would join her? The idea excited Klein and she agreed to try to enlist her current boss, a senior antitrust lawyer named Joe Tringali.

A tall, reserved man in his late thirties with fashionable wire-rims and a wry smile, Tringali worked hard and managed important clients. But he enjoyed a reputation for dry humor and composure that had earned him the nickname Joe Cool. His office was crowded with antique toys, including a spring-mounted rocking horse and a red wooden truck parked on a file cabinet, and he had a trendy downtown loft, where he occasionally held Simpson events for junior attorneys.

Grateful as he was for his lucrative practice, Tringali still wondered at times if he shouldn't have become a teacher or public interest lawyer. Perhaps because of this ambivalence, he went out of his way to take on pro bono causes. In one recent suit, he had represented two gay men beaten up by federal drug enforcement agents. Tringali had a special interest in the case, for he was openly gay himself, making him somewhat of an outsider even at a relatively liberal law firm like Simpson.

The idea of a suit for the Haitian refugees intrigued him. He'd kept his eyes on the Guantánamo situation through the newspapers, and believed White House policy on the Haitians was outrageously unfair. Though he'd been working long hours on Viacom's suit against Time Warner over the cable movie market, he asked the firm's pro bono committee for authorization to get involved. It was not a typical case for Simpson. Suing the Bush administration carried the potential to alienate certain corporate clients, particularly if it attracted media attention. But with support from Cyrus Vance, Conrad Harper, and the pro bono committee, Tringali got the green light.

Back at Yale, Koh's jaw dropped. Michael Barr had delivered exactly what he'd promised. Ratner was ecstatic. He'd dealt with heavy-hitting private firms a number of times in his two decades of practice, but rarely had one been on his side. He knew better than anyone what a difference Simpson could make. "It gives us a deep pocket, endless resources, the capacity to deal with almost any problem that comes along," he crowed. And as Koh and Michael Barr both saw, there was another advantage to Simpson Thacher's involvement: credibility. If an old, established firm appeared on the court papers, the suit would have some weight to it. It wouldn't seem like a desperate, left-wing gambit.

Joe Tringali, though, remained cautious about the new partnership, foreseeing a number of possible problems on the horizon. With other lawyers involved, Simpson wouldn't have control over case strategy and court documents. That made Tringali uneasy. The firm had meticulous standards, and Tringali wasn't prepared to sign any pleading that did not meet his expectations. On the other hand, he was adamant that Simpson not remain in the background, simply bankrolling the case. That might have been the practice at some other firms, where attorneys wanted credit for pro bono work without any of the real responsibilities. But if Simpson were going to be involved, Tringali intended to play a major role.

One matter he didn't give much thought to was the role of the students. He'd worked with plenty of kids during their summers at Simpson Thacher. Young people with a couple of years of law school behind them could be fun to have around, but usually weren't much help on anything besides simple research tasks. They lacked judgment and precision, and the only antidote for that, Tringali believed, was years of legal practice. Given the stakes of the case Yale was contemplating, he did not expect much from the students. Tringali figured he'd be dealing mostly with Koh and Ratner.

Lisa had never been in a major private firm before, and its wealth astonished her. A spacious, gleaming elevator whisked the students to Simpson's top floor and opened onto a soaring reception space overlooking Lexington Avenue. There was original artwork on the walls, and office messengers silently made their rounds through the hallways. State-of-the-art printers waited, humming softly, flanked by skyscrapers of fresh white paper. There was even an outbox for dull pencils to be resharpened.

Lisa, Graham, Sarah, and the other students piled into a conference room reserved for them by Jennifer Klein. Backpacks were unzipped, new packages of legal pads ripped open, computers commandeered. Within an hour, a corner of Simpson Thacher & Bartlett's thirtieth floor had been transformed into the Manhattan office of the Lowenstein International Human Rights Clinic.

Believing that private firms were a tool of capitalist oppression, one of Lisa's friends had insisted that it was wrong even to set foot in an institution like Simpson. The hell with that, thought Lisa. If this place is going to give us all its resources to fight the U.S. government, I'm going to take everything we need. Her first trip to the firm's well-stocked cafeteria netted a fresh oatmeal raisin cookie and an imported Italian soda. "You people just don't get it," she muttered as she passed a couple of Simpson Thacher's lawyers. "But thanks for the snacks."

Sometime later, Klein arrived to find the students swarming over the secretaries' desks and crumpled paper and coffee cups scattered about. Her guests, who struck her as both frantic and self-righteous, had no time for even the most basic of courtesies. The only thing anyone could talk about was the refugees—and why Simpson Thacher's stupid computer system wouldn't let them save documents on a floppy disk. Klein took a deep breath. Michael Barr had been the consummate diplomat when he'd first called about the suit a week or two earlier, and she wanted to pull him aside. But he was nowhere to be found.

After tossing a few things into a wastebasket, Klein went back to her office with a copy of the court documents to review before Tringali arrived. They were a disaster. The main brief tried to address every argument imaginable, and the result was a one-pound stack of paper that read like a half-finished treatise on refugee law. Klein had been practicing for a couple of years now and knew that no judge would have the patience to read a one-hundred-page brief. None of the documents met the rigid court rules of formatting, either, and the case citations, which Simpson Thacher expected to be flawless, were a mess.

When Tringali came in, he wondered just what kind of role Simpson was supposed to have in the drama playing out in front of him. Lisa, Sarah, and the others believed they were taking great care to express their gratitude for access to Simpson's facilities, but that was part of the problem. Tringali thought he had made it clear that he was not furnishing ready-to-use office space. If the circus in the conference room was any indication, his initial worries had been accurate, though with a twist. Someone other than Simpson was indeed running the show. But it wasn't other lawyers. It was a bunch of law students.

Koh's eyes wandered around the room, from Lisa, Graham, Sarah, and the other students to Michael Ratner and Joe Tringali. The group suddenly seemed very small to him, and the contingent from Yale even more like kids than usual. Koh's arrival had given Tringali a little more comfort about things. But on the other end of the handshake, Koh couldn't help worrying about how young Tringali looked. He'd been expecting someone older—gray hair, creases around the eyes. He wanted visible evidence that the Simpson Thacher partner had been through a few dozen trials and really knew what he was doing. For now that Koh was in Manhattan, just across the river from the Eastern District courthouse, his nerves had seized him with a new force.   *TRO*

Meanwhile, the weekend was more than half over and there was still a massive amount to do if they wanted to go to court on Monday. Filing the TRO required a seemingly endless number of documents. There were lawyers' affirmations, a special motion for Koh to appear in court, a filing fee, specific numbers of copies for everything, signatures here, signatures there. With guidance from Tringali and Klein, the students were slogging through each of the documents, and third year Chris Coons, a *Yale Law Journal* editor who knew all the byzantine citation rules, was doing his best to clean up the case references. But the team was nowhere close to finishing.

Gathering information about Guantánamo had been particularly frustrating. When Koh taught a case in class from his textbook, the facts were neatly set out in the judicial opinion in a few pages. And in most lawsuits, lawyers had access to their clients and could get their side of the story before preparing the initial court papers. None of that was available here. For the last two weeks, Sarah and other students had been playing detective, relying on newspapers, the Coast Guard's public affairs office, and a couple of Creole translators eager to describe the problems they'd witnessed as INS subcontractors on Guantánamo. The story Yale had pieced together was complex.

From early November 1991 through mid-March 1992, over fifteen thousand Haitians had been intercepted and ferried to Guantánamo. Eight thousand had been screened out, many of them already sent back to Haiti, and another six thousand had qualified to go to the United States and make their case for asylum. A thousand more were still on the naval base waiting for their screening interviews, and additional refugees were arriving all the time. According to a United Nations observer, the screening process had descended into chaos. The translators reported that hundreds of interview records had been lost. Screen-in rates varied drastically from one asylum officer to the next, and as Kurzban had suspected, government higher-ups were apparently pressing to send more people back to Haiti. There was also the continuing mystery of second interviews: the INS seemed to be questioning some refugees twice. But why?

All the details of the Guantánamo situation remained sketchy, but now, on the verge of filing, the team finally got some critical inside intelligence. It came through Robert Rubin, a San Francisco civil rights lawyer Lisa had worked with the previous summer. He'd obtained an internal government document from another human rights attorney with contacts in the Bush administration. Rubin faxed the two grainy pages to Simpson and everyone crowded around the conference room telephone to talk things over with him.

What Rubin had sent was a memo from Grover Joseph Rees, the general counsel of the INS, revealing that a number of the Guantánamo refugees had "a communicable disease of public health significance."

"What's that mean?" someone asked.

"It probably means," Rubin said, "that they have AIDS."

Several students winced. Koh sat motionless, processing the news. This was a new problem, and a big one. Haitian boat people were hardly a popular group. Haitians with AIDS would be the most unsympathetic plaintiffs imaginable. The stereotypes and fear surrounding HIV remained extreme at the time, the tail end of an era of panic and desperation, of angry protests by ACT UP radicals, the traveling display of the AIDS quilt, families chased out of small towns after their children contracted the illness. Some people still believed they could get the disease from casual contact; others thought of it as a problem mostly for the gay community. Certain religious conservatives continued to call it a punishment from God.

Haitians in America faced particularly harsh prejudice relating to HIV. Years earlier, the federal Centers for Disease Control and Prevention had branded them as a high-risk group for the disease, along with intravenous drug users, gays, and hemophiliacs, who often needed blood transfusions. It was an ugly stigma for all the groups, but along with the gay community, Haitians found themselves under especially vicious attack. Some watched their businesses fail; others were evicted from their apartments; Haitian children were beaten in school. Graffiti in Brooklyn proclaimed: "Haitians = Niggers with AIDS."

Haitian Americans responded with bitter protests, and the CDC later rescinded its assessment of them as a special risk, stating that it was no longer statistically justified. By 1992, a Harvard physician who'd spent years in Haiti would publish his conclusion that AIDS had most likely been introduced there by tourists from the United States—not, as some believed, the other way around. But the pernicious myth that all Haitians carried AIDS lingered.

Lisa, Koh, and the rest had barely absorbed this first aspect of the Rees memo when Rubin revealed another piece of big news, solving the mystery of the second interviews. Rees had directed that for the screened-in Haitians who were HIV-positive, the INS was to hold final asylum hearings on Guantánamo—without lawyers.

Until that point, the screened-in refugees had all been flown to the United States for the actual asylum hearing.* It was a more formal proceeding before an INS bureaucrat, and the applicant had the right to an attorney and, if necessary, an appeal. As an immigration expert, Robert Rubin knew that the right to counsel was absolutely crucial. Government statistics showed that legal representation more than doubled the chances that an individual would win asylum.

The students could easily see why. Even U.S. citizens without legal training could never present their cases the way an American lawyer would. But foreigners dealing with the American legal system were at still greater risk. An alien bureaucracy with mysterious rules, a strange language, the highest possible stakes: even with a translator, it would be a harrowing experience, and who knew what the chances of success were?

But the HIV-positive detainees on Guantánamo would have to go through their asylum hearings alone.

"I think we need to be very careful with the HIV issue," Koh said. "Making a big deal of it is not a good idea." He didn't want the case to become a debate about bringing Haitians with AIDS into the United States. That struck him as legal and political suicide.

Ratner disagreed. He'd spent his whole life litigating unpopular issues, and he wasn't interested in hiding the problem. If the INS was treating HIV-positive refugees unjustly, then the courts and the public needed to know about it. Fear of losing was not a reason to avoid the matter.

Lisa backed Ratner—loudly. The Rees memorandum was just one more violation of equal protection, she snapped. The INS was already

*See List of Terms, p. 317.

treating Haitians worse than any other group of refugees on earth. Now the agency was simply piling on the abuse. If Koh wasn't willing to fight this policy, why go to court at all?

Koh cut her off. He'd already agreed to include an equal protection claim in the papers, though he was certain it would fail.

Ratner finally suggested they seek advice from lawyers in town who specialized in AIDS advocacy. This was an issue many people had a stake in, he pointed out, and they would have to be consulted no matter what the team decided to do.

He called a colleague at the ACLU, Judy Rabinovitz. For years, Rabinovitz had been fighting to get rid of a federal regulation that banned HIV-positive foreigners from the United States. The brainchild of Senator Jesse Helms, the HIV rule was the basis for the Rees directive not to fly the ill Haitians off Guantánamo. Most medical experts criticized the ban as founded on fear, not science, and it seemed useless in practice, since millions of people entered the United States each year without testing. But support for the ban remained high, particularly among conservatives, who had defeated a recent attempt to take it off the books.

Given the volatile history of the issue, Rabinovitz asked Yale to soft-pedal it in court. Challenging the HIV rule before a judge, she warned, was risky and might undercut whatever support was left in Washington to change it.

Ratner remained skeptical. He believed that only a judge, someone not subject to political pressure, might dare set aside the bar on people with the virus. But both he and Lisa deferred to Rabinovitz, respecting her long-term agenda. For now, anyway, they would only mention HIV in passing, if they said anything at all.

"I can understand holding off on AIDS," Lisa went on, "but that still leaves open the way we frame the rest of the case."

"We're *not* going to take on everything at once," Koh said.

"So you're just going to limit it to the First Amendment issue?"

"It's a major step asking for lawyers for these people."

Lisa shook her head. "But the point is to get them off Guantánamo!"

"No," Koh said, his voice rising in frustration. "The point is to have lawyers for everyone to ensure that those who deserve asylum get it."

He'd only been working with Lisa for two weeks on the case but was already exhausted by her constant harping. This was not just another one of her political stunts. It was a federal lawsuit with terrible odds. The

team had worked out a strategy that gave them a reasonable shot at winning. Getting the Haitians lawyers would be a huge victory, and he wasn't
going to ask for more.

"You whittle the objective down enough," Lisa complained, "and it
won't matter if we win. Litigation by provisional goal would make sense
to me if I saw the reason to wait, but I don't."

"Forget it, Lisa." Koh threw her a hard stare. "I'm not fighting about
this anymore. I'm the one who has to sign the papers. I'm the one who
has to argue the case. I'm not going to ask the judge to declare the whole
Guantánamo operation illegal, because he's never in a million years going
to do it. He's got to have some workable option in his mind, and it can't
be airlifting thousands and thousands of people to Florida."

Lisa stalked off, and soon afterward, Koh, tired and annoyed, learned
that Judge Weinstein was in the hospital.

———

The rain came down in a wall. It was gray and hard and made a roar as it
hit the water. The heavy drops slapped at Yvonne's face. She shook with
cold. The boat pitched through the waves, shooting up a crest, plunging
into the trough behind it. Her nausea had sharpened into a fine, hard
point, and she could feel she was about to throw up once more. A wave
rolled under them and she doubled over, retching into the sea. She gathered her strength to lift her head and held out her tongue in the rain,
washing away the acrid taste. She was grateful, at least, to be at the edge
of the boat. A person could breathe there. The middle was a crush of
bodies lying in a stew of vomit, diarrhea, and urine.

The captain had promised that Cuba was no more than two days
away, but they no longer seemed to have a destination. Yvonne mumbled
a prayer and adjusted her grip on the gunwale. Her joints were stiff from
holding on, but she permitted herself no time to stretch her fingers. Earlier, a wave had hit her head-on, the briny water exploding against her
chest and nearly knocking her off the boat.

All she wanted was stillness and warmth, a place to lie down, a ray of
sunlight. The boy beside her leaned between his legs and heaved, and as
the boat rolled, his head jerked toward her. A trail of vomit slapped against
her leg. He looked up, eyes a haze of pain and apology, then fell forward
and threw up again. Yvonne let go with one hand for just a moment and
stroked the boy's head. She didn't believe they would ever see land again.

Three
PICKING A JUDGE

MICHAEL RATNER HURRIED into One Pierrepont Plaza, a teak-colored skyscraper that housed the U.S. Attorney's Office for the Eastern District of New York. The 150-lawyer office, among the largest and most prestigious of its kind, prosecuted federal crimes committed in Brooklyn and other parts of New York, including many celebrated Mafia cases. There was also a civil division that handled everything other than criminal prosecutions, from civil fraud and asset forfeitures to lawsuits filed by private citizens against the government. The civil division's chief, a bearded, energetic Brooklynite named Bob Begleiter, was the man Ratner had come to see.

The two shook hands warmly. Years earlier, Begleiter had worked at a public interest law firm that helped needy Brooklyn residents, and he'd crossed paths several times with Ratner's organization, the Center for Constitutional Rights. Despite serving under a Republican president, Begleiter considered himself a liberal, and he was quick to remind Ratner of his past work. The lawyers traded a story or two, and then Ratner handed him a sheaf of papers. At the top was the caption, *Haitian Centers Council, Inc., et al. v. Gene McNary, Commissioner, Immigration and Naturalization Service, et al.*

"We're filing for a TRO to get access to the Haitian refugees on Guantánamo," Ratner said.

Begleiter sighed. Sue the president, sue the State Department. This was Ratner, after all. After leafing through the papers, Begleiter decided the case was a surefire loser. He'd kept track of *Baker,* and knew it had been kicked out of court just weeks earlier. But Ratner was a likable guy and Begleiter didn't see the need to get combative. He called in Scott

Dunn, a stocky, earnest-faced young lawyer who handled the office's immigration cases.

"This is the truth-and-justice brother," Begleiter said, introducing Ratner. "The other one, Bruce, he owns the building. Really."

Dunn's eyes widened.

Ratner took the kidding with a smile. His brother was a hugely successful real estate developer, and the stark contrast between siblings—one sued presidents, the other dined with them—made for good gossip.

"Yeah," Ratner joked. "If the case doesn't go well, I'll have you all evicted."

He shook hands again with both men, then double-timed it over to the courthouse. The meeting put him in a good mood. He could work with these people, he figured, and that was no small victory. It was one of Ratner's strengths that he made friends easily and could find common ground with most of the lawyers he met. This get-along attitude might have seemed to contradict his strident politics, but he'd learned long ago that good relations with the other side made litigation easier. And Ratner was glad to have met them alone. He'd begun to fear that both the students and Koh might get carried away with demonizing the government lawyers. That would only interfere with the day-to-day handling of the hundreds of disagreements, large and small, that they would have to resolve if the case went forward.

Koh peered out the taxi window. The Brooklyn sidewalks overflowed with people of countless nationalities bundled up against the late winter chill. Ratner was right, he realized. This was definitely the place to file the *McNary* case. Koh still wasn't sure, however, just what he was going to tell the judge. With all the time he and the students had spent finishing up the papers, there'd been no opportunity to practice his argument, and his anxiety began to build as they neared the federal courthouse. The driver swung over to the curb and Koh looked up. Above him loomed a huge concrete box, six stories high and nearly a city block in length. He was disappointed. Though he knew plenty of courthouses were not all that impressive, for some reason, he'd imagined a columned marble edifice with a sweeping staircase. This building looked like a warehouse.

Still, he had one reason to feel upbeat. The judge substituting for the ailing Weinstein was the Honorable Eugene Nickerson, in Koh's mind the most desirable alternative of the other judges available. Nickerson was a smart, liberal jurist, known for his scrupulous fairness and even temperament. He was also confident enough not to duck complicated questions of international law. In fact, his landmark 1984 decision on torture as a violation of the law of nations was the basis for a number of the Lowenstein Clinic's cases. One of his law clerks even happened to be a recent Yale graduate with an interest in refugee law. Koh was delighted at all this good fortune.

A small cheer erupted from the students as Koh shuffled up to them. They had taken the subway and were waiting outside in their interview suits, hugging themselves in the cold.

"Hey, you almost look like real lawyers," he said, only half-kidding.

Lisa yawned and tried to will away her headache. She still wasn't persuaded of Koh's legal strategy, but was glad to see he looked ready for court, his dark suit lending him gravity and his white shirt brightening his appearance despite the bags under his eyes. Even so, he seemed slightly disheveled to her. It might have been the way his hair flopped over his ears or the off-center knot of his tie. While he wore the clothes of the establishment, there was always something that didn't seem to fit quite right.

Lisa herself certainly didn't look the part. After working on the court papers all night, she had dozed for an hour on a pullout bed in Michael Ratner's home, and was wearing the same wrinkled, flower-print cotton dress she'd had on for the last four days. There'd been no time to head back to New Haven for a change of clothes, but the work was done, and that, she figured, was what mattered.

The team headed into the courthouse, Koh with his father's briefcase, everyone else carrying canvas backpacks.

The deputy court clerk eyed Koh.

"Don't you need a complaint for this?"

"Rule 50.5 includes emergency motions," Koh said over the din of voices and ringing telephones. "All we have are the affirmations and a proposed order."

The clerk studied the papers again.

"I don't know." She hesitated.

Ratner looked from Koh to the clerk. She thumbed through Koh's affirmation and the exhibits, her mouth twitching from side to side.

"All right," she finally said, sounding less than convinced. She stamped the papers and directed Koh to Judge Nickerson.

Ratner was amazed. He'd been sure they would end up before the wheel.

An hour later, they were in Nickerson's sweeping courtroom. It had a forty-foot ceiling; heavy, pewlike seats in the gallery; and a massive, elevated bench for the judge. The wall behind the bench was paneled in green marble, with an enormous seal of the United States of America painted in gold.

The students filed into the first two rows of the gallery, shoes silent on the carpet. Lisa smoothed her dress and pulled out a legal pad. Koh and Ratner were conferring in the courtroom's enormous well, and they seemed small and very far away to her.

Two men strode past the students and joined Koh and Ratner. One was short and stocky, and looked very young; the other was tall and thin, with a clipped beard. Lisa had been expecting a battalion of scowling attorneys in charcoal suits. These two government lawyers didn't look imposing at all. She watched the shorter one shake hands with Ratner and Koh. He appeared to be making small talk, and Ratner smiled. Lisa couldn't believe it. This man stood for everything she loathed, that she thought Ratner loathed, too.

Koh was only slightly less taken aback. Ratner could be a ferocious advocate, but, on the brink of the argument, he was playing the nice guy as Scott Dunn shot the breeze in a nasal Brooklyn accent. Koh was about to turn away when Dunn asked if he'd be willing to postpone the hearing for twenty-four hours. "We'd like to get the right folks from Washington in here to deal with this," Dunn explained, "and that could take a day."

Koh considered him for a moment, then said no. He was not about to give the Coast Guard any more time to return people to Port-au-Prince. Dunn paused, surprised. It was common practice to ask for a short postponement, and common courtesy to grant it. He went back to defense counsel's table, wondering if his adversary was simply trying to be a "hard-ass."

Back turned, Koh began laying out his papers, almost as he would before class. And there was, perhaps, a slight classroom feel to it all. Students were seated around him, notepads out, waiting for Koh to begin speaking, just as he had hundreds of other times. Even Nickerson's Yale clerk, who had now appeared, had once been in Koh's course, and Dunn was not much older than the students themselves.

Koh was just beginning to breathe a little easier when Nickerson shot through a door behind the bench. Seventy-three years old and silver-haired, with even features and deep-set eyes, he looked like the kind of judge Norman Rockwell might paint. Everyone snapped to attention. Nickerson shoved his chair aside and fixed Koh with a stare.

"I've glanced at your papers," he said. "Can you explain to me what exactly you're doing here?"

Koh stepped toward the bench but Dunn was too quick.

"Scott Dunn for the government, Your Honor. Before we get to the merits of this action, the government must raise a preliminary point. We believe plaintiffs are judge shopping. It's our understanding that they used the Miscellaneous Judge rule to get this case before you instead of going to the wheel."

Dunn went on as Koh scrounged for something to say.

"Plaintiffs already litigated this case down in the Eleventh Circuit, and they lost. They've come up here for a second go-round—and they're trying to get you, Your Honor, as the judge in this case by framing it as a TRO without filing a complaint. Totally improper."

Nickerson nodded.

"Your Honor," Koh began. Nickerson held up his hand.

"How'd this get on my docket, Mr. Koh?"

"This is an emergency," Koh said. "The rule assigning matters to the Miscellaneous Judge authorizes—"

"Do you intend to file a complaint and try this case to judgment?"

". . . authorizes you to hear this emergency application. As we speak, the U.S. Coast Guard—"

"What I'm asking you, counsel, is are you going to file a complaint and try this case to judgment?"

"Yes, Your Honor."

"Then you had better file it," the judge said sharply. "You should have gone to the wheel."

Nickerson beckoned Koh forward and thrust the TRO papers into his hand. Then he whisked out the door, robe billowing.

The team gathered in the courthouse library, thick with the smell of old books and dust. The students had reached the limit of their physical and emotional reserves, and they hunched around a reading table, blue-black circles beneath their eyes, brows knit in concern. One of them suggested returning to New Haven to regroup. Why opt for the wheel and get a judge who was almost certain to throw out the case?

Ratner calmly scratched his beard. He'd been waiting for Nickerson to bounce them from the moment they'd walked into court, and to him, it was one big shoulder shrug. After all, they hadn't *lost* anything, other than a little face.

"Okay, look," he said. "Our first option failed, but we knew there was no guarantee. Let's be realistic here. Brooklyn's still the best place to file this thing. So we get a lousy pick for a judge. So what? The Second Circuit's still a good appeals court for us, if it comes to that."

Lisa stole a glance at Koh. He looked nervous, and she wondered whether he'd have the resolve to keep going. While Lisa was no stranger to confrontation, even she had been taken aback by the severity of Nickerson's response, and admitted to herself that she was glad not to have been in Koh's shoes.

"He really seemed to think we were manipulating things, didn't he?" Koh mused. He followed up with a joke and a couple of students chuckled.

There was a long pause, and Koh's expression changed.

"This is an emergency," he finally said. "Michael's right. We can't start over now. We have to go to the wheel." His voice rose. "We're right. And if we're right, we're going to win."

Lisa leaned against the wall of the clerk's office with Graham Boyd, Sarah Cleveland, and the other students. Scott Dunn seemed to be gloating. And why not? she thought. He'd just watched a bunch of bleeding hearts from Yale get shot down by one of the most liberal judges in the Eastern District. Now their case would likely be assigned to someone who'd toss them out of court even faster than Nickerson had.

Koh's mind was swimming with possibilities, all of which seemed bad. When he reached the front of the line, this time for civil proceedings, he presented the TRO papers to a deputy clerk. She stamped "92–1258"on the front page—the 1,258th civil case filed in 1992—and handed a copy back to him.

Then she turned to the wheel, an old contraption that would soon give way to a computer. It was an eight-sided, polished oak barrel about a foot in diameter that rotated on a metal spindle. The barrel held some one hundred tiny manila envelopes the size of a credit card, and inside each envelope was a small card bearing the name of one of the court's dozen or so judges. The clerk spun the wheel in a matter-of-fact, almost bored fashion, and the envelopes made a soft, ruffling sound. As Koh watched the wheel turn, he struggled to think of the other judges in the

Eastern District. Jacob Mishler . . . Thomas Platt . . . Reena Raggi. Was there *anyone* to hope for after Weinstein and Nickerson?

The wheel slowed down. *Fft, fft, fft* went the envelopes.

A Carter appointee came to mind: Judge Charles Sifton. Was he a liberal? Koh couldn't remember a thing about him.

Fft . . . fft . . . fft. The wheel fell still.

The clerk opened the door, pulled out an envelope, and tore it open. "Judge Sterling Johnson Jr.," she said in a flat voice.

Koh looked over at Ratner, who shook his head. *Who?*

They both glanced at Dunn.

"Interesting pick," he murmured. "Very interesting pick."

They had been on the ocean for almost two days. By late afternoon, the sea had calmed but the waves kept up a rhythmic slosh against the boat and a light rain fell. Land was still nowhere in sight. What food and water they'd brought was gone. People huddled in heaps of arms and legs, lost in misery. Some were bailing out vomit and rainwater to prevent the waterline from rising any higher.

Yvonne's clothes, soaked through, clung to her skin, and her body shivered in protest. A young mother near her had fallen ill and Yvonne was cradling the baby in her arms. She was whispering to the child when someone started to shout. It was the captain.

"A light!" he cried, pointing into the gloom. "A light! A light!"

Yvonne squinted and saw a white pinprick blinking on the horizon. She gave a soft cry, and the people wedged around her came to life.

The captain sliced an empty plastic jug in half, jammed a candle into the spout, and held it up in a vain attempt to send a distress signal. Then he turned the boat in the direction of the beacon, but for what seemed like hours, they made no progress toward it. The boat's weak engine had failed and the wind wasn't cooperating.

Finally, as daylight began to fade, a ship emerged on the horizon. It was tiny at first, no more than a toy, its lights twinkling in the mist. But as the minutes passed, it grew larger and its details began to take shape. A white tower bristling with black metal antennae jutted high above the deck. There was a large gun turret on the bow, and flags strung from the tower hung limply in the drizzle.

It was Bondye, someone cried. God had been looking out for their boat.

But as the vessel plowed toward them, relief became concern—and then panic. Passengers tumbled into one another and the sailboat jerked to one side. The captain shouted for everyone to lean the other way before the boat capsized. The huge ship kept coming, the roar as it plowed through the surf overpowering the screams in the sailboat. Yvonne tightened her grip on the baby. She could feel herself slipping out.

But just as the ship appeared certain to ram them, it veered around, churning the water, and eased its engines. The people beside Yvonne fell quiet, and the sailboat at last righted itself. Heart still pounding, she gazed up at the hull, a white metal wall that rose high above her. Near the bow was a diagonal slash of red paint and enormous block capital letters that spelled out "U.S. COAST GUARD."

A few moments later, a motorized raft from the cutter came buzzing toward the sailboat. As the raft pulled alongside them, a man wearing a blue uniform hollered through a megaphone in broken Creole.

"This is the United States Coast Guard. We need everybody to sit down!"

Excited young men on Yvonne's boat were fighting to get to the raft.

"Sit down!" ordered the megaphone man. "Sit down! Sit down! You're all safe!"

Other members of the Coast Guard crew tossed puffy orange life vests to the passengers and demonstrated how to put them on. As people fumbled with the vests, the megaphone man called for the children. Someone reached for the infant in Yvonne's arms and she gingerly passed it forward. A basket on a cable descended from the big ship. The men on the raft tucked the baby in the basket and it rose into the air.

A rope ladder spilled down from the cutter and flopped into the sailboat. People surged forward, grabbing, shouting. One by one, they pulled themselves up. Yvonne tightened her backpack and climbed. It was only a short distance, but with her fatigue, the ladder seemed to stretch to the sky. Men in gloves and breathing masks helped Yvonne aboard. She teetered forward, weak and disoriented, and leaned against a railing. A line formed and she shuffled along with the others until she came to a table with several more men in gloves and masks.

One of them dug through her backpack, then returned it and gestured for her to keep moving. Someone offered her a blanket; someone else, a cup of water. Yvonne gulped it down and nodded in thanks, then followed the others toward the stern. To her amazement, hundreds of

Haitians were crammed together under a huge tarp, dozing beneath blankets or talking in small groups—a floating refugee camp in the middle of the Caribbean.

She picked her way through the crowded deck, searching for a place to lie down. She was about to curl up in her blanket when an explosion rocked the boat. A fireball erupted against the dark sky, bathing the faces around her in a brilliant orange. Flaming splinters trailed into the black sea and the thick aroma of burning wood flooded her nostrils.

"Yo detwi bato a." They blew up your boat, someone muttered. Just like ours. Just like all the rest.

The rain had stopped and the air was cool. The engines rumbled below deck, mingling with the sounds of the wind and the ship cutting through the surf. Yvonne lay down and tugged the blanket around her. She mouthed a prayer and then, stretched out on the landing pad of the cutter, drifted into a fitful sleep with a question hanging over her: Where were they going?

Koh, Ratner, and the students powwowed over lunch in the courthouse cafeteria, a dreary, windowless space in the building's basement. What they'd learned about Judge Johnson was not good. He was a Bush appointee, so he was almost certainly conservative, and he'd only been confirmed a few months earlier. That meant he was still adjusting to the heavy demands of the position. It seemed unlikely that he'd want to probe a complex foreign policy operation ordered by the president who had put him on the bench. Worse yet, Johnson had served as New York City's special narcotics prosecutor for the past fifteen years. That background probably meant a judge sympathetic to the government, and jaded, if not downright hostile, when it came to claims of federal wrongdoing.

They could not have done worse, Koh decided. And yet there had been that curious remark by Dunn at the wheel.

Before going to court again, Koh finally took a moment to run through his argument for Ratner and the students. He started to go on as if he were in class, launching into a complex lecture that seemed to cover all of immigration law. There were long lists of concepts and principles; references to a dozen cases; caveats, qualifications. After a few minutes, Ratner held up his hand.

"Harold, look. You've got the law down cold, but that's not what matters. Get to the point: These people are being sent back to Haiti even as we speak, and they could be tortured or killed. You just have to repeat that twenty different ways."

The students looked at one another. Harold getting criticized: that was something new.

Koh listened in silence. He started wondering if Ratner should take over. He was the experienced lawyer, after all. He'd been through dozens of these hearings. But then Koh shook off the thought. He'd agreed to be lead counsel. It was his responsibility. He had to argue the case.

It was mid-afternoon when the team arrived outside Johnson's court-room. Koh dropped his heavy briefcase on the floor, tired of lugging around pounds of documents, and the students waited nervously, checking their watches.

Ratner wandered over to the courtroom door and peered through the small window. He froze.

"Harold," he hissed. "Harold, come here."

Everyone crowded around as Koh pressed his face against the glass. There, at the far end of the courtroom, sat Judge Johnson. He was addressing several lawyers. He looked to be about fifty-five or sixty years old, with a puffy face and a broad frame. And he was black.

Adrenaline bolted through Koh. Interesting pick indeed, he thought.

The Eastern District was undergoing major renovations, and Judge Sterling Johnson Jr. was temporarily stuck in a first-floor annex. His court-room was a drop-ceilinged box with blue carpeting and heavy support pillars that blocked the view from the wide, shallow gallery.

He was conferring with his two law clerks when everyone filed into the courtroom.

"*Haitian Centers Council versus McNary*," called the courtroom deputy, and Johnson nodded to the lawyers.

"Good afternoon," he said in a firm, friendly baritone. "Welcome to the Eastern District."

Unusually polite judge, Koh thought. Even nice. He stole a glance at Scott Dunn, then stepped to the podium and introduced himself.

"May it please the Court," he began, hoping to cut off a burst from Dunn.

"We are here today on behalf of Hatian refugees who have . . . have fled their homeland to, uh, escape political persecution," Koh stammered.

"This case grows out of a coup that forced out Haiti's first democratically elected president last . . . last September."

Back in the gallery, Lisa fidgeted with her pen. The run-in with Nickerson seemed to have thrown Koh off balance. She'd never seen him, a man of such intellectual confidence, this nervous before.

"Over fifteen hundred supporters of the ousted president, Jean-Bertrand Aristide, have been killed in politically motivated violence, and the Haitian military is hunting people down. Many have left the country by boat, and what the U.S. government is doing is sending Coast Guard cutters into the waters off of Haiti to intercept them."

Koh paused. Johnson was listening intently, so he plunged in again, describing Guantánamo, the screening process, and the repatriations. The judge appeared to be getting the picture, and he started asking questions in an easy, conversational tone.

"You say they are on Guantánamo. How are they holding these people?"

"Well, I haven't been down there, Your Honor. None of us have. The reports say there are tents, and they're surrounded by razor wire."

"Razor wire?"

"Yes, Your Honor. These aren't prisoners of war. They're refugees, unarmed people who're fleeing violence and persecution in their own country."

"Now, what are these interviews you're talking about?"

"They're screening interviews, Your Honor, to determine whether someone has a possible claim for political asylum."

"And you're saying these interviews aren't being conducted properly?"

"That's right, Your Honor. They're interviewing some people twice and there's just a lot of confusion. They've lost interview records, they're sending people back by mistake—"

"Who's doing this? You said the United States military?"

"It's the INS who's in charge of screening. The Coast Guard stops the boats and takes people back to Haiti. But the military, it's the military running the camp."

"Well, they're on a naval base. There's a need for order."

"Yes, Your Honor. We don't dispute that. And we don't dispute that the INS can be conducting these interviews. All we're saying is, the interviews have to be fair, and these people have a right to speak with a lawyer before being sent back to a place where they might be killed."

"And they've asked for you to represent them, Mr. Koh?"

"Yes."

"And you have been denied access to your clients?"

"Yes, Your Honor," Koh said, for the INS had not responded to Yale's demand to meet with the Haitians. "That's one of our primary concerns. Our claim here is there's a First Amendment right for lawyers to communicate with their clients. That right has been denied, even though the government's letting others on the base, other nonmilitary people. For instance, they're letting on priests."

"Why not lawyers?"

"Well, that's our question, Your Honor."

"I have a question about—what was the name of the case?" Johnson's law clerk whispered to him. "Right. *HRC versus Baker.* Now, do we have res judicata here?"

No, Koh said. These were new lawyers demanding First Amendment access to Guantánamo. Also, the INS was now conducting final asylum hearings on the naval base, as directed by the recent Rees memorandum, something not at issue in *Baker.* That new INS procedure, implemented just weeks earlier, had never been reviewed by a court.

Before Koh could continue, Johnson cut him off. "I'd like to hear from the government before we go any further," he said.

Deflated, Koh sat down. It was coming home to him how little time a lawyer had in court to make a point; how absolutely critical it was to distill everything down to a few words. Ratner leaned over.

"We're doing fine," he whispered. "At a minimum, he won't boot us today, and frankly, I think we're doing a lot better than that."

Dunn was up now, and talking quickly.

"Scott Dunn for the United States, Your Honor. You just touched on the most important thing when you asked if there's a preclusive effect here. Absolutely. Res judicata bars this whole suit. This is exactly the same case that the plaintiffs brought in Florida and lost. Despite what they're telling you, there's no difference. They're trying to relitigate issues and claims that were decided against them by the Eleventh Circuit just last month."

As he spoke, Dunn gestured with his right hand for emphasis. It was, one of the students thought, almost a karate chop.

"Since filing *Baker* last November, plaintiffs have been trying to use the courts to decide matters of national security, in place of the Defense

Department, the Department of State, and the president himself. The courts have already decided that's improper and this case is over and done with. But they're trying to start it all over again here in Brooklyn."

Lisa thought she heard condescension in Dunn's voice, but the truth was that he was on edge. This was the biggest case he'd ever worked on and there'd been no time to prepare. After Ratner had arrived with the TRO papers that morning, Dunn had gone straight to the courthouse with his boss, Bob Begleiter, resolved to do the best he could under the circumstances.

"Unless Your Honor decides to dismiss the case immediately," he went on, "the government will request a continuance of the hearing until tomorrow morning. As I think is abundantly clear, Your Honor, this is a case of national importance."

Koh stole a glance at Johnson. He couldn't be sure, but the judge's eyes seemed to be narrowing.

"The solicitor general himself," Dunn said, "who oversaw the government's case in *Baker,* will come in from Washington, D.C., tomorrow to address this court."

Lisa nudged Graham. Kenneth Starr was coming in? Tomorrow?

"I don't think I have to tell you how uncommon that is. The solicitor general rarely, if ever, appears in district court and—"

"Mr. *Dunn.*" The judge leaned forward, his knuckles pressed into the hardwood, and stared at the attorney. "You go right ahead and bring the solicitor general in here, or anyone else you want. But don't think that's going to change one thing that happens in this courtroom. I'm from Bed-Stuy, and I am *not* going to be intimidated."

Dunn looked as if he'd been punched.

The hearing, Johnson added firmly, would resume the next morning at nine.

The students bounded out of the courthouse, ebullient. Their judge was new to the bench. He was a Bush appointee; they were challenging a Bush policy; and there was a long, long way to go. But Bedford-Stuyvesant was one of the toughest neighborhoods in Brooklyn, and Sterling Johnson Jr. hadn't survived there by letting people push him around.

———

Southern Florida was teeming with college students on spring break. Jeeps rumbled along the Fort Lauderdale strip blasting Guns n' Roses and daiquiri-fueled crowds spilled out of the neon-lit bars. But when Tory and her friends landed at the Miami airport, they headed straight for Little Haiti, a scrappy quarter of town with a bustling open-air market, tiny homes in aqua and pink, and corner restaurants with handwritten Creole signs. Well after dark, they pulled into the Budget Inn on Biscayne Boulevard, a run-down fifties-style motel that reeked of chlorine.

The students were planning to visit a Haitian advocacy group the next day. But by a stroke of good fortune, the Budget Inn had contracted with the government to house Haitians who'd just arrived from Guantánamo. Dozens were gathered around the courtyard's rickety picnic tables to smoke and debate. The students would not have to spend any time hunting down people to interview about camp conditions.

After a day of investigation, Tory and fellow student Michelle Anderson found someone who seemed to know a lot about the interview process, a tall, gaunt man named Claudel Pierre. But their interpreter was nowhere to be found, and the two students were growing frantic. Graham Boyd had called earlier to say that Yale was going to court the next day, and he needed the Guantánamo information immediately. The interpreter finally showed up late at night, and Michelle and Tory went to work.

Pierre told them he was a writer and a staunch supporter of Aristide and his Lavalas political movement. He said he'd plastered his neighborhood with political posters, and when soldiers had not been able to find him, they had killed his father and brother. Several days later, he'd fled Haiti. It was the kind of story INS asylum officers on Guantánamo heard so often that some doubted if it was ever true. The students, though, listened with mouths agape, horrified.

When they turned the topic to Guantánamo, Pierre shook his head with disgust.

"Se kankou lanfè . . ."

"It's like hell," the interpreter relayed. "We are treated like animals. There are thousands of us. Children everywhere. There is so much confusion. Nobody knows what's happening."

He'd spent almost a month on Guantánamo, he said, before being interviewed. Someone from the INS had asked him questions for about fifteen minutes and then screened him in. Ten days later he was flown to Miami. He was one of the lucky ones. Most of the people Pierre knew had been sent back to Haiti.

Had he been interviewed more than once? *Non.*
Had others? Yes.
So there were definitely second interviews on Gitmo?

Pierre gave a grave nod. The interpreter listened to him for a long time, then turned to Tory and Michelle and spoke in his Creole-tinged English.

"If a cutter heading for Port-au-Prince still has space, more screened-in people will be questioned again. If a person's story has even a small inconsistency, then he is told 'you are lying' and sent back to Haiti. The same thing happens if the camps are getting too crowded. Some of the screened-ins, if it's too crowded, they take them away and put them on the cutters for Haiti."

Tory hunched over, writing as fast as she could. Every answer was like a flashlight shining into another dark room, revealing a new secret. The students felt as if they were uncovering something very important, but after a time, Michelle began to realize she had no idea what was true and what might be an exaggeration. How, she kept asking, did Pierre know everything he was telling her? His response much of the time was that "everyone knew."

The interpreter went on to explain that after Pierre had been screened in, "military men" had taken his blood.

"For a test?" Michelle asked.
Pierre nodded.
"And then what?"

Two days later, he said, they had repeated the blood test, though he wasn't sure why. After that, he'd been flown to the United States.

"Were other people being tested?" Michelle asked.
Pierre nodded.
"What happened to them?"

"Lòt yo? Mwen pa konnen." The others? I don't know.

It was now two in the morning. The team up in Brooklyn would be going to court in less than eight hours. Although Michelle had lugged her 1990 Apple Macintosh desktop computer down to Florida, there was no point in typing up her notes because she had no access to a printer. She ended up writing out the information by hand and signing it herself because Pierre insisted that he remain anonymous, afraid of saying anything negative about the INS.

Tory looked doubtfully at Michelle's handiwork:

AFFIRMATION OF MICHELLE ANDERSON ON
BEHALF OF ANONYMOUS HAITIAN REFUGEE

There wasn't even a notary public available to witness Michelle's signature. Could it be filed in this haphazard condition? Who knew?

Tory pounded on the motel office door. A young clerk appeared, rubbing his eyes. Apologizing, Tory explained that they had to send a fax to New York. Immediately. He gave her a blank look, then nodded to the machine. She and Michelle fed in the papers, dialed Simpson Thacher's number, and waited for the electronic *beep-whirr-hiss* from the receiving end of the line. The firm had dozens of fax machines running twenty-four hours a day, and a little after three a.m., Graham Boyd had the document in his hands.

To mark the end of their Florida visit, Tory and her friends went swimming at a nearby beach. They were pale and exhausted after so many hours bent over their legal pads, and the turquoise water and blinding light seemed surreal. Tory left Florida with a hint of a sunburn to show for her week away, while Michelle and the others spent one more night with relatives of one of the students. They had a huge home overlooking a canal in Fort Lauderdale, with a luxury boat and a guesthouse. The hostess smoothed fresh sheets on the students' beds while her beagle, who was getting chemotherapy, waited in the corner.

"I think it's just so interesting what you're doing," she said brightly. "And I feel for all those poor people from Haiti. But we just don't have room for them here."

When Koh reached the courtroom the next morning with Ratner, he was more amazed than anxious. Nearly empty the day before, it was now buzzing with activity. Haitian activists and community leaders were in the gallery, and reporters were canvassing the crowd for leads. Several new lawyers flanked Dunn and Begleiter, though Kenneth Starr was nowhere to be seen. Dunn was struggling with a large pushcart piled high with boxes. He pulled out stack after stack of papers, dropping them on defense counsel's table with a thud.

Lisa and Sarah ran up the aisle, breathless, and plunked their own set of papers on the table in front of Koh. Their faces were gray, their eyes swollen. They'd finished proofreading and copying the complaint at five in the morning. In a rare move, Koh had stopped working before midnight in order to be sharp for court, leaving the students in charge of the final draft of the documents. Lisa had considered it a signal moment, making the students closer to equals with the lawyers. While Koh had been visibly concerned about surrendering so much control, he'd given in. There was simply no way he and Ratner could keep track of everything.

But to Koh's great relief, the students had somehow pulled it all together. They'd even squeezed in the affirmation from Tory and Michelle, tucked in as Exhibit 10, confirming that final asylum hearings were taking place on Guantánamo.

Ratner flipped through the papers. "This is beginning to look like a real case," he grinned.

When Johnson resumed the hearing, Koh ran through all the papers he was submitting to the judge, including the document from Miami. "We have students who are working with us down in Florida," Koh explained. The judge nodded with a hint of a smile.

Starting to feel more comfortable, Koh began to tick off the legal claims in the complaint with his usual one-two-three approach. By the time he reached the last claim—Lisa's equal protection theory—he was in full throttle.

"We think what is really going on in this case is separate but unequal," Koh said. "There are now two asylum tracks. There's one asylum track for everybody else and then there's a separate asylum track for black Haitians that's being administered on Guantánamo. If you're a black Haitian on Guantánamo, you don't get a lawyer, you don't get an appeal, you don't get anything. What's the harm of letting lawyers talk to their clients? What's the harm of having clients talk to their lawyers? What's the harm of giving one asylum process to everybody?"

Koh seemed to be making progress. What grabbed Johnson's attention, as it had the day before, was the ban against lawyers on the base.

"You mentioned yesterday," the judge said, "that there are other people who've been granted admittance to Guantánamo."

Koh nodded quickly. "The people that have been allowed on are priests and the press. So newspaper reporters are there and people from the television media are there," he said. Then he remembered something he'd learned from Ira Kurzban. "A piano tuner was allowed on Guantánamo."

Johnson's eyebrows shot up. "Piano tuner?"

"Yes," Koh said.

"What's a piano tuner being allowed on Guantánamo for?"

Koh couldn't resist. "I guess the Haitians are allowed to play the piano but not allowed to get a lawyer before they file for asylum, Your Honor."

Johnson cracked a grin. Koh could feel the momentum swinging his way.

"It may be one thing to say we can't let anybody come on the base," he said. "But to let some people come on and not others because you're afraid of what they might hear or say, that's a content-based denial of First Amendment rights."

Content-based denial: the government allowing some forms of speech but not others. As the students knew from class, the Supreme Court rarely allowed it.

"The government has put our clients in limbo," Koh summed up. "They are people without a country. They can't get in. They can't get out. They can't get help, and now the government is saying no court can review what's going on. We think, Your Honor, that that's an emergency situation that requires judicial intervention."

Dunn was no longer the government spokesman. That job fell, for one day, to Steven Valentine, an official with the Civil Division of the Department of Justice. Valentine repeated the res judicata argument. Everything in the new *McNary* case now before Judge Johnson had already been decided in the government's favor in *Baker,* Valentine said. To drive home his point, he waved repeatedly at the mass of documents from the earlier lawsuit piled on the table beside him. In the right court, before the right judge, Valentine might have carried the day. But Johnson was now plainly concerned about the situation on Guantánamo.

The naval base, the judge pointed out, was under the "complete control and jurisdiction" of the American government. Didn't that mean the Haitians had at least some legal protection?

Valentine's answer was simple: no. "Guantánamo is a military base in a foreign country," he declared. "It is not United States territory."

"But United States law is applicable there," said the judge.

Valentine shook his head. "All the sources of law that the plaintiffs claim here, the INA, APA, U.N. Article 33, all of those do not create any judicially enforceable rights on the part of the individual Haitians on

Guantánamo. They're outside the United States and therefore they have no judicially cognizable rights in United States courts."

Johnson looked incredulous. Guantánamo was controlled exclusively by the U.S. government, he repeated. And the U.S. government derived its authority from the Constitution, and was therefore limited by it as well. Was Valentine really insisting "that Haitians, or anyone else at Guantánamo Bay, have no constitutional protection *at all*?"

That's right, Valentine repeated. They're outside U.S. territory, so they have no rights.

"You're saying, if I hear you correctly," the judge said slowly, "that an agency like INS, assuming that they are arbitrary and capricious and even *cruel,* that the courts would have no jurisdiction because the conduct did not occur on U.S. soil? That's what you're saying?"

"That's correct, Your Honor."

Johnson sat back in his high leather chair, momentarily quiet. To the students, it seemed as if the judge couldn't quite believe what was coming out of Valentine's mouth. When the government lawyer called on the judge to dismiss the case immediately, Johnson said no, he was going to reserve his decision. He wanted written arguments from both parties. He wanted time to think it over.

———

Several times that morning, Yvonne asked the cutter's crew where they were being taken. She didn't trust them, especially after finding one of her countrymen, an outspoken activist named Pierre Charles, handcuffed to a railing. Yvonne tried to give Charles some water, but one of the uniformed men turned her away. The crew had a slew of other problems to handle—people with high fevers, pregnant women. Yvonne Pascal was just one person out of dozens jabbering at them for one thing or another as they attended to the sick, handed out endless plates of rice and beans, and tried to maintain some semblance of order.

The crews on all the cutters in the Carribean were drunk with exhaustion. "Migrant vessels," as they called them, were streaming into the Windward Passage at a faster rate than ever before. Just as the Haitians on one boat had been taken aboard, instructions crackled over the radio with orders to proceed to the next vessel. It was a round-the-clock operation, with crew members working six hours on, six hours off for weeks at a time.

The refugee boats appeared as silent blips inching across Officer Jim Carlson's flickering radar screen, deep inside the 270-foot medium-endurance cutter *Mohawk*. Carlson coordinated the radar and air surveillance of the Alien Migrant Interdiction Operation, or AMIO, the name for the U.S. policy of intercepting Haitian vessels. A massive undertaking, the AMIO required over a dozen Coast Guard cutters and heavy air support from Dolphin and Sea King helicopters, Guardian Falcon jets, and several mammoth C-130 Hercules turboprop planes.

Under Carlson's direction, each Coast Guard aircraft patrolled a certain sector of the Caribbean, radioing him to report sightings of new refugee vessels. After verifying that the boat was in international waters, beyond Haiti's twelve-mile territorial limit, Carlson would select a cutter to intercept it. The exercise played like a high-stakes video game, with Carlson juggling planes and cutters to keep up with the endless stream of electronic blips.

In Carlson's mind, the purpose of the AMIO was not to block access to the United States. It was to save lives. Boats that the Coast Guard failed to reach sometimes made it to Cuba or the Bahamas, but Carlson knew they were just as likely to sink. They lacked navigation and communications equipment, and their crews often had only a vague idea of how to get to Florida. On Carlson's first day, he'd been on a helicopter that had spotted a small Haitian boat fighting its way through angry seas. As the chopper flew past, the passengers below waved frantically for help. Carlson and the crew returned later to hunt for the vessel, but it had vanished.

After intercepting Yvonne's boat, the Coast Guard cutter she was on had reached its capacity. The deck was packed and the ship was running out of food, fresh water, and blankets. The commanding officer ordered that they plot a new course, and the ship steamed northwest through the night. The next morning, the cutter eased into the waters between Leeward Point and Glass Beach, then cruised around Fisherman's Point and headed toward a series of piers.

Yvonne studied the shore, relieved finally to see land but unsure of where they had arrived.

"I think," someone said, "this is Guantánamo."

———

Now the Yale team had a new task to worry about: responding to the government's motion to dismiss the case. Anxious for a quick ruling, the

Justice Department had agreed to file a brief by Friday, just two days away. Judge Johnson had given Yale until Monday to respond, a tight time frame under any circumstances, and almost absurd in a case of such complexity. But Koh had quickly agreed to the schedule. With hundreds of Haitians being returned to Port-au-Prince every day, there was no choice.

While waiting for the government's papers, the students converted one of the law school's clinical offices into their case headquarters. They set up a filing system, a calendar, mailboxes, and a telephone list of all the volunteers. Beside each name was the amount of time the person had offered to the cause, from spot duty to what the students called "full-body commitment." The office boasted a battered IBM PS2 computer with no hard drive, a frayed couch, some telephones, and a couple of scratched wooden desks from mid-century. Cold air seeped through fissures in the leaded-glass windows overlooking the law school courtyard, and the ancient radiator bucked and hissed, straining to heat the room.

The operation may not have met Simpson's standards, but it was more formidable than it appeared. The dormitory where many first years lived was across the law quadrangle, which meant fresh brainpower was immediately available any time of the day or night. The colossal library was close at hand. Every student had unlimited access to the high-priced computer databases necessary for legal research. And just down the hall were world-class specialists on every legal theory in the case—the Yale law faculty, some of whom had already agreed to provide advice.

But the team was still missing one key element, and that was a case manager: someone who could organize all the student labor power, ensure deadlines were met, and solve all the logistical problems that were bound to spring up. Sarah Cleveland suggested third year Ray Brescia, and Koh readily agreed. A square-shouldered New Yorker with bulldog tenacity, Ray had devoted himself to human rights work at Yale, even spending a summer in Guatemala documenting abuses by that country's military. Sarah had worked with Brescia to support a strike by Yale's service workers, and in her view, Ray was the rare person who always got the job done.

That night she and Lisa pleaded with him to join the cause. Ray wasn't sure. He was troubled about the situation on Guantánamo, but like Lisa, he had an avalanche of work to do if he was going to graduate on time. He was also annoyed at Koh for denying him a spot in the

Lowenstein Clinic the semester before. While Koh had reasoned that
Brescia was already directing another clinic, Ray had taken the slight personally. He could be touchy, showing an aggressive streak in the law
school's Friday-afternoon football games, and was one of the few students to challenge Koh in class. But he told Sarah and Lisa he would
think it over.

The next morning, Brescia stopped by Koh's office.

"I'm with you, man," he grinned.

Koh pounded him on the back. He liked Ray's intensity, and his addition would immediately plug a gap: Michael Barr was gone. After pushing so hard to file the case and bringing in Simpson Thacher, Michael
had flown out west for a long-planned family ski vacation. His departure
just before the team went to court did not sit well with the others. Koh,
in particular, wasn't pleased. No one else was taking a break, and he
hadn't put his own reputation on the line only to have key people disappear at such an important juncture. Michael began to feel guilty the moment he got on the plane, and kept calling back to Yale to check in. But
his case duties had to be reassigned, and the culture of complete dedication he'd helped create began to turn against him. The team needed his
help now, not later.

Two days after the argument before Judge Johnson, Lisa took the train
down to New York to pick up the government's motion to dismiss the
case. She was chatting with Ratner in his office on lower Broadway—a
dingy room decorated with newspaper headlines from his old cases—
when a deliveryman arrived. He was struggling with a large brown cardboard box. Ratner signed for it, then ripped it open. There was a
mountain of paper inside, including a document entitled Motion for
Sanctions.

By the time Lisa had lugged the box back to Yale, she had an ugly
bruise on her hip. Koh grabbed the sanctions motion, his eyes racing
from line to line. According to the Justice Department, none of the legal
claims in McNary had any chance of success because the Eleventh Circuit
had rejected all of them and the Supreme Court had refused to intervene.
Yale therefore had no good-faith basis for filing a follow-up case in New
York. As a penalty for the "frivolous" suit, the Justice Department demanded payment of all its attorneys' fees and court costs—a potentially
astronomical amount. No fewer than fifteen government lawyers had

signed the document, including an assistant attorney general. A lot of people in Washington were angry.

Koh felt sick. He *taught* about motions for sanctions. They were filed under Rule 11 of the Federal Rules of Civil Procedure, which authorized fines against both lawyers and parties for bringing frivolous lawsuits. Since Koh's signature was on Yale's papers, he was personally liable for any resulting sanctions. His bank account could be on the line, he thought to himself. Perhaps even his house. It was unlikely to go that far, but who knew?

Lisa and several other students were watching him, and he tried to stay calm. He didn't want them to know how frightened he was.

Alone in his office, Koh called Michael Ratner for reassurance.

"Those bastards at DOJ," he said to Ratner. "They're trying to destroy my reputation."

Ratner wasn't that concerned. He thought Koh was overreacting.

"Look, Harold," he said, "it's simply part of the deal when you engage in aggressive litigation like this. It's going to happen."

Ratner had been the target of a number of Rule 11 motions over the years. Indeed, radical civil rights lawyers faced the threat of sanctions so often that Ratner's Center for Constitutional Rights relied on a special group that did nothing but Rule 11 defense work. And reputation was rarely an issue for Ratner, who saw Rule 11 motions as so much squawking by his opponents. He knew, though, that Koh hadn't been through the mill before, so he let him vent.

But as Koh continued talking, Ratner began to realize that this particular Rule 11 motion might pose a real threat. The first concern had to do with Yale's Legal Services Organization, or LSO, the law school entity that ran most of the student clinics. LSO was part of the lawsuit, which meant it could be on the financial hook if the government won the Rule 11 motion. LSO was also tied to Yale University—and its endowment. Depending on the extent of Yale's insurance policy, if everything lined up the wrong way, it could produce a nightmare scenario: the government raiding school coffers because Koh and Ratner had filed an ill-planned lawsuit.

But there was also the issue of Koh's own professional liability. Practicing lawyers like Ratner had insurance that protected them from Rule 11 motions. Koh, however, was a professor, and neither he nor Ratner knew how Yale's insurance policy would shield him if something went wrong. There was likely a deductible involved, Ratner figured, and it could be huge.

It was Friday at six o'clock. They had three days, minus one hour, to submit their response to Judge Johnson.

A dozen students gathered at Koh's home that evening, a handsome colonial in the faculty neighborhood a mile from campus. Spring officially began the next day, but Connecticut remained cold and dark. A fire crackled in the living room and the group nursed coffees and Cokes. Word about the sanctions motion had spread, and everyone was on edge. Koh passed out copies of the government's brief, which at eighty-two pages was nearly half an inch thick.

"They think they can just scare us off with this thing," Koh began. "But they have no idea who they're dealing with. Every one of you is as smart as those people at Justice, and we're willing to work a lot harder than they are." The students were perking up now.

"If we lose this case, we may or may not get Rule Eleven-ed," Koh went on. "But if we win, there's no way that can happen. If we win, then by definition this wasn't a frivolous lawsuit. So that's what we're going to do . . . we're going to win this thing."

People nodded, throwing in an "all right" or an "okay."

"So I can keep my house," Koh added, the dimples returning to his face. The room exploded in nervous laughter.

Koh then pointed to Adam Gutride, the first year who'd been working on the claim that lawyers had a First Amendment right to speak with their Haitian clients.

"This is DOJ's response," Koh said to him, flipping to page forty-three of the brief. "Start here. I want you to read every single case they cite. Check them all. We need an answer to everything they say and then write it up in five pages that destroy their position. I need it by noon tomorrow."

Next Koh turned to Lisa. "Same thing with equal protection," he said to her. "Every case, every point. Attack everything. Rip what they say to shreds."

He put several more students to work on a new, high-stakes issue. Along with the sanctions motion, the government had demanded that Yale post a ten-million-dollar bond with the court, meant to cover the cost of halting the repatriation process. If the Coast Guard were prevented from returning anyone to Haiti, the brief warned, then more Haitians would pour out of their homeland and head for the United States. According to the government, this was what had happened during the *Baker* case—and it had cost the Coast Guard about four million dollars a week in extra operations.

"Find out if there's ever been a larger bond demand," Koh directed. "I doubt it. There've got to be cases that say we don't have to put up some huge amount like this."

The students grabbed their backpacks and headed off into the New Haven darkness. It was Friday night, two days before the end of spring break, and the rest of the school was still away on vacation. The law library's soaring Gothic reading room waited, empty and silent.

Everyone fanned out to work, and Adam Gutride was soon surrounded by stacks of legal decisions on the First Amendment. His disgust grew with every case that he read. The Justice Department brief was misconstruing the precedents—even, he believed, flat-out lying about them—to justify its policy of refusing access to Guantánamo. It was a moment of overwhelming disillusionment for him. Many of the other students on the team were quick to charge the Bush administration with sinister motives and unethical conduct. As a college debater accustomed to looking at both sides of an argument, Adam hadn't shared their view. He'd been sure that the Justice Department attorneys were reasonable people and would eventually negotiate with Yale to improve the situation on Guantánamo. But even he didn't see it that way anymore.

Moments after the last student left his house, Koh sat down at the keyboard. Tense and tired, he began to type. At three a.m., he stopped to refill his coffee mug. Sometime after six, the sky turned from black to a feeble gray. By nine, his eyes dry and his shoulders cramped, he had written forty pages. At eleven, Ratner, who'd come up from New York, called from the law school to suggest he'd better look at the draft. Koh splashed water on his face and rushed to campus. He had a quick bite while Ratner read through it.

The news wasn't good. Koh had gotten caught up in the need to explain everything again, covering the most minute details of the case. Great for teaching. Not for court. Ratner paused. "You've got to start over, Harold."

After a moment of shock, Koh realized Ratner was right. He was furious at himself. He'd wasted the entire night, lost even more sleep, and now had only forty-eight hours before the deadline. To make matters worse, he'd gotten some bad news about the Rule 11 problem from Jay Pottenger, another professor at Yale. The university had an insurance policy that protected him up to $1 million. But it had a deductible of $250,000.

Great, Koh thought. *After they take our house, we're covered for the next 750K.*

He collected the comments on the brief from Ratner and a couple of professors, along with the work of all the students—over a dozen computer disks, each with a chunk of research. As it turned out, Koh had been right about the ten-million-dollar bond. It was the largest in the history of the New York federal courts.

Koh began typing again in the mid-afternoon on Saturday. He wrote until late, slept a few hours, kept writing. On Sunday evening, he jumped in his car and roared back to the law school.

Ray Brescia had already organized teams of students to review each section of the argument. He circled past Koh's office every hour to collect new pages and hand off revisions. Koh kept at it, but around midnight, he started to lag. Soon he was typing in slow motion, losing his place, his head bobbing up and down as he tried to stay awake. At four, Ray began pushing him to finish. They had to start the final citation check, he warned. Koh grunted . . . and kept typing. Most of the other students, even Lisa, were too tired to continue, and by five, Ray was standing alone next to Koh, staring at the screen with him. Just after dawn, Koh collapsed. The notes on his desk were a jumble of incoherent scribbles and he couldn't hold a thought. He stumbled out of the office, unsure if the brief would even get done. All he could think about was sleeping.

As Koh drove home, trying not to weave over the yellow line on Prospect Street, snowflakes flitted against his windshield. *Oh, shit,* he thought. *Now we'll never get the brief to Brooklyn on time.* At home, he dragged himself upstairs and fell into bed. *This might be the end of the case,* he figured, too numb to be upset. *I went ahead, I took a risk, I blew it.*

He fell asleep in seconds and began to dream of terrible things. Then he tumbled into a black abyss.

Ray had watched Koh limp off sometime after six a.m. that Monday, leaving him with a mass of paper and computer disks. Two days earlier, Brescia hadn't even been involved in the case. Now, at crunch time, he was the only one working on it. Ray had brought in a small stereo to keep up his energy, and he cranked it up, took Koh's chair, and started typing in the edits.

Ratner and several students straggled in by eight a.m. to help, but without the lead author, the brief was turning into a disjointed, Frankenstein-like document. As the morning wore on and classes resumed, the hallways filled up with students, their faces tan, their hair bleached from days in the sun. Lisa shuffled into the office to help, so fatigued she felt ill. The floor was covered with paper. Everyone was on their hands and knees editing in pen, with Ray still poking at the keyboard.

Suddenly, Koh burst in. He'd had two hours of sleep.

"Ray," he said with a grin, "Michael Jordan wants the ball."

Just before one-thirty, Koh hit the print key for the final version: seventy-five pages, eighty-four footnotes, and references to more than one hundred cases and exhibits. Students dashed to the law school copy center with the brief, and minutes later, Ratner jumped into a taxi with the finished product and raced for the train station. He caught the early-afternoon train to Manhattan moments before it left and collapsed into his seat, a dozen copies of the mammoth submission beside him. He would be in New York City by four o'clock, giving him just enough time to reach the courthouse in Brooklyn.

Now it was Judge Johnson's move.

With the brief out of the way, Koh had to tell Dean Guido Calabresi about Yale's potential liability under the Rule 11 sanctions motion. Calabresi knew the Koh family well—he was already a professor when Harold's father arrived in New Haven with his wife and children in 1961—and had long supported Harold in his career. Koh hoped the dean would feel some personal stake in the suit. Calabresi came from a family of refugees who had fled Italy just before World War II.

Koh brought Ray Brescia and Sarah Cleveland with him to the meeting, figuring that if the dean became really upset, he would at least feel obliged not to show it with the students around. They filed into the dean's office—oriental rugs, oil portraits of esteemed scholars—and Calabresi welcomed everyone with a concerned smile. An energetic, elfin man with wise eyes and a goatee, the dean had been tied to Yale University for over forty years and cared deeply about the law school as an institution. Nurturing its faculty and students and protecting its reputation were profoundly personal concerns to him.

Koh began by giving Calabresi some background, describing things as positively as possible. They had a judge who seemed sympathetic to the suit. A huge number of students had been working with great energy, including Sarah and Ray. Simpson Thacher had committed a partner and a few associates to the project. But the candy coating could only cover so much.

"The government has filed a Rule 11 motion against us," Koh finally admitted.

Calabresi clasped his hands together and brought them to his chin. His brow furrowed.

"Harold, what's our potential exposure?"

"We think we'll succeed in opposing their motion to dismiss. This should—"

"But what's our potential exposure?"

"We doubt the court will even decide the sanctions motion right now, and we believe it's meritless."

"Harold. How much are we talking about?"

Koh returned Calabresi's gaze. "It could be significant," he said.

The dean tended to show distress more than anger, and at the end of their meeting, he seemed distressed. With Ray and Sarah looking on, Calabresi calmly told Koh to keep him informed about how things were going. The implied message was stronger: *Don't let this get out of hand.* That was, perhaps, Koh's own greatest fear.

Later that day, Koh went to see the manager of New Haven Savings Bank's Hamden branch. He and Mary-Christy were hoping to redo their kitchen soon, but he wondered if he'd even qualify for a loan now. He went into the bank partly out of sheer curiosity.

He knew the manager vaguely, having taken a loan out some years before. He reminded the man of his position at Yale, his salary, his wife's income, their home in New Haven. Given that information, Koh asked, would the bank extend him a loan?

The manager was all smiles. He had just a few routine questions, he said, including whether Koh had any contingent liabilities.

"Well," Koh replied, "I recently filed a lawsuit against the United States government. They're demanding that I post a ten-million-dollar bond, and I face financial sanctions for bringing an allegedly frivolous case."

The manager looked at Koh in surprise. After a moment, he set his pen down.

"I'm sorry," he said.

Koh went home and told his wife the situation. Mary-Christy understood financial pressure. Some of her public interest work involved helping impoverished people to deal with their debts.

She was quiet. If they had to, she finally suggested, maybe they could protect their house by declaring bankruptcy.

The call finally came on Friday afternoon.

"Harold?" It was Ratner, breathless.

"Michael."

"Harold, we won."

Koh leapt out of his chair.

"I'll call you back," he said, then slammed down the receiver. He raced down the hall.

"Hey! Hey! Hey!"

Lisa and Sarah were the first to hear him shouting.

"We won! We won! We won!"

The news whipped through the halls and students streamed into the Lowenstein office. Koh grabbed a clinic phone and pounded out Ratner's number. Down in New York, Ratner had started running the decision through the fax machine, but Koh couldn't wait for it to come through.

"Just read the thing!" he demanded.

More than a dozen people were now crammed into the room, sitting on desks, leaning against file cabinets, wedged against the windowsill.

Ratner raced through the opinion, and Koh relayed the words to everyone around him. There was silence until he reached the first ruling: res judicata did not apply. *Baker* did not bar the new suit. The room exploded.

Koh had to call out the next ruling just to be heard. The judge had rejected DOJ's demand for a bond and declared the sanctions request "premature." *"This is not a Rule 11 case!"* Koh yelled. The cheering erupted again.

"Hold on, hold on!" Koh shouted. Ratner had more. "Hey!" Koh pumped his fist in the air. "The government's barred from returning any screened-in people to Haiti! Johnson's halting the asylum hearing process! That's the ball game!"

The judge had sided with them on everything. It was a total victory. The students roared and pounded on the tables and file cabinets.

There was, though, one issue left. Koh waited as Ratner explained something for a long moment, then turned to face the group.

"We won the right to discovery. *They have to let us onto Guantá-namo.*"

The cheers started up again, but Koh shut everyone down with a wave.

"We've only got four days," he said, his voice suddenly sober. "We've got to go to court again on Wednesday."

It was now Friday afternoon. They had to fly to Guantánamo Bay to meet the Haitians, which also meant tracking down Creole translators. They needed lawyers who could go to Miami and Washington, D.C., to take depositions of U.S. immigration officials. They had to assemble deposition transcripts and affirmations and other documentary evidence, write another brief, possibly prepare witnesses for examination in court, and give Koh the research support for an extended oral argument before Judge Johnson. And it all had to happen in less than 120 hours.

Koh put the receiver back to his ear.

"Uh, Michael? What do we do now?"

"I don't know," Ratner said. "I've never won one of these before."

Four

FIGHTING THE STAY

ON THE MARCH morning that Michael Ratner dropped off Yale's initial TRO papers at the U.S. Attorney's Office in Brooklyn, Scott Dunn and Bob Begleiter called the Office of Immigration Litigation in Washington. The Justice Department arm responsible for representing the government in federal immigration cases nationwide, the office went by the unfortunate acronym of OIL. Public interest lawyers who dealt with OIL viewed it as an insulated group with a fanatically anti-immigrant culture. "They never met an alien they didn't want to deport," said ACLU lawyer Lucas Guttentag, who was advising the Yale team. "They fight every case to the nth degree, whether the end result is just or not. They don't care what damage they do to individual lives. They know no shame."

When the OIL lawyers learned of the Yale lawsuit, they immediately notified their superiors at Main Justice, an immense columned office complex several blocks from the White House. Word of the suit shot up the hierarchy and within hours had reached the highest levels of the department. Sometime later that day, the court papers arrived on the desk of Paul Cappuccio, an associate deputy attorney general who at just thirty years old was one of the Justice Department's rising stars.

Cappuccio didn't know Lisa Daugaard or Michael Barr, but he'd long despised their sort. At Harvard Law School, nothing had irked him more than liberals holding forth about the plight of the underprivileged as if they were bringing down Truth from the Mount. The offense was personal for Cappuccio, for his parents were among the people that this "*New York Times* crowd" thought it was helping. He'd grown up in a traditional Italian family in blue-collar West Peabody, north of Boston, the grandson of immigrants from Salerno. His father cleaned fluorescent lights at Harvard as a university serviceman and his mother worked in a candy factory. Cappuccio had risen quickly, excelling in Catholic school while working in a shoe store and then winning a college scholarship to Georgetown. Along the way, he'd cast aside his support for Senator Ted Kennedy in favor of Reagan's ethic of individualism. As far as Cappuccio was concerned, his family was doing just fine without a bunch of Harvard bleeding hearts figuring out their lives for them.

Boisterous, unkempt, and very, very smart, Cappuccio left Harvard intent on making his mark in the conservative world, and he started out in grand style, pulling off a rare double clerkship at the Supreme Court. After a year working for the court's leading conservative, Antonin Scalia, he served in the chambers of the newest justice, Anthony Kennedy. Cappuccio allegedly wielded great influence as a leader of "the Cabal," a group of conservative clerks aiming to drive the court to the right— limiting civil rights statutes, questioning last-minute execution stays— and a clerk in Justice Blackmun's chambers even credited Cappuccio with changing the outcome of a key race discrimination case. By the time he left the court, Cappuccio had established a reputation as hard-driving and well-connected, with an agile mind and the ability to get things done.

Soon afterward, he was tapped for an associate deputy post at Justice by Attorney General William Barr. It was a stratospheric position for someone Cappuccio's age. But while he was charged with the influential task of overseeing President Bush's nominations to the federal judiciary, he let Barr know he didn't want to give up the rough-and-tumble of courtroom practice. Weeks later, Cappuccio was knee-deep in the *Baker* case filed by Ira Kurzban, and working beside the man who would soon be the most famous lawyer in America, Solicitor General Kenneth Starr.

Traditionally, the solicitor general, or SG, was a supremely talented lawyer whose presence in court was reserved for the government's most important cases, and then only after they had reached the Supreme Court. It was remarkable for the White House to ask the SG to appear before a Miami federal trial judge in a preliminary hearing. But the administration was more anxious about *Baker* than perhaps any other case in America. President Bush himself repeatedly summoned the attorney general to the White House to inquire about the case, worried that a court order might interfere with the Coast Guard's repatriation of the Haitians.

With Cappuccio at his side, Starr had argued *Baker* first in Miami and then in Atlanta before the Eleventh Circuit Court of Appeals. After the case was thrown out, the two lawyers had dusted their hands of it and turned to other matters. But then some law students and a professor from Yale had popped up in Brooklyn, complaining about Guantánamo all over again. The reaction at Justice ranged from frustration to disgust. The general belief among attorneys who'd worked on *Baker* was that res judicata—the rule of one bite at the apple—barred the case. For Cappuccio personally, it felt like a replay of law school: a bunch of sanctimonious liberals wanted to save the world, only this time it meant interfering in a major foreign policy crisis.

It was Cappuccio's idea to draft the Rule 11 sanctions motion challenging the Yale lawsuit as frivolous. He wanted Koh and his goody-two-shoes students to realize that the Justice Department meant business. "This damn thing was costing the department a lot of money," he later explained. "There are rules in litigation, and everything they'd raised was already decided in *Baker*." Given Judge Johnson's background as a tough New York drug prosecutor, Cappuccio thought the government would have a sympathetic audience. So he was amenable when word bubbled up that Steven Valentine, the lower-level political appointee who oversaw OIL, wanted to argue the initial TRO hearing. Cappuccio thought neither he nor Starr should come in too quickly, anyway. It might suggest that the Justice Department believed the case had merit, and Cappuccio didn't want to send that message. The plan was simple: send Valentine to Brooklyn, let Judge Johnson know the case was a no-brainer, get it dismissed ASAP.

But Johnson had issued the TRO anyway, the order coming down on a Friday afternoon, just in time to ruin Cappuccio's weekend. Now, with crews of law students and public interest lawyers lining up for flights to Washington, Miami, and Guantánamo Bay, Justice was scrambling.

The alarm went off at four a.m. Mike Wishnie, a trim Yale second year with long sideburns, stumbled into the motel shower, dizzy from lack of sleep. He'd been awake most of the night, pacing the hotel room, wondering what to expect. While he'd scanned the TRO papers and talked to several fellow students about the case, he still had only a general idea of what was happening. That limited knowledge would have to do. The military flight to Guantánamo was leaving from South Carolina's Charleston Air Force Base in only a few hours.

Like Ray Brescia, Mike had been recruited for the case after it was already under way, and he'd initially been skeptical. Motivated more by concrete problems than legal theories, Mike was passionately involved in helping New Haven's indigent. His clients were people living just blocks from the law school, struggling with eviction threats, drug-infested housing projects, inadequate medical care. International human rights cases held little appeal for him. They felt disconnected from reality, and the Haiti project seemed particularly remote. Nor did he have any interest in cozying up to faculty kingmakers like Koh. He preferred his clinical professors—down-to-earth guys with plaid shirts and beards.

But after some prodding from his college buddy Graham Boyd and others, Mike ducked into the team's Friday-night strategy session following Judge Johnson's TRO. The Lowenstein office was giddy with excitement, the room so packed that Mike had to stand in the doorway. He was soon drawn in by Koh's enthusiasm and intensity, though he remained doubtful about the case itself. In his clinic work, Mike had been trained that a lawyer's efforts should center on the concerns expressed by the client. No one had even spoken with the refugees Yale supposedly represented. How, Mike wondered, could anyone be sure that a federal lawsuit was the help they wanted or needed?

Koh had very different matters on his mind. Judge Johnson's order had halted the current process of interviews and repatriations for just five days. The Yale team now had to persuade him to keep that order in place for the coming months. Under the law, that required a showing of "irreparable harm" to Yale's clients. So the goal was to gather as much evidence as possible of Koh's initial claims to the judge: that the screening interview process was unfair and chaotic, and that refugees were being sent back to Haiti and suffering persecution.

To complete all this factual investigation, or "discovery" work, the team needed a few more experienced students. That was where Mike Wishnie came in. Michael Barr and Graham Boyd had both recommended Mike to Koh, praising their former roommate's smarts and steady temperament. With so many high-strung students around, Koh was relieved to bring on a cooler-headed person. He was especially intrigued to learn that Mike had once visited Miami's Krome Detention Center, an INS facility that immigration lawyers saw as a deportation prison for Haitians who'd reached Florida by boat. Koh figured Mike's Krome experience would make a good point of comparison with the refugees' current conditions.

"We need another person to go to Guantánamo," Koh said. "Mike, can you do it?"

All eyes in the room fell on him, and Wishnie cringed. He'd already sensed the students jockeying for desirable assignments, and there was no question where everyone wanted to go. But in Mike's first hour at the clinic office, Koh had offered him the plum job on the case.

As the motel van motored toward the Air Force base in the predawn darkness, Mike grew tense. On a telephone call the day before, the government had clashed with Koh over every aspect of the trip, and Wishnie was convinced the military was going to do all it could to thwart the eleven-person team of lawyers, students, and translators. But to his shock, everyone from the base's guardhouse security official to the people at the check-in counter proved eerily agreeable. It appeared that nobody on the base cared what the Yale people were doing, or even knew who they were.

Then, however, the government lawyers arrived. To Mike, they all seemed to be glowering. The group included Allen Hausman, a career OIL attorney, along with a lawyer in uniform from the military's Judge Advocate General's Corps and a couple of younger attorneys from Justice. "Close-the-border freaks," Mike later called them. "Their attitude was 'Fuck the immigrants.' And they were *pissed.*" After a few cold introductions, the two teams were directed to a hulking military transport plane waiting in the early gray light.

They hiked up a ramp into the gaping, unfinished cabin. Fold-down seats ran along the sides of the aircraft, facing inward, with parachutes above them. Mike buckled himself in with the four-point restraint belt, and minutes later, they roared down the runway. The bumpy two-hour flight, thunderously loud, made him nauseous, but he was intent on showing no sign of weakness because he thought Hausman was watching him. Less than one hundred miles south of Key West, the plane banked into a tight arc to avoid Cuban airspace, then touched down on Guantánamo Bay's leeward side, which was separated from the main base by a wide stretch of bright blue water.

Queasy, Mike wobbled out into the warm, humid air, along with fellow student Sarah Cleveland and Robert Rubin, the San Francisco lawyer who'd come up with the Rees memo. Barren hills rose in the distance and GIs working on the tarmac cast long shadows in the morning sun. Wishnie felt as if he were heading into combat.

A military escort arrived to take the Yale team to its quarters, but Rubin cut him off. "We can't do that right now," he said. "We're on a tight time schedule and the plan you're describing is going to take—"

"This is a military base," snapped an OIL attorney, "and we're going to stick with military procedure."

The two men were soon shouting at each other, and Mike grew suspicious. The previous afternoon, OIL had claimed confusion about whether the Guantánamo flight was leaving from Maryland or somewhere in the Carolinas. The Yale delegation had been forced to wait at LaGuardia Airport in New York until the last commercial flight of the evening. Now the team had reached Guantánamo, but with the flight home just thirty hours away, OIL seemed intent on wasting as much time as possible.

Rubin finally agreed to a quick luggage drop-off and everyone piled into a military van. Wishnie was expecting to see tanks and troop carriers along the way, but instead, they passed drab office buildings and warehouses. The Justice Department's complaints about base security, like the supposed uncertainty about the flight, seemed like a sham to him.

Back at the airfield by late morning, the team was directed to two rooms on the second floor of a building near the hangar. "You can't go anywhere else," Allen Hausman declared. "You stay here and the bathroom. That's it. And one other thing: we consider all personnel on this base to be our clients, so you can't talk to anyone about anything."

Why, Mike wondered, was the government so paranoid? What was everyone trying to hide?

Growing frustrated himself, Rubin asked where the refugees were.

"We haven't sent for the migrants yet," said a military official. "We didn't know when you'd be here."

Rubin's face went dark. "We gave you a list of our clients' names two days ago," he said, trying to remain calm.

"Well, no one told us," the official said.

"Under the court order," Rubin countered, "you were responsible for making them available. We'd appreciate it if you would do that immediately."

The hours ticked away, Mike anxiously checking the time. It was mid-afternoon before the official at last reappeared. "The migrants don't want to come," he announced, handing Rubin a note in English from the refugees. The team crowded around to read it.

> *MRs lawyers,*
> *We say Hello To you all and the name of Jesus Christ. We very Please to meet your. Reason why we don't want feel like to come so we're afraid to trust those people. we Please to do us a favor to call the Juge see if they could give your chance to come and the camp to talk to us as your come to defend us. thanks your. God blest your. Please do your best For us. Sign. Frantz Guerrier.*

"My God," Rubin murmured. "They think this is some kind of trick." He looked at the official. "We have to go to the camp," he said.

The JAG lawyer cut in. "I'm sorry, sir, but we can't let you do that," he said.

"Why not?"

"Military security. We also can't guarantee your safety."

"Forget our safety," Rubin said, his voice sharp. "We have a federal court order that grants us the right to meet with our clients, and one way or another, we're going to talk to them. If you can't bring them over here, we're going over there!"

The JAG lawyer's face turned hard. "You're a civilian on a military base, *sir,* and we are not compromising security."

With the afternoon slipping away, Rubin at last convinced the government to let one of the Yale team's translators, a Haitian American advocate named Johnny McCalla, cross the bay to the refugee camp.

It was almost dinnertime when he returned. Trailing behind him were several small Haitian men in flip-flops. They scanned the room, quiet and tense. It had been nearly impossible to coax them onto the ferry, McCalla reported. They thought he was a U.S. operative scheming to take them back to Haiti—and it hadn't helped that "McCalla" happened to be the name of Guantánamo's main refugee camp.

Mike and Sarah joined Rubin as he introduced himself to the Haitians. Rubin had dealt with refugees from many countries and knew it usually took time for them to become comfortable with an American lawyer. But he didn't have that luxury. With McCalla translating, he hurriedly tried to explain the lawsuit, the discovery process, the court hearing.

The Haitians stared silently at Rubin, then turned back to McCalla—and lit into him. Fingers were pointed, voices raised. Mike didn't have to speak the language to know things weren't going well. Rubin tried again, but it only produced another fusillade from the refugees. Finally, McCalla held up his hands for quiet.

"Despite what you might think," he told them in Creole, "we're not military agents. We have nothing to do with the U.S. government, but there's little else we can do to prove it. We came down here at great cost to ourselves, and we're trying to help you. But if you're not going to listen, if you don't want to work with us, that's fine. We'll all just leave. It's up to you."

A few minutes later, Mike was seated beside Frantz Guerrier, a slight man with a goatee and smudged dress shirt. His serious, guarded look suggested he'd been through a lot. Mike had a long outline of questions to cover with Guerrier, and was trying to explain himself when the refugee interjected.

"*Avan nou kòmanse, mwen vle poze w yon kesyon.*"

"Before we start, I want to ask you a question," repeated the translator, a Brooklyn nurse named Evelyne Longchamp. "Your military has told me that I have HIV. Is this true?"

Mike froze. He'd understood from Sarah Cleveland that AIDS might somehow be involved in the case, but this was not what he'd expected. He paused and then looked to Longchamp. She leafed through Guerrier's medical file, studying charts and reading notes.

"He's taken the blood tests," she told Mike. "The results are here. . . ." She paused. "Looks like they're positive."

Longchamp spoke to Guerrier in Creole, gesturing to the file. Guerrier fell silent. After a long moment, he asked Longchamp something. She turned to Mike.

"He wants to know if we think the lab results are real."

Off balance, Mike struggled for what to say. He didn't know that much about AIDS, but understood that even with treatment, most people died within a few years of the diagnosis. He guessed that Guerrier's question was a sign of desperation, a man looking for any reason to avoid the truth. Mike didn't understand the deep Haitian mistrust of military authority; he didn't know that some refugees even demanded the American soldiers taste the food served to them.

"Well," Mike stammered, "Evelyne's an experienced nurse and there's nothing here to make us think the record's false." He paused. "Anything's possible, I guess. They could have used someone else's blood to make it look more plausible."

Guerrier sat motionless, staring at the table. Mike waited, then cleared his throat. After a few moments of silence, he suggested they start talking. He felt terrible but didn't know what else to do. There wasn't much time, and he had a lot of ground to cover if he was going to be of any help.

Guerrier nodded, then unfolded a crinkled piece of paper.

"I want to make a statement first," he said, Longchamp translating. "There are many others in the camp in my situation," Guerrier read. "I have come here as a leader of the Association of Haitian Political Refugees, but I am no better or worse than the others. This meeting is not for me. It is for all of us."

Mike was surprised—and impressed. He had met with a lot of clients through his clinic work, but he'd never seen anything like this.

Guerrier then told his story in a flat, matter-of-fact voice. A dentist from Port-au-Prince, he'd supported Aristide, but his brother was the real democracy activist. After the coup, he said, soldiers had torched Guerrier's dental clinic when they couldn't find his brother. His mother and his child were in the basement and had died in the blaze. Weeks later, his wife had been kidnapped and killed. He'd fled Haiti on December 24, 1991, and was picked up by the Coast Guard on Christmas Day.

Guerrier's experience on Guantánamo had been one of confusion and fear. After three weeks on the base, he was screened in and told he was heading for the United States to file for asylum. But a month after taking a blood test, he was still waiting to leave. There were rumors about AIDS, and when the military announced further blood tests were necessary, Guerrier turned suspicious. Doctors had taken his blood by force a second time, he said, and he'd been told he was HIV positive. But Guerrier didn't believe it. He figured he'd been singled out for forming a group to protest the refugees' confinement.

His worries had turned to panic when a soldier said his "lawyers" were coming to see him. Though a priest had helped him fax a note to New York seeking assistance, he'd never heard a word about lawyers. All he knew was that when people left the camp, they were returned to Haiti. Sensing a plot, Guerrier had sent over the message in English earlier that day, pleading for the attorneys, if that's what they really were, to come to the camp.

As he talked, Guerrier grew more animated. He described mass chaos, rough treatment by soldiers, the use of a punishment compound. And now, Guerrier said, the government was pressing people with positive HIV tests to go through a second review of their asylum claims. He believed it was a subterfuge to send him home, and he urgently wanted Mike's advice. What should he do?

This was it, Mike thought. This was what the other students had been talking about—the final asylum hearings without lawyers.

Mike offered the same opinion that Robert Rubin and Sarah Cleveland were giving to other refugees in the room. It's our view, Mike told Guerrier, that the government can't force you through a final asylum hearing without us here to represent you. You shouldn't have to do it. That's what we're fighting for in court. Guerrier gave him a relieved nod, and finally, for the first time, seemed to relax a little.

Mike spoke with several more refugees that evening, all as frightened and bewildered as Guerrier. They, too, described threats, intimidation, even physical abuse. Mike remained quiet as he listened, but inside he was boiling. While representing his clients at Yale, he'd battled many different defendants, from acrimonious landlords to vindictive businesses. But he had never encountered, as he later recalled, the "terrible things our own government can do—and in such stark, concrete terms."

The Haitians went to sleep on cots in the adjoining office, but Mike stayed up all night with Robert Rubin, pounding out declarations for the refugees to sign in the morning. The next afternoon, he watched helplessly as the soldiers led Frantz Guerrier away. When Mike boarded the plane back to the United States, exhausted and still fuming, he vowed that somehow or other, he was going to get him released.

On Friday night at Yale, after Koh had handed out the discovery assignments to Wishnie and the rest of the older students, Tory and several first years still had no tasks. When the meeting broke up, she summoned her courage and approached Koh. She always felt as if she were wasting his time when she spoke with him, but believed he had missed something important. If he wanted to know more about the camps, Tory ventured, the place to go was Miami—specifically, the Budget Inn hosting the Haitians who'd just flown in from Guantánamo.

"Okay. That's a good idea," replied Koh, distracted. Tory turned to go, but then he grabbed her.

"Wait!" he said, eyes suddenly alive. "Find me this: find me someone who was screened in but sent back by mistake, and then got hurt in Haiti. Because that's the guts of this case."

The Bush administration had maintained from the start that no one returned to Port-au-Prince by the Coast Guard was suffering persecution. Though journalists and human rights groups continued to report stories to the contrary, they were often vague—and Koh wanted something more than a newspaper to bring into court. Tory raced to make plane reservations, thrilled to have the assignment. But on the plane down to Miami with Michelle Anderson and a couple of other students, she began to wonder how they could possibly satisfy Koh's request.

Hours later, they pulled into the Budget Inn and Tory jogged to the courtyard, expecting to find the usual crowd of Guantánamo veterans at the picnic tables. The place was empty.

Tory tracked down the clerk at the front desk.

"Where are they?" she demanded.

He blinked at her. "Who?"

"You know, the Haitians!" Tory could feel her stomach knotting. "Ten days ago, there were, like, a ton of people here!"

"Oh, them. They're gone."

Tory stood there, stunned. For once, she'd figured she was a step ahead, not just playing a bit part, but making a strategic contribution to the case. Now she was stuck at a vacant, run-down motel in Florida with no Haitian refugees in sight and no idea what to do next. We've just spent sixteen hundred dollars of our own money on plane tickets and we've got nothing to show for it, she thought. The idea of telling Koh, and then asking for reimbursement, filled her with dread.

Determined not to go home empty-handed, she and the others headed to the local office of Church World Services, a charity service where they had interviewed several Haitians the last time around. A young lawyer there explained that the refugees who'd once been at the Budget Inn were now going through the arduous process of resettlement, many of them in New York. But another group from Guantánamo was expected in the evening. Tory cried out in relief.

Back at the motel that night, she and Michelle Anderson pounced on the weary new arrivals as they filed off a bus, belongings in hand. Several Haitians brushed them off, but at last, a stocky, tense refugee named Decoste Veillard agreed to sit down with them. He spoke English reasonably well, which reduced the confusion that always seemed to result with translation. If Veillard's account was accurate, the refugees on Guantánamo were divided into several different camps. One camp, he said, held new arrivals awaiting asylum screening. Two more were for refugees bound for the United States, and another held the screened-out people destined for Port-au-Prince. Veillard also claimed there was a punishment facility for troublemakers and a separate camp for those whose interview files had been lost.

"There's one more place, away from the other camps," he said in his Creole accent, "where sick people are sent. It's called Bulkeley."

"Buckley?"

Veillard shook his head and spelled it out for the students. B-u-l-k-e-l-e-y. What kind of sick people?

Veillard wasn't sure. But a lot of people were talking about AIDS.

Tory traded glances with Michelle.

The students moved on to other refugees, and at the end of every interview, they asked the long-shot question from Koh. Do you know anyone who was sent back to Haiti and then attacked?

Over and over, they got the same confused look and the same response: no. But the night before they were scheduled to leave, a young man told Michelle that he had met a woman on Guantánamo by the name of Marie Zette. Zette, he said, had been returned to Port-au-Prince by the Coast Guard—and the Haitian military had killed her.

Michelle's eyes went wide. It was late and the translator had been planning to go home, but she convinced him to stay and then took the refugee aside.

I need you to tell me everything, she said.

Yvonne lived in lines. The line for an identification bracelet. The line for an identification card. The line for flip-flops. The line for soap, the line for the latrine, the line for food, where, after an hour or longer, someone would hand her a plate of gloppy rice with shreds of gray meat. Sometimes she would just give up and leave.

From a makeshift facility in late November, Camp McCalla had expanded by the spring of 1992 into a city of over ten thousand Haitian refugees. Row upon row of olive-drab canvas tents and yellow portable toilets stretched along the broiling cement tarmac of the old McCalla Airfield. Yvonne's senses were under constant attack: the glare of the sun, the scream of military jets, the biting ocean wind. Her tent was an improvement over the Coast Guard cutter deck, but not by much. During the day, the dark canvas soaked up the sun's rays, baking the musty interior. The heat lingered in the evening, and she would lie on her cot in a pool of sweat, the stench from nearby latrines hanging heavy in the air as the people around her argued into the early-morning hours.

More than the crush of noise and confusion, however, it was her family that kept Yvonne awake. She'd never spent more than a day apart from Daniel and Jacques, and when she saw kids their ages in the camp, her guilt became almost unbearable. Bringing them with her had seemed too dangerous, yet she couldn't fathom how she'd left them. Strung out from lack of sleep, she walked the trash-littered tarmac, trying to stay calm, telling herself that her sons were safe with Thérèse.

To get off the base, she now understood that she would have to go through some sort of interview. She waited for days, watching those who'd been scheduled for screening shuffle away under military escort, grim looks on their faces. Everyone shared the fear of being sent back to Port-au-Prince, and the rumor mill about the interviews was constantly churning: "No one who supports Aristide is going to the U.S." . . . "The only way to get to America is to talk about Aristide" . . . "Cedras has sent Macoutes to spy on the camp." On and on it went. Yvonne's worries multiplied. What was she supposed to say?

One morning, finally, her name was called and she was escorted with several dozen others to an immense hangar. Desperation hung in the air. All around her, refugees were facing off against INS officials at small tables. There were mothers with babies squirming on their laps and a few people in gaunt middle age, but young men made up the vast majority. Some had been vocal supporters of the ousted president and feared for their lives if returned. Others simply sought freedom from the misery and random violence in Haiti.

But the INS interviewers were required to reject people from the latter group, no matter how desperate their circumstances at home had been. Under the law, fear of persecution based on one's political beliefs was the key to reaching the United States, and while some refugees had latched on to this basic principle, the interviewers did not explain how they made their decisions. It was a process for which only the INS knew the rules.

A tall black man introduced himself to Yvonne and announced in perfect Creole that he would be her translator. "They want to know about your political activities and your connections to Aristide," he said. "And you should give them any papers you have." She eyed him nervously. He sounded Haitian, but what was he doing working for the U.S. government?

Her mind raced as he led her to an open interview table. She wouldn't have dared mention her activism to any official in Haiti, and after what she'd seen of the American military, she wasn't ready to trust the United States either. She knew the Coast Guard sent many people back home. What would they do with the information she revealed if they returned her to Port-au-Prince? Someone had told her that the interview was confidential, but she had no reason to believe it.

The translator introduced her to a white INS asylum officer, who gestured for her to sit down. Like his colleagues, the officer was working up to ninety hours a week under immense pressure from the military to move the refugees off Guantánamo as fast as possible, whether to the United States, Haiti, or anywhere else. He was overwhelmed with paperwork and meetings, and while his direct supervisor encouraged fair interviews, senior officials were demanding that more people be sent back to Port-au-Prince. Yvonne Pascal was just another in an endless stream of Haitians with a story to tell, a story that might or might not be true, and the asylum officer would have only thirty minutes to decide her fate.

He began with the usual questions: Where was she from? How old was she? Did she have any family at Guantánamo or in the United States?

She answered at a slow, deliberate pace. Port-au-Prince. Twenty-eight. Yes, a cousin in New York and a cousin and an aunt in Florida.

He watched her closely. "Why did you leave Haiti?" he asked.

Yvonne hesitated, looking from the translator to the interviewer and back again. The translator gave her a coaxing nod, and finally, she pulled out her papers and set them on the table—her *manda,* which designated her as an election observer, her party membership, other documents.

He flipped through them doubtfully and pressed for more details, jotting down notes on some form. Growing worried, Yvonne recounted her work for KID and the night the soldiers had come for her. She tried to tell him about what had gone on inside Recherches Criminelles, but she didn't want to concentrate on it, didn't want to think about what had happened to her baby. She began to shake, and finally, unable to say anything else, simply pushed her sleeve above her shoulder.

Her bruises were healing, but the cigarette burn was still fresh—a yellowish hole in the groove between her shoulder and slender tricep muscle. The officer peered across the table at her arm. Consumed with the blunt task of survival over the last month, Yvonne had ignored the wound and the memories it brought back, but now she, too, found herself staring at it, suddenly nauseous. She began to choke and then collapsed in tears.

The interviewer offered her a small towel. He didn't ask any more questions.

———

On Wednesday, April 1, just five days after Judge Johnson had issued his temporary restraining order, the Yale team trooped back to Brooklyn for the next hearing in *McNary*. The Justice Department was demanding that the judge lift the order and allow the INS to resume the final asylum hearings for people like Frantz Guerrier—without lawyers involved. Yale's task was to persuade Judge Johnson to keep his order in place, ensuring that Guerrier and everyone else who'd been screened in had access to an attorney in their fight for asylum.

When Koh and the students entered the drab courtroom, they found the usual battery of government attorneys, along with a new adversary— Paul Cappuccio, a hefty man of about five foot ten with a boyish face and flushed cheeks. He seemed remarkably relaxed, joking with his colleagues, but Koh already knew firsthand how aggressive Cappuccio could be. On an earlier conference call with the judge, the Justice attorney had grabbed control of things, forcing Koh to play catch-up for the rest of the argument. That experience, coupled with Dunn's quick-draw speech before Judge Nickerson and the subsequent Rule 11 motion, had convinced Koh that he had to be ready to attack.

Koh's other challenge was that his students and fellow lawyers had achieved almost too much over the last several days. They had produced piles of evidence to assimilate: a dozen refugee affidavits from Guantánamo and Miami, hundreds of pages of deposition testimony by government officials, stacks of documents from Washington, more legal research. Assembled by the students at dawn, the result was another mammoth submission for Judge Johnson, this one almost the size of a telephone book.

But Koh knew by now that he had to keep the argument simple. Rising to address the judge and a gallery filled with Haitian activists, he reduced everything to one crucial point. Yale now had proof that refugees with credible asylum claims were being sent back to Haiti and indeed suffering persecution.

In the last two days of depositions, Koh charged, the INS itself had admitted the screening process was in disarray. The interview records of over twenty-five hundred people had been lost, leading to mass confusion, and the Coast Guard had mistakenly returned more than fifty screened-in refugees to Haiti. No one knew what had become of them.

"Your Honor," Koh said, "I think we need to understand the real-life consequences of what's happened here, and I turn you to document fifty-two in our exhibit book, the affidavit of Marcus Antoine. This was taken in Miami by a law student intern." Koh held a copy of the affidavit from Michelle Anderson in his hand.

"I knew one girl named Marie Zette," Koh read aloud. "She was a friend of mine. She told me that if she was sent back to Haiti she would be killed. She also told the immigration officials this fact."

The courtroom was still.

"At the beginning of February, she was called to be sent back to Haiti, even though she had been screened in. She had long black hair and was very beautiful. Before she was sent back to Haiti, she sang a song to us."

Koh's voice cracked. He fell silent.

Back in the gallery, Tory looked around, confused. What was going on? Was she missing something? Had Koh lost his place? Then she realized: he was struggling not to cry.

The same thing had happened late the night before, when Tory and Michelle had briefed him on the story they had uncovered in Miami. Tory was shocked. She had assumed he would be interested in Marie Zette only as a means to help make his argument to the judge. It had never occurred to her that he might have such intense emotions about the refugees.

Now he had choked up before a packed courtroom, and Tory was actually worried that he'd become too emotional and might be hurting their case. The stenographer waited, hands poised to type.

Koh cleared his throat. "I'm sorry, Your Honor," he said. "The next day the guards called her name to be sent to Miami. It was too late. She had already been sent away. In mid-February, a new group of Haitians arrived at Guantánamo. That boat contained relatives of Marie Zette. They said she had been murdered by Macoutes—Haitian military police. The police came at night and killed her while she slept."

Koh looked up from the affirmation.

"In other words, this is a person who had been screened in. Through the clerical errors of the people on Guantánamo, she was inadvertently sent back, and her relatives then reported that she had been killed."

If she'd had a lawyer to point out the mistake before she was returned, Koh said, Marie Zette might still be alive. Protect the refugees who remain on Guantánamo, he urged Johnson. We'll send a lawyer to the base at our own expense to advise them. If they must go through a final asylum hearing, if they suffer abuse, if they are about to be mistakenly repatriated, they will have representation. It's like the criminal process, Koh concluded: "A lawyer is there to stand between you and the government."

Whatever Johnson may have thought of Koh's plea, he didn't betray it as he called for a recess. His only comment, when he returned a few minutes later, was to ask that the courtroom doors be kept open. With so many people in the gallery, the air had grown stifling.

It was now Cappuccio's turn. He didn't want to focus on Marie Zette, and he didn't want Judge Johnson focused on Marie Zette, either. Cappuccio had grave doubts about the credibility of Koh's story. But there was no way to disprove it on the spot, so he didn't mention it at all. Instead, he took up where Steven Valentine, the DOJ attorney, had left off in the previous hearing. He aimed to convince Johnson that U.S. law didn't apply on Guantánamo in any circumstance. Therefore, no matter how the screening interviews were being conducted, no matter what mistakes Koh claimed had been made, the case would have to be thrown out.

Cappuccio began by passing around a written outline of his argument. It wasn't common practice and struck Koh as an amateurish move. But Cappuccio told Johnson the outline would clarify his argument.

"It's kind of convoluted," Cappuccio said.

Great, thought Koh. You be convoluted. Convoluted isn't going to get you anywhere.

Cappuccio faced a tricky problem. Had Judge Johnson been inclined to dismiss the suit, he could have argued his case in broad terms—there are no legal constraints on Guantánamo, period—and avoided bogging himself down in the mass of legal theories in Yale's brief. That approach had worked in *Baker* because the conservative Eleventh Circuit judges had been receptive to it. But Valentine had tried the same route with Johnson five days earlier at the TRO hearing and failed. So Cappuccio had opted for a new strategy. He would slog through Yale's legal claims one by one and show Johnson precisely why each of them should be thrown out.

Even with an outline, and Cappuccio's keen analytical abilities, it turned out to be an impossible task. Koh and the students had put into play over a half-dozen legal theories that applied in different ways to the three groups of plaintiffs: the refugees themselves, their U.S. relatives, and the advocacy groups (including the Yale team itself) that wanted to represent the refugees on Guantánamo. Had Koh diagrammed the whole thing on a blackboard, it would have taken an entire class period. To argue against it would take no less.

Sure enough, Cappuccio lost Johnson in a matter of minutes. The judge went from polite to confused to annoyed, but the Justice attorney couldn't seem to dig himself out of the situation.

And yet, while Cappuccio had nothing so compelling as the Marie Zette story, Koh feared for the outcome because he still believed the law favored the government. Despite all the efforts of Lisa, Graham, and the others, Yale still hadn't found a single case clearly holding that refugees on an overseas military base should have access to lawyers.

The team's solution to this problem had been to argue from a basic sense of justice. Beginning with the TRO hearing, Koh had kept asking the judge: How could the refugees have *no* rights? Shouldn't they at least be able to speak with an attorney before being sent back to possible persecution in a land of such terrible violence? To Cappuccio's evident dismay, those questions continued to strike a chord with Johnson.

Neither the Constitution nor any other law gave the refugees a right to counsel, Cappuccio responded. "The United States has decided two things," he said. "Number one, that it just won't work on a military base. It will be too meddlesome. And you could disagree with that, but that's our decision." Lawyers, he declared, would also complicate the processing of the refugees. "It would make it too adversarial. It would slow things down, and it would affect the integrity of the process to have lawyers nitpicking everything," he said. "As long as that decision to bar lawyers isn't crazy—"

"You don't think it is crazy," Johnson asked, "not to allow the refugees access to an attorney?"

"The reason why I don't think it is crazy is because the immigration people are helping the Haitians," Cappuccio protested. "They are trying to get their stories out. The sideshow that we have about coercion and duress and everything is just that, a sideshow."

Back in the gallery, the students were buzzing. Thanks to Cappuccio's aggressive, outsized presence, they had at last found themselves a real villain. Tory considered him evil incarnate. It didn't matter that the responsibility for Guantánamo ultimately stopped at the White House. Cappuccio was the man standing up in court to defend the administration, so he was the target of everyone's ire. Everyone hated the Pooch.

Lisa was seething because she felt Cappuccio had twisted the law beyond recognition. The last straw for her was his argument that the refugees had no equal protection claim because of a case known as *Bertrand v. Sava.* The idea that equal protection should apply on Guantánamo had become Lisa's obsession. She had almost memorized the *Sava* decision and was convinced that footnote twelve supported her, not Cappuccio. As Lisa read the footnote, the court was talking about the power the Constitution gave *Congress* to discriminate against national groups in immigration matters. But Cappuccio was suggesting the *president* had that power, and could, without Congress, set up a special asylum process on Guantánamo just for Haitians.

Unable to sit mute anymore, Lisa jotted down her point on a legal pad and tore off the page with a loud *rrrrip*. The government attorneys stared disapprovingly as she leaned over the railing and handed her note to one of the lawyers sitting beside Koh.

That started it. Every time Cappuccio mentioned a case or a key fact, another student whipped off a response.

Johnson v. Eisentrager? It involved *enemy* aliens—German prisoners of war, not civilian refugees. *Rrrrip.*

United States v. Verdugo-Urquidez? It was based on the Fourth Amendment, not the Fifth. Different constitutional language, different application. *Rrrrip.*

Government testimony claiming no harm to repatriates? *Rrrrip. Rrrrip. Rrrrip.*

On and on it went, scraps of paper and Post-its moving from hand to hand in a bucket brigade meant to help Koh in his rebuttal.

A note came back from Lucas Guttentag of the ACLU, who was next to Koh. "You guys," he wrote, "are the human Lexis machine." He finally waved everyone off. He was unable to keep up with the paper coming over the railing and the noise was distracting even the judge.

But the students were not silenced for long. Late in the afternoon, Mike Wishnie took the stand. The judge had given each party the opportunity to put on one witness, and Koh had asked Wishnie to testify about his trip to Guantánamo.

"Do this with controlled fury," Koh said.

"You don't need to tell me," Mike answered, eyes blazing.

He'd been both surprised and a little concerned when Koh had told him late the night before that he would be on the stand during the hearing. Now, though, spruced up with a fresh shirt and borrowed tie, he couldn't wait to tell Johnson everything on his mind. He wanted to point out Allen Hausman and the other attorneys from OIL, who were sitting in the courtroom, and reel off the ways he felt they'd stalled the investigation. He wanted to describe the HIV-testing mess and the refugees' accusations of military brutality. Most of all, he wanted to tell everyone the story of Frantz Guerrier—and how outrageous it was for the United States of America to hold democracy activists like him in a detention camp.

But on the stand, before the judge and all his fellow students, Mike was hamstrung. When Tringali asked Wishnie what he'd learned from Guerrier, Assistant U.S. Attorney Bob Begleiter jumped in to object. That was all hearsay, Begleiter snapped: the impermissible practice of repeating someone else's words in court. Tringali had feared this would happen. He'd been skeptical about putting Mike on the stand at all—not because Wishnie wouldn't do a good job, but because the rules of evidence would get in the way.

Tringali shifted course, asking that Mike simply read from the declarations he had prepared with Guerrier and the other refugees. Begleiter objected again. Judge Johnson could read the declarations himself, Begleiter said. He didn't need Wishnie's help. Nor, in the end, could Wishnie describe the refugees' conditions, since the government hadn't allowed him to see the camp itself. After about fifteen minutes, Tringali decided enough was enough. "I have nothing further, Your Honor," he said.

It was a brutal introduction to the way courts really worked, and Mike left the stand brimming with frustration. Koh felt Wishnie had made a powerful impression on Johnson as an idealistic law student acting on principle, and Sarah Cleveland and the other students were amazed at how calm and poised he had seemed given the stakes. But Mike believed he'd contributed nothing.

The government then put on its own witness, Brigadier General George Walls Jr., the man who'd set up Camp McCalla. An African American with classic military bearing, Walls strode to the stand and sat ramrod straight in the witness chair. In a confident tone, he testified that the military was making every effort to care for the "migrants" and had worked diligently to solve a raft of logistical problems, from camp governance to meal quality. He also commended as "very professional and compassionate" a Marine officer whom Guerrier had complained about, and assured the judge that the medical treatment provided at the "humanitarian" camp met U.S. standards.

The students stared in disbelief, amazed at what they saw as a transparent attempt to pander to the judge by bringing a "Colin Powell clone" into court to testify for the government. It was evening by the time Walls finished, and the team headed back to New Haven on a late train, all smiles and happy chatter. Koh was convinced they'd blown Cappuccio out of the water, and everyone else agreed. The question seemed to be when, not if, Johnson would rule for them.

It was a rare moment to take stock. Tory realized that at some point she had to go to class again, for she was falling further and further behind. Michael Barr was grateful just to be back in the groove of things. The first few days after his ski trip had not been easy. He'd taken plenty of ribbing for his tan and was still fighting with his own guilt about leaving. The chance to go to Washington two days earlier to help with the depositions had been a welcome one, and he quietly promised himself he wouldn't walk out on the case again.

Mike Wishnie stayed behind in New York to see his girlfriend, and they went out to dinner in Greenwich Village. Finally coming down off the adrenaline rush of court, he managed to relax for the first time in five days. But he couldn't stop thinking about Frantz Guerrier.

Five days after the hearing, Judge Johnson announced he would stand by his initial decision. While he never mentioned Marie Zette by name, he declared that repatriated Haitians faced persecution and even death on return, and he took Yale's side on most every issue. The Yale team, Johnson said, had a First Amendment right to communicate with the plaintiffs on Guantánamo. And since the government had already let priests, journalists, doctors, and other civilians meet with the refugees, lawyers alone could not be barred from the base.

The judge also rejected Paul Cappuccio's contention that the Constitution's due process clause had no force on Guantánamo. Courts in the past had applied certain parts of the Constitution beyond traditional U.S. borders, he said. That was appropriate here because the refugees were detained on territory under the "complete jurisdiction and control" of the American government. The Fifth Amendment, the judge pointed out, was a broadly worded provision, prohibiting the government from depriving any "*person*" of "life, liberty, or property, without due process of law." While the Haitians were not American citizens, he said, they were "certainly 'persons.'"

Accordingly, Johnson ordered the government to give Yale immediate access to the screened-in refugees, and prohibited final asylum hearings on Guantánamo unless their attorneys were present. In legal parlance, the court's temporary restraining order had now become a "preliminary injunction" and would remain in place until trial.

There were plenty of grins at Yale, but no shouting and hollering. The agenda now was to get back down to Cuba as fast as possible. The team had a huge class of people to represent. Over three thousand screened-in Haitians remained on Guantánamo, and there was no telling how many of them the INS planned to subject to a final asylum hearing. The Lowenstein Clinic telephones were tied up as Koh and the students recruited immigration lawyers and Creole translators for the next visit to the base. Reporters were calling; more volunteers were showing up; and Ray Brescia was struggling to organize all the teams of people and piles of paper. Michael Ratner and Mike Wishnie, meanwhile, pressed the government for information on flights to Guantánamo.

And then came the fax from the Justice Department.

Paul Cappuccio had appealed the case to the Second Circuit Court of Appeals in Manhattan, which sat in review of Judge Johnson's court. More worrisome, he'd asked for an emergency stay of Johnson's order. The term was familiar to Tory. But she couldn't recall exactly how a stay worked.

The details became clear to her during the tense discussion that followed. Cappuccio was not only challenging the judge's order in a higher court. He also wanted to circumvent the normal scheduling process for the argument. Since under appellate court procedures the case would not be heard for about four weeks, Cappuccio had asked the Second Circuit to bar Judge Johnson's order from taking effect in the interim. In lawyers' language, he wanted a stay.

A stay was an innocuous-sounding term, but it packed a wallop. If the government prevailed on the stay, Johnson's decision would count for nothing until the Second Circuit reviewed it in a month. It would be as if Johnson had never issued his ruling. The government would have a window of time to bar Yale from Guantánamo again while it geared up the asylum hearing process, and people like Frantz Guerrier could then be subjected to a hearing without a lawyer. Everyone understood what that meant: the INS would start returning refugees to Port-au-Prince as fast as possible.

The clinic office was filled with scowls and looks of despair. More briefs had to be written, more court arguments made, and all simply to protect Judge Johnson's ruling. Tory now realized that every step of the way, there would be a fight.

Sarah Cleveland went out for more Dunkin' Donuts, Ray Brescia turned up the music, and everyone got to work.

———

Yvonne didn't know for sure why they were calling her name, but she had a hunch. Along with a group of other refugees, she was directed to a separate section of the camp, where an official then announced that they had been screened in and would be going to the United States. Surrounded by jubilant cries, Yvonne exhaled in relief and mumbled a quiet prayer. She'd had her doubts about the INS man even after the interview, and she was grateful her story had been taken seriously. But as she began her wait anew, her mind hummed with worries. How was she going to get the children out? And what about Antenor and her parents?

A few days later, her name was called again. Her blood had to be tested, she was told. They were checking for diseases. A man wearing a camouflage uniform and rubber gloves examined her identification bracelet and took out a small vial. In his hand was a syringe with a hypodermic needle. She shuddered but finally extended her arm.

Several weeks later, she was still counting the days. People in group after group packed up their belongings and left. They would ride a bus down to the water, take a ferry to the leeward side of the base, and then board a plane to Miami. But Yvonne's name was never on the list. It became an exhausting cycle: the tension of waiting, the disappointment of hearing other names called on the loudspeakers, the renewed hope for the next plane. She volunteered at the supply station to pass the time, handing out soap, toothpaste, and flip-flops, telling herself that sooner or later, she would go, too.

But when Yvonne finally heard her own name once more, it was the medical people who wanted to speak with her.

"We can't find the results of your blood test," one of them said through an interpreter. "We have to do another for you."

"No," she protested, pulling away. "You're not testing me again. You already did whatever you had to do."

The translator took her aside. "If you don't agree to this," he said quietly, "you'll never get on the plane."

Trembling, Yvonne sat down and waited for the needle.

Some days later, they asked her to collect her things and sent her back to the medical clinic. She was directed to a private spot where several people were waiting for her. Someone closed a drape and a white woman in uniform began speaking to her in English.

"You have some germs in your blood," the interpreter translated. "We're going to take you to a specialist. He'll help you."

Yvonne's mind raced back to the testing. The needle. They'd done something to her.

"But you may have to spend a long time here," the woman was saying. "Or you can sign a paper and return to Haiti."

Back to Haiti? The woman couldn't be serious. "What's this problem I have?" Yvonne interrupted. She waited as the translator repeated her words.

"It's a virus," the woman told her.

"What does that mean?" Dizzy, Yvonne reached for a chair.

"We have medicine for you."

"I don't understand what you mean," she repeated.

"We're going to take you to a doctor."

"Tell me what you mean!" she implored.

They threw open the drape. Two soldiers were waiting, and they marched her out of the clinic to a bus.

"What's going on?!" she cried, struggling to yank free.

They pushed her up the bus steps. Several other refugees were already inside, cowering in their seats, faces twisted in fear. The door squealed shut and the bus lurched away.

———

On April 14, a week after Judge Johnson's preliminary injunction order, Koh, Ratner, Lisa, and the rest of the team convened for the stay hearing at the federal courthouse in Manhattan. The argument was held in a stately, wood-paneled chamber lined with bronze busts of former judges. Court TV was providing live coverage of the event, its cameras trained on the lawyers' lectern. Lisa didn't like the feel of things from the outset. The three-judge panel was made up of nothing but old white men. She was certain they'd have no clue about what was going on in the Caribbean. All that effort on the stay brief, she thought, was a waste of time. They're just going to give the government whatever it wants.

Cappuccio was stuck in Washington, so Steven Valentine had returned to make the argument for the Justice Department. Yale's lawsuit, Valentine claimed, was acting like a magnet, encouraging more refugees to flee in the belief that they now had a better chance of reaching the United States. If the appellate court didn't stay Johnson's order, he warned, refugee interdictions would soar even higher, costing the Coast Guard millions.

Koh considered the "magnet effect" argument ridiculous. How could people living in a country with no free media learn about legal proceedings in Brooklyn in just a few days? There were other obvious reasons for the uptick in refugee boats, Koh told the court. "In Haiti in the last several weeks," he said, "there has been the collapse of an international plan to reinstall Aristide. There has been violence. There have been threats to people in the streets, and Castro has expelled a large number of Haitians who had originally sailed to Cuba."

Koh had more to say, but moments later, the presiding judge interrupted him. The government's request for a stay, the judge announced, was denied.

Lisa looked at the old white men in shock, then laughed to herself. Not bad, she thought. Three court arguments, three victories. They'd be back to Guantánamo within days. And she couldn't help feeling excited. She was on the list to go this time.

Late to the hearing, Tory Clawson ran into the team on the courthouse steps. The bright faces told her everything. The group squeezed together for a few celebratory photographs in the chilly spring sun—Koh, Ratner, and a dozen students in suits, frayed backpacks slung over their shoulders—and then trooped off for lunch. Tory recalled the moment many years afterward with a slow shake of her head. "We were beginning," she said, "to feel invincible."

Three days later, the Lowenstein fax machine spit out yet another filing from the government. Koh glanced at the heading and paused. Having lost at the Second Circuit Court of Appeals, Cappuccio had now asked the U.S. Supreme Court to issue the stay.

The "Supremes" had the power to step in if a court of appeals declined to intervene in a lower court proceeding. But as a former clerk, Koh knew it rarely if ever happened. Surrounded by the students, he flipped through the brief, which had officially been filed by Solicitor General Kenneth Starr. The government had again made the "magnet effect" argument: refugees were streaming into the Windward Passage in greater numbers because of Judge Johnson's ruling. If the Supreme Court didn't order Johnson to stop interfering with Guantánamo, the price would be millions of extra dollars in Coast Guard cutter operations. Included with the brief was a declaration by a State Department official, Caribbean specialist Donna Hrinak, attesting to the lawsuit's magnet effect.

Koh had a bad feeling. Things worked differently at the Supreme Court. He knew politics mattered more there than in the lower courts, and when the solicitor general put his name on the papers, it carried a lot of weight with the justices.

He was troubled, too, by the Hrinak declaration. Under long-standing practice, new evidence could not be submitted on appeal. Judge Johnson had already rejected claims about the supposed magnet effect, and the Second Circuit had agreed with him. Cappuccio was trying to sidestep those rulings. What proof did this person Hrinak have of the magnet effect? Her statement didn't say, and there would be no chance for Yale to challenge her before the Supreme Court made a decision. Cappuccio, Koh felt, was telling the justices: Trust us. You have to take what we're saying at face value. But according to the Kurzban team, the government had pulled the same maneuver in the *Baker* case, and the information, the lawyers said, had later proved false.

Koh and the students fired off a hasty letter to the Supreme Court. The Hrinak declaration, they argued, had been "manufactured" to "mislead" the justices. A sense of dread began to build as the afternoon wore on. Sarah felt that the high court wouldn't get involved, but Michael Barr wasn't so sure, and Lisa was downright grim. They eyed the fax machine, checked the time.

That evening, the Supreme Court spoke. The ruling came during a fight between Koh and Cappuccio, who were on a call with Judge Johnson. Another government lawyer interrupted with the news. The students in Koh's office leaned in to listen.

With the rest of the court split, four justices against the stay and four in favor, the deciding vote had been cast by Justice Clarence Thomas, the conservative Yale Law School graduate. Nominated by President Bush, he'd taken the seat vacated by civil rights champion Thurgood Marshall just six months earlier.

Justice Thomas had voted for the stay. Judge Johnson's order was scrap paper.

The next day, Robert Rubin got a call from a contact on Guantánamo. The final asylum hearings had begun. Some of the refugees were refusing to participate, and the INS was preparing to send them all back to Haiti.

A dark anxiety settled over the clinic. Tory, in particular, was a wreck, convinced that people were going to die. She stomped through the hallway, demanding to know how the justices could be so flippant about people's lives. Mike Wishnie sat on the clinic couch, biting his lip. He had a gut feeling that Guerrier was one of the "refuseniks," as the team started calling them.

The question now was what, if anything, Yale could do. Everyone hurried over to Yorkside Pizza, a nearby campus eatery, for a strategy session. Several students argued for seeking another TRO from Judge Johnson based on a different legal theory. Technically, he had only ruled on a few of Yale's legal claims. He'd left the rest to decide later, such as Lisa's equal protection claim.

Koh shook his head. The Supreme Court's message to Judge Johnson was clear: Stop what you're doing. "We've already pushed Johnson as far as he'll go," Koh warned. "We push him any further, we'll destroy our credibility."

Then Paul Sonn, the quiet third year who'd worked on the res judicata question, offered an intriguing thought. They could file a new case, a petition for habeas corpus, before a different judge in another court. The proposal drew support from the students, but it would be an aggressive move, challenging the refugees' confinement on the base as illegal and demanding their release.

Koh sensed it would never work. He also worried about angering Judge Johnson, for the new suit would be like going behind the judge's back.

"We have to do *something,*" Lisa responded. The team had told the Haitians that they didn't have to go through an asylum hearing without lawyers. That made Yale responsible for anyone who refused. Lisa had fought a lot of battles against Koh on her own, but this time, most of the students backed her up. They believed they had an ethical obligation to act, no matter how slim the chances of success.

A group led by Paul Sonn raced back to the library, but the going was rough. A habeas petition had all sorts of odd rules to follow. For technical reasons, it seemed they would have to file the case in Washington, D.C., but even that wasn't clear. They were soon bogged down, stuck on long phone calls with criminal procedure experts, and as the work went on, Mike Wishnie began to develop doubts. He, more than anyone, wanted to save Guerrier. But if this was as wild a gambit as Koh was suggesting, then it wouldn't help any of the refuseniks and the team's goodwill with Johnson would be lost.

At dinnertime several days later, Tuesday, April 28, Rubin got another call from Guantánamo. "*They're escorting eighty-nine people onto a cutter,*" the contact whispered. "*Right now. In twelve hours, they'll be back in Haiti.*"

Panic seized the students. The habeas petition had to be filed that night or not at all, and it would take several more hours to put the papers in order. That meant someone would have to pound on a judge's door at home, after midnight.

"We have to get a lawyer in Washington," Lisa insisted. "Right away."

His two-year-old son squirming on his lap, Koh finally suggested some former students he thought might be up to the task, including a Georgetown professor named David Cole. But something was telling Koh that it was time to stop.

He left to put his son to bed. As he drove home, he became convinced that the habeas petition was a mistake. For weeks, the students' enthusiasm had been fueling him, but the situation at hand called for dispassionate judgment, not another wild-eyed declaration that everyone would work all night if necessary. Lisa's harping, Tory's hand-wringing, the endless strategy discussions—Koh was getting sick of it all.

If any of them paused for a moment, he thought, they'd realize that researching the habeas petition was simply a way to relieve their consciences. Yale had responsibility for thousands of refugees on Guantánamo, and they couldn't save everyone. This group of Haitians was lost, and the students would just have to deal with it. He had to start imposing some discipline on the case.

He drove back to the law school late that evening. The clinic was filled with haggard faces and the stale smell of reheated coffee. One of the students had managed to reach David Cole, and Koh got him back on the phone. Cole sounded tired, perhaps even annoyed.

"Look," he said. "You file this case down here, and the government comes in and says, 'Hey, this is the same as the action up in Brooklyn.' The judge looks at it. He sees it's the same and the stay has already been issued by the Supreme Court. Then you've got Rule 11. Checkmate."

Koh thanked Cole and hung up.

Lisa started to argue and Koh cut her off.

"It's the middle of the night," Koh said. "No judge is going to order a Coast Guard cutter in international waters to turn around now."

"Harold—"

"None of you is a lawyer," Koh snapped, gazing around the room from one face to another. "And I'm *not* going to sign the petition. It's *over*."

He eyed Lisa. "If any of you does anything with those papers, you're off the case. Got it? Everyone just go home and get some sleep."

He limped down the hallway without another word.

Five

THE FLOATING WALL

THE IMMIGRATION AND Naturalization Service wasted no time. At six a.m. on April 23, just twelve hours after the Supreme Court stayed Judge Johnson's ruling, the Guantánamo asylum officers were roused out of bed. They went through a hurried training session to learn the difference between the screening interviews they'd been doing—which required only a "credible fear" of persecution—and the more rigorous "well-founded fear" standard of an asylum hearing. Then they received counseling on the risks of contact with people who had HIV.

At 4:30 p.m, they began hearings for Frantz Guerrier and the two hundred other screened-in Haitians with a positive HIV test. The hearings went late into the night and resumed at eight the next morning. The entire process took just two days, with senior officials rushing things from start to finish. "The haste was just unseemly," one asylum officer later charged. "Do it now, do it fast."

Frantz Guerrier pleaded for his attorneys from Yale. Told he had no right to see them, he refused to submit to a hearing he believed was rigged. Others followed his lead. When they would not yield, Guerrier and his compatriots were escorted up the gangway of the Coast Guard cutter *Tampa,* fists raised in defiance. The government also forced aboard the refugees who'd submitted to the hearing and failed it. The *Tampa* steamed out of Guantánamo on the evening of April 28, bound for Port-au-Prince with almost one hundred Haitians huddled on its aft deck.

Remaining behind on Guantánamo were about 120 HIV-positive refugees and their relatives, perhaps 200 people in all. They had established their right to asylum in the United States during the final hearings, and by law could not be repatriated. But because of their illness, they were still barred from America under the HIV ban. The only way off the base was if Attorney General William Barr personally authorized their release, and he was unwilling to do that. Stuck in legal limbo, the group presented a logistical problem that no one, least of all the Pentagon, wanted to handle: housing, feeding, and providing medical care to political refugees with a fatal illness.

As it turned out, General George Walls had already decided how to handle the HIV-positive population. For some time, he'd been concerned about AIDS spreading to the thousands of other Haitians on Guantánamo. Acting on his operations director's recommendation, he'd finally decided to "concentrate the HIV-positive migrants and their families in one camp." So in early March, several weeks before the asylum hearings, they'd all been confined to Camp Bulkeley—a primitive training facility in a remote eastern corner of the base, named for the commander who'd stood watch after Castro cut off the water in 1964. But there had been reservations about the isolation plan from the start. "We could," the operations director predicted, "have a serious medical problem if any type of infectious disease hits the camp." He advised that higher officials be warned of the situation.

After rising through the chain of command, the matter finally reached the desk of Admiral Leon Edney, head of the U.S. Atlantic Command in Norfolk, Virginia, and the man ultimately responsible for Bulkeley. The admiral sent several urgent messages to General Colin Powell's staff in Washington, seeking guidance. But Edney and his subordinates were left to deal with the situation on their own.

The Bush administration also received warnings from Dr. Paul Effler, a physician with the federal Centers for Disease Control and Prevention in Atlanta. After a stint supervising the HIV testing on Guantánamo, Effler notified his superiors that given the possible spread of tuberculosis and other communicable diseases among people with compromised immune systems, Bulkeley was "a potential public health disaster." His concerns ultimately came to the attention of Dr. James Mason, the assistant secretary for health at the Department of Health and Human Services, who evidently advised the INS to get the HIV-positive refugees off Guantánamo as soon as possible. As far as Effler knew, Mason never got a response.

Mike Wishnie's mind drifted in class. He was worried about Frantz Guerrier. It would have been so easy, Mike thought, to have saved him.

The morning Mike had left Guantánamo, he could simply have taken Guerrier along. The OIL lawyers and the military guards could have just quietly let him go. But now, he was somewhere in Haiti—perhaps in prison, maybe even dead.

Mike was all the more frustrated because the Second Circuit Court of Appeals had come within a few weeks of saving Guerrier. After finally reviewing Judge Johnson's order, the appellate court agreed that the refugees were protected by the due process clause and therefore entitled to counsel. The Supreme Court stay was now officially "dissolved," as lawyers said. Yale again had access to the Haitians.

The Second Circuit decision was a landmark. No higher federal court had ever ruled that the Constitution applied on Guantánamo, and it would be a key legal precedent for the future. The court seemed especially troubled by the government claim that the detainees had no legal recourse even if they were subjected to "physical abuse." Echoing Judge Johnson, the Second Circuit emphasized that the U.S. government was holding the Haitians incommunicado on land entirely under American control. In those circumstances, said the court, the due process clause guaranteed the refugees access to a lawyer.

The team was ecstatic with the ruling, and Koh took everyone out to a lobster shack on the Connecticut shore to celebrate. As favorable as the ruling was for Yale, however, it had a Pyrrhic taint. Were Guerrier and the other refuseniks still on Guantánamo, they would now have had the right to counsel. But it was too late. They already had been hauled back to Haiti.

Still, Mike realized that the new court decision would have an immediate impact. More refugees had fled Haiti. Some would be screened in, and like Guerrier, a few would probably test HIV positive. During their asylum hearings, those individuals would now enjoy the right to a lawyer that Guerrier had been denied.

But as Mike discovered in the weeks that followed, Bush officials weren't about to let anyone from Yale back on Guantánamo. Since the Second Circuit had only granted lawyers access to the base during the hearing process, the government halted the hearings altogether. Instead, HIV-positive Haitians who made it past the initial screening interview and were thus eligible for an asylum hearing were now simply bused to Camp Bulkeley—and left there.

Among the terrified new arrivals to the camp late that spring was a

woman whom no one from the Yale team had ever met. The military referred to her as migrant T00105. Her name was Yvonne Pascal.

Mind still racing with the positive HIV test, Yvonne stumbled off the bus.
Guards directed her past Bulkeley's main gate and toward an array of one-
story buildings. She was farther from the ocean now, hemmed in by hills,
the heat more intense.

As she shuffled along, she became vaguely aware that someone was calling her name. She looked up to find two women gesturing to her—Christa
Micles and Armelle Nelson, distant cousins she'd come across on the island of La Gonâve, just before leaving Haiti. They had been sent to the
camp several weeks earlier, and now past the initial shock, they'd adjusted
to the routine, from the morning head count to the medical clinic visits.
Their reunion with Yvonne was a mixture of relief and despair, and they
gently led her to their plywood hut, or *kay,* as they called it in Creole.

The main area of Bulkeley, called Camp Alpha, had perhaps forty
such huts—*kay yo,* in the Creole plural. Each was about twenty feet by
forty feet, with cement bases, tin roofs, and wire-mesh screen windows.
They were arranged in close rows, cement walkways running among
them, with a nearby shower room and a mess hall, all enclosed by razor
wire. Portable latrines were scattered throughout the living area. Close by
were a U-shaped cinder block command post; a white, barnlike structure
that served as a medical clinic; several Quonset storage huts; and a dusty
expanse that some of the men used as a soccer field. More razor wire and
a high chain-link fence surrounded the broader camp perimeter, and sen-
tries in guard towers kept watch over the refugees, arms folded in bore-
dom as the sun inched across the sky.

A dozen people lived in Christa and Armelle's *kay*—men, women, and
children jumbled together in a sweltering pen. Seeking privacy, families
had draped sheets from the ceiling to separate their olive-drab canvas
cots and belongings, adding to the claustrophobia. A few people were
using flattened cardboard boxes, laid out on the cement floor, for beds.

Distraught, Yvonne could only absorb her new surroundings in
strobe-light flashes. The place smelled of sweat and diapers. A toddler
was crying in a metal crib. Flies buzzed in the rafters. A little girl warily
eyed Yvonne from behind Armelle's skirt, a bar-code bracelet hanging
loosely from the child's ankle.

Christa pointed to the corner where she and Armelle slept with their four young nieces and nephews. There was an empty cot nearby and Christa steered Yvonne toward it. Sleep here, she suggested. Yvonne dropped her bag on the cot, her breath tight and shallow, then pushed her way outside. Christa called after her but Yvonne ran up the pathway until she was alone. She dropped to her knees, fighting back tears, begging God for some explanation of what was happening to her.

Several days later when a military man who called himself Dr. Malone reiterated her diagnosis, she took the news with little emotion. Yvonne didn't know what to believe anymore. She understood little about AIDS and listened doubtfully as Malone explained to her what a T cell was—a tiny thing in her blood that helped fight disease—and the way HIV attacked T cells. She had a T-cell count of 235, he told her. That was low, he said. She was in danger of becoming sick.

The actual prognosis was more dire, though Malone evidently didn't give Yvonne all the specifics. Yvonne's T-cell level was under 13 percent, which meant that by definition she had full-blown AIDS. Given her impaired immune system, she was susceptible to a swarm of potentially fatal "opportunistic infections"—tuberculosis, which had already struck several others in the camp; pneumonia; cancers; parasites that destroyed the gastrointestinal system; funguses that attacked the brain.

Malone gave Yvonne a bottle of pills that he called AZT, a nucleoside reverse transcriptase inhibitor that slowed reproduction of the virus. At the time, it was the best drug available for fighting AIDS, although there were new doubts about its effectiveness. He also gave her something called INH to prevent tuberculosis, and Septra, an antibiotic to ward off pneumonia.

Back at her *kay,* she asked about the drugs.

"They hand them out to everyone," somebody shrugged.

"Do you take them?"

"Some do, some don't. How do we know what they're giving us?"

Yvonne stared at the strange little bottles, pondering what to do. Then she went down to the washhouse, filled her cupped hand with water, and slipped an AZT pill between her lips.

Later, she wrote to her mother, trying to explain her situation, though she did not go into her medical condition. A camp guard who spoke Creole told her the return address to put on the envelope and promised to mail the letter for her.

A week passed. Then another, and another. She never heard back.

Koh was late for class, but when the phone rang, he picked it up. It was Dudley Sipprelle, the consul general for the American embassy in Haiti. "I'm trying to track down a Marie Zette here, someone I think you mentioned in a court hearing," Sipprelle said in a chatty tone. "I just wanted to get a sense for who this person is and if you had any more information about her."

Koh broke into a sweat. Over the last couple of weeks, he'd started to worry about the Marie Zette story. Was she a real person? Or was the whole tale something an excitable student had come up with after talking to a refugee who'd heard a rumor?

"I'm the lawyer for the other side in this case," he snapped. "I don't know how many privileges you've waived by calling me like this, but you'd better be careful. I don't want to have to put you on the witness stand. You're represented by counsel. You don't call me directly."

Sipprelle hung up in a hurry, but Koh had the warning he needed. Instead of relying primarily on reports of repatriate abuse from Amnesty International and other groups, he had personalized the case for Judge Johnson by focusing on the specific story of Marie Zette. Now the government was out to discredit the Zette story and undermine the claim that anybody was suffering persecution upon return to Haiti. After class, Koh called Michelle Anderson, the student who'd dug up the Marie Zette information in Miami. He asked her how quickly she could get back to Florida to try to corroborate the story.

"I don't want to eat that affidavit," he said. "But if I have to eat it, we need to have a good reason for this failure of information."

Michelle promised to do everything she could, but Koh began to think he was in serious trouble. The idea of telling Johnson that none of it was true made him sick.

Down in Miami, Michelle searched out the translator she'd worked with her last time in town. He looked skeptical when she told him the situation, but took her to a processing center with a planeload of new arrivals from Guantánamo. They walked into a room packed with refugees and the translator shouted for attention. He pointed to Michelle and gave a quick speech in Creole that included the words "Marie Zette."

All Michelle could see were blank stares.

"This is crazy," the translator muttered.

Trying not to panic, Michelle insisted they keep looking. She firmly believed in the Marie Zette story. The man who'd told it to her had sounded so earnest, and his account had included so much detail, including a precise description of Zette's appearance: pretty, short, and plump, with light skin and long hair.

The translator repeated his request to another group of refugees: Has anyone heard of Marie Zette, who was sent back home from Guantánamo?

This time, to Michelle's amazement, a woman slowly raised her hand. Michelle soon had another declaration supporting the story, and before the day was out, three more people had confirmed that they'd heard about Zette. It was all secondhand information, ultimately little better than rumors. But the stories were strikingly similar, Michelle reasoned, down to Zette's age, appearance, and hometown, and she had conducted each interview separately.

She called Yale and reached Tory, who relayed the news to Koh. He relaxed—a little. At a minimum, they would have a response to anything the government filed with Judge Johnson. But he knew that as a strategic matter, the Marie Zette story was dead. We don't know the truth, he decided. They've raised legitimate questions and we can't rely on this anymore.

As Koh had feared, Paul Cappuccio sent a letter to Johnson soon after Dudley Sipprelle called. Marie Zette was alive and well in Haiti, Cappuccio assured the judge. He included a statement from Sipprelle claiming to have met Marie Zette in person.

The woman's full name, Sipprelle said, was Marie Zette Joseph, and she'd been repatriated on February 12, 1992. A team from the U.S. embassy had tracked her down in Port-au-Prince and brought her in to speak with him. "We had a cordial conversation," Sipprelle reported. "I asked her if she had had any problems since her return to Haiti and she replied that she had not beyond her leg hurting." He also said that Marie Zette Joseph perfectly matched the physical description of the refugee identified by Michelle Anderson.

Koh was shocked by the amount of energy the government had put into discrediting the story. He dashed off an angry response, relying on the new declarations collected by Michelle. Zette *had* been killed, Koh insisted. The government's information about Marie Zette Joseph, he wrote, "tells us no more about the fate of Marie Zette than the story of Martin Luther King would tell us about the life of Martin Luther."

Koh never mentioned Marie Zette to Judge Johnson again. But while the State Department claimed no repatriates were getting hurt, he was certain there were real Marie Zettes out there.

To Mike Wishnie's astonishment, Frantz Guerrier called from Haiti in early May. He and his fellow resisters had left Guantánamo peacefully, he said, but when they arrived in Port-au-Prince twelve hours later and found Haitian soldiers prowling the docks, many had refused to disembark. The Coast Guard had broken the standoff by dragging several people ashore—and then charging up fire hoses to blast the rest off the cutter. With the nozzles trained on them, Guerrier and the others had surrendered to the Haitian military.

As the cutter departed, an officer had forced Guerrier to the ground, then led him away to be fingerprinted. He was finally released, but when he returned to his old neighborhood later that day, a soldier recognized him. The next night, paramilitary thugs attacked him in his grandmother's home, striking his head with a pistol butt and cracking his left wrist. Neighbors barged in after hearing his cries, and he managed to get away. Guerrier was now in hiding.

Determined to help, Mike began searching for a way to get Guerrier to Canada, perhaps, or Venezuela. He called immigration experts, aid workers in Haiti, foreign lawyers, anyone who would listen to him. Finally, after weeks of dead ends, he found a Belgian priest in Port-au-Prince willing to arrange secret passage for Guerrier into the Dominican Republic. Money had to change hands, and the trip could be dangerous: soldiers on both sides of the border were ready to use their weapons if they saw a problem. Nor, despite U.S. government claims to the contrary, was the Dominican Republic interested in giving asylum to Haitians, so Guerrier would have to remain in hiding once he got there. But he was desperate to get out of Haiti, so he agreed to the plan.

Before Guerrier left, Lisa Daugaard arranged for him to meet Elliot Schrage, an American attorney monitoring human rights conditions in Haiti. On a Sunday morning in mid-May, Guerrier slipped into the Hotel Montana, a white, terraced refuge perched high among the palms above Port-au-Prince. Schrage brought Guerrier to his room, examined the refugee's wounds, and took notes on his story.

The meeting left Schrage shaken. "I've met a lot of people who've been beaten or tortured," he recalled. "I've done human rights work in

El Salvador, Kosovo, and Uganda. I've seen scars from machete attacks, women who were raped, children who've witnessed their parents get killed, and worse. In each case, as someone from the United States, I was the good guy. I was on their side. This was the first time I had met someone who was returned by the United States to be tortured. My government had brought this man back."

Using Schrage's notes, Lisa wrote up a declaration, referring to Guerrier as "M. Bertrand" in case Haitian authorities ever got their hands on it. Schrage signed the declaration when he returned home to the United States. If the Marie Zette dispute ever came up again, the Yale team could put the broader point to rest: repatriates were in real danger.

Guerrier's meeting at the Hotel Montana coincided with a frantic period at Yale—final exams. Students from the litigation team now had to cram for courses they'd quit attending and pound out papers that should have been researched weeks earlier. Sarah Cleveland and Michael Barr, who both had judicial clerkships lined up, raced to graduate on time. Lisa was now so far behind that she couldn't possibly do the same, nor did she care that much about her academic situation anyway. The *McNary* case remained her main concern, and she had just won an ACLU fellowship in Manhattan on the strength of her clinical work and glowing recommendations from, among others, Harold Koh.

Tory was still worried about finals, but after the stress of the past three months, school seemed neither as threatening nor as important as it had the first semester. When she was through, she hugged Koh good-bye and headed to Nepal for the summer. She would be interviewing Tibetans who'd fled from their Chinese-occupied homeland. While she worried about the people marooned on Guantánamo, it didn't appear there was anything Yale could do for them at the moment. On the long flight over the ocean, the Haitians faded from her mind.

While the third years were welcoming their parents to New Haven and preparing for graduation ceremonies, the Bush administration faced a new problem. Haitians were now fleeing their homeland in greater numbers than ever, and the Coast Guard was intercepting hundreds of people each day. By mid-May, more than twelve thousand refugees were crammed onto the McCalla Airfield, up from just two thousand in March. With the power and water systems taxed to the limit, the military finally announced it had run out of space on Guantánamo.

Reports of violence continued to emerge from Haiti. But some in the

Bush administration blamed the refugee exodus on the U.S.-backed economic embargo, which, while still having no impact on Cedras, had plunged the country into new depths of misery. Food prices had doubled, and aid workers in Haiti were finding all the signs of severe malnutrition among children—orange hair, distended bellies. As Deputy Secretary of State Lawrence Eagleburger admitted, this put the White House in an awkward spot. If the Haitians were simply economic migrants, as Bush claimed, then United States policy was helping to drive them out of the country.

The administration considered building a permanent camp at Guantánamo or moving refugees to other Caribbean nations. But the Pentagon was adamantly against expanding refugee operations on the naval base, and no other country in the region wanted the Haitians. As the boats kept coming, the White House scrounged for another solution.

Yale's graduation ceremonies were scheduled for Memorial Day, and by tradition, Koh threw a brunch the day before in honor of the graduates from his first-year civil procedure course. It was a bittersweet afternoon. While this graduating group had been fiercely loyal to him over the last three years, taking his higher-level courses and seeking his advice as they prepared for life after Yale, that devotion had faded with the Guantánamo case. He'd repeatedly asked his most promising protégés to help out, but every one of them had declined. Koh was deeply hurt. They'd been happy to work for good grades and a recommendation, but were unwilling to sacrifice anything in return. "What's with those guys?" he'd asked Sarah Cleveland.

Amid his doubts about student loyalties, the commitment of Yale's public interest crowd had come as a revelation to him over the past several months. In February, he'd barely known some of the third-year leaders of the Guantánamo case. Now, they, too, were guests at his graduation brunch. It made for an odd mix of people, with Graham Boyd and Lisa Daugaard sitting a few feet away from well-known campus conservatives. Earlier in the year, Lisa would never have imagined attending an event hosted by Koh, let alone one packed with students of this sort. But not only had she come, she'd even brought her parents, who beamed as Koh heaped praise on her.

The party was an occasion of great relief for him, even though the departure of the graduating students had initially been one of his chief concerns in filing the *McNary* lawsuit. Despite team discussions on transferring duties to younger students, he'd worried all along about the impending loss of knowledge, talent, and labor. Yet the transition was coming at a manageable time because, for once, there was no emergency bearing down on the team. While the HIV-positive refugees were stuck in Camp Bulkeley, they were nevertheless safe from repatriation. And the screening of newly arriving refugees continued in the main camp at McCalla Airfield, ensuring that at least some who genuinely feared persecution would receive safe haven in the United States. As Koh saw the last guests out the door, he told himself that with Michael Ratner, Joe Tringali at Simpson Thacher, and a student or two around for the summer, the team could hold everything together until school resumed in September.

Then, shortly after brunch was over, Ratner called Koh.

"The sons of bitches," Ratner said. His tone was high-pitched, intense.

"What?"

"They're just returning them all now."

Hours earlier, President Bush had announced a new Haitian refugee policy from his vacation home in Kennebunkport, Maine. From that moment on, no one would be brought to Guantánamo. There would be no more screening interviews, no more inquiries to check if anyone deserved asylum. The Coast Guard's new orders were to intercept every boat leaving Haiti, take all the passengers aboard, and immediately return them to Port-au-Prince. Not only would the president block Haitians from entering the United States, he would now prevent them from leaving their own country. Refugee boats were not equipped for long sea voyages, a White House press release warned. The safety of Haitians could best be assured if they stayed home.

The White House urged those fearing persecution to seek asylum through the U.S. embassy in Port-au-Prince. But as human rights monitors who'd been to Haiti had advised the Yale team, both the embassy and the consulate were high-walled fortresses in areas swarming with Haitian soldiers. Serious activists wouldn't get near either, and the odds of winning safe haven through the consulate, which handled the applications, were next to nothing. In the four months the United States had taken applications in Port-au-Prince, it had granted asylum to just eleven people.

Ratner was stunned by Bush's decision, but for Koh, it had all begun to feel inevitable. Egged on by the students, he had started out seeking

lawyers for a limited group of refugees on Guantánamo whose fate lay
with mid-level INS bureaucrats. Now the team had to confront a major
foreign policy operation ordered by the president himself, and the timing
could not have been worse. The younger students were already scattered
from Washington to Hong Kong for the summer, and graduation for the
third years was just eighteen hours away.

Koh gunned his Subaru out of the driveway and tracked down Sarah
Cleveland at a dinner party. Over the past two months, she had become
his chief aide; he valued her judgment and dependability and appreciated
that she didn't argue about every last little issue with him. Just as important, she was also the student responsible for researching a complex law
that up to that point had not been a focus in the litigation—the United
Nations Refugee Convention of 1951, which the United States had
adopted in the late 1960s.

Article 33 of the U.N. Convention recognized the fundamental principle
of refugee law, the rule of non-return or non-refoulement, which barred a
country from sending political refugees back to a place where they might be
persecuted. Up until the watershed day of the new Bush policy, May 24, the
administration had observed Article 33, however imperfectly, through the
Guantánamo screening process. But the new White House policy simply
ignored that law, making it a central issue in the case. And Sarah, who knew
more about Article 33 than anyone on the team, was scheduled to leave
New Haven for good soon after the graduation ceremony.

Sarah had a dim view of the Bush administration, but had never imagined the president would take so extreme a measure. Most striking of all
to her was that, when Bush made his decision, the INS had been screening in about one-third of the refugees intercepted by the Coast Guard.
The administration *knew* it would be returning people with a credible
fear of persecution.

The last thing Sarah wanted to do at that moment was legal work.
Her parents were in town for graduation, and she was heading to Florida
for a summer job in two days. She wanted to sit back, finish dinner, take
it easy. But as she put it, "There's no way in hell we're going to let the
president get away with this." She polished off her dessert, postponed
her flight, and went straight to the library.

As word of the new White House policy traveled from student to student, the reaction was shock, disgust—and the swift rearrangement of
plans. Lisa was burned out, but didn't think twice about returning to

full-body commitment. Ray Brescia, who was intending to study for the bar exam in New Haven, began recruiting other students. It didn't always go smoothly. When Michael Barr told his girlfriend he had to get back to work that evening, she was furious. First it had been the lawsuit. Then he'd had to scramble to finish his courses. After barely seeing Michael in three months, she'd taken several days off so they could spend *his* graduation together. Now he was walking out on her in the middle of the weekend because of another damn emergency with the Haitians.

Graduation day turned out gray and cool, the wind slapping at the blue and white balloons festooning the law school courtyard. The faculty speaker was Koh's sister, a popular clinical professor, and while she singled out the students on the Haiti case for praise, many were too distracted to fully appreciate her words. The new Bush policy was on the front page of every newspaper and the Coast Guard cutters were already sending people back to Port-au-Prince. Following the ceremony, most of the class of 1992 milled about in the courtyard, sipping champagne with family and friends. Lisa, Sarah, Ray, and several others on the case gave their parents a squeeze, tore off their gowns, and hurried upstairs to the clinic office with Koh.

Some of the newly minted graduates, though, decided that enough was enough. They gave one last day or two to the suit and then quit. Each person had a good reason—the bar exam, a clerkship, sheer exhaustion. But Koh was still frustrated, particularly with some of the third years who'd pushed to file the case, and he groused to Sarah about it. He felt they'd never fully appreciated the commitment that would be necessary over the long haul, yet that hadn't stopped them from pressing for the lawsuit. Now they were leaving Koh and Ratner with the mess.

A decade afterward, the scene on Memorial Day continued to haunt one student. "I still remember Ray coming to me after the ceremony and saying, 'We've got a meeting in twenty minutes, the government's just done something, we're going up to Harold's office.' And that's when I finally broke. It was like, I've got to take the bar. I've got a moving van here and I'm supposed to pack up and be home tomorrow. My bar class started forty-eight hours later. I ended up staying a week, but with each passing day, I got more and more terrified. Still, when I left New Haven and was driving down I-95, I kept thinking of turning around. So if it sounds like I feel bad about this ten years later, that's right."

Locked in Bulkeley with no news of the outside world, Yvonne was un-
aware of the change in White House policy. Days passed at the camp and
she drifted into a routine. She ate what they offered, though the strange
food often made her stomach hurt. She helped Christa and Armelle care
for their nieces and nephews, tutoring the older ones in reading and writing. She worried constantly about her children and Antenor, and had
nightmares about the baby she'd lost. And while she was conscientious
about taking her AZT and the other drugs, she wondered if she really was
sick—and how she might have gotten the illness. I felt fine when I left
Haiti, she reasoned. What had happened since then? The camp was
buzzing with rumors that the military had deliberately infected everyone
during the blood tests. But she quickly determined that the other refugees
had no better grasp of the situation than she did. In fact, nobody seemed to
have hard information about anything—including when they could leave.

After a month in Bulkeley, Yvonne's anxiety hardened into frustration. She decided to organize a protest, though she expected little help
from the refugee leadership. Camp president Wilson Edouard had been
elected by his peers for his English, not his political skills. An easygoing
man with a slight paunch, he'd lived in Florida for several years before
returning to Haiti around the time of Aristide's election. Every week,
Edouard and his makeshift cabinet met with the camp commander to
discuss their concerns. The refugees had their worries about AIDS, but
Edouard spent most of his time repeating a single question pressed upon
him by the rest of the camp: *How long must we stay here?*

The INS is in charge, Edouard was told again and again. People in
Washington are responsible for your situation. The military is just following orders. "I do not see Bulkeley as a prison camp and do not see this as
punishment," a man named Captain Engler said. "Our job is to provide a
decent, humane place to live, with quality housing, food, and medical attention. My goal and the goal of my staff is to treat you with respect."

For weeks, the other refugees had been pushing Edouard for better
answers, and Yvonne now joined in that demand. But Edouard didn't
have the stomach to confront the military, and he was convinced the
Haitians couldn't remain at Bulkeley forever. He'd seen America, he reminded them. It wasn't like Haiti. People didn't just sit in prison for no
reason. Sooner or later, he promised, something would change.

It did. Edouard lost his job, replaced through a camp vote by Vilsaint Michel, a small man with a high-pitched, reedy voice who'd been a political activist in the seaside town of Petit Goâve. Serious and organized, he was forever carrying around a clipboard with notes of his discussions with the military—a habit that eased others' suspicions about what went on during the meetings with the American soldiers.

As part of the same election, Yvonne was chosen to speak for the women. She had only been in Camp Bulkeley a few weeks, but had already earned a reputation among the other refugees by clashing with the commander at one of Edouard's last meetings. She's willing to take on the military, people said. She's going to get things done.

Several days later, the refugees packed into a bare *kay* that they used as a chapel. Yvonne had encouraged everyone to wear white to symbolize their innocence, and many were in tunics and headbands cut from their bedsheets. Some had scrawled messages on their outfits: "Georges Bush Racist," "FREDOM." Others held aloft pictures of Aristide or Jesus. Over the din of urgent murmurs, the Haitian American camp chaplain read from a Bible, recounting the story of Moses leading his people out of slavery. Then the protesters streamed out into the blazing sun, a throng of bodies clad in billowing white cloth, singing hymns of deliverance.

As the march wended its way past the inner gate and onto the road leading to the main base, the Haitians switched to a Creole political chant. Some of the angry young men—the *militan,* the refugees called them—shuffled in unison to a drumbeat, repeating a dance step from Port-au-Prince street rallies. A one-legged refugee nicknamed Bacon fought to keep up on his crutches. The children trailed behind, clutching an adult's hand or a sign asking President Bush for help. Yvonne stayed in the middle of the pack, hoping to keep a low profile. She wanted her captors to see the demonstration as a collective effort, not something she'd spearheaded with a few other radical activists.

A half mile later, the boisterous procession reached the camp's perimeter fence. Beyond, Yvonne could see nothing but dusty hills, scrub trees, and the white-capped ocean. Some refugees dropped to their knees; others lay down on the hot asphalt as if to block traffic. The chaplain offered a prayer, shouting to be heard over the wind whipping off the water, and then the protesters joined in, calling toward the water for someone, anyone, to help. But the gate remained locked, and the soldiers unmoved, and finally, the refugees retreated to the *kay yo.*

The next day, nothing had changed. Yvonne paced the camp, brooding. In Haiti, the government always responded to a demonstration. Even when she had performed as a youngster in a school play called *The Cake Is Not Shared Equally,* Macoutes had broken up the performance. Hateful as the repression was, it did signal that officials were paying attention. Guantánamo was something new. Yvonne could exhort her fellow refugees to spend hours making protest banners and then chant until their voices gave out. But no one was listening.

In the days after President Bush issued his new direct return order, the effects rippled through Washington and beyond. Human rights groups denounced the White House while dismayed U.N. officials declared Bush's policy a clear violation of Article 33. But the State Department asserted that most Haitian asylum claims were "nonsensical," and Republicans on Capitol Hill emphasized the strain that the refugees would put on social services.

Compared with other refugee crises around the world, however, the number of Haitians that had fled their homeland since the coup—34,000—was tiny. From Afghanistan to Cambodia to Somalia, hundreds of thousands, sometimes millions of people, crossed international borders seeking safety and were granted temporary asylum in countries with nowhere near the resources of the United States. The U.S. itself, in fact, had welcomed over 321,000 refugees from other nations over the previous three years, along with 4.4 million immigrants. But Haitian refugee boats heading for Florida made for threatening images in the news, and as one Senate aide told the *Miami Herald,* White House policy reflected a simple political calculation. "It's an election year," he said. "They want this genie to stay in the bottle."

Out on the campaign trail, President Bush was challenged in Marietta, Georgia, by a man who asked if the new return policy didn't run counter "to what America has stood for over the last couple of hundred years."

"I am convinced the people in Haiti are not being physically oppressed," replied Bush, perched on a stool in a stifling hot school gym. He assured the questioner that "the Statue of Liberty still stands," and declared, "I would not want it on my conscience that anyone fleeing oppression would be victimized on return."

In response came a new voice, that of a charismatic young governor from Arkansas, the surprising front-runner for the Democratic presidential nomination. His name was Bill Clinton, and as it happened, he had graduated from Yale Law School. "I am appalled by the decision of the Bush administration," he said. "This policy must not stand." He called the White House move a blow to "America's moral authority" and charged that if the Haitians were fleeing for economic reasons, it was due to the embargo supported by the administration. Bush, he added, "wants to send them back, even if some of them die on the way."

Michael Ratner was ecstatic when he heard Clinton's comments. He was not in the habit of trusting politicians of any stripe, but he considered Clinton's statement extraordinary because it was so unequivocal. Ratner was all the more pleased because Clinton had been fighting to make his name as a "New Democrat," tougher and more practical than traditional East Coast liberals. It signaled to Ratner, who was usually on the radical fringe, that Yale might be closer to the mainstream than he'd thought in challenging the White House.

Whether that challenge should come in a courtroom was a different question. On a postgraduation conference call that included Yale and human rights advocates around the country, an NAACP lobbyist warned that racing to a judge wasn't always the answer. In fact, he suggested, Yale might have contributed to the new Bush policy by interfering with the asylum process on Guantánamo. This time, the lobbyist argued, they should try to negotiate a solution in the less adversarial environment of Capitol Hill.

Congress would never do anything for the Haitians, Koh shot back. There was no political gain in it for them.

But some litigators on the call worried, as they had before Yale sought the first TRO, that going to court could end up creating bad precedent. They didn't want conservative judges putting constraints on Article 33.

"When else are we going to do this?" Koh asked, growing testy. Bush's order was *exactly* what the U.N. Refugee Convention was meant to forbid. If they were ever going to challenge that practice, now was the time to do it. Yale was already before the right trial court judge in Sterling Johnson, he said. The team even had clients who'd been returned to Haiti and beaten—and the same thing was about to happen to countless others now.

There was no grand burst of enthusiasm from the other lawyers after

Koh had finished his pitch. But in the end, no one stood in the way, either, and when the call ended, Yale's plan against the White House was set: "We're going to sue the bastards."

The new goal in court would be to seek a second temporary restraining order from Judge Johnson, this time to halt the immediate repatriations. Another massive research effort was necessary, but the work for the second TRO marked a turning point. Three months earlier, when the students had first researched the legal theories for the Guantánamo case, they'd faced a remarkably complex set of issues—particularly the question of how American law applied to the base. The result had been days if not weeks of wasted effort on creative but impractical ideas.

For the new case challenging the direct returns, the law was much clearer—and the students far more efficient in their work. Article 33 of the U.N. Refugee Convention imposed a flat prohibition: refugees could not be returned to a place where they might suffer persecution. Congress had adopted the same principle as a matter of domestic law by passing the Refugee Act of 1980. Yale's fifty-page brief, completed in just three days, argued that Bush was in flagrant violation of both laws.

Graham Boyd came up with the theme that tied it all together. Everyone had been looking for a name for the direct return policy—something that made it sound brutal, heartless, downright un-American. The collapse of Communism in Eastern Europe was still fresh in everyone's mind, particularly the defining image of the time: crowds in Berlin toppling the wall that had blocked East Germans from fleeing their repressive government for three decades. "That's it," Graham told Ray Brescia. "Bush has created a floating Berlin Wall!"

They now had one night to prepare for their new opponent, Solicitor General Kenneth Starr, who would be flying in from Washington to argue the case himself. The law school hallways were empty, the rest of the student body gone for the summer, but the atmosphere in the Lowenstein office was electric. Starr's appearance would be one of only a handful of times in history that a solicitor general had argued at the trial-court level. And Koh, who'd briefly served with Starr at Justice under President Reagan, couldn't wait to challenge him.

In the time they had overlapped, Koh had come to see Starr as more of a well-connected politician than a great legal mind. Often described as gracious and courtly, but also eager to please and openly ambitious about a Supreme Court seat, Starr was only in his mid-thirties when Reagan appointed him to the federal appellate court in Washington. Six years later, President Bush chose Starr as his solicitor general, evidently to groom him for the high court. But then came *Planned Parenthood v. Casey,* a crucial abortion case in which Starr asked the justices to overrule *Roe v. Wade.* The bid failed, and after *Casey,* the White House feared Starr's confirmation hearings would be a political bloodbath. He was passed over for the Supreme Court twice in the next two years, but remained a high-profile figure with strong support in conservative circles.

Koh, drinking from another jug-sized cup of coffee, strategized with Ratner and the rest of the team about how to handle the solicitor general in court. He believed Starr was at his best when he stood above the fray, relying on the lingering aura of his years on the bench to present himself as an impartial adviser instead of an advocate. So Koh made a calculated decision: he would be as aggressive as possible, aiming to make Starr fight and scrap like any other lawyer.

Before they went to court, Mike Wishnie gave Koh a photograph, obtained from a government contact who'd just returned from Guantánamo. It showed the refuseniks being loaded onto the Coast Guard cutter *Tampa* on April 28, just four weeks earlier. Wishnie pointed to one of them, a slight figure under the escort of two guards. "I swear," Mike said quietly, "that's Frantz Guerrier."

The hearing took place in the Eastern District's immense ceremonial courtroom to accommodate all the spectators and reporters on hand. Koh hammered home one main point in his argument to Judge Johnson: President Bush was not a king. He had no right to ignore the law simply because he found it inconvenient. Congress had mandated that people fleeing persecution were not to be returned to their persecutors, and the White House was bound to honor that legal obligation. Just as the president could not persecute or drown the Haitian refugees, neither could he put up a floating Berlin Wall that prevented them from leaving their country.

Conditions in Haiti were a nightmare, Koh went on. Just two days before, the *New York Times* had reported a sharp increase in nighttime military raids and multiple killings in Port-au-Prince. "The U.S. government itself sent Navy SEALs in to rescue people," Koh said, referring to media reports of secret military maneuvers to extract Aristide officials. "And these are the same people who are saying, 'By the way, we don't notice any political persecution going on.'" How, Koh asked, could everyone from Haiti have suddenly become an economic migrant when just days earlier, the INS was screening in one-third of them as potential political refugees? All you have to tell the government, Koh said to the judge, is that "this option that you have chosen is illegal—sending people back to their persecutors to be tortured and killed."

There was a hush as Solicitor General Starr took the podium. Evidently unruffled by Koh's attacks, he wore a mild, composed expression. Backed by a phalanx of government lawyers and uniformed Coast Guard and Pentagon officials, Starr calmly informed the judge that Bush was sending all the Haitians back to Port-au-Prince because he had no other choice. The president, he declared, didn't have the luxury of philosophizing about refugee policy the way they might at Yale Law School. He had to make real-world decisions about real-world problems, and the direct return order was the only reasonable option available to him. Anyone fearing persecution, Starr assured the court, could seek asylum through the American embassy or flee to the Dominican Republic—only a "two-hour car ride from Port-au-Prince."

Two months earlier, Judge Johnson had promised he would not be pushed around by anyone in Washington, and to the students, he seemed to be making good on his word. The judge suggested the new White House policy smacked of racism and demanded repeated explanations from Starr.

Wouldn't lives be lost under the new return policy? he asked.

"We have conducted over two thousand in-country interviews with repatriates," said Starr. "We have found no evidence of persecution or attacks on these individuals, none in our two thousand interviews."

"The Navy SEALs went into Haiti to rescue friends of the ousted president," Johnson shot back. "If that is so, then how can you really say that conditions are not that bad?"

Starr had no answer for the judge. But when Johnson pressed him about the two laws against returning refugees—Article 33 and the Refugee Act—he responded emphatically that they had no force outside American borders. As the students recognized, it was, in essence, the same position Paul Cappuccio had taken in earlier court arguments. On the high seas, as on Guantánamo, President Bush could do with the Haitians as he wished. He was bound by no law.

Johnson looked incredulous. As the Yale brief had pointed out, the purpose of both Article 33 and the Refugee Act was to protect refugees wherever they might be found. The Jews aboard the *St. Louis,* the original inspiration for Article 33, did not lose their right to safe haven simply because they were on the open ocean instead of in Miami Harbor. Sending them back to Hitler's Germany would have been reprehensible—and illegal—in either instance. But when the judge pushed Starr on the reach of Article 33, the solicitor general held his ground.

"Your Honor," Starr said, "when I was a judge, there was one thing that I knew I had to do and that was to follow the law." And the law, he insisted, did not give the refugees any rights.

The solicitor general closed by assuring Johnson that despite appearances, the government had no anti-Haitian bias.

"Well, I will tell you one thing that I was always told," the judge replied. Perceptions, he said, mattered as much as reality. And his perception was that Haitians were being singled out.

"Then we need to do a better job at correcting a perception," Starr said.

Johnson nodded. "You need to do a better job."

Everyone from Yale believed Koh had bested the solicitor general. Graham Boyd, who'd been impressed by Cappuccio at previous hearings, didn't think much of Starr at all. What's all the hoopla? he shrugged. There'd been no flashes of brilliance, no dazzling rhetoric. He'd expected more out of the lawyer he initially imagined as Yale's archenemy, especially given the solicitor general's résumé. Ray Brescia left the courthouse bristling. "Starr clearly didn't think Johnson was smart," Ray told a classmate. "He was so patronizing, and he had this accent like he was Thurston Howell III from *Gilligan's Island* or something. His whole presence was: I'm here, the government knows what it's doing—and it was just so off-putting."

But when Judge Johnson issued his opinion a few days later, he ruled for the government. He said his decision, based largely on a technicality in treaty law, was compelled by a precedent from the Second Circuit—a higher court whose rulings he was bound to follow. And yet the judge was plainly troubled. He called Bush's direct return policy "unconscionable" and said he was "astonished that the United States would return Haitian refugees to the jaws of political persecution, terror, death." The government's conduct, Johnson declared, "is particularly hypocritical given its condemnation of other countries who have refused to abide by the principle of non-refoulement. As it stands now, Article 33 is a cruel hoax and not worth the paper it is printed on."

Koh took the judge's unusually harsh words as an invitation to seek a reversal from the Second Circuit, and hours later the Yale team was at work on an appeal.

———

Days after President Bush's order, KID leader Evans Paul tried to leave Haiti for an international summit. The military arrested him at the airport and interrogated him for two hours. French and Canadian diplomats intervened when soldiers announced they were taking him to police headquarters, and Paul was escorted back to Port-au-Prince in a Canadian embassy car. He went into hiding again. Antenor Joseph, meanwhile, slipped from one safe house to another in Carrefour-Feuilles. He had no idea where his wife, Yvonne Pascal, was and he couldn't visit the family. It was too dangerous. Yet he refused to think about fleeing the country. He mapped out plans with other members of KID and prepared for the future, still convinced that Aristide would ultimately return.

Few shared his optimism anymore, and people kept taking to the sea. But under the new White House policy, the Coast Guard methodically intercepted the boats, delivering everyone aboard to the Port-au-Prince docks. As word of the forced repatriations spread through Haiti, the number of vessels leaving the country plummeted. There was simply no point in fleeing. By the end of June, the cutters patrolling the Windward Passage found themselves nearly alone.

With no new arrivals at Guantánamo, the administration announced that it was closing down Camp McCalla. The remaining refugees were screened for fear of persecution and then either returned to Haiti or taken to the United States. On the first of July, Brigadier General Richard Neal told the press by telephone that fewer than a thousand refugees were left on the base, down from over twelve thousand just a month earlier. A number of them would be flown to Florida within two weeks, Neal said, leaving only three hundred Haitians on Guantánamo.

The last three hundred were the HIV-positive refugees and their relatives, isolated among the hills in Camp Bulkeley. Neal did not say what would happen to them.

Amid the crush of bodies, it was impossible to tell whether a refugee or a soldier struck first. But in seconds, the new protest at Camp Bulkeley had exploded into a riot. Soldiers chased after refugees, pounding them with batons. The *militan* grabbed anything they could find—a stone, a scrap of wood, a broom—and hurled it at their captors. One refugee kicked a soldier in the face, breaking his nose, and military police then rushed into the fray, driving the refugees back to the inner camp and slamming the barnyardlike gate at the entrance.

The *militan* regrouped and threw it open again. This time, the soldiers responded with a fire hose, blasting people to the ground. Covered in mud, hands shielding their faces, the young Haitian men fought through the spray to hold their position. The hose finally ran dry, leaving a murky pool at the camp entrance and a knot of refugees, still on their feet, shouting in triumph. After more effort, they at last knocked over the gate, but no one tried to flee, for they were still locked inside Bulkeley's perimeter fence and had nowhere to go.

Evidently realizing the Haitians weren't looking to escape, the MPs trudged away. With no enemy to fight, the soaked protesters slogged back to the *kay yo,* where Yvonne and the others had waited out the riot. Dusk had fallen, and she watched as a few mud-caked *militan* tried to right the damaged gate in the failing light. It was beyond repair, and they finally gave up, leaving the disjointed remains sagging from the gatepost.

Yvonne went to bed with one thought on her mind: The soldiers are coming back. They're coming back, and we had better be ready.

She was praying the next morning when a fighter jet screamed overhead, a few hundred feet off the ground. The camp shook with the thunderous flyby and Yvonne sprinted for her *kay,* head ringing. She stopped short at the main walkway. Soldiers were everywhere—hundreds, it seemed, brandishing shields and batons, guard dogs trotting beside them.

Translators threw open the *kay* doors. "Get out!" they shouted. "Out! Out! Out! Now!"

People hurried away in flip-flops and T-shirts, belongings stuffed into plastic garbage bags or rolled-up sheets. Children clung to their parents, sobbing.

A translator pointed at Yvonne. "You!" he yelled. "Down here with everyone else!"

Yvonne ran into her *kay* for her backpack and rushed to join the others.

They're going to shoot us all, someone cried.

Don't be stupid, another responded. But nobody could explain the two soldiers standing on a rooftop, armed with machine guns.

The refugees were herded against a fence, and the troops then stormed into the empty huts. They tore apart cots, threw aside tables and chairs, ripped down sheets hanging from the rafters. Under orders to seize anything that might be used as a weapon, they grabbed every metal tube, every wood scrap, every jar or can.

After the injuries sustained in the melee the day before, the soldiers were in no mood to treat the Haitians' possessions with care. They only sounded angrier when they found stashes of sharp rocks and planks with rusty nails driven through them. The members of the Guantánamo Joint Task Force had been feeding and housing the refugees for months. It wasn't a job they wanted, but they were carrying out orders as best they could. This was the payback?

Over the loudspeakers, military translators ordered the young male refugees who'd instigated the riot to turn themselves in. When no one came forward, the names were repeated, but the Haitians stood together in defiant solidarity. Yvonne eyed Pierre Charles, who'd been on her Coast Guard cutter. He'd become one of the fiercest opponents of the guards, but she wasn't about to help them identify him. Finally, the troops shoved their way through the crowd and seized a couple dozen men, including Charles. Two soldiers forced him to the ground, bound his wrists with plastic flexcuffs, and marched him to a waiting van.

Yvonne was ordered into line with the rest of the refugees and forced to surrender her belongings for yet another search. Then she was sent to the mess hall with the other women and children. MREs—meals ready to eat, which the military relied on in the field—had been set out on the tables, but few seemed interested in food. Some people were shouting; some, crying; others sat, silent, staring into space.

She tried to stay calm and assess the situation. There was, she knew, a fine line between protest and violence, and some of the men had lost their discipline the day before. But she was astounded by the soldiers' response. All their talk about respect and dignity, she thought to herself, was so much propaganda. As far as she was concerned, the refugees were now at war with the American military.

For the appeal to the Second Circuit on the direct return order, Koh faced off against Kenneth Starr again. This time, Yale won. The judges pelted the solicitor general with questions, and he stumbled along, agitated, trying to get his point across. When he argued that the laws protecting refugees didn't apply on the high seas, Judge George Pratt turned apoplectic.

We can do whatever we want to the Haitians, Pratt challenged, as long as they're outside our borders? We're forbidden to return them once they're here, but the law is meaningless if we get them out on the ocean? How can that be?!

In late July, the court issued its opinion declaring Bush's direct return policy illegal. The president was absolutely forbidden from returning political refugees to their persecutors, Judge Pratt wrote. And the Refugee Act of 1980 was so clear on this point that there was no need to get into the Article 33 complexities that had concerned Judge Johnson. Pratt even referred to the direct return order as "the Kennebunkport order," a term cooked up by the students to emphasize that Bush had adopted the policy while at his vacation home.

Hours after the opinion was issued, Bill Clinton, who had now won the Democratic presidential nomination, responded with a press release. "The Court of Appeals made the right decision in overturning the Bush administration's cruel policy of returning Haitian refugees to a brutal dictatorship," he said. "We respect the right of refugees from other parts of the world to apply for political asylum, and Haitians should not be treated differently."

The next day, Starr and Cappuccio again asked the Supreme Court to intervene. The Second Circuit Court of Appeals had overstepped its bounds, the solicitor general argued, misreading the law and meddling with the president's authority in foreign affairs.

Yale's skeleton summer crew—Koh, Ratner, Lisa, and a pale, stubbly Ray Brescia, straight from the bar exam—raced to respond. But they already knew what to expect.

Just seventy-two hours after the Second Circuit handed down its decision, the Supreme Court issued another stay in favor of the administration. This time, only Justices Harry Blackmun and John Paul Stevens voted against it. President Bush was once again free to continue the direct returns until the Supreme Court heard arguments from Koh and the solicitor general in person. That would be many months later.

It was August 1, 1992, and after three hearings before Johnson, three arguments before the Second Circuit, and two emergency applications to the Supreme Court, the case was briefly at a standstill. The students were scattered around the country and beyond. In New Haven, Lisa packed up all of her things and went over to campus for one last pizza with Koh and Ray Brescia. Then she flew home to Seattle—broke, exhausted, and still four papers away from graduating.

All summer long, Mike Wishnie had been in Manhattan trying to learn more about Camp Bulkeley. He and Graham Boyd wanted to pitch the major media outlets on stories about the refugees. They believed Koh had too much faith in the court system, and that it was a mistake to direct so much of the team's efforts into legal action alone. There were other ways to force change, they reasoned, and one of them was ugly publicity about the camp. News articles about Bulkeley would force politicians to pay attention and bring sympathetic people to the refugees' cause.

The problem was one of access. No Yale lawyer could go to Guantánamo, and the government had barred reporters for weeks. Seeking intelligence, Mike and Graham tracked down government Creole translators and chaplains who'd worked in Bulkeley. They reported harsh conditions, assaults by the guards, and an atmosphere of fear and anxiety. One source led to another and Mike ultimately found himself on the telephone with a Justice Department employee who wanted to help but insisted on anonymity. There'd been protests, she confirmed. Military police had responded with force, and many refugees were now being detained in a punishment compound.

Wishnie couldn't persuade anyone to write a major story on such scant information, but he knew all of his research was bound to lead somewhere. He and Graham kept working their contacts and Mike developed a relationship with *Washington Post* reporter Lynne Duke, building the case for a future piece about the camp. Then late in the summer, Wishnie got a rushed telephone call from a source on Guantánamo. Within minutes, he knew there was enough for a major story.

It was August 29, six weeks after the fire-hose riot, and some of the *militan* were still locked up in Camp VII, a "segregation area" of small razor-wire pens, cardboard mats, and crude tents. Late in the morning, camp president Vilsaint Michel, Yvonne, and other refugee leaders went to their weekly meeting with the military. They pleaded, as they had several times already, for the release of the "segregated" Haitians.

"I won't talk about Camp VII," declared Colonel Joe Trimble, yet another in the parade of military officials the refugees had dealt with during their captivity. "I've laid out the guidelines and I will go case by case on September 4."

Over twenty guards had been hurt during the fire-hose riot, and Trimble's men had recently found more homemade weapons in Bulkeley. He made clear that he wasn't about to let the refugees he considered the most dangerous rejoin their comrades.

"The people in the camp are restless," Michel went on, referring to Bulkeley as a whole. "If we could give them something concrete about their status. . . ."

"As the general and I have told you before, we can only provide food, clothing, and shelter," Trimble said. "We don't control when you leave. I wish I could answer that for you but I can't."

When the rest of the Haitians in Bulkeley learned that no one would be allowed out of Camp VII, they charged the compound en masse and freed the men themselves. Then they returned to the main camp in a triumphal procession, chanting in broken English. An hour later, Colonel Trimble strode into Bulkeley and demanded that the escapees surrender. The entire camp rebuffed him, forming a human barrier to protect the men, and the colonel called for backup. Troops clad in riot gear fell into formation outside the entrance.

This time, the refugees were ready. They'd been siphoning gasoline from the camp generators, and they now fanned out among the *kay yo*. Yvonne double-checked to make sure her own *kay* was empty—everyone had already removed their belongings—and then smeared Vaseline over the sheets and ignited them. The heat was sudden and intense. She ran out the door, coughing. Huts were aflame all around her and dark smoke billowed into the sky.

She'd dimly hoped that the burning buildings would somehow get the attention of the United Nations, perhaps through a news report. But it wasn't the U.N. that responded. Instead, several tanks rumbled into the camp, troops marching in behind them. Yvonne had been keeping a journal and she yanked it out of her backpack and uncapped her pen. Hand shaking, she counted the armored vehicles and the men and began to record everything. She was still writing when the soldiers fell upon her.

There were more arrests that afternoon; more people thrown to the ground, hog-tied, and dragged to Camp VII; more shouting from the *militan*; more sobbing from the children. Yvonne was among those taken down, a boot pressed against her neck while her wrists were bound. The

guards were about to haul her away when an officer whom Yvonne recognized stepped in. She'd learned enough English by now to understand
that he was telling them to let her go.

Another guard pointed at Yvonne, his voice sharp.

"They said you have to stop writing," an interpreter repeated to her in
Creole, "or next time, you'll pay for it."

She held her tongue until a tense, campwide meeting later that day. A
Joint Task Force officer was trying to broker a peace.

"We don't want to fight with you anymore," he said through an interpreter. "Let's just talk. What do you want?"

Everyone shouted at once, a cacophony of demands and accusations.
The officer called for order. When it fell quiet, Yvonne took the floor.

"I'll tell you what we want," she said in rapid-fire Creole. "We want to
get out of this place. And if you don't have the power to let us go, we
want somebody from the U.N. to come here. We want other countries to
know what America is doing."

The others murmured in agreement.

"We want to speak with someone outside the military. Someone who
can really tell us *what is going on.* How come you won't let anybody in
here? What are you trying to hide?"

"We've told you," the officer said, "it's not up to us. All we can do is
maintain order and protect you."

"*Protect us?* You're not protecting anyone! We live day to day wondering what you're doing to our bodies. You're experimenting with us.
Testing drugs on us like we were animals!"

The others joined in, a chorus of angry cries.

"You call yourselves the country of freedom and democracy. You're
lying. *This is all a lie!* We're tired of your food, your head counts, your
orders, your prison!" Yvonne yelled. "But we're not going to stop. We
won't rest. We won't sleep. We'll keep fighting, and we are not going to
die here!"

Six

GOING TO GUANTÁNAMO

THE FALL OF 1992 brought a changing of the guard at Yale. The third years had graduated, and Tory Clawson and the other younger students now became the new leaders. The "Next Generation," as the group called itself, had a different character from its predecessor. The students who'd launched the suit had been especially self-confident. But Koh was pleased, and perhaps more comfortable, with the people who were taking over. They were a warm, modest bunch—less contentious, yet just as committed to the case.

Koh considered Tory exceptionally dependable, so he picked her as one of two student directors for the Lowenstein Clinic, which was now officially back in session. While Tory herself was shocked, Koh saw her as the clear choice. Time and time again in the spring, when something needed to be done at four a.m., she'd been there, eager to help. Tory soon became his chief aide, as Sarah Cleveland had been before graduating. The role fit Tory well. She didn't like squirreling herself away in the library; she wanted to be in the thick of things.

Her new co-director, Steve Roos, balanced out her frenetic energy. An introspective second year with deep-set, worried eyes, Steve had been on the case since the first trip to the Budget Inn in Miami. He was a rarity among his peers in the clinic, skeptical and pessimistic, and had a far more detached view of the case than the others. The Yale team orthodoxy—Cappuccio and the INS were pure evil; the Haitians were all heroic democracy activists—struck him as simplistic, and he quietly harbored doubts about the litigation. Should the Bulkeley refugees really be allowed into the United States? What about the tens of thousands in Haiti who still wanted to flee? Was it sensible to let them all enter the country? These were all legitimate questions in Steve's mind, but as he saw it, debate wasn't welcome within the team. He focused on the work and kept his thoughts to himself.

There was, in fact, skepticism in the clinic, but it was directed at the fresh volunteers. Veterans questioned whether the new people really cared about the refugees or just wanted to get in on a high-profile lawsuit. The crisis in Haiti was routinely in the national newspapers, and the litigation at Yale had drawn considerable media attention the previous spring. There'd even been features on the students themselves, including a column by Anthony Lewis in the *New York Times*. Now that working for the Haitians had become sexy, even staunch conservatives were popping up at the new team headquarters—an aging suite in a law school dorm with room for all the paper generated by the case.

But as recruits poured in, older hands departed. Michelle Anderson, for one, decided she'd had enough. She wanted to be a law professor, and felt she had to devote her time to classes rather than an all-consuming lawsuit. Other students were disappointed, even angry, when she quit. In Tory's view, Michelle "just didn't get it." When it came to coursework, Tory merely wanted to make sure she didn't flunk. She enrolled in the same courses as other members of the Lowenstein Clinic, and they formed note pools, with students planning to attend class on a rotating basis.

The team reconvened with Koh for the first time on a hot August afternoon to dole out autumn assignments. Litigation would now proceed in two cases in two different courts.

The original *McNary* lawsuit, for the HIV-positive refugees detained in Bulkeley, was set for trial in late October in Brooklyn, just seven weeks away. After all the preliminary skirmishes of the last several months, Judge Johnson would issue a final decision on the question that had first brought Yale into court: Did the refugees have a right to counsel during a final asylum proceeding on Guantánamo?

Some of the new students were confused. Hadn't the Second Circuit just decided that question? Didn't the court already rule that the refugees had a right to a lawyer? Yes, they were told. But like all the other court orders in the case, that, too, had been just a temporary decision. Judge Johnson would make the ultimate call at trial.

The second lawsuit was the direct return case, challenging President Bush's May 24 order to repatriate all refugees fleeing Haiti by boat. That case, which for technical reasons was also called *McNary,* was now on its way to the Supreme Court, and Yale would have to submit a brief to the justices in a few months. In the meantime, the Coast Guard would continue sending Haitians back to Port-au-Prince.

Up to this point, Koh, feeling compelled to manage everything himself, had served as lead counsel in both cases. But he now realized that had to stop. In the Guantánamo case, there were constant arguments with the OIL attorneys over documents, depositions, and scheduling matters. After one fight, Koh had even come late to his own class, and he finally took Joe Tringali's gentle hint that a sharper division of labor was necessary. Since Koh had no trial experience, he agreed that Joe would take the courtroom lead in the Guantánamo case. Koh would stay involved with Guantánamo, but would focus on the direct return case at the Supreme Court.

Despite all the work to be done, there was a renewed optimism around the clinic. Developments in the presidential race had raised the tantalizing prospect of victory without going back to court at all. Democratic candidate Bill Clinton was now the front-runner for the White House, with a pre–Labor Day lead over President Bush in the low double digits—and he was still speaking out for the refugees. In early September, he attacked the Bush direct return policy yet again, charging that innocent civilians in Haiti were being tortured and executed. Clinton also announced he would lift the immigration ban on foreign nationals with HIV, convincing Koh that if he won, everyone in Camp Bulkeley would be freed.

One refugee that Clinton's promise wouldn't help was Frantz Guerrier, and Mike Wishnie waited anxiously for news from him. Not long before school started, the phone call finally came: Guerrier was safe. He'd made it across the Dominican border with two other Guantánamo returnees, and they were now camped out at a pro-Aristide radio station, Radio Enriquillo, surrounded by sugarcane fields.

Mike was ecstatic, but there were already new complications. The station manager, a radical Catholic priest, had been expecting to send the three men to Santo Domingo, the Dominican capital. But the contact there had vanished, and the priest—who had his own problems with the Dominican government—was anxious about harboring the refugees himself for very long. With renewed hopes of bringing Guerrier and the others to the United States, Mike enlisted a Florida immigration expert to help prepare their asylum applications. As a backup strategy, he and other students investigated the possibility of asylum in various Caribbean countries.

Wishnie was worried, though. On the telephone, Guerrier sounded demoralized and listless. While the other two refugees were helping out at the radio station, he seemed to have lost purpose—worn down after losing his family and living on the run for so long. Mike, now living near his girlfriend in Brooklyn and commuting to Yale, did everything he could to speed along Guerrier's asylum request. He hoped to get him out as fast as possible.

Lisa was now in New York as well, crammed into a tiny Greenwich Village apartment with other young public interest attorneys. There weren't enough bedrooms to go around, so she slept in a cubbyhole next to the staircase landing. It was loud and uncomfortable, and she rarely got much sleep. While some of her classmates were pulling in close to six figures in their first year at firms like Simpson Thacher, she barely made enough at the ACLU to pay the rent and buy groceries.

Work was another struggle. Though she was expected to help out on everything from death penalty work to reproductive rights, Lisa instead threw all her effort into preparing the Guantánamo case for trial. Her superiors weren't pleased, but Lisa didn't care. A new legal theory for the refugees had seized her attention, keeping her late at the office and occupying all her thoughts. Since Judge Johnson had avoided a ruling on the equal protection claim, Lisa had moved on to a more promising option: the due process theory. Johnson's tentative decision was that the due process clause applied on Guantánamo, and he would make a final ruling on that issue at trial.

The question for Lisa was exactly what rights the refugees were guaranteed under due process. Up to that point, Yale had focused only on the right to counsel. But Lisa knew from constitutional law that the concept of due process encompassed other rights, too. People in government custody had the right to proper medical care, for instance, and the team was now planning on raising that claim at trial.

Lisa, though, wanted to go further still, and she was now researching the right to be free of indefinite detention. It was a restricted right, particularly when it came to aliens. Earlier cases on the issue almost always sided with the government. But a few paid lip service to the idea that even foreigners couldn't be detained forever without good reason.

Lisa was convinced this principle applied to the Haitians. After all, she thought, where did the president get the power to detain innocent people just because it was politically convenient? The point, she believed, was that he *didn't* have that power—that's what "due process" meant in this instance.

After many days of research, she realized it would not be an easy argument to make. But she was not deterred. As far as Lisa was concerned, Yale had to quit focusing on the claim about lawyers and take a more aggressive position: all the refugees on Guantánamo should be released.

———

In mid-September, two weeks after the *kay* burnings, Army colonel Stephen Kinder, a tall man with gentle, dark eyes, assumed command of the Joint Task Force at Guantánamo. A member of the 18th Airborne Corps based at Fort Bragg, North Carolina, Colonel Kinder had trained in many countries, from Egypt to Jordan to Honduras, and he'd visited a number of refugee camps along the way. Kinder's superiors at the U.S. Atlantic Command had a favorable impression of him, and they thought he might be the one to solve a problem they'd come to see as interminable—keeping Camp Bulkeley under control.

If the INS wasn't going to process the refugees, if they were really going to sit on Guantánamo indefinitely, the military had to figure out how to deal with them for the long haul. The Pentagon wasn't going to limp along from month to month anymore, hoping for a quick solution from the courts.

When Kinder first arrived at Bulkeley, he was met with tight frowns and cold stares. Trust between Haitians and soldiers was at an all-time low. The camp had a lockdown atmosphere, and over a dozen of the *militan* were still imprisoned in Camp VII. Some of the refugees had now been on Guantánamo for over nine months, and the INS had yet to give them any information about when, if ever, they were leaving.

Kinder told the GIs guarding the inner-camp entrance that he was going in alone, unarmed, to speak with the Haitians.

One of them shook his head nervously. "Sir," he said, "we can't guarantee your safety."

But Kinder hiked up to the newly built mess pavilion with an interpreter and climbed up on a picnic table. A small crowd surrounded him, wary but curious.

"It's not my choice that you're here," he shouted, waiting for the interpreter to repeat his words. "And it's not the military who's keeping you here. I want you to have a resolution to your situation as quickly as possible, but that's not in my control. All I can do is make your life as pleasant and decent and safe as possible. I'll do everything in my power to see that that's done. You tell me what you need, and I'll try to get it for you."

The Haitians eyed him, murmuring.

"Nou ta vle kola," someone finally called back. "We'd like soda. The soldiers have it. Why can't we?"

The translator explained to Kinder. He nodded.

"I think we can do that," he said.

Soon afterward, cases of Coke arrived at the camp. There were looks of surprise and then excitement. As everybody cracked open cans, they watched Kinder hike over to Camp VII, about a hundred yards from the main camp.

He found a young Marine guarding the fifteen detainees, who were confined like farm animals in small razor-wire pens. Kinder reviewed each of their files. Some had been accused of throwing rocks or hitting guards. Others had done nothing more than use the camp soda machine, which had been reserved for the Joint Task Force. The colonel met with the Haitians one by one, obtained promises that they would remain peaceful, and welcomed them back to the main camp with a handshake. Then he sent in bulldozers to destroy Camp VII.

Yvonne watched as the open tents and razor wire were crushed into a heap and carted away. She wasn't sure yet what motivated Kinder. But he'd promised to make changes, and he was keeping his word.

Days later, he installed a television in one of the *kay yo* so people could stay abreast of current events. Then he gave everyone telephone access so they could let loved ones in Haiti know they were alive. Meals went from dehydrated meat and rice to fresh chicken, vegetables, and fruit, and he put the refugees in charge of cooking their own food. He brought in tools and wood and joined them in converting a *kay* into a makeshift church. He encouraged nonviolent protest, and the camp was soon covered in graffiti, with references to Haiti's revolutionary heroes, Toussaint Louverture and Jean-Jacques Dessalines. Some people even wrote their T-cell counts on their clothing. The camp English school and the dirt soccer field were reopened, and Kinder organized trips to the

Navy Exchange, where the refugees could buy clothes with money he paid them from a small discretionary fund for doing camp chores. The Haitians soon began to call the camp commander Kinder, Gentler, a play on President Bush's promise to run a "kinder, gentler" government.

As far as Kinder could tell, the Marine commander in charge before him had taken a don't-cross-this-line approach to Camp Bulkeley. The Marines, Kinder later explained, maintained a "hard-assed, battle-ready culture." As he saw it, they'd been trained to kill the enemy, not house and feed refugees. In contrast, Kinder had made a point of reviewing recent humanitarian missions by the Army in order to prepare for his stint on Guantánamo. His conclusion was simple. He had to establish trust and communication as fast as possible. As he later said, "I was going to treat 'em like human beings."

Kinder's Joint Task Force subordinates, who came from all branches of the military, did not uniformly adjust to his methods. Some protested when he took away their M-16s and sidearms, but he believed weapons weren't necessary at the camp, nor did he want the refugees to get their hands on a gun. He also got rid of several men he felt weren't suited for working at Bulkeley—including one who'd almost beaten a Haitian for asking for a different choice of meal.

For reasons Kinder couldn't fathom, the INS officials on Guantánamo thought he was being too lenient with the refugees. But no one could deny that the trouble at Camp Bulkeley halted the day he took over.

As the weeks passed, Yvonne warmed to Kinder. He was one white man she decided she could trust. He kept the camp gate open during the day, ate all his meals with them, and didn't wear rubber gloves when he touched people. But his decision to let everyone use the telephone was the most important gesture of all. She waited in line, patiently, as one person after another cried with joy, greeting someone from home.

Then it was Yvonne's turn. She called the pawnshop, and someone sent a runner over to her shanty. She waited, listening to her own breath in the receiver, praying for the familiar sound of her mother's voice. It had been almost five months since she'd spoken with Thérèse or heard anything about her children.

Someone picked up on the other end of the line. Her heart jumped. It was the runner. No one was home, he said.

Did it seem like they were just out somewhere, she asked, or did it look like they had gone away?

The runner didn't know.

Well, had he seen Thérèse recently?

No, he said, but he didn't go near Yvonne's place much.

Was it safe there now?

Not at all, he said. The Macoutes were everywhere.

"If you see my mother or someone else, tell them I'm okay," she said. "I'm on Guantánamo."

"Guantánamo?"

"Yes."

"Okay."

"You'll tell them," she pleaded, "right? You'll tell them?"

"Yes."

Distraught, she began to suffer bad headaches, a sharp, needling pain behind her eyes, and would stop by the medical clinic for Tylenol. Whenever she went, the staff pushed her to take a Depo-Provera injection for birth control. She had no need for it and didn't want them putting any more needles in her, but the doctors persisted. Mistakenly believing it was good for those with a low T-cell count, she finally agreed. She didn't really understand the potential side effects of the drug, however, and she was terrified when she woke up in the middle of the night, bleeding profusely and racked with stomach cramps.

Yvonne's health problems only exacerbated her anxiety about what would happen to her and how she would ever reach her family. These questions had come to define her existence, and no one had answers for her. She had asked so many different INS officials, soldiers, and interpreters the same thing so many times that it had become a ritual, each side playing the same, tightly scripted role.

When will you let us go?

We don't know.

When will you know?

We're not sure. We're waiting for Washington to tell us something.

Some of the others in the camp pressed their case for asylum to Kinder. He had done so many other good things, they said. Couldn't he get them out of Bulkeley? He would listen sympathetically, but all he could advise them to do was speak to their lawyers.

Who are our lawyers? the refugees asked. Where are they? How can we reach them? Yvonne, for one, didn't believe these mysterious people even existed.

Around the time Colonel Kinder arrived at Bulkeley, the Yale team and the government went back to Brooklyn. With trial only a month away in the Guantánamo lawsuit, Judge Johnson had called a status conference. Koh and Ratner made the trip, but it would now be Joe Tringali's job to handle the courtroom arguments.

Paul Cappuccio and an OIL lawyer named Lauri Filppu were on hand for the government, along with a pack of their colleagues. A small man with short, dishwater-blond hair and even features, Filppu would be in charge of the trial for the Justice Department, and he did most of the talking. Since graduating from law school nineteen years earlier, Filppu had worked exclusively as an attorney for the United States government, most of that time at OIL, where he was now a deputy director. As a colleague later recalled, Filppu had never had a human being for a client. "It affects the way you think about cases," the colleague sighed. "And I just don't think Lauri could empathize with the people whose lives were being affected by the INS."

When Filppu got up to speak for the government on this particular fall morning, his objective was immediately apparent to everyone from Yale: delay.

"The case simply is not ready for trial right now," Filppu told the judge. "We've had to scramble and try to prepare ourselves for a trial date not knowing all the issues to be raised." He complained that Yale was now focusing on camp medical care as an issue, and that would change the character of the case. There were dozens of new witnesses to prepare, he said. He talked about procedures, rules, schedules. He brought up the direct return case, saying that would affect things as well. There was no reason to move ahead, anyway, he added, because the Haitians weren't suffering any harm. "Right now," Filppu said, "the people on Guantánamo are protected."

Steve Roos, watching from the gallery, was fuming. As the team's document czar, he'd been reviewing piles of paper from the government for the last several weeks. But Yale was still waiting for much of the material it had requested, and Steve was sick of Filppu's foot-dragging. All he ever seemed to do was send letters packed with excuses and conditions. Now, seeking to delay the case even longer, Filppu was throwing in every reason imaginable to push off the date. A key government witness had vacation plans. Filppu himself needed to attend a wedding. In one recent letter to Yale, Filppu had actually suggested that trial be put off for another six months.

When Filppu finally finished, Joe Tringali got up to respond for Yale. Until now, neither Steve nor any of the other students had given him much thought. To them, Tringali was little more than a curt voice on late-night conference calls. Tory thought he was "just some corporate law guy," and though Steve had been working on the document review with Tringali, he viewed the Simpson Thacher partner as distant and unengaged. He worried that in court, Tringali would never match Koh's intensity.

But to Steve's astonishment, Joe cleared his throat, paused, and then, icy and indignant, declared, "With much arrogance and little candor, defendants come before you today and request that you reward them for doing nothing to get this case ready for trial. Their conduct merits a reprimand, not a reward."

Then he proceeded to rip Lauri Filppu to pieces. Tringali plowed through every obstructionist tactic he believed the government had used, pausing only for dramatic effect. Filppu hadn't allowed mail access to Yale's clients. He'd delayed answering Yale's interrogatories, then provided meaningless responses. He'd held back military surveillance video of the camp. And he'd refused to give Yale the full medical files of the refugees because they hadn't signed privacy releases. How, Tringali asked, are we supposed to get those releases? We're not even allowed on the base!

The Immigration and Naturalization Service could act quickly when it wanted to, Tringali went on. He'd recently taken depositions of INS officials from Guantánamo. He knew that the INS had moved like lightning when it came to running the asylum hearings after the Supreme Court stay and forcing people like Frantz Guerrier back to Haiti. But now that trial loomed, it was drag, drag, drag.

How could Filppu carry on about attending a wedding, Tringali demanded, while claiming that the Haitians were just fine sitting on Guantánamo? They had no access to their lawyers. They had no idea what their legal situation was or when it would ever change. They were facing a deadly illness. And yet they were forced to remain in a modern-day leper colony.

It was time for trial, Tringali said, and it was time for trial *now*.

The presentation dazzled Steve Roos. Who knew? It was as if Tringali had dammed up his emotions for months and then released them in a torrent at the exact right moment, to maximum strategic effect.

When it was over, Judge Johnson declared that the trial date would remain October 19.

After Steve got back to Yale, he passed on the word about the "real" Joe Tringali to the other students. A week or two later, Tory was in New York and she dropped by Joe's office. With great ceremony, she presented him with a lacquered wood box. It was filled with tiny red beads given to her by a Tibetan refugee in Asia.

He thanked her with a bemused smile.

"They've been blessed by the Dalai Lama himself," Tory said seriously. "Only use them when you really need help."

With trial pressure mounting, Cappuccio called Michael Ratner. He had a proposal to make and offered to meet in New York to discuss it.

The two men had kept up a friendly banter from the start of the lawsuit. Nobody else at Yale could stand Cappuccio, including Koh, who took the litigation so personally he could barely speak to him. But Ratner managed to kid around with the Justice lawyer, swapping the occasional anecdote, and though he had no illusions about Cappuccio's politics, Ratner still believed Paul had a heart. "He's conservative," Michael said. "Very, *very* conservative. But he's human on a lot of levels." Cappuccio had his own fondness for Ratner. Politics aside, he thought, Ratner's a little like me: We're both nice, storytelling guys, one Jewish, one Italian. As radical as Ratner was, Cappuccio never saw the older human rights lawyer engage in the "holier-than-thou crap" he found so loathsome among the Yale crowd. At one point, Cappuccio had even joked to the attorney general, "Why don't we just bring in the Haitians and deport all the students?"

A few days after his call to Ratner, Cappuccio arrived with other Justice attorneys in one of Simpson's elegant conference rooms. Waiting for them were Koh, Ratner, and several students. Along with the usual soft drinks and bottled water, the firm's staff had brought in plates of gourmet cookies, and everyone munched on them as Cappuccio made his pitch.

The Justice Department, he said, was determined to get rid of the Second Circuit's interim decision that the Constitution had force on Guantánamo Bay. The solicitor general was about to ask the Supreme Court to review the case, and Cappuccio felt pretty confident the justices would overrule the Second Circuit. But he said he'd consider a deal if the Yale team would agree to have the Second Circuit opinion vacated—removed from the books—so the government didn't have to go to the high court. If vacated, the decision would cease to exist. It would have no bearing on any future case involving the naval base. Everyone from Yale understood the upshot: the Bush administration wanted to preserve Guantánamo as a land without law.

In return, Cappuccio said, he would give Koh and Ratner exactly what they had been demanding in court all along: the refugees would get access to counsel. Lawyers from Yale could represent them during the asylum hearing process. There would be no need for a trial before Judge Johnson.

Ratner flinched. He'd worried that Cappuccio might make this offer at some point. It raised the question of the Yale team's ultimate goal—a question the team itself had not resolved. All along, Koh had been focused on getting lawyers for the Haitians, to ensure a fair hearing process and thus asylum for anyone in Bulkeley who met the precise legal requirements. But for Ratner, as for Lisa Daugaard, the demand for lawyers was ultimately just a "wedge issue," a way to get into the courthouse. Though he hadn't yet focused on Lisa's due process research, Ratner shared her ultimate goal of freeing everyone in Bulkeley—an objective Koh still considered too extreme and bound to fail.

Ratner pushed Cappuccio for more information. The refugees who won asylum would still need a humanitarian waiver from the Justice Department to get into the United States because of their HIV status. Could Cappuccio guarantee those waivers?

No, Cappuccio said. That would be Attorney General William Barr's decision, and Cappuccio conceded that Barr would probably issue only a few of them. Most of the refugees would be sent back to Haiti.

Ratner told Cappuccio that the Yale team needed to talk in private. Everyone shuttled out of the room, leaving the Justice lawyers alone with the cookies.

Down the hall, Ratner closed the door and looked at Koh.

"What the hell do we do now?" he said.

The only thing they'd demanded in court was the right to represent the refugees in their asylum hearings, and Cappuccio had just given that

to them. But access to lawyers meant little without assurance that everyone who won asylum would get a waiver. Otherwise, they'd remain stuck
on Guantánamo or get sent back to Haiti. That made Cappuccio's offer
unacceptable even to Koh.

The critical question, though, was whether the refugees themselves
might take the deal. Aside from Wishnie's trip to Guantánamo almost six
months earlier, the team hadn't been allowed to visit the Haitians and the
government had barred telephone contact. As the group now puzzled
over what to tell Cappuccio, it dawned on everyone that his offer had
given them the opening they'd needed all along.

Under the ethics of the legal profession, the Yale lawyers could not
settle the case without presenting the offer to their clients. The refugees
had to make the decision themselves. "And that," Ratner said, "gives us
the chance to say, 'You've got to let us go down to Guantánamo.'"

Back in the conference room, Cappuccio wasn't happy to hear their
demand. But Ratner and Koh were adamant. They had to meet with their
clients.

"I won't make any promises," Cappuccio finally said. "All I can do is
look into it."

Sometime after Cappuccio got back to Washington, he called Ratner.

"We can get you to Guantánamo," he said.

Yvonne conferred with camp president Vilsaint Michel and other leaders
to choose the people who would speak for the Haitians when they met
the lawyers, or *avoka yo.* High on the list were deposed camp president
Wilson Edouard and others who understood English well. No one
wanted to rely on military interpreters or anyone the lawyers might bring
with them. Suspicions were too high. If these people come, they come,
Yvonne thought, imagining sinister people with pale skin. But white men
are for white men. Why would they bother?

On the appointed day, October 6, Yvonne boarded a crowded bus to
the cavernous hangar near the site of her screening interview almost a
half-year earlier. She'd bought some clothes at the Navy Exchange for the
occasion—a blouse and pants in a brilliant yellow, and a matching ban-
danna for her hair. Believing yellow to be the color of treason, she'd chosen the outfit to show she wasn't going to be duped.

The military had set out folding chairs in the middle of the hangar, and the refugees arranged themselves in several rows, with the leaders, including Yvonne, in front. Vilsaint Michel had changed into his best white shirt and dark slacks, and as usual, he was carrying his clipboard. He wore his sunglasses, both to hide an ugly eye infection and as a traditional Haitian gesture of power, for it was impossible to read his eyes.

The group was chattering nervously when a number of people appeared at the gaping entrance to the hangar. Yvonne studied them as they approached. To her surprise, she saw several individuals who appeared to be Haitian, a man she figured was Chinese, and a couple of very young white women.

As Tory's eyes adjusted to the dim light, she discovered that armed guards were patrolling on a catwalk above her. Faint voices echoed off the distant walls. She followed the sound. Perhaps forty yards away, seated in neat rows as if waiting for a class lecture, were the Haitian refugees.

There were fewer than three hundred of them, and squeezed together inside the immense building, the group seemed remarkably small to Tory. That's it? she thought. These people are the reason the government is fighting so hard? We could bring them all to the United States on a single airplane and that would be the end of everything.

As she drew closer, individual people began to emerge—a slight, dark man in sunglasses, clutching a clipboard; a taller man wearing a hand-painted T-shirt; a beautiful, well-groomed woman dressed all in yellow.

The woman had high cheekbones, dark, sad eyes, and a café-au-lait complexion. Tory couldn't stop gazing at her. The phrase "Haitian refugees" had always conjured up images in her mind of desperate souls in rags. Some of the people she'd interviewed in Florida had matched that image, but not this group, and certainly not this woman.

High-pitched shouts rang out from a corner of the hangar. Kids were chasing one another in circles. After a moment, Tory realized they belonged to the Haitians.

The man in sunglasses tapped at the microphone, testing it for sound. Then he signaled the others, most of whom stood up.

"*Yon sèl nou fèb, ansanm nou fò,*" they chanted, the words reverberating through the hangar. "*Ansanm, ansanm nou se Lavalas.*"

Tory recognized only the term "Lavalas," the name of Aristide's political movement, but Ronald Aubourg, a tall, gravelly voiced Haitian American with the Yale team, repeated the rest of the Creole for everyone: "They're saying, 'Alone, we are weak, together we are strong; together, together we are Lavalas'—the flood." It was the slogan of the Aristide movement, the promise that the people could wash away the injustices of the past.

Tory paused. While working on the case, she'd slipped into a mentality she described as "saving the poor Haitians." It was a way of thinking encouraged by the television ad she'd seen years earlier depicting a Nepalese child in misery—the idea that the people she was trying to assist were helpless without her. The demonstration by the refugees threw her off. They seemed organized and disciplined. She recalled their protests over the summer, which she'd learned about after returning to school in the fall. We may be fighting the legal battle here, she thought, but it's not like they're powerless.

There was an awkward silence as the Yale group took the row of empty chairs facing the Haitians. Vilsaint Michel introduced himself as camp president, but the other refugees did not come forward, and Tory and the others from Yale kept a respectful distance. Koh finally limped to the front, with Ronald Aubourg joining him to interpret. Koh had spoken with Michel on the phone a few days earlier, and the camp leader's wary, standoffish attitude had been a warning signal. This was not, Koh realized, going to be easy. On the plane down, he had pondered how he might break through to Michel.

"I bet you're asking yourselves, who is this Chinese guy, and what's he doing fighting for us?" Koh said into the microphone, trying to smile.

His voice died away and Aubourg repeated the words in Creole.

"Well," Koh went on, "I'm actually Korean American."

Some of the refugees murmured. It sounded to him as if they were saying, *Kore, Kore.*

Koh told them that many years earlier, his father, Kwang Lim Koh, had supported a democratic government in Korea and that, just like in Haiti, the elected leader had been ousted by the military. My father sought refuge in America, Koh said, as you are now doing. "Any of you could be my father," he concluded. "That's why I'm here."

There were some nods and a few words of support, but many of the refugees simply stared at him. Tory scanned their faces, concerned. She had assumed they would be grateful, even thrilled, to finally meet the people fighting for their release. Instead, they seemed cold and cautious.

As she was puzzling over what the team could possibly do at that moment, Koh approached the first row of refugees.

"Bonjour," he tried, using what little French he knew. He reached for

someone's hand and clasped it. Then he reached for another, and another. As people got to their feet, he started to hug them.

"Harold Koh," he said. "Hi. *Bonjour.* Harold Koh. Harold Koh."

Tory, Lisa Daugaard, and the rest of the team plunged in after Koh, shaking hands, repeating their names. Tory was surrounded by curious faces and the staccato rhythm of Creole. Some people hung back, eyeing her suspiciously, but a few smiled, and she tried to smile in return.

While she'd been through this before, at the Budget Inn in Miami, something was different. There she had felt nothing but exhilaration, but now, as Tory's clients closed in around her, another emotion took over: fear. She'd never been in contact with someone she knew had AIDS, and while she understood very well that the disease couldn't be spread through casual contact, she was still on edge.

You're being ridiculous, she told herself. She stole a glance at Koh.

As it turned out, he was dealing with the same anxieties and self-criticism. Was there some kind of precaution I should have taken? Koh thought. Is this really smart? It's too late anyway, he decided. If we're going to convince these people we're on their side, we can't show any hesitation.

The story about Koh's father did not impress Yvonne. She had no interest in heartfelt speeches or handshakes, and she was troubled by the whole setup. Why, she wondered, are they hiding us in this hangar? Why keep the media away? If this man Harold Koh is telling the truth, she thought, let him say everything out in the open. Let him visit the camp. Bring in reporters. Bring in the U.N.

A meeting between the lawyers and the camp leadership did nothing to allay her skepticism. Worried about client confidentiality, Koh had demanded that they confer away from the military police standing guard above them. Michel, Yvonne, Wilson Edouard, and others were escorted with the Yale team to a sweltering office, where Koh explained the lawsuit before Judge Johnson and the government's settlement offer.

The refugees had three options, Koh said. They could return to Haiti, which he expected they wouldn't want to do.

When Ronald Aubourg translated that alternative, the refugees looked at him in disbelief. Was he kidding?

Or, Koh continued, they could take the settlement offer. In that case, everyone would go through a new asylum hearing with a Yale lawyer representing them. But those who won asylum would need something called a "humanitarian waiver" from the attorney general, an official in Washington, to enter the United States.

Yvonne listened carefully. What was this waiver thing? She'd never heard a word about it.

It was a special exception to the HIV rule, Koh explained. Unfortunately, he said, the attorney general would issue only a few of the all-important waivers, though the Justice Department had refused to give him exact numbers. This meant that even after the asylum hearings, most people would either remain on Guantánamo or be sent back to Haiti.

Nobody sounded happy with the settlement option, and Koh then moved on to the third alternative. They could reject the offer, put the lawsuit on hold, and wait for the presidential election in early November.

Vilsaint Michel cocked his head, a look of recognition on his face. Election politics—this was something he understood.

Koh explained that the Democratic candidate, Bill Clinton, had criticized President Bush's Haitian refugee policy and had also promised to lift the HIV ban. He held up Clinton's campaign book, *Putting People First,* and read aloud from it. Ronald Aubourg described the book in Creole as the Haitians passed it among themselves, examining Clinton's picture on the cover and puzzling over the English words.

We cannot be sure, Koh told them, but we believe that if Clinton becomes president, he will release you.

Several refugees leaned forward, eyes widening.

"Delivre nou?" Free us?

"Probably, yes."

Koh did not say directly that Clinton was their best hope, but he presented the option as favorably as he could. Given the candidate's repeated, adamant statements on the Haitians, Koh now considered it the wisest move, though he was careful to stress that Bush could still win. If that happens, he said, we'll go back to court.

Yvonne was incredulous. *Putting People First* didn't interest her. Wilson Edouard was reading the text as best he could, but it was obvious he couldn't really tell what it meant. And she was not about to trust her fate to some mysterious book she could understand only with the help of an unknown translator.

After everyone else was done with their questions, she pushed her chair aside and stood up.

"Words are not going to be enough," she told Koh, pounding the table. "The most important thing to me is my freedom. What we want is to get out of here."

The next morning, Lisa was squeezed inside a portable, air-conditioned trailer with a translator, a law student, and twenty-five refugees. Now that she was at the ACLU, Lisa was serving in the same lead role for the day as Koh and Ratner, who were each meeting with other groups. The plan was to explain the settlement offer in further detail to all three hundred people in small gatherings, giving the refugees a chance to ask additional questions.

Lisa had been looking forward to this moment for months, and she was especially pleased to be speaking with some of the Haitians on her own. To her mind, Koh's presentation of the various strategic options had been far too rigid. She felt it was critical to have more of a give-and-take with them about the situation, no matter how little they might understand about American law. The refugees, she reasoned, were the clients. Not only did they presumably have their own objectives, but they probably had their own strategic ideas as well. Yale had to be receptive to them.

She opened the meeting in this spirit, eager to hear what the Haitians had to say. They had placed a single chair directly across the table from her, and after she introduced herself, they sat down, one after another, and hammered her with questions.

Why is the U.S. accusing us of having AIDS?

Don't you work for the government?

Why has it taken you so long to come here?

Why should we believe anything you say?

Lisa tried to keep her composure, but the onslaught continued.

"You're just doing this for yourself," one person accused. "This is for your own advantage. Look at how young you are—this is for experience or something. But it's not for us."

"Actually," Lisa tried, "we're doing this because we think our government is mistreating you."

"No. You're in this just to get rich."

"That's not true," she said, off balance now. "We're not getting paid anything. We're all volunteering to help you."

When the translator explained, Lisa's interrogator glared at her.

"*You're not getting paid?* You must be terrible lawyers if you can't make money!" he shouted. "No wonder we're still here!"

Dumbfounded, Lisa tried to respond but could only choke back a sob.

They don't understand a thing about what we've been doing, she thought. I've been killing myself for these people and they don't even give a damn.

Feeling the tears coming, she pushed her way outside into the blinding midday sun. There was a chair beside the trailer and she flopped into it, burying her face in her hands.

Great, she cried to herself. Now they think you're not just a shitty lawyer, but unstable, too. An attorney is *not* supposed to behave like this.

She sat there, alone, staring at the parched hills in the distance. She had no idea what to do. Should she go back in? What could she possibly say?

Then the trailer door squeaked open. A slight Haitian woman in flip-flops padded over to Lisa and rested her hand on her shoulder.

"Come," the woman said in English, gesturing to the door. "Come, come."

Lisa wiped off her face and followed the woman back into the trailer. She sat down at the table, cheeks still flushed, and tried to look at her clients.

"Nou fè w konfyans," the woman said in a gentle voice.

"We trust you," Lisa's interpreter translated. "If you didn't care, you wouldn't be so upset."

The people who'd been so harsh to her a moment ago were now gazing at Lisa sympathetically. She managed a meek smile.

Someone cracked a joke in Creole. Lisa didn't understand, and everyone seemed to find that funny itself. One by one, the refugees began to open up.

Lisa listened respectfully and tried to answer their questions. They wanted to know how the American legal system worked. Could it be trusted? Was it fair? Didn't it favor the government? What were their chances in this court case she was talking about? How much longer would it last? What did she think of Clinton? How was he different from Bush? What were the prospects of a Clinton victory?

As time went on, Lisa felt she was making real progress. And then the topic of AIDS came up.

"They're telling us we're HIV positive, but we know we're not," one of the refugees said. Others nodded in agreement.

"It's all a lie."

Again at a loss, Lisa turned to her translator, Adrien Marcel, for help. Marcel was a physician, although Cappuccio and the other government lawyers didn't know it. They had refused Yale's request to let independent doctors on the base, so the team had brought Marcel, a Haitian American, along as a translator without revealing his medical credentials.

Lisa knew Marcel's job would not be easy. He had to be supportive and maintain the refugees' newfound trust, but he also had to help them understand that they might really be ill. Their HIV diagnosis was not the fabrication of a government conspiracy, but very likely a medical fact.

In a nearby trailer, Koh and Tory were dealing with the same problem. Koh knew it was going to be an uphill battle. Days earlier, Ratner had obtained an internal government memo written by CDC physician Paul Effler, who'd worked in Bulkeley back in March. Effler had warned that many of the Haitians hadn't been properly counseled on HIV and didn't even understand they were being tested for the disease.

When Koh now raised the topic of AIDS, the Haitians dug into their pockets and held out fistfuls of brightly colored pills.

"They're trying to poison us with these," someone said.

One by one, the refugees dropped their medications on the table. Tory stared at them in dismay. Unsure what else to do, she jotted down the color and shape of each new pill. Based on what she'd learned, she thought she recognized INH, used to treat tuberculosis, as well as AZT. But numerous others were a mystery. They piled up like children's Halloween candy—red, yellow, green, pink, white, purple—and she finally tossed her notes aside in frustration and grabbed a camera to photograph the multicolored jumble.

Koh tried to explain to the refugees that the people treating them were indeed doctors, despite the military uniforms they wore. He also offered that Yale's Haitian physician would check their health if they wanted. But the *militan* brushed him aside.

"That's not what we need," someone spat. "We want to leave Guantánamo, not see another doctor."

"They're fake tests," another declared.

"We don't think they're fake," Koh replied. "We don't know everything for sure, but we don't believe your doctors are lying."

"So what's that mean?" someone else asked.

"You need to be tested again," Koh replied. More grumbling followed.

"What about the medicine?"

"You should take it," Koh said. "It won't hurt you and it might save your life."

Tory echoed Koh's advice. But it was obvious to her that the Haitians wanted confirmation of their own view of the situation, not the message of the military doctors.

To her distress, when the meeting ended, the pills remained on the table.

If Koh and the students were having trouble winning the refugees' confidence, they weren't alone. The Haitian American translators were doing no better, despite Yale's hope that they could bridge the divide. Ronald Aubourg, who was working with Koh and Tory, faced heckling from the start. "You don't know a thing about the way we have to live here," he was told over and over. Aubourg protested that no one from Yale was allowed into Bulkeley. But the refugees weren't interested in his excuses. The attacks grew sharper, and Aubourg finally decided he'd had enough.

As one of the groups prepared to head back to Bulkeley, Aubourg ripped off his dress shirt and borrowed a pair of flip-flops and a T-shirt. A refugee gave him a towel to wear around his head, which some of the men did on the hottest days. Then he joined the people boarding the buses to the camp, staring at his feet as he passed the guards. Lisa knew what Aubourg was doing, but said nothing to Koh or Ratner. She was sure they would try to stop him.

Before the buses left, an official took a headcount. His numbers were off by one. He shot off the bus and grabbed Lisa.

"What's going on?" he asked.

Lisa looked back at him, trying not to blink. "What are you talking about?"

"There's an extra migrant or something."

"Huh?"

The official jerked his head toward the bus. "What are you trying to pull?!"

"I'm sorry, but I really don't understand," Lisa said.

The official gave her a disgusted look and stalked off. He went through another headcount, shook his head, then signaled the drivers. The buses pulled away.

Aubourg sank into his seat, sweating. When they reached Bulkeley, he slipped past the soldiers and through the main gate. News of his presence whipped through the camp. Refugees scurried toward him from all directions, calling for his attention.

"*Rete! Pa fè sa!*" he hissed, eyes blazing. "Stop it! Just one or two people with me. No more!"

Aubourg poked his way through the *kay yo,* testing the flimsy cots and checking on babies asleep in cribs. He examined the showers, water pooled on the concrete floors, and the rows of plastic portable toilets reeking in the sun. His stomach was in knots. If everyone were really as sick as the doctors said, how could they be kept like this?

Yvonne watched his surreptitious investigation, surprised and pleased. This was more than talk; it was action that would have real consequences if he got caught. She began to wonder if the lawyers might be credible after all.

When Aubourg returned on another bus, Koh and Ratner were frantically hunting for him. "Damn it, Ronald," Koh said, exhaling. "You could have gotten us kicked off the base."

"They didn't see me," Aubourg assured him. "The guards, they think we all look alike. That's the way I live my life. I'm just one more black man."

Aubourg's gesture seemed to mark a turning point. At a meeting the next day, a gaunt man named Harold Michel, one of the sicker refugees, stood up to speak. He announced in a quiet, serious voice that an angel had come to him in a dream. The angel, he said, had told him to put his trust in the lawyers. There was a ripple of support from the other Haitians. Lisa was grateful for the sentiment but didn't take his words at face value. She thought he was indirectly acknowledging Aubourg's visit to the camp.

But whether because of its timing or perhaps its dramatic impact, Michel's declaration catalyzed the refugees around him. They addressed their legal team with a sudden energy and openness, thrusting out barcoded wristbands and tattered political documents. One refugee gave Koh a photograph of an activist lying dead on the floor, drenched in blood, an Aristide poster draped over her body. The Haitians told stories of terror and death back home and made earnest pleas for help. By late afternoon, a nascent understanding and even camaraderie had finally developed between lawyers and clients.

In the day's last meeting, Vilsaint Michel, Yvonne, and the other leaders agreed that they would reject the settlement offer. "You know the American legal process," Michel told Koh. "We're going to take your word on what to do." The refugees understood there was little point in lawyers representing them in asylum hearings if the attorney general wouldn't guarantee the waivers necessary to enter the United States. They would wait for the presidential election, now just four weeks away, in hopes that Clinton would win.

Koh nodded, pleased. After such a rocky start three days earlier, he could not have hoped for more progress. But Michel had a question. He wanted to be clear on how the Yale team would proceed if Clinton lost.

Before Koh could say anything, Lisa jumped in.

"We'll seek your release at trial," she said.

Koh stopped short. "We're not asking for your release at this point," he said to Michel in a deliberate voice, trying to send Lisa a message. "So far, the lawsuit itself has focused on making sure you have lawyers."

Aubourg was still translating when Lisa cut in. "Harold, that's not what they want—"

"This isn't the time," Koh said under his breath.

"What they want is to get out of here. That's all they've been saying for the last several days!"

Michel's face clouded.

Koh turned to Lisa. "Just. Stop. Talking," he ordered. The refugees were now murmuring among themselves. Koh apologized to Michel and hustled Lisa away, so angry he was shaking. Everything they had achieved was suddenly at risk because she couldn't keep her damn mouth shut. When they were out of earshot, he unloaded on her.

"Never, ever fight with me in front of the clients!" he shouted. "They're going to get confused and you'll destroy their faith in us!"

"They don't want *lawyers*!" Lisa yelled back. "They want their freedom!"

"We can't oversell what we're doing in court! We haven't amended the complaint and we don't know if we can! We haven't done enough research on this yet!"

"Yes, we have! I—"

"I don't care what you think! We can't raise their hopes like that!"

"But getting out of here is what *they want*!"

* * *

It was silent on the van ride back to the group's quarters. Koh had done his best to smooth things over with Michel, but he was seething about Lisa. Her badgering and tantrums were bad enough back home, but the most damage she could do there was drain his energy and waste time. This was different. She had questioned his authority and the team's litigation strategy in front of the refugees after everyone had spent dozens of painstaking hours fighting to win their confidence. The goals of the case might now be in flux, but it had been neither the time nor place to address that issue.

He expected more of Lisa. She was effectively a law school graduate and working as an attorney for the ACLU, yet in his view, she still hadn't shed the take-no-prisoners, argue-all-the-time mentality of a hard-core activist. The professional discretion so necessary to good lawyering remained alien to her.

His patience, already frayed from the pressures of the last several days, had worn away to nothing, and his empty stomach only made him testier. When they neared the McDonald's, he grunted to the van driver to stop. Koh hopped out and made his way to the restaurant entrance.

The door wouldn't open. He tugged at it again with no luck. The only other option would be a military MRE back in his room, and he wasn't about to settle for dehydrated potatoes au gratin when he was twenty feet from a Big Mac.

Koh pressed his face against the glass, then pounded on the door with his fists.

"Open up!" he hollered.

An employee looked up.

Koh pounded again, harder. The employee shuffled to the entrance.

"We're closed, sir," he said.

"All we want is a few burgers."

"Everything's gone."

"I know you've still got food," Koh said, squeezing into the door frame. "We'll pay you whatever you want, but I'm not leaving until you give us something."

"Sir, I can't do that."

Koh had never felt hungrier in his life. He eyed the kitchen. "Just give me whatever's back there," he said.

"It's against the rules, and if you don't leave, I'm going to call the MPs."

"I'm here on the order of a United States district court judge!" Koh shouted. "And I want something to eat!"

Tory, Lisa, and the others were out of the van now, watching as Koh went after the McDonald's man.

The military driver shifted nervously from foot to foot. "Your guy here's going to get kicked off the base if he keeps this up," he muttered to Tory.

She had never seen Koh like this, and it scared her. Harold's the leader of this whole thing, she thought. He's got all of us depending on him all the time; he can't go to pieces now. He can't afford it. *We* can't afford it.

The situation, Tory feared, was playing right into Cappuccio's arguments about base security and disruptive lawyers. If the Pooch finds out about this, she said to herself, we're all going to get thrown off Guantánamo. That will be the end of the lawsuit and the Haitians will be stuck here forever.

She was trying to decide whether to go in after Koh when he emerged with a triumphant grin on his face, clutching a grocery-sized bag of food.

Back at the officers' club, where they were quartered, Koh handed out burgers and fries with a forced jolliness. He was embarrassed about his outburst and struggled to talk about something, anything, that would take his mind off it.

The familiar aroma of McDonald's filled the room, but Tory was too jittery to take more than a few bites. She eyed the door, expecting soldiers to burst in at any moment and drag Koh away.

Lisa sat apart from the rest of the group, red-eyed and sullen. She'd never felt so insulted by Koh, and when she couldn't take his banter anymore, she stalked away. People murmured good night, their eyes fixed on Koh. A few minutes later, he grabbed a salad from the McDonald's bag and went to knock on Lisa's door.

She let him in and he offered her the food. She picked at it in silence.

"You've come a tremendous distance in this case," he finally said. "And you're going to be a great lawyer. But you just can't talk like that in front of the client."

Lisa eyed him skeptically.

"Do you really respect me as much as everyone else?"

"Yes, Lisa. Listen, you're as smart as anyone on this case. Probably smarter. But you don't think like a lawyer. You've got to learn to work within the system. It's the only thing holding you back."

"I know we shouldn't have fought like that," she said quietly.

They turned from their quasi-apologies to a discussion of case strategy, but resolved little. Lisa again insisted they had to demand the release of everyone on the base. She'd done the research, she said. There was enough legal precedent out there to make the argument. Koh, though, wasn't prepared to toss such an extreme claim into the case without serious thought, and he felt it wasn't the right moment anyway. He didn't want the team pouring time into something that might never be necessary. They would wait for the election.

The flight back from Guantánamo was quiet, everyone mulling over the new developments. For the last six months, they'd been fighting for access to the Bulkeley Haitians, but the reality was that lack of client contact had in some ways made the case easier. Since March, they'd been free to litigate as they saw fit, unburdened by the refugees' concerns and expectations. Now, however, their clients were available. And as Lisa was insisting, the Haitians' desires had to be addressed—even if that wreaked havoc on the legal strategy.

———

Back home, Koh and Ratner formally rejected Cappuccio's settlement offer, and Yale and the government then jointly asked Judge Johnson to postpone the trial until after the election. No one wanted to commit thousands of hours to trying the case only to have Clinton become president and shut down Camp Bulkeley.

That did not, however, mean an end to the work for the Lowenstein Clinic. The students returned from Guantánamo with a bundle of requests from the Haitians: shampoo, clothes, batteries, headphones, cassette tapes, art supplies, and a dozen other items. Tory didn't want to say no to anyone, and she spent long afternoons wheeling shopping carts through discount stores. But preparing care packages for the refugees became a drain on the Lowenstein bank account, and there was also the problem of the telephone bills. The students had given out their home phone numbers before leaving Guantánamo, and they were now inundated with collect calls from the refugees, often lasting several hours. Steve Roos skipped classes to churn out expense reports, and pleaded with an associate dean to pay a student phone bill totaling three thousand dollars—for one month.

None of it was exactly legal work, and some students grumbled that they hadn't signed up for hours of menial labor. Second year Adam Gutride had committed many nights to legal research, but he considered this new phase of assistance, dubbed Guantánamo Client Services by his classmates, to be ridiculous. Adam saw himself as a law student, not a volunteer aid worker, and he refused to make excursions to buy flip-flops and hairbrushes. He also considered it a matter of drawing emotional boundaries. He didn't want the Haitians taking over his whole life.

Tory could see there was no use in arguing with him, but it left her wondering about her own role. What kind of help, exactly, did a lawyer provide? What *was* "legal work"? In the end, she decided, it didn't matter. They had three hundred miserable clients to help. If sending shampoo to Bulkeley made them happy, that's what she was going to do. She couldn't help noticing, though, that most everyone helping with the nonlegal tasks was female. She wondered how exactly that had happened, and a couple of her friends started to ask the same thing.

Down in Manhattan, Mike Wishnie was consumed with the most complex nonlegal problem of all. After a baby born on Guantánamo had died of pneumonia, Ratner negotiated a deal with Cappuccio: the pregnant women could be flown to the United States following their eighth month of pregnancy. Resettling them, however, was not an easy process. INS officials demanded proof that each one had housing and medical care arranged before she arrived, and it could not be at federal expense.

The first few pregnant refugees released from Bulkeley arrived in midfall and moved into a New Jersey AIDS shelter discovered by Tory's friend Laura Ho. Laura had poured weeks into the effort to get the pregnant women out, and after sleeping on military cots and using portable latrines during their pregnancies, they were grateful for real beds and a bathroom. But no one in the home spoke Creole and there was no Haitian community nearby. Having left behind husbands or relatives, they felt alienated and alone.

Joining Laura in the hunt for a solution, Mike called nonprofit groups all over the area and ended up speaking with a major Catholic charity that specialized in refugee assistance. An official told Mike they could handle resettlements. But they expected a set fee that would run into the thousands of dollars—to be paid by the government. Mike hung up, disgusted. He couldn't tell Cappuccio to make a cash outlay for each woman who was released.

After exhausting a long list of other options, Wishnie's luck turned

when an old college friend introduced him to William Broberg. A strident, self-described "big fag" in his mid-twenties, "Bro" was a high-
energy Manhattan activist at the Coalition for the Homeless who
specialized in finding housing and medical help for street people with
AIDS. He often teamed up with Betty Williams, a radical Quaker thirty
years his senior, and together they set out to resettle the pregnant refugee
women in New York, which had a large Haitian community and better
AIDS services than New Jersey.

It was an arduous process—endless paperwork, long lines—but Bro
and Betty shared a talent for working the bureaucracy, and after a number of resettlements, they managed to win a rare private meeting with the
czar of New York City's welfare department, Barbara Sabol. Helping the
Haitians, they told her, was a chance for the city to do some real good at
a moment when almost no one else, including the federal government,
was willing to help. Sabol bought the idea, and with her approval, Bro
and Betty were able to line up housing, medical care, counseling, and
other assistance for the refugees with a single request. Resettlements that
had required weeks would now take only a day.

One by one, the pregnant women arrived from Guantánamo, and
Betty, Ronald Aubourg, and aid workers from the Haitian American
community would meet them at LaGuardia Airport, keys in hand for
their new apartments. They would teach them how to navigate the city's
public transportation system; help them buy food, clothes, and supplies;
take them to their medical appointments; support them as they gave
birth; and then meet with the women almost every day as they struggled
to care for their newborns in a foreign world.

In addition to the deal for the pregnant women, Ratner negotiated another agreement with Cappuccio: refugees with severe medical problems
that couldn't be treated on the base would also be flown in. Ratner took
this as one more sign of Cappuccio's decency; Tory saw it as a cover-your-
ass move. She thought Cappuccio didn't want to look bad by allowing
anyone to die on the base. Over the course of the fall, a few of the sickest
refugees arrived in the United States for treatment, though when one of
them rapidly improved, the INS took him out of the hospital and sent
him to a Manhattan detention center.

Koh and the team saw an important side benefit to moving people out
of Bulkeley on a piecemeal basis. If they could just keep the system running, they would be able to cut down the camp population, perhaps sig-

nificantly. At some point, they figured, Bulkeley might become small enough that bringing in the rest of the refugees would not be that controversial, especially because Yale was proving it could be done without a hassle.

The October resettlement efforts took place amid obsessive concern about the presidential polls. Like the Haitians, Tory and her friends fretted about the slightest erosion in Clinton's support as they counted down the days until the election. The numbers showed Bush closing in, but the team took it as a good omen when Hillary Clinton visited campus on a brilliant afternoon in mid-October. A 1973 graduate of the law school like her husband, she was scheduled to deliver a speech as part of alumni weekend, and she met with Koh and several students beforehand to talk about the refugees.

Clinton impressed and inspired them. She already knew the issues, seemed genuinely concerned, and promised to advise her husband about the situation. As she got ready to leave, Koh pressed a briefing book in her hands and made a final appeal.

"You're right," she told him. "And I'm proud of you all for doing this."

———

Every day after the Yale team left, Yvonne and the others piled into the *kay* where Kinder had set up the television. The children wanted to watch movies, but the adults insisted on CNN, monitoring Bill Clinton's campaign speeches and debating election polls late into the night. Election Day had finally given Yvonne a fixed point in time, and as much as she wanted to restrain her anticipation, as cynical as she'd been when Koh had first mentioned Clinton, she could now focus on nothing else.

On November 3, as America went to the polls, the refugees held their own vote to choose the new U.S. president. Only 55 percent of Americans voted, but all of the refugees in Camp Bulkeley cast a ballot, dropping scraps of paper in a cardboard box and then tallying them up on Vilsaint Michel's clipboard. Bill Clinton picked up over 260 votes from the Haitians on Guantánamo Bay. President George Bush received none.

For the real election, Colonel Kinder brought in an extra-large television and erected a tent. By dinnertime, the entire camp had assembled to wait for the results. As the polls closed and the tallies were announced, the states on CNN's large U.S. map flashed blue for Clinton or red for

Bush. With each state that turned blue, the Haitians roared; when a state turned red, there were jeers and curses.

Anticipation began to build at nine o'clock, as CNN anchor Bernard Shaw suggested a decision was near.

"With polls closed in thirty-nine states and the District of Columbia, Democrat Bill Clinton has opened a commanding electoral lead over President George Bush. He is well within striking distance of that magic number—270," Shaw said. "The Democratic standard-bearer and his running mate, Al Gore, both sons of the South, have loosened the longtime Republican lock on Dixie, scoring wins in Georgia, Kentucky, and Tennessee."

After a translator repeated the news, chants of *Clin-tawn! Clin-tawn! Clin-tawn!* erupted. Some shouted for quiet, demanding there be no celebration until they knew for sure that he had won.

Finally, at 10:48 p.m., CNN announced that Ohio had gone to the Democratic challenger, giving him 286 electoral votes.

"Governor Clinton is now President-elect Bill Clinton," Bernard Shaw announced.

The tent exploded and Yvonne threw her arms around Christa and Armelle, crying with relief.

At Koh's house in New Haven, there was pandemonium. Most everyone working on the case was Democratic, and as young adults in their mid-twenties, the only presidents they'd really known—Reagan and Bush—were Republican. Tory bounced around the room, whooping with joy, and Koh slapped backs and gave everyone bear hugs. Then he dialed Guantánamo and got Vilsaint Michel on the line. He could hear the celebration in the background as he shared the news with the camp leader.

A short time later, Clinton appeared on an outdoor, floodlit stage in Little Rock to address the country. The refugees in Bulkeley crowded around the television in anticipation, a military translator standing by to interpret.

"My fellow Americans," the president-elect began, "on this day, with high hopes and brave hearts, in massive numbers, the American people have voted to make a new beginning."

Clinton described the election as a "clarion call" for the country to face the challenges of a new century and address "problems too long ignored, from AIDS to the environment."

The refugees nodded, waiting.

"And perhaps most important of all," Clinton said, it was a call "to bring our people together as never before so that our diversity can be a source of strength in a world that is ever smaller, where everyone counts and everyone is a part of America's family."

The whole camp cheered.

Seven

WAITING FOR THE PRESIDENT

WALTER DELLINGER, A respected constitutional law scholar from Duke University, was munching on peanuts and sipping a beer, his face splashed with the blue light of a flickering television. It was nearly midnight, and he was stretched out on the bed of his northern Virginia apartment, a few miles from Clinton's transition team offices in Washington. He'd arrived in town less than a week earlier and would soon be appointed to serve in the White House Counsel's Office. Dellinger had just wrapped up another eighteen-hour day and was on the verge of nodding off when the telephone rang.

It was Harold Koh. The two professors had become friends several years earlier during a Yale alumni weekend. Dellinger yawned as he described the transition chaos and then asked what he could do for Koh.

It's the situation on Guantánamo, Koh said. We need your help.

After the Clinton victory, Koh expected an access to power that human rights lawyers couldn't have imagined under the Reagan or Bush administrations. Just two months earlier, Michael Ratner had been taken away in handcuffs from the White House gates after protesting U.S. policy on Haiti. But for years, Koh had been developing ties with liberal standouts in the legal profession, and they were now streaming into the nation's capital to join the new Democratic administration. He diagrammed it all on a blackboard for the students with chalk boxes and arrows, and then explained the influence each person might have on Haiti policy in the Clinton White House. Second year Adam Gutride didn't know much about the inside world of Washington, and he sat back in his chair, amazed. If this is how it works, he thought, the litigation is practically over.

As the days passed, the different parts of Koh's diagram started falling into place. Drew Days, a Yale professor who'd consulted with Koh on the direct return case, was put on the short list for a top post at the Justice Department. Koh's friend Kathleen Sullivan, a professor at Harvard, was chosen to review the personnel in the Solicitor General's Office and help select Kenneth Starr's replacement. While Starr had wanted the Yale team kicked out of court, Sullivan sought Koh's guidance on how to handle the refugee crisis. The team also had access to Clinton's choice for secretary of Health and Human Services, Donna Shalala, and various other White House and Justice transition officials. Koh was ebullient. After months spent fighting a hostile administration, he was now dealing with friends and colleagues who shared the team's values and would, he was certain, ensure that the Haitians received justice.

Believing there were open lines of communication between New Haven and Washington, the Yale team churned out briefings for every transition official within reach. Koh worked the telephone constantly, and within weeks, he and Michael Ratner were in Washington lobbying key Clinton aides in person. Ratner had never been comfortable with the idea of being an insider, but he was intoxicated by the reception they received. The administration's new AIDS policy adviser told them they were doing "God's work," and a State Department official promised Haitian advocate Johnny McCalla that resolving the refugee issue was merely "a matter of the details."

Hopes climbed higher still when two lawyers on the Yale team, Robert Rubin and Lucas Guttentag, were asked to assist the immigration transition "cluster" at Justice. Proposals for shutting down Bulkeley and reversing Bush's direct return order evidently made it onto a high-level list of measures Clinton could take the day he became president. The immigration cluster even suggested shutting down DOJ's Office of Immigration Litigation and firing its chief attorney, whom some transition officials considered to be too anti-immigrant.

Then, in the midst of all this activity, Koh received a call from the search firm responsible for vetting Clinton appointees. At a hastily arranged interview in Washington, he learned that he was under consideration for his dream job, legal adviser to the State Department. Almost giddy with optimism, Koh wondered if the Clinton team could persuade Bush to release the Bulkeley refugees before the inauguration. If everything went right, he figured, they might even be free by Christmas.

Ratner, meanwhile, kept up his negotiations with Cappuccio to move pregnant women and some of the sickest refugees off the base. Cappuccio seemed more willing than ever to help, and by mid-December seventeen people had been freed—though Cappuccio now believed with some cynicism that the military was using medical evacuations simply to empty the camp. In any event, whatever sympathies Cappuccio had for the refugees did not extend to the new president, and he was quick to tell Ratner so.

The issue wasn't Clinton's ideology, Cappuccio said. After all, Ratner was a liberal, and Paul liked him plenty. What irked Cappuccio was that the president-elect seemed driven by political expediency, not principle. During the campaign, Clinton had flown home to Arkansas to oversee the execution of Ricky Ray Rector, a brain-damaged man convicted of murder. Rector was so confused that he'd saved the pecan pie from his final meal to eat after his lethal injection. Cappuccio himself strongly supported the death penalty, but felt Clinton had endorsed it in Rector's case merely for political gain.

Cappuccio warned Ratner that despite Clinton's promises on the campaign trail, he would never change Bush's direct return policy when he got into office. The new president, he insisted, would now have to grow up and face the fact that there weren't any other reasonable policy options available. Just you wait, Cappuccio said.

———

```
Guantanamo Bay, Cuba 11/17/92
Dear Mr. President,
It is with great respect that the Haitian refugees
on Guantanamo Naval Base greet you. How are you Mr.
President? we hope that God will help you in your
duties.
  Mr. President, we are asking you to do everything in
your power to see us out of this base, God willing.
  May God bless you and your family as well as the
Lawyers. We are waiting for your response.
                                          Signed
            The Haitian Refugees on Guantanamo Base
```

The letter, written by camp president Vilsaint Michel and sent to the Clinton transition team by the students, tried to sound upbeat. But morale around Bulkeley had plummeted, and the rumor mill was churning again. Some refugees whispered about an INS plan to return everyone to Haiti before Clinton was sworn in. Others revived the story, first heard months earlier, that no one could leave the camp until a cure for AIDS was developed. The departure of the occasional sick or pregnant refugee only made those left behind more anxious.

Yvonne was disgusted with herself. Despite all her doubts, she'd let her guard down in the days leading up to the election; allowed herself to believe in Clinton. But the new president had said nothing about Guantánamo during his acceptance speech, and then Koh had called to remind Michel that there would be a transition period: Clinton wouldn't actually take office for almost three more months. Everyone seemed to have lost sight of this fact, and when Michel relayed the news to the rest of the camp, they lit into him.

"I'm only telling you what the lawyers said," he protested.

"Just shut up," came the reply. "Nobody wants to hear your talk."

The excitement of the election gone, Yvonne began to sleep more and more, imagining that one day she might not wake up at all. She sank deeper still after a friendly female soldier invited her home for dinner with the permission of Colonel Kinder. The woman's house had soft carpet, a refrigerator, a big color television, even air-conditioning. Yvonne was astounded that a military guard could live so well, and it made her own surroundings seem that much more miserable.

Two weeks after Clinton's victory, one of the *militan,* Jean Benedict, jumped off a chair with nylon parachute cord wrapped around his neck. The cord sliced his throat and he was rushed away, vomiting and bleeding. The doctors saved him, but another halfhearted suicide attempt followed, this time by a young man named Robert Henry. After returning from the hospital, Henry tried to cut himself on the razor wire, and Colonel Kinder had to step in to restrain him.

As their hopes for freedom dwindled, some people retreated to the makeshift chapel to pray or sought help through *vodou*—voodoo, as Americans called it. Melding African rituals with elements of Christian worship, *vodou* dated back to Haiti's colonial era and was practiced alongside Catholicism by many of the refugees. Near the chapel, they set up a special space known as a *peristil* for their ceremonies, with some old bongos and a fifty-five-gallon fuel container serving as drums. Special entreaties were made to Agwe, the *lwa*—or spirit—of the sea, in bleak hopes that he would ensure safe passage out of Bulkeley, and Bawon Samdi, *lwa* of the dead, to ask that he not claim anyone from the camp.

In this atmosphere of despair, another delegation from Yale arrived in late November, and Cappuccio finally agreed to let the team visit Bulkeley itself. Aside from Ronald Aubourg's surreptitious reconnaissance mission six weeks earlier, this group would be the first to see the camp. Koh had stayed home to keep up the lobbying effort, so Joe Tringali of Simpson Thacher took his place, joined by second year Steve Roos and several other students who had yet to visit Guantánamo.

After taking the ferry over from the leeward side of the base, the group piled into a military van and headed for Bulkeley. Since beginning work on the suit, Steve had imagined the naval base as a mysterious, alien world. Paul Cappuccio had only reinforced that idea in court, pounding home the point that Guantánamo was sovereign Cuban territory—and therefore not subject to U.S. law. But now that Steve could see things for himself, it was obvious, as Yale had argued, that the naval base was under the "complete jurisdiction and control" of the United States.

There were suburban neighborhoods with tidy homes, neatly trimmed lawns, and gleaming Fords and Buicks in the driveways. Kids pedaled their bikes on the sidewalks, played hopscotch, dribbled basketballs. The van cruised by the McDonald's Steve had heard so much about, as well as a Baskin-Robbins and a large discount store that resembled a Wal-Mart. Guantánamo—this part of it, anyway—felt just like the U.S. mainland.

When they pulled onto a highway running out of town, however, the landscape changed radically. It was hilly and parched and a stiff wind blew in off the water. Military jets screamed overhead and the *rat-tat-tat* of gunfire echoed from a shooting range. Several miles later, the fences and guard towers of Camp Bulkeley emerged in the distance, shimmering in the heat. Steve had seen images like this before, but they were in history books and documentaries about World War II.

He joined Tringali on the hike into the camp, on edge after a government lawyer had warned that the Haitians might try to take them hostage. As it turned out, however, many of the refugees barely seemed to care that the lawyers were back. Yvonne, Vilsaint Michel, and several dozen others gathered at the mess-hall pavilion to hear an update on the lobbying efforts. But many other refugees drifted in and out of the meeting with little apparent interest, and Steve saw weariness and frustration in the faces gazing back at him. When Tringali played a videotaped greeting from Koh, some in the crowd made an exaggerated show of turning their backs to the screen.

The refugees finally came to life when Tringali and the students asked to see their living quarters. Steve trudged through the dust, joined by Haitians trying to communicate with him in a mishmash of Creole and English. He ducked into cinder block *kay yo,* held his nose as he passed the latrines, swatted away flies. Despite the improvements Colonel Kinder had struggled to make, all Steve could see was laundry drying on razor wire and black plastic garbage bags taped over broken *kay* screens. With just a little money, he thought, the government could have at least made things tolerable—plugging the roof leaks, replacing the flimsy cots with mattresses, doing away with the knife-sharp coils surrounding the compound. As it was, he felt the refugees were being treated like prisoners of war.

Back in New Haven, Steve reported on the situation, and Tory and the others agreed that it was time to press their clients' case in the media. Koh was not enthusiastic. This wasn't a popular cause, he reminded them. The safer move would be to keep the story quiet, given that Clinton already supported Yale and the lobbying strategy was going smoothly. But the students insisted on going ahead. Over Thanksgiving break, they put together a press packet with a photograph of the camp children behind razor wire and sent it to a hundred media outlets across the country.

A few days later, Steve answered the clinic telephone and found himself speaking with an Associated Press reporter. He'd never dealt with the press before, and stumbled over his words as he tried to come up with just the right thing to say. The next day, the story went out on the AP wire with a headline that read, "Guantánamo Haitians in 'HIV Prison Camp'"—along with a quote from Steve. Guantánamo suddenly became a hot topic. Barred from the base for months, journalists sued in court for access with help from lawyers lined up by Ratner and Mike Wishnie, and the Justice Department agreed in early December to open Bulkeley to the media. Lisa Daugaard called every major newspaper and network, pushing them to send someone to Bulkeley, and a week later, a planeload of writers and photographers streamed into the camp.

Yvonne had been yearning to speak with the press, but the day the journalists finally arrived, she lay curled in a fetal position on her cot. Her headaches had grown worse, and she felt as if someone were pounding a nail into her brain. In her absence, the others made the case for their freedom. Colonel Kinder, too, spoke with reporters, openly frustrated that the INS had refused to fly four seriously ill refugees, including a seven-year-old girl, to the United States for treatment.

An AP reporter later telephoned INS spokesman Duke Austin to ask about the four patients. "We have no policy allowing people with AIDS to enter the United States for treatment," Austin said. "They're going to die anyway, aren't they?"

When the AP story came out, another reporter called Austin to check whether the quote was accurate. "I did say it, yes," Austin replied. "But it would be so unfair to print that. All I meant to say was that the outcome would be the same either way, so what would they gain from coming to the U.S.?"

Lisa was so pleased with the press she could hardly contain herself. In her view, the government's strategy with Guantánamo had been "out of sight, out of mind." But that, she thought, was impossible now. Camp Bulkeley was everywhere—newspapers, magazines, even CNN and ABC News. A *USA Today* columnist had declared Guantánamo a "national disgrace" reminiscent of "a Nazi stalag." And at the center of all the coverage was Colonel Kinder, cradling a refugee baby and announcing that he'd shut down Bulkeley himself if he could.

Down on Guantánamo, though, the mood remained dark, for Kinder was now leaving. He explained to the distraught refugees that he had no choice. He had completed his tour of duty; his orders required him to go. He promised them he would meet with his replacement, Colonel Larry Zinser, about how to run Bulkeley, but Yvonne's bad memories of past commanders were still fresh. She feared the worst.

As a last gesture of respect, Kinder invited everyone to the soccer field for a ceremonial transfer of command. Loudspeakers blared "The Star-Spangled Banner" while the soldiers marched in formation through the dust. The Haitians, assembled in bleachers beside the field, then joined in a salute to the American flag. When the ceremony was over, the Lee Greenwood country hit made famous during the 1991 Gulf War, "Proud to Be an American," poured forth from the speakers. As the song swelled to its refrain, celebrating America as a beacon of freedom around the world, the Haitians hoisted Kinder on their shoulders and carried him off the field. He left the next morning with an empty suitcase, having given away all his civilian clothes and personal belongings, down to his wristwatch.

———

With the lobbying effort under way to change Bush's direct return policy, Koh hoped Yale's case against the direct return order would soon be moot. But since Clinton had issued no official statement on the matter, the Supreme Court would not suspend the briefing schedule. The team would have to file a brief with the justices, and it was due just before Christmas. That meant still more legal research and drafting, all for a document that Koh figured the justices would likely never read.

Tired and irritated, he met with Ratner and the students on a dreary November afternoon to dole out responsibilities. Tory could feel a distinct tension in the room, for whether or not the case was ever argued, everyone wanted a piece of the Supreme Court work. But with so much to do and so little time to do it, Koh was focused on efficiency. Several fresh volunteers were on hand, all male, and he asked them to take various tasks on the brief. Given the tight deadline, he felt it was impractical for students working on the Guantánamo litigation to do research that new people could handle instead.

Koh's decision, though, left some veteran women stuck with their current menial jobs, from document review to clerical tasks that a college sophomore could have handled. There were frustrated whispers, and as the meeting broke up, Tory's friend Christy Lopez called out, "I don't think this is fair. Why do the men get all the hard-core legal work?"

Koh, mind already on the heavy workload awaiting him, stared at her in disbelief.

He could accept that the Justice lawyers were going to be difficult. He could tolerate frustrated clients. He could take sleepless weekends and an annoyed spouse. In the end, he could even tolerate Lisa Daugaard's maddening outbursts, for she was only trying to do the right thing. Yet he'd always depended on the trust and goodwill of his students, and now, when things couldn't have been more stressful, he had someone charging him with sexism.

"You chose that work on your own!" he exploded. "We've got hundreds of clients on Guantánamo! We're up to our ears with the transition team! And now we've got to write this damn brief, and you're worrying about who's doing what? I'm not going to stand for this crap!"

He stormed out the door.

There was a stunned silence. Ratner finally tried to defuse things with a little joke, but no one laughed, and he decided it was best to let the students sort out this issue on their own. The discussion went on for a long time. Some accused Koh of favoritism. Others charged that he was too controlling or self-absorbed: the case was all about him and his trying to prove himself to his father. Several women agreed that men who hadn't paid their dues on the project were getting the best assignments. Koh just didn't value women the same way he valued men, and like so many supposed liberals, he didn't even *realize* it.

Steve Roos could only roll his eyes in disgust at his classmates. He'd been stuck with Guantánamo-related bullshit for months and he didn't think it had anything to do with his gender. He'd taken on the work because it needed doing, intending to make a niche for himself on tough logistical issues. The result had been one thankless task after another, but he wasn't complaining. The other students had more or less chosen their work just as he had. As far as Steve was concerned, this was Yale at its worst—political-correctness prosecutors hurling charges of sexism, racism, or some other "ism," where anyone with a bit of common sense wouldn't have seen a problem.

Christy Lopez quietly finished her assignment—the clerical duty of coordinating the Supreme Court amicus briefs to be filed by human rights groups—and then quit the team. She was tired of feeling like a "trained chimpanzee," taking care of address lists and the like, and wasn't comfortable around the office anymore. Christy was shocked when Mike Wishnie called to say Koh wanted her back, but she declined. She'd had enough.

Tory found herself wanting to defend Koh but wondering at the same time if the charges of male favoritism had some truth to them. He did have a way, she thought, of typecasting people and then steering them toward work he considered a good fit. She didn't see the point of discussing it any further, but then the rest of the team appointed her to speak with him about the incident. While it was not a responsibility she wanted, everyone seemed to think she was the best person for the job. She finally mumbled a few words in passing to him.

Over the next few days, Koh thought about it. The sexism charge roiled him because he considered himself acutely sensitive to issues of prejudice. But he was more receptive to another possible failing: that he hadn't geared the clinic enough toward teaching the students. Though the case work had to get done, he wasn't running a law firm. Was it fair that one person had to fill out travel reimbursement forms while another investigated an important point of international law?

He had no easy answers and there was no time to reshuffle major assignments before the December deadline. Still, he made some changes, and Tory, who'd done almost no legal work up to this point, now got an important task on the Supreme Court brief. It didn't excite her that much. But she drove herself to do it, believing she should try, for once, to be engaged by the law.

The team filed the brief just before Christmas, following yet another all-night session at Simpson Thacher. For a moment, everyone relaxed. There were holiday chocolates around the law firm, and as Koh and Tory downed some sweets, they joked that even if the justices never read their brief, it would still make a good law review article.

Clinton, meanwhile, wasn't saying much about the refugees. A few days after the election, he told the *Washington Post* that Bush's direct return policy was an "error" and that he would "modify that process." But the incoming president had been quiet since then, and as Koh started to think more carefully about Clinton's comment, it struck him as strangely lukewarm.

There were other danger signals as well. Some transition officials proved surprisingly cold during meetings with Koh and Ratner, particularly Michael Cardozo at the Justice Department. A former lawyer in the White House Counsel's Office under President Jimmy Carter, Cardozo steadfastly kept Koh at arm's length, refusing to discuss the Haitian situation with him one-on-one. An NAACP lobbyist subsequently warned Koh and Ratner that Clinton was unlikely to "put three hundred HIV-positive Haitians on an airplane and bring them into the United States." And while the NAACP had fiercely criticized the direct return policy just months before, the lobbyist now said his organization had other priorities and would no longer press the issue. The turnabout disgusted Ratner, who dismissed it as "typical Washington talk" from one of "the compromise groups."

Ratner considered the media another problem. Coverage of Bulkeley had been sympathetic, but reports about the situation in Haiti seemed custom-made to create a refugee backlash. General Cedras remained firmly in power, and news stories warned that an armada of refugee boats would head for the United States if Clinton reversed the direct return policy. While touring the Haitian coast, one U.S. congressman predicted a "human tidal wave," and Defense Secretary Dick Cheney told reporters, "The evidence is there that thousands, perhaps hundreds of thousands, of Haitians are in fact preparing to descend upon Florida." Other sources suggested such warnings were based more on fear than reality. The U.S. Coast Guard advised that fishermen might be responsible for the boatbuilding, and a *Miami Herald* reporter found that Haitians who wanted to flee now faced a black-market boat fare as high as seven hundred American dollars—far beyond what most could afford.

Still, Florida was taking no chances. State officials prepared to detain tens of thousands of refugees in vacant fairgrounds, airports, and old department store buildings. The Pentagon assured Governor Lawton Chiles that it could move a hundred thousand refugees away from South Florida if necessary, but U.S. congressman E. Clay Shaw of Fort Lauderdale would have none of it. "We've lost our damn minds if we think the military can handle this," he told the press.

Debate about a possible exodus from Haiti took hold at Yale as well. Graham Boyd, one of the graduated third years, had stayed in New Haven to clerk for a judge, and he raised the issue during a dinner at Tory's house. He agreed that the direct return order violated the law, but also pointed out that the entire Haitian population couldn't come to the U.S. Simply reversing Bush's order wasn't the whole answer, he insisted. The team had to think in broader terms about a humane, workable solution to the situation.

"It's not our job to solve that problem," Tory shot back. "We're here to tell the INS what they *can't* do. They can't return everyone." In fact, she now believed that the Yale team's obligation was to obtain asylum for everyone who fled Haiti. Political refugees, economic migrants, whatever we call them, they're all suffering, she thought. Let's just get them out of there. As far as she was concerned, Clinton couldn't act fast enough.

But others on the team were starting to wonder if the president-elect would really honor his campaign promises. Mike Wishnie didn't trust any government official to reform a policy just because it was the right thing to do. Lisa wasn't even thinking of waiting for Clinton. She wanted to go to trial for the Bulkeley Haitians right away. But she was the only person who favored that plan and knew she would never change Koh's mind. For once, she held her tongue and hoped for the best.

––––––––

As time crept forward and the holidays approached on Guantánamo, Yvonne felt emptier and more alone than ever. Even in lean years, Christmas in Haiti had always been happy for her. She'd cut out paper decorations with Jacques and Daniel—a cross, a small figure of Jesus—and her brother, Jean, would make glowing paper lanterns known in Creole as *fanal.* Her boys chattered about the gifts Papa Nwèl would bring them, and Yvonne would slip off to a nearby market to buy them whatever she could afford—a little plastic truck, some balloons, maybe a cookie or two. On Christmas Eve, the family went to midnight mass at the nearby cinder block church, returning home for a very late dinner known as Reveyon. Yvonne and her mother would make a feast of *griyo,* or fried pork, along with rice and beans, and everyone would celebrate all night long, Antenor and Yvonne's father setting off homemade fireworks for the kids.

But the tilted Christmas tree near the mess-hall pavilion reminded her that for the first time in her life, she would not spend Reveyon with her family. Desperate for a distraction, she immersed herself in a holiday pageant for the camp youngsters. She used bedsheets to make angel outfits for them, and another refugee, an artist named Michelet, fashioned wings from yellow construction paper. People crowded into the plywood chapel for the show, which also featured Bible readings and music on an old guitar from Colonel Kinder.

In the story Yvonne had written, a little girl on Guantánamo cries for her freedom and goes to church to pray. On her knees, she begs of God: "Why have you put me in bondage? Why am I enslaved?"

Three angels alight on earth to answer her.

"Be strong," they say. "Deliverance is near."

The girl musters her will and waits, repeating the words of the angels whenever she begins to lose faith. A month later, the angels return and lead the girl and the other children in the camp to freedom.

Yvonne whispered cues to the little performers from beside the makeshift chapel stage. The star was a six-year-old girl from Yvonne's *kay,* and the angels, played by younger children, tiptoed before the audience with timid smiles. The play drew laughter and warm applause, but Yvonne left the chapel lost in thoughts of her family. Reveyon would begin at home in just a few hours. Would anyone dare to go out? Was there even a reason to celebrate?

Mike Wishnie went home to suburban Boston for the holidays and drifted through family events with little enthusiasm. He'd visited Bulkeley a few days before Yvonne's pageant, and the despair of his clients had lingered with him.

But he was even more depressed because of Frantz Guerrier, whom he'd spent the rest of the fall struggling to get out of the Dominican Republic. Periodically, Mike had called him at Radio Enriquillo with updates. But as the weeks passed, Guerrier sounded progressively more demoralized. Then one day, a man on the other end of the line told Mike that Guerrier had left the radio station. No one was sure where he'd gone.

Mike's heart sank. He had no way to find Guerrier or even be certain he was alive. Perhaps, Mike thought, Guerrier had simply grown tired of running. Maybe he'd returned to Haiti, despite the danger, to search out his remaining family members. Mike harbored a small hope that Guerrier might contact the Lowenstein Clinic office at some point. But he never heard from him again.

———

Right after Christmas, Koh got a call from transition team lawyer Walter Dellinger. Dellinger was on Hilton Head Island for Renaissance Weekend, a yearly schmoozefest for the well-connected. The event had reached a frenzied pitch now that Clinton, a Renaissance regular, was headed to the White House. Dellinger had no inside information about Haiti policy, but there was some news on the position of legal adviser at the State Department. "Three people are on the short list," he told Koh. "You're one of them."

Koh wanted the job—badly. Yet while it might have paid for him to shake hands down at Hilton Head for a few days, he was determined to spend the holidays at home in New Haven. In the past nine months, while he'd been surviving from one litigation crisis to the next, his young son had transformed into an energetic toddler motoring around the house. He'd recently promised to tuck William into bed only to get tied up fighting with the INS for refusing to fly a sick Haitian child out of Bulkeley. He'd missed school functions for his daughter, Emily, now halfway through first grade, and had left his wife, Mary-Christy, to handle most everything, large and small, around the house. Patient as she was, she'd blown up at him—in front of Tory. They'd also lost any semblance of a private life, with people pounding on their door about case matters at all hours.

At school, his international business transactions students had been grumbling that he wasn't prepared. He was hopelessly behind on his other academic duties. And while most of the faculty supported his work for the Haitians, some professors were grousing that he'd become too much of an advocate.

Koh was just starting to put his life back together when he got a call from the American Immigration Lawyers Association. A delegation was headed to Port-au-Prince to assess human rights conditions. Could Koh join them?

The timing was terrible and the State Department had issued travel warnings for Haiti. But Michael Ratner and ACLU lawyer Lucas Guttentag were going, and after talking it over with his wife, Koh decided he had to join them. If for some reason he did have to argue the direct return case at the Supreme Court, Koh wanted to tell the justices he'd seen the situation in Haiti for himself. He'd never forgotten what Justice Blackmun would ask about the legal principle of a case: "How will this affect real people?"

On the flight down with Ratner, Guttentag, interpreter Ronald Aubourg, and others, Koh plowed through a book that several people had told him he had to read: Graham Greene's novel about Haiti, *The Comedians*. The book left Koh deeply troubled. The violence was so severe; the poverty, so extreme—if the current conditions even approximated Greene's earlier portrayal, it was obvious why someone would flee. And yet, as the plane descended into Port-au-Prince, a conflicting thought began to take hold of him. Had he been overstating Haiti's problems in his court arguments? He gazed out the window at the bare mountains and the sprawling capital beside the Caribbean. Perhaps, he thought, it's not that bad here.

After arriving, Koh drove down with Aubourg and Guttentag to the slum of Cite Soleil, where Yvonne's family still lived. Koh knew well by now that it was an Aristide stronghold, and one of the places hit worst by the embargo. What he saw left him numb: a sea of rusting shanties, waist-high filth, grim faces. People flocked like seagulls to the SUV, pressing their palms against the windows, crying for handouts, and when Koh stepped outside, he was overcome by the stench of rot and waste. Gaunt women were cooking rice over feeble fires and squatting to wash clothes in the open sewers; hollow-eyed children darted through the sludge. The air tasted of disease, and even with a bright sun, the sky was gloomy with smoke. Koh had visited some poverty-stricken ghettos in Korea earlier in his life, but Cite Soleil was the most wretched place he'd ever seen. It looked, literally, like hell.

The next morning, the delegation split up to conduct investigations, and Koh headed with Aubourg and Lucas Guttentag to Hinche, a small town about ninety miles northeast of Port-au-Prince in Haiti's central plateau. The trip took all day, their SUV jerking along the rock-strewn trail that was once a road. They passed dozens of handmade signs supporting Aristide, most of them beginning to fade. Village after village was patrolled by paramilitary *attachés*. As the SUV rolled by, the *attachés* would shoot into the air, the townspeople around them scattering like mice, and Koh and Guttentag would instinctively duck, anxious for Aubourg to step on the gas.

Several miles after the village of Thomonde, they were jouncing along when Aubourg nearly ran into a chain strung waist-high across the road. He slammed on the brakes and the truck skidded to a halt, throwing dirt on a large, muscled man with a rifle slung over his shoulder.

Aubourg swore under his breath.

The gunman stalked up to the truck. *"Nou pa wè chenn sa?!"*

"Dezole," Ronald said calmly.

The man put his hand on his rifle. *"Pouki sa nou vin isit?"*

Aubourg nodded at Koh. *"Li se biznismann."*

The gunman eyed the lawyers. Sweat was pouring down Koh's brow and back, and he fought to keep his breathing steady.

"Biznismann?" the gunman repeated. He ordered Aubourg out of the SUV.

Good Lord, Koh thought. He leaned forward to say something but Aubourg spun around, face taut. *"Let. Me. Handle. This,"* he said between his teeth.

The gunman's interrogation seemed to go on forever, Aubourg responding to each question in a slow, respectful cadence. He gestured to the SUV, nodded, gestured again.

A short distance away, people were climbing onto an overloaded truck that appeared to be doubling as a bus. For some reason Koh couldn't determine, a soldier was hitting them with a baton—winding up, then unloading for all he was worth. There were yelps and cries, and someone fell to the ground.

Aubourg's own ordeal finally ended and he got into the SUV. Koh fell back against his seat, his shirt drenched. The gunman removed the chain and they eased away, Aubourg clenching the steering wheel, his eyes fixed on the rearview mirror.

Koh and the group finally reached Hinche at nightfall, where they met with the brother of the town priest in a run-down rectory. He recounted killings, disappearances, bodies hacked to pieces with machetes. People slipped into the meeting, whispered their own gruesome accounts, then vanished into the darkness. It now seemed obvious to Koh why the State Department had no evidence of harm to repatriated refugees: the U.S. government conducted its own interviews in public—a town square, for instance, with the police watching.

Back in Port-au-Prince, Koh again discovered that reality didn't jibe with official U.S. assessments of the country. He went to the American consulate, where Haitians were supposed to file for asylum, and found the area swarming with *attachés*. And when he joined other lawyers who'd been searching the coast for boats, they reported finding only a few vessels under construction, along with a flock of American photographers shooting the scene from every possible angle.

The delegation spent its last evening at the lavish home of a *boujwa* couple who owned a string of Port-au-Prince gas stations. Unlike most of the Haitian elite, the host professed to want a freely elected government. But it didn't show in his weary assessment.

"Democracy cannot succeed in Haiti," he declared. "We're too corrupt. What's here is beyond repair and what the Americans do doesn't matter."

When Koh left the country the next day, he was plagued by images of terror and want and overwhelmed by Haiti's pervasive hopelessness. Haitians' lack of faith that anything would improve seemed to him a key reason why so many had fled before President Bush cut off their ocean escape route. Hope made a huge difference. Few people had left during the nine months of Aristide's presidency, and the economic situation at the time had hardly been good. The United States had to quit worrying about attracting refugees, Koh thought, and give people in Haiti a reason to stay home. Clinton had to help restore the country's fledgling democracy.

Koh didn't discuss his career situation with the students, but his trip to Haiti carried special importance for them. They knew his name was in play for the post in Washington and some were concerned about how his loyalties and ambitions would play out. Lisa and Steve Roos, among others, had wondered whether the "old Harold Koh" might resurface now that a high-ranking position at the State Department was on the line. The trip to Haiti offered them a new perspective. Steve was now convinced that no matter how the job played out, Koh wouldn't abandon the cause. A person didn't go to a place that dangerous, he thought, without a very good reason.

But career matters were on the students' minds as well. As people following the traditional law school track discussed future plans, Steve began to sweat. He'd thrown everything else at law school overboard to work on expense reports and schedule charter flights to Cuba. None of that seemed fit for a résumé.

In angrier moments, he resented the departed third years who had dreamed up the lawsuit in the first place. Michael Barr, Sarah Cleveland, Graham Boyd—their postgraduation jobs were set when the litigation began, and now they were all comfortably ensconced in their judicial clerkships. Even Mike Wishnie, who was entering his final semester, had made it through most of the second year before the case had swallowed him up. The current crop of second-year students had enjoyed no such luxury. They'd been in law school all of six months when the case started and were just beginning to grasp how Yale operated. Now they were hopelessly behind everyone else.

When he went to the financial aid office to pick up his student loan check, Steve wondered why he was bothering to pay tuition at all. Don't try to succeed by the narrow standards of this place, he muttered as he trudged back to the law quad. If you get caught up in that, it's going to eat you alive. He reminded himself that he'd entered law school to become a public interest lawyer. That's what I'm doing right now, he thought, and I'm sure I can get one of those jobs after graduation.

The Haiti work was wearing on people in other ways, too. Tory's life had never been so busy, but in another sense, never more lonely. Several of her friends on the team had boyfriends, including Laura Ho, who was now dating Steve, and it depressed her to catch them whispering or sneaking a kiss when they thought no one was around. Without a romantic interest of her own, the case absorbed all of Tory's emotional energy. She found herself carrying on about the Haitians when some students were sick of even hearing the word "Guantánamo."

For a change of pace, Steve ventured to a new table in the dining hall a few times, hoping to chat about sports, classes, whatever. But he could tell that the others on the team weren't pleased. Though he hadn't planned it this way, he was now an integral part of what the rest of the school called "the Haiti crowd," a clique some students saw as holier-than-thou do-gooders and others thought of as just plain nuts.

As the semester drew to a close, Steve quietly wondered what it would feel like to walk away from the grind of the last nine months. A few did, including one of his roommates. But in the end, Steve knew he couldn't do the same. If everyone focuses on their own needs, he thought, this whole team's going to fall apart and the Haitians will be screwed. We need to see this thing through until Clinton takes care of it.

On January 14, six days before the inauguration, a transition aide called Koh to say that the president-elect was going to make an announcement. For the last few days, top Clinton officials had been holed up in Arkansas, dealing with foreign policy. The news, the aide warned, wasn't good. The students hurried over to Koh's house to watch CNN, and they didn't have to wait long. Reporter Wolf Blitzer appeared on-screen, live from Arkansas with the breaking story.

"The big news out of Little Rock today," said Blitzer, "is President-elect Bill Clinton's very dramatic about-face on this whole Haitian-refugee policy issue, a policy that he now says is designed to stop Haitians from fleeing aboard unseaworthy boats. He fears that thousands of Haitians could die if they try to seek political asylum coming to the United States aboard these boats on the high seas. He's continuing the Bush administration's approach, an approach that he criticized strongly during the campaign, of summarily returning Haitians who are picked up on the high seas by the U.S. Coast Guard. They will not have a chance to apply for political asylum."

CNN cut to Clinton. "For the time being," the incoming president said, "I think this is the best policy while we try to get political reform, while we try to take care of as many Haitians as possible in Haiti, and I want to pursue this policy. I still believe, and I—just exactly what I said, that everybody is entitled to a hearing who seeks to become a refugee in this country, and I want to give it to them."

Haitians would be able to apply for asylum inside Haiti, as they had under Bush, but the direct return policy would stay. The president-elect uttered not a word about the people on Guantánamo.

"No doubt," Wolf Blitzer said, "this new policy does come as sort of an embarrassment to the Clinton people here in Little Rock, who, as I said, were bitterly critical of the Bush administration's approach during the campaign." The new administration, said Blitzer, was now facing up to "the realities of governing."

The group in Koh's basement sat in crushed silence. Tory had gone pale.

Koh looked around at everyone, his face blank.

"No one said this would be easy," he finally said.

Long after the students had filed out, Koh remained slumped on the couch. He glanced around the room. They had celebrated in the very same place on election night. Tory had been jumping on the furniture. They had won. He'd been sure of it: they had won.

He began to sob—huge, heaving moans—and then hurled the couch pillows across the room.

"How could he do it?!" he yelled. "How could he do it?!"

He dropped his head into a pillow. He hadn't cried so hard since his father had died. Mary-Christy came down and held him as he sobbed. He'd dared to believe what Clinton had said. He'd staked everything on it. And he'd been duped, betrayed, sucker-punched.

William Jefferson Clinton was inaugurated as the forty-second president of the United States on January 20, 1993, a brilliant, frigid day. He took the oath of office on the U.S. Capitol steps, surrounded by family, friends, and members of Congress, with five immense American flags hanging from the Capitol as the backdrop. After he'd been sworn in, Clinton shook hands with Chief Justice William H. Rehnquist and stepped to the podium to address the American people, including several disgusted Yale students who'd decided to make the trip despite his change of heart.

"Our greatest strength," he declared, "is the power of our ideas, which are still new in many lands. Across the world, we see them embraced— and we rejoice. Our hopes, our hearts, our hands are with those on every continent who are building democracy and freedom. Their cause is America's cause."

As Clinton spoke, the Coast Guard's new operation in the Caribbean, dubbed Able Manner, was running at full force. At least seventeen cutters and patrol boats and a dozen airplanes and helicopters were engaged, hunting for refugee boats that had reached the international waters twelve miles off Haiti's coast. The Florida Marine Patrol had also set up additional defenses, instituting twelve-hour work shifts and issuing a statewide alert.

But the exodus so many had feared never came. Perhaps, Koh thought, it was Clinton's radio address on Voice of America advising the Haitian people not to flee. Or perhaps it was the Haitians' hopes that the new U.S. administration would indeed bring Aristide back to power. Whatever the cause, on the day Clinton took office, the Coast Guard intercepted only a single vessel about twenty miles off Haiti's northern coast. The 163 refugees aboard were scheduled to be returned to Port-au-Prince the next day, where, as usual, the Haitian military would be waiting for them.

A week before the inauguration, Yvonne turned twenty-nine. She was eight months into her captivity and had forgotten that it was her birthday. January 13 was the same as every other day—she got up, stretched out the kinks in her back from sleeping on a sagging cot, prayed, presented herself for the morning headcount, ate breakfast, and then wondered if she'd hear something about leaving. The only difference was her appearance.

Yvonne had cut her hair. For the past several months, she had tried to wear it longer, straightening it with one of the discount hair products Kinder had brought to the camp, but she finally gave up. She chopped it all off and buzzed what was left down to her scalp. When she was done, she stared into her little mirror, amazed. Her high, wide cheekbones now seemed more prominent than ever, her face more severe. She almost looked, she thought, like a soldier.

It was with this martial appearance that she learned of the president's decision to maintain the Bush direct return policy. Afterward, she stumbled back to her *kay* and fell onto her cot in dismay. If Clinton had gone back on this promise, she thought, what would he do about Guantánamo?

Eight

THE HUNGER STRIKE

E VERYONE AT THE ACLU had packed into a conference room to watch Clinton's inaugural address, but after the first few words Lisa Daugaard stalked off, too disgusted to listen. She called her mother in Seattle seeking consolation and ended up in an argument instead. While Mrs. Daugaard was disappointed by Clinton's reversal on the direct return order, she was still thrilled that he'd won. "On balance," she told her daughter, "his victory's a good thing. We can't criticize him for not being perfect."

He betrayed us, Lisa fumed, but we're so beaten down by the Republicans that we think he's treating us well. Not that she was surprised by Clinton's decision. She'd seen Seattle politicians jettison a cause once it became inconvenient and hadn't expected the new president to be much different.

As it turned out, the decisive moment for Clinton had been an early January meeting with the CIA and his top advisers. Repeating the reports in the press, CIA officials had warned that hundreds of thousands of Haitians were preparing to flee on inauguration day. Their intelligence briefing included dramatic aerial photographs of half-built boats lining Haitian beaches like whale skeletons, and advised that people were even tearing apart their shanties for construction material. The looming mass migration would prove catastrophic, the CIA stressed, with up to one-third of the refugees drowning.

Years later, Deputy National Security Adviser Sandy Berger, who'd been at the meeting, expressed doubts about the CIA report's accuracy. But he said it had gone unchallenged at the time. Berger stressed that before taking office, Clinton was still dependent on the Bush bureaucracy for information. And if refugees were in fact about to flood into America, as the CIA claimed, the new president understood from bitter experience that it could mean political disaster.

Back in 1980, then-Governor Clinton had lost his bid for reelection after Cuban refugees rioted to protest their detention at Fort Chaffee, an Arkansas military base. The refugees had been detained there by order of President Jimmy Carter, who was struggling to handle the influx of over 125,000 Cubans after the Mariel boatlift of 1980. The president's decision enraged Clinton, who'd loyally supported Carter. "You're fucking me!" the young governor had screamed at a White House official. Clinton blamed his ouster by Arkansas voters in large part on the president—and told the press that he was "coming to Washington with a few refugees" for Carter to resettle.

Harold Koh knew all about the Fort Chaffee incident, and he kicked himself for not having recognized how it might affect the new president. Clinton was not about to start his presidency in the way his first term as governor had ended, so he adopted the Bush direct return policy that he'd called both immoral and illegal during the campaign. Promising new efforts to restore democracy in Haiti, Clinton now claimed that direct return was meant to save refugee lives—the same rationale Bush had used. But Clinton looked profoundly uncomfortable to Koh as he defended his decision. Watching a videotape of the president's fumbling explanation years later, Koh stabbed a finger at the image on-screen. "Look at his eyes," Koh said, as if talking to a jury. "He knows he shouldn't have done it."

With no other way to stop the Coast Guard from sending refugees back to Port-au-Prince, the Yale team now had to press ahead with the Supreme Court case against the direct return policy. That put Koh in the awkward position of challenging the president who might soon appoint him to the State Department. But with the argument just six weeks away, he had little time to ponder the irony of his predicament.

Despite the turn of events, Koh still believed Clinton would free the refugees on Guantánamo. "They're screwing us on the big policy, but they'll assuage their guilt by going with us on Bulkeley," he reassured the students. There were now just 267 refugees left on the base, thanks to all the negotiations between Ratner and Cappuccio. Yale's new hope was to keep the system of case-by-case releases humming along until that number fell below two hundred, which everyone seemed to feel would make it easier for Clinton to shut down the camp. "Fewer than two hundred people": Koh liked the phrase. It didn't sound like a lot.

But there was a problem with this strategy. The day before Clinton's inauguration, Paul Cappuccio had left the government. He'd packed his things into a few cardboard boxes, flicked off the lights, and walked out of Main Justice for good. The transfer of power was that simple, that complete, that sudden.

Like Kenneth Starr and many others, Cappuccio was trading in government service for the fat salary of private practice. Wooed by the elite firm of Kirkland & Ellis, he was soon representing corporate giants like General Motors, earning more in a month or two than either of his parents had made in a year. After buying them a home in Florida, he got himself a luxurious house in a tony Washington neighborhood, complete with a swimming pool, a Mercedes, and a yacht to cruise the Potomac.

Ratner and the rest of the Yale team, meanwhile, had assumed a sympathetic liberal would replace Cappuccio. But the Clinton transition people were woefully disorganized. No one at the Justice Department seemed to know what was happening on Guantánamo or even who was in charge of the issue. The result was a total breakdown in Ratner's efforts to move sick and pregnant refugees out of Bulkeley. Cozy calls to Cappuccio gave way to long waits on hold with his transition successors, followed by an "I'm not sure" or an "I'll get back to you." Far from improving under Clinton, the situation had turned worse.

By the end of January, Yvonne had lost all faith in both her lawyers and the new president. The Yale people had told her to wait, to have patience, but the inauguration had come and gone, and still, nothing had happened. As far as she could tell, Clinton had completely forgotten about Guantánamo. After languishing in the camp for nearly nine months, Yvonne was not going to bide her time any longer.

An idea had seized her the previous fall. She'd even mentioned it to Lisa Daugaard during the Yale team's first visit, though at the time she had no intention of acting on it. She considered the plan a dangerous and difficult last resort, and more than a little frightening. But now she believed it was all the refugees had left.

Yvonne made her case to Vilsaint Michel and the other camp leaders before their weekly meeting with Colonel Zinser. "We have to go on a hunger strike," she announced. "We have to free our bodies of everything that is a part of the military. We can't eat their food, take their medicine, or sleep in their *kay yo*. If we're going to get out of here, we've got to put real pressure on Clinton. But we have to be prepared to die."

Everyone stared at her in silence.

"No hunger strike's going to free us," someone finally said. "We protested, we fought, we burned the camp. Nothing happened. The lawyers haven't done anything, and Kinder couldn't get us out, either."

Others nodded.

"If you don't want to do this," Yvonne replied, "then don't do it."

She returned to her *kay,* grabbed her sheet and pillow, and hiked out to the barren, dusty soccer field. Then she spread out her bedclothes on a flat, unprotected patch of ground and sat down under the burning midday sun.

Back in Port-au-Prince, refusing to eat in the name of a cause was not uncommon, from demands that a school reopen to the famous 1987 fast protesting Father Aristide's transfer from the Saint Jean Bosco parish. For the most important political causes, a hunger strike, or *grèv grangou,* was a far more dramatic and sustained statement than any street rally— and while Haitians had control over little in their lives, they could still do violence to their own bodies.

Over the course of the hunger strike's first day, most of the refugees joined Yvonne. The *militan* swaggered onto the soccer field as if they were looking for a fight, then claimed a space in the dirt. Bacon showed up on his crutches. Mothers appeared with their children, pulling toddlers along by the hand, cradling infants in their arms. Even the pregnant women came. Some sought the shade of the nearby bleachers; others challenged the sun with Yvonne. The field became a patchwork of sheets and blankets, plastic bags and canvas tarps.

Afternoon faded into evening. Only a handful of refugees went to dinner, eating alone, quietly, beneath the mess-hall pavilion on the other side of the camp. Everyone else remained on the soccer field. As the sun dipped below the hills, camp guards appeared and fanned out to talk with them.

"It's time to head back," they said through the interpreters. "It's late, and you've got to be inside the gate. Let's go home."

Yvonne jumped to her feet. "This isn't home!" she shouted in a hoarse Creole.

"What if it starts to rain?" one interpreter asked. "What about the animals? Why not come back inside? See if we can compromise."

Yvonne stood her ground, arms crossed. Finally, after conferring among themselves, the soldiers left.

Darkness fell and people huddled in small groups, debating their new situation. Others stretched out to sleep. Suddenly, bright security lights flooded the field. Yvonne stood up and looked around. Bodies in white sheets were scattered about in twos and threes, like dead who'd fallen in battle. After a few moments, everyone gathered up their belongings and headed for the shadows beneath the soccer field bleachers, the youngest children carrying their pillows with both hands.

Yvonne joined the others and hunted for a new spot to lay her sheet. The ground was uneven and she shifted around, trying to get comfortable. Insects whirred and clicked. A baby was crying. Several people around her were eating fruit or crackers they'd slipped out of the mess hall, and the *militan* were scolding them for cheating.

Yvonne herself was not going to touch any food, and she knew it was important to conserve her strength. She tried to close her eyes and rest, but felt too energized to lie still. After months of waiting, she was *doing* something. Clinton had broken his promise, but now they would take the fight to him, and whatever happened would be on his conscience.

She thought of Daniel and Jacques and murmured a prayer. As a gentle breeze blew in from the ocean, drowsiness at last descended on her. Just before drifting to sleep, she felt the first pangs of hunger.

In a panic, Tory raced to the Lowenstein office after class and dialed Guantánamo. Camp president Vilsaint Michel had called earlier to notify Yale about the hunger strike, and now the students were pleading with the refugees to call it off. It's not safe, Tory warned her clients. You're sick. Denying yourself food will only make it worse. Desperate to get the women and children eating, she stressed that Americans weren't going to support the Haitians if their kids were part of the strike. But the refugees had no interest in lectures from their lawyers.

Hurried research by the students revealed that a healthy adult could last between fifty and seventy-five days on a hunger strike. While there was little information about how long a person with HIV might survive, a doctor advised it could be less time, perhaps much less. The doctor also warned that before death, a fast could lead to muscle wasting, kidney

failure, and brain damage as the body began to tear itself down to produce energy.

Koh sided with the students opposed to the strike. He considered it not
only dangerous but a political drawback. Yale was still lobbying the Justice
Department for the refugees' release, he stressed, and negative publicity
from Guantánamo was not going to help the effort. Mike Wishnie and Lisa
Daugaard, though, saw the strike as a political choice that belonged to their
clients, and they believed media coverage would be a plus. If the refugees
had chosen to fast, the point was to figure out how to make the most out of
their protest. Indeed, Lisa insisted that if people did start eating again, they
would lose the "special moral authority" they'd acquired by fasting, leaving them with even less political leverage than they had before.

The disagreement over the strike became an argument, and the argument became a fight, with Tory shouting at Lisa that Yale could not sit by
if the kids were refusing food. In the end, though, even those most opposed to the idea conceded that if the refugees wanted to fast, the team
couldn't stop them. The consensus was to encourage as safe a strike as
possible: get down to Guantánamo and urge the children and pregnant
women to eat and everyone else to drink plenty of fluids and stay in the
shade.

In a stroke of good fortune, a new delegation of lawyers and students
had already been slated to visit the base, including Adam Gutride and
Cathy Powell, a young African American attorney who'd graduated with
Lisa Daugaard's class. They arrived on Groundhog Day in the scorching
heat to find most of the refugees camped beneath the soccer field bleachers. When the visitors introduced themselves, reactions ranged from
tepid to hostile. Cathy stumbled through a few words of French only to
have a refugee thrust a letter into her hands. It had been translated into
English, perhaps by another Haitian in the camp:

> You said you are my lawyer. Can you tell me what have you done
> for me since you are defending me? Since President Clinton had
> took power, what have you done for me? Counsel, it is now 14
> months since I left Haiti. May I say if you cannot defend me, it's
> better to leave my case in the government hands.

More angry messages to the lawyers, scribbled on cardboard, were
propped against the bleachers.

Off balance, Cathy and the rest of the team tried to assemble the refugees for a meeting. They were interrupted by the collapse of a hunger striker named Berince Georges, a big man who wore a towel on his head like a turban. He writhed in the dirt, vomited blood, then fell unconscious. An ambulance rolled up, clouds of dust behind it, and military paramedics squeezed through the crowd hovering over him. They tried to ease Georges onto a stretcher, but the Haitians elbowed them away with angry shouts. It was impossible for the interpreter to keep up, and Cathy waited, bewildered. Two other strikers fainted soon afterward, followed by more paramedics and more interference from the refugees. By now, the situation was clear: the Haitians were intent on severing all ties with the camp, even if it meant rejecting medical care.

Nor, it seemed, did they want any help from their lawyers. Harold Koh said President Clinton would free us, one refugee after another charged. Harold Koh promised us that. But Clinton has done nothing.

The promises came from Clinton, not Harold Koh, a Yale attorney replied. We're still trying to get the White House to free you.

But the refugees weren't convinced, and after Cathy spoke with INS officials in hopes of freeing more pregnant women and children, the Haitian men grew belligerent. If the women get to go, then we all get to go, one man insisted. But if we have to stay, they stay, too.

Adam Gutride feared there might be a similar kind of coercion behind the hunger strike, and he quietly raised the issue with the refugees one by one. He was relieved to learn that no one was forcing the children to fast, and as far as he could tell, both the youngsters and the pregnant women were eating, though mostly on the sly. But the mess hall had given up serving meals at regular hours, and as a safeguard, Adam and others met with the staff to ensure that food was always available to anyone who chose to eat.

Another discovery left him more troubled. The military seemed to be building new, sturdier barracks to replace the slapdash huts the refugees had vacated when they'd launched the hunger strike. So that's the plan, he said to himself with a shudder. The government's going to keep them here forever.

On a call back to New Haven, Adam and Cathy went over the bleak situation with Koh. People were sick, losing weight, and angry—and they were especially angry with him. Koh sank into his chair. He was sleeping only a few hours a night, but between his lobbying efforts and preparations for the Supreme Court, there simply wasn't enough time to do everything. Yet he felt he had no choice. He packed a change of clothes and was soon on his way to Cuba.

It was late afternoon on a Friday when he reached Bulkeley with Ronald Aubourg and Michael Ratner, a hazy sun casting long shadows across the camp. The refugees lay on the soccer field or under the bleachers, listless in the warm air. Shaken, Koh picked his way through the bodies, looking for familiar faces. He met the dejected gaze of a young refugee he didn't know. He wondered what he could possibly say, acutely aware that he could not create any more false expectations.

Finally, he reached out with his hand.

"I'm sorry," he said quietly.

Dezole, Aubourg repeated for him.

Moving from one Haitian to another, he apologized and promised Yale would not give up. When he finally found Yvonne, he was dismayed. Her face was drawn, her body limp. She did not respond to his embrace, and her expression was one of doubt and distrust.

At no point in the lawsuit had Koh been more afraid. Things were spiraling out of control. The physical toll on people after more than a week of fasting was obvious, and even though the children were eating, they didn't look right. From Yale's first visit in October, he recognized a mischievous boy named Wadson Fortune. A healthy twelve-year-old stuck in Bulkeley because his guardian was sick, Wadson had an easy laugh and he'd clowned around with the students in the hangar. But over the last four months, the boy had changed. His smile was gone, his eyes were sullen, his energy had drained away. Koh left the field at dusk, agonizing over what Yale might do to restore the refugees' hope.

Some weeks before the hunger strike, Lisa had contacted a friend who worked for the Reverend Jesse Jackson. Lisa didn't care much for Jackson personally. Years earlier, after pouring time and energy into his Rainbow Coalition, she'd concluded it was less a genuine political movement than a vehicle for Jackson's own agenda. But she knew how well he worked the press and figured he could dramatically increase the camp's visibility.

At the time, he was already pressing for Aristide's restoration, and after Lisa's call, Jackson began slipping Bulkeley into his speeches. It was an encouraging start, but she wanted him to do more. The hunger strike gave her the opportunity she needed. If we present him with an eyewitness report about what's going on down there, she thought, maybe he'll visit the camp.

Lisa was in luck, for Cathy Powell happened to be flying in from Guantánamo an hour before Jackson was slated to speak at a New York City rally on the Haiti crisis. When Cathy called in to the ACLU office after landing at Newark airport, Lisa barked out new directions: Get in a cab and meet me at the U.N. Plaza—*now!* The two women soon joined up on First Avenue, but it was eighteen degrees outside, with driving snow, and Cathy had no winter clothes along. By the time the protesters marched up the street an hour later, she was growing faint from the frigid weather, and Jackson was still nowhere in sight.

Finally, a limousine eased up to the curb and Jackson emerged in a long coat, flanked by bodyguards. In his familiar baritone, he demanded that Cedras step down and vowed to fight for Aristide's return.

"We met with Secretary Warren Christopher yesterday!" he shouted to the demonstrators, the snow swirling in the air. The applause rose.

"We are in New York today!"

More applause.

"And next week, we will go to Guantánamo Bay, Cuba, to visit our brothers and sisters there!"

Lisa shot Cathy a grin. Jackson was one step ahead of them.

Minutes later, the two women were huddled in his limousine along with several local politicians and reporters. As Cathy, still shivering, described the hunger strike to an intent Jackson, another idea popped into Lisa's mind. A visit to Guantánamo in a week would be great, but maybe he could do something right now. What they needed was a tape recorder.

That evening, Ratner, who was still on Guantánamo with Koh, received a call from Lisa. She reported that Cathy Powell had been treated for hypothermia after waiting for Jesse Jackson in the snow, but they had persuaded him to tape a greeting to the refugees. While the words were not exactly what Lisa had hoped for, she figured the sound of Jackson's voice was what really mattered. She played the message over the telephone to an astounded Ratner, who recorded it on his Dictaphone.

He grabbed Koh and they headed over to Bulkeley's public address system. The two men weren't quite sure what to expect, but after two days of angry accusations from their clients, playing the tape seemed worth a try.

A full moon glowed above the soccer field lights, and sleeping bodies dotted the dusty ground. Koh leaned into the microphone. "We have a message for you," he said tentatively. "From Reverend Jesse Jackson."

The refugees murmured in recognition. They'd seen Jackson over and over on CNN for the past several months. They knew he was a powerful black man in America, and that he'd been calling for Aristide's restoration.

Ratner threw Koh a here-goes-nothing look and flipped on his Dictaphone.

"My brothers and sisters in Guantánamo," the authoritative voice reverberated across the camp, *"we need you to live for the struggle, not die for the struggle."*

Ratner paused the Dictaphone for translation. Several people sat up, still wrapped in their sheets, like ghostly figures awakened from the dead. Koh watched them, transfixed.

"Eat your food and take your medicine, because when Father Aristide returns to Haiti, he doesn't want to take your corpses back to Haiti."

Another pause, more translation. All across the field, bodies stirred to life.

"We will be coming to Guantánamo to visit you next week on February fourteenth."

A soft chant rose up from the field. "Jess-ee . . . Jess-ee . . . Jess-ee . . ."

"Yes, that's right . . . Valentine's Day. This will be our own special Valentine's Day gift to you."

The chant grew in strength, the refugees up now, alive, energetic. "Jess-ee! Jess-ee! Jess-ee! Jess-ee!"

Suspended between elation and astonishment, jaw slack and eyes wide, Koh threw his arm around Ratner.

"I love you!" Jackson's voice thundered into the night air. *"Je vous aime beaucoup! Keep hope alive!"*

The students did not wait for Jackson's trip to publicize the hunger strike. Now veterans at working the media, they issued press releases and called the major news outlets to pitch the unfolding story. Lisa knew fasting refugees made for good drama, and sure enough, reporters demanded access to Guantánamo again and began churning out sympathetic stories. The *Boston Globe* devoted an entire article to Yvonne, recounting her torture and the uncertain fate of her family. "I am no longer sure what is in Mr. Clinton's brain," she told the *Globe* reporter. "So far, everything he says is a lie."

Colonel Zinser also vented to the press. For weeks, he'd been calling for the evacuation of five refugees with severely depressed immune systems, including one, Joel Saintil, whose liver was on the verge of collapse. Saintil's father, who lived in Florida, was pleading to take care of his dying son, but the INS had rejected all of Zinser's requests to fly him to the United States for adequate medical treatment. "Let's say I was upset," Zinser declared in one interview. "I could use other jargon."

The hunger strike, he made clear, only made his task harder. Even if many people were eating, as he suspected, there was still the possibility of serious injury. He didn't want that happening on his watch. He'd even approached Yvonne privately to discuss the matter.

"You can stop this," he pleaded with her. "They follow you."

She shook her head. "If they don't eat," she said through a military translator, "that's their choice."

Finally, Zinser agreed to have Yale bring in outside physicians. Ratner had already contacted a New York AIDS expert, Dr. Douglas Shenson, to advise on the case, and Shenson and a Haitian American physician flew to Guantánamo representing Doctors of the World. As Shenson understood it, Zinser wanted him to talk the Haitians out of the fast, but the doctor had no such plans. While he would explain the medical risks involved, Shenson shared Lisa Daugaard's view that it was ultimately the refugees' decision.

After examining the hard-core fasters, several of whom had passed out, Shenson concluded they were in grave danger. But his concern was not limited to the hunger strike. In his view, Bulkeley as a whole didn't even come close to meeting the standards of an American prison. The lack of flush toilets and nearby running water for the refugees to wash their hands meant infections could spread like wildfire; there were no barriers to separate the children from the razor wire; the water pooling in the shower room could be a breeding ground for disease. Bulkeley, Shenson reported to the media, was "a medical and public health outrage."

As Shenson was wrapping up his investigation, Tory arrived at the camp for a weeklong stay. With the military's consent, Yale had decided to maintain a constant presence at Bulkeley. It was not an easy trip for her. The refugees' indifference made her feel superfluous at times, but she tried to brush it off and do what she could—counseling a suicidal teenager, playing with the children, and monitoring the hard-core fasters, who had retreated under a shelter they'd built out of the soccer goal-posts, garbage bags, and tarps.

She could tell some strikers were eating at least a bit, but others were visibly malnourished, and she was worried about one in particular—Yvonne. The energetic, beautiful woman she remembered from four months earlier was wasting into a wan stick figure. Tory had been intimidated by her during the first visit, but in Yvonne's fragile state she seemed more approachable, and the two ended up sitting together on the soccer field bleachers with an interpreter. They talked about Yvonne's children, about life in Haiti, about the INS.

Finally, Tory broached the real issue, asking her to think about eating something, or at least drinking fruit juice.

Yvonne was silent for a moment. "I know you care about us," she finally said. "And I know you've tried very hard to help."

Tory did not push the matter. Back at Yale, the strike had seemed like a pointless act of self-destruction. Here, though, amid the plywood *kay yo,* the latrines, the fences, Yvonne's protest somehow made sense to her. There was both a defiance and a dignity to it that she hadn't understood before.

Yet Tory's respect for the woman huddled beside her was mixed with a growing fear. If Clinton didn't act soon, Yvonne could die.

Jesse Jackson stepped off the jet into the Guantánamo heat, and Tory and her friend Laura Ho waited impatiently as the cameras flashed away. He wore a dark Nehru shirt and carried himself with a bearing that announced his importance. He surveyed the airfield with an authoritative squint and then, trailed by aides, reporters, and the Yale students, he took the ferry across the bay and boarded a gray school bus for Bulkeley.

As they all rode toward the camp, Colonel Zinser presented Jackson with the military's version of the situation, including his conviction that most of the refugees were eating again. While Tory and Laura had hoped to rebut the colonel's account in a private meeting with Jackson, they sensed there'd be no chance. At a pause, they cut in with their side of the story. Zinser did not look pleased, but the students ignored him. They had too much to tell Jackson before the bus reached Bulkeley.

The camp was decorated with balloons and a big welcome banner. The Haitians were buzzing, and many who'd quit the fast were back on the soccer field. Others anxiously waited near the main gate. As Jackson arrived,

Tory noticed several refugees affecting expressions of great distress, even though earlier they'd seemed fine. The strategy bothered her. She understood their determination to send a strong message to their visitor, but she thought things were bad enough. The dramatics weren't necessary.

Press in tow, Jackson strode to the goalpost shelter and embraced the hard-core strikers. They were ecstatic, even overcome, and not just because this larger-than-life figure had taken up their cause. He'd made a promise to them—he would come to Guantánamo—and he'd kept it. After Clinton's cold silence, the gesture by Jackson carried special significance. He could be believed; he could be trusted; he would help.

After joining them in a Creole hymn, Jackson made his way to the bleachers to address the rest of the camp. His appearance produced an almost biblical effect. The refugees swarmed him, crying out his name, and when he made his way with a translator to a waiting podium and called out a traditional Haitian greeting—"*Sak pase,* my people!"—they exploded.

Tory waited anxiously in the crowd, expecting that Jackson would finally repeat the message he'd taped in his limousine eight days earlier— eat so you can maintain your health.

"I am working for your release," he shouted. "I did not understand how bad your situation was, but I have seen it now and in the name of Christ, I will take up the struggle for you and join your fast for the next week!"

Tory froze.

"The soldiers are not your enemy!" Jackson went on. "They do not want to keep you here! So when you protest, protest with your words and not your fists! Keep up the fight, keep up your will, keep hope alive!"

Applause poured forth around her, but Tory was lost in worry. Jackson was supposed to put an end to the strike, not join it.

And yet she'd never seen the refugees so hopeful. Some had been on Guantánamo for more than a year now, their contact with the outside world limited to lawyers, doctors, and a delegation of U.S. officials from Jamaica who'd peered at them as if they were zoo animals. But today, a famous American black man, *Jesse,* had come to Bulkeley. He'd listened to them, held them, prayed with them. And then he had announced that he would go to the White House himself to plead their case. Enveloped by little children chanting, "Guantánamo no good," and the rest of the refugees cheering for their new champion, Tory tried to believe that Clinton might free them after all.

If anyone in the camp remained doubtful amid the throng, it was Yvonne. Jackson could fast along with them if he wanted. That was fine. In any case, she was not about to stop her own strike. The question in her mind was what, if anything, Jackson could really do once he left Guantánamo.

"Is Jesse Jackson coming in today?"
    "I don't believe so."
    "He said so."
    "Reverend Jackson said he was coming in?"
    "I believe so."
    "It's not on the president's schedule, but it may get added."
    Clinton's press secretary, Dee Dee Myers, was briefing reporters at the White House.
    "What's your reaction to the hunger strike that Jesse Jackson—"
    "We're still reviewing it at this point."
    "What's the dilemma here?"
    "Well, there are a number of things that have to be considered. Again, the situation at Guantánamo is under review and the broader policy is under review. Beyond that I can't say anything else."
    Jackson was not able to see Clinton, but he managed to meet with White House Chief of Staff Thomas McLarty. It did not go well. Bringing in the Bulkeley Haitians, McLarty told him, was "not a popular issue," and he refused to say when the president would deal with Guantánamo. Jackson nevertheless told reporters he expected the White House to make a decision within the week. Then he went on CNN to press the refugees' cause in a debate against Congressman Lamar Smith, a Texas Republican.
    Smith wanted no part of the Haitians, charging that each one would cost $100,000 to treat in the United States. The students watching the broadcast yelled at the screen. Smith was leaving out that the United States routinely admitted immigrants with more expensive conditions, such as kidney ailments and cancer, and that Camp Bulkeley had cost the government more than $55 million to maintain. Instead, he warned that the Guantánamo refugees would "inevitably" spread AIDS if they reached America.
    The show's host, Sonya Friedman, asked the congressman for a solution.

"I would certainly have them go back home," Smith said. "I don't think Haitians should get special treatment."

"So," Friedman asked, "the fact that they may be of a political refugee status means nothing?"

"Right," Smith said.

Jackson interrupted and the two men began shouting.

"If somebody landed here on a boat or a plane from Cuba," Jackson managed to say, "whatever disease they had, they would be received." But there was no time for him to mention that Cubans seeking asylum had recently slipped onto Guantánamo and promptly been flown to Florida, without talk of testing or medical expenses.

More shouting followed and Friedman cut in to take a telephone call from a viewer who identified himself as Jim from Ohio.

"Go ahead, Jim," Friedman said.

"You know," said Jim, "when we come to the border, from Canada or anyplace else, and we have vegetation of any kind, it's refused. It might be infected." So why, he went on, would we allow a sick human being into the United States?

Jackson's fight with Smith was part of a larger battle over the president's campaign promise to lift the ban on HIV-positive foreigners, Haitian or otherwise. The ban already had a Swiss-cheese quality to it, because people who didn't know or reveal that they were infected could enter the country. The Public Health Service favored lifting the ban because AIDS was not spread through casual contact and there were concerns that the ban was discouraging foreigners in the United States from seeking medical care.

But fear of AIDS still ran high on Capitol Hill, and when lawmakers got wind that Clinton might act on his campaign promise, the Republican-led Senate voted to make the ban permanent. Jackson's deadline for the president to reach a decision about Guantánamo passed without a word from the Oval Office, and Clinton later signed the congressional bill on the HIV ban into law, caving on yet another preelection pledge.

Yale's grand lobbying strategy was down to one last hope. Despite the overall HIV ban, the Justice Department could still release the refugees through humanitarian waivers or the attorney general's special "parole power." The latter was how Cappuccio, with authority from his boss, had brought in the pregnant women from Guantánamo. But Clinton still had no attorney general. His first choice, Zoë Baird, had seemed ideal for helping the refugees. A superstar liberal corporate lawyer, Baird was the spouse of a Yale law professor and lived just blocks away from Koh. But she'd been forced to withdraw her name over a tax issue with her nanny, and Clinton's current nominee, a little-known Florida prosecutor named Janet Reno, was weeks away from confirmation. That meant the team would have to return to the same transition officials who'd become increasingly hostile to Yale.

Mike Wishnie joined Koh and Ratner on a final trip to Washington to meet again with Michael Cardozo, who was now advising the temporary chief at Justice, Clinton pal Webster Hubbell. After walking along endless polished hallways, the Yale group was directed to a conference room dominated by an immense table. To Wishnie, it all felt very official and important, and he wondered if the team might finally swing the momentum in the refugees' favor.

But Mike could tell something was wrong right away. Cardozo came across as formal and distant. He'd brought several aides with him and they sat in a row, stone-faced, as Koh offered Yale's new solution to the situation.

You don't have to shut down the camp all at once, Koh told Cardozo. You can fly the refugees in over time, quietly. We've already proved it can be done this way. We'll place them with relatives or in city-sponsored housing in New York. We'll get them proper medical care. The press doesn't have to know about it and the political fallout will be minimal.

Wishnie had come to answer any questions Cardozo might ask about resettlement, but it never got that far. Before Koh had finished, one of Cardozo's aides shook his head and ticked off several legal technicalities that barred humanitarian waivers or parole for the Haitians. When Koh pointed out the flaws in his analysis, another aide jumped in to list more difficulties.

Mike looked on, seething. It was all a sham. Everyone in the room knew the refugees could be brought into the United States if Clinton wanted it to happen. The law just wasn't that complicated.

Refusing to give up, Koh methodically stripped away the Justice Department's legal pretenses one by one, until at last, Cardozo cut him off. There was a momentary pause.

"In the view of those close to the president," Cardozo said, "he can weather dead HIV-positive Haitians on Guantánamo better than the political fallout of letting them into the U.S."

* * *

Mike Wishnie did not go in for drama. His laugh was soft. He rarely shouted. When he got angry, it was usually in a quiet, smoldering way. He was silent as he walked out of Main Justice.

Earlier defeats in the case had left the students shocked, hurt, disgusted. But after Cardozo's final words, there were no more outbursts in New Haven, only a lock-and-load determination. If Clinton would not honor his campaign promises, if his officials were going to string along the refugees for months and ultimately sell them out for the crassest of political reasons, then Yale was going to drag the new administration back to court and settle things there once and for all.

Koh was dismayed that he'd taken Clinton at his word on anything. At least with the Bush officials, he and everyone else at Yale had known where they stood. He was all the more upset because he'd felt such a strong sense of destiny following the election. Clinton was going to reverse the direct return order, free the refugees on Guantánamo, and then appoint Koh as the chief lawyer of the State Department. But any question that Koh might forsake the final battle to accept the appointment at State now was answered after he received another call from Washington.

"We just wanted to let you know you're still in contention for legal adviser," a Clinton official told him.

"You're kidding me," Koh said, astonished.

"You can't assume there's a connection between the placement people and the Justice lawyers working on Haiti," the official shrugged.

Koh called to break the news to Ratner and Tringali.

"I think you should withdraw from the case and go for the State job," Ratner said.

Tringali agreed.

"You've taken things far enough," Ratner continued. "You've wanted this for a long, long time. Someone else can argue at the Supreme Court."

Koh understood that Ratner was advising him out of friendship, telling him, in effect, not to throw away his career—despite the fact that Ratner had always counseled against working for the government. But Koh had already made up his mind, haunted by an incident his father had often retold. After South Korea's democratic government fell in 1961, Kwang Lim and his colleagues at the Korean embassy in Washington all vowed they would never serve the new military regime. One by one, however, the others broke their promises until the elder Koh found himself standing almost alone against the coup.

"There will always be people like eels," Kwang Lim told his son. "They slither toward power on their bellies."

Now, thirty years later, Koh knew he was through with Clinton.

As the students had learned early in law school, only a small percentage of federal lawsuits actually go to trial, and a far smaller number—a tiny fraction of one percent—make it to the Supreme Court. Trial in a district court usually takes place years after a case is filed, if ever. And in the rare event that the Supreme Court hears a case, that stage is reached years later, following post-trial motions, an appeal to a circuit court, and then a petition asking the justices to review the case.

Yale's lawsuit could not have been more different. *Haitian Centers Council v. McNary* had played out with such speed and intensity that it might have been the legal equivalent of a perfect storm. In less than one year, the case was racing toward both a trial for the Bulkeley refugees *and* a Supreme Court argument on the direct return order. And there would be only five days between the two.

Though few had believed it would come to pass, the team had begun preparing for such a possibility when Koh and Joe Tringali had split up the Supreme Court and trial duties six months earlier. Koh was now pouring all his effort into the Supreme Court case, with a cadre of students to handle extra research and help arrange his practice oral arguments, or "mootings." Meanwhile, Tringali and another pack of students were gearing up for trial along with ACLU immigration expert Lucas Guttentag. Tringali may have been a gifted, meticulous attorney, but immigration law was a mystery to him. That was where Guttentag, who'd spent ten years in the field, came in. A tall, lean litigator who'd gone to law school with Koh, he knew the ins and outs of running a class action suit against the INS and was all too familiar with Lauri Filppu and the other lawyers at the Office of Immigration Litigation. He didn't like them one bit.

Well before Michael Cardozo slammed the door on the Guantánamo refugees, the team had begun trial preparations by reexamining why they were in court. Everyone, Koh included, agreed that securing the right to an attorney had become almost pointless. Even if the Haitians all won asylum with lawyers representing them in their hearings, they would remain locked up in Bulkeley because of the HIV ban.

With Yvonne and her compatriots pleading for freedom, Yale now committed to the goal Lisa Daugaard had researched so tenaciously and championed for so long: the unconditional release of everyone in the camp. Relying on the Constitution's due process clause, Yale would argue that it was illegal for the government to imprison the refugees indefinitely and without proper medical care.

The irony of the new strategy escaped no one. The strength of the refugees' case now rested on their having suffered for so long.

As Joe Tringali saw it, the trial team's task was to present a clear, well-organized account of the situation in Camp Bulkeley. Yale had a devastating story to tell—and a sympathetic audience in Judge Sterling Johnson, who would try the case himself, without a jury. As Koh taught his first-year students, the Constitution generally didn't provide for a jury trial in civil cases unless the plaintiff was seeking money damages. Going with Johnson alone was just fine with Tringali. The judge already seemed to favor the refugees, and if anything, a jury might have made the case trickier. A few anti-immigrant jurors could have thrown everything in doubt.

Unlike Lisa Daugaard, Joe had few qualms about the precise scope of the legal principles at issue. He knew a trial was less about the law than the facts. In his mind, the problem was that the sheer mass of evidence threatened to overwhelm the team's argument, burdening the judge with a lot of unnecessary information. Yale's task would be to dig through everything and select only the most dramatic, damning details. Tringali was confident that if Johnson understood what was happening on Guantánamo, the judge would rely on one or another of Yale's legal theories to get the Haitians out.

The biggest challenge involved the depositions. There were hundreds of possible witnesses scattered around, and outside, the country: refugees on Guantánamo, doctors in New York, public health and immigration experts in New England, government and military officials all over the place. Yale had taken about twenty-five depositions the previous spring in order to figure out the INS processing system on Guantánamo. Another thirty were now needed to document all the aspects of Bulkeley, and Tringali and the team would then have to decide on the list of witnesses to call at trial. But to leave time to pore through the deposition transcripts and prepare witnesses to testify, they had to finish all the remaining depositions in less than three weeks.

Lisa Daugaard set up a command post in her ACLU office. Working nonstop, she scheduled depositions; assigned team members to question and defend witnesses; suggested material for each witness to cover; ordered, reviewed, and organized transcripts; and tracked everything with a huge trial chart. A lot of it was grunt work, but that didn't bother her. She was learning how all the evidence fit together, angling to help write Yale's crucial post-trial summary of the case for Judge Johnson. The "proposed findings of fact and conclusions of law" would suggest rulings for the judge on every issue, and if all went well at trial, would serve as the foundation for Johnson's opinion. Lisa knew several of the legal arguments better than anyone on the team, and she wanted to work on the first draft herself.

With lawyers and students fanning out from Boston to North Carolina for depositions, two other team members headed back to Bulkeley: San Francisco attorney Robert Rubin and Tory's friend Veronique Sanchez, a sunny second-year student born to immigrants from Peru and Belgium. Rubin and Veronique had a pressing task. The government would not let any of the refugees fly to the United States to appear in court, so depositions taken in Bulkeley would be their only chance to testify about the camp.

Given her fluency in French, Veronique was a logical choice to join Rubin on the trip. The refugees would require plenty of preparation before testifying, and she wouldn't need an interpreter to work with them. But while she'd been to Bulkeley before, she was far more nervous this time, for she had only a rudimentary understanding of how a deposition worked. She'd never even seen one in person. Before leaving for the airport, she stuffed several books on pretrial practice into her backpack and tried to tell herself everything would be fine.

When she arrived on Guantánamo, the giddy optimism of Jesse Jackson's recent visit had faded. Talk of suicide was spreading and refugees were even turning on one another. It was just shouting at first, but then one man stabbed another in a fight, and Rubin had to intervene before the military resorted to force. Medical complaints were on the rise as well, with more people succumbing to full-blown AIDS. A few women were also suffering from searing cramps and heavy vaginal bleeding, as Yvonne had earlier. Apparently these were the side effects of Depo-Provera birth control injections, which some of the women claimed they had been pressured to get. Modeste Valme was faring the worst, and she lay outside her *kay,* whimpering, her children huddled beside her in fear.

Yvonne and the other committed fasters on the soccer field had grown still weaker. Most of those left were women, clad in white to symbolize their cause, and their tenacity had changed the balance of power among the refugees. Vilsaint Michel was still camp president in name, and the *militan* could still claim the legacy of last summer's uprising. But the moral authority in Bulkeley now belonged foremost to Yvonne and the quiet, weary women surrounding her.

The Yale visitors did what they could to comfort the Haitians, and Veronique, a devout Catholic, joined them in prayer. With trial looming, though, the focus of the visit had to be the depositions. They planned to conduct almost a dozen in three days, with Veronique handling three or four. No matter which refugees she questioned, it would be a challenge. But to her surprise, Rubin suggested she be responsible for Yvonne. Of all the depositions, Veronique felt Yvonne's had the highest stakes. Now an icon for the students and perhaps the most eloquent person in Bulkeley, she would surely have taken the stand at trial had that been possible. Instead, it would fall on Veronique to capture her story for the court.

Rubin had faith in Veronique, but he was less than certain about Yvonne. After hearing so much about her strength and charisma from everyone at Yale, he was stunned when he saw her for the first time—a frail, passive figure in a white nightgown, so thin now that she was seeking cover in the shade of a telephone pole.

Well into its third week, the strike was growing harder for her. She kept telling herself and everyone around her that she felt strong, that her body did not need food, that God and the cause would sustain her. She sang with the other strikers—"When we stand firm, our hearts are not troubled; We know the road is not easy, but hard"—recited passages from the Bible, prayed for her children.

But Yvonne's fears were building. There was no sign that Clinton might change his mind, and she was growing feeble. Her muscles ached, her knees hurt, she ran fevers. Her skin felt strange, like paper, and her mouth was so dry at times that her voice would become a raspy whisper. Yet after being rushed to the medical clinic and put on an IV, she'd pulled the needle out of her arm and marched back to the field. She felt she had no choice. The strike was all she had left.

Rubin had serious doubts about whether Yvonne could handle the stress of a deposition. He warned that the government lawyers might be hard on her during cross-examination. There are other people who can testify instead, he told her. You don't have to do this.

Yvonne said she understood but was not about to give up her one chance to question a lawyer from the INS. Rubin paused. It actually doesn't work that way, he explained. If you have some things you want to ask the government, I'll try to get answers for you.

Yvonne shook her head in disbelief. She was the one in prison. They had all the answers. She didn't know anything. Why would they be grilling *her*?

In the end, she decided to go ahead. She wanted to have her say, and despite Rubin's description of the deposition as a procedure to prepare for trial, she clung to a private hope. She believed that if she conveyed her situation forcefully enough to the INS lawyers face-to-face, they would let her go—not after some mysterious legal proceeding in a city called Brooklyn, but immediately.

It was early in the evening when Rubin and Veronique guided Yvonne to a trailer at the edge of the camp. The office inside was air-conditioned and she hugged herself to stay warm. She was tired and nauseous, but her anxiety made her more alert than she'd been in days.

Three men from the government introduced themselves, including the lawyer who would cross-examine her, OIL attorney Lauri Filppu. Yvonne shuddered as he approached her. He had a cold gaze, she thought, as if he were probing for a weakness.

Veronique had her own anxieties, but Filppu and the court reporter receded from her mind as she tried to develop a natural give-and-take through her questioning. Answering through an interpreter, Yvonne recounted the work she and Antenor had done for Aristide and all that had followed: the beatings and the cigarette burn, the midnight flight on the crammed boat, the news that she might have a fatal illness, the endless frustration of waiting, the pain after her Depo-Provera shot, the soldiers attacking in riot gear.

She kept her composure through it all, even the miscarriage, but after Veronique asked her to read a letter she'd written to her children, Yvonne turned away, fighting back tears. It was painful enough to reveal the private details of her life to this stranger Filppu. But the skepticism she saw in his eyes as she testified was too much to bear. She'd even shown him the scar on her arm. What else could he possibly want?

Filppu, it turned out, wanted a lot. With Robert Rubin taking over to defend Yvonne on cross-examination, he demanded to know about her arrival on Guantánamo, the confusion surrounding her multiple blood tests, even her INS identification card and bar-code bracelet. He then dragged her through the details of her initial HIV diagnosis—a traumatic event she tried to keep out of her mind—and pressed her, repeatedly, to explain what happened to people with her illness.

Yvonne's stomach churned. Everyone knew what happened to people with HIV, she thought. They got sick. They died. What could this man possibly gain from asking her that?

Filppu then interrogated her about the details of the previous summer's riots. Hundreds of soldiers had marched into Bulkeley that day, and she couldn't tell him who had thrown her to the ground, who had handcuffed her, or who had dug a boot heel into her neck. Yvonne could see that he doubted her story, but there was nothing more she could add.

The military cut the deposition short at nine, ordering her to return to the camp until the next morning, and she shuffled back to the soccer field, exhausted and consumed with worry. How could she persuade Filppu she was telling the truth? Was there something she shouldn't have said? Had she made some kind of mistake?

Veronique, deeply troubled herself, rode home with Rubin to her quarters at the main base for the night. By nature, she had a strong impulse to understand and forgive. For months she had tried to believe that the government lawyers were just doing their jobs, that they couldn't be as evil as her fellow students were making them out to be. But she was appalled by what Lauri Filppu had done to Yvonne.

The next morning, Yvonne felt terrible. Now twenty-five days into her fast, her head was cloudy and she had trouble focusing, but she went forward with the cross-examination anyway. If there were any chance of persuading Filppu to free her, no matter how slim, she was going to take it—and if he merely intended to interrogate her, she just wanted to get it over with. She'd had enough.

Back in the trailer, Filppu prodded her about returning to Haiti.

"As long as there is democracy at home," Yvonne offered, "I will go back."

"Would you be willing to stay at Guantánamo until there is democracy in Haiti?"

"I will *die* here before there is democracy."

"Is that because you expect to die on the hunger strike?"

We started the hunger strike because of our mistreatment, she replied.

"What is the mistreatment that you speak of?"

Her pulse began to rise. What did she have to do? Walk him around the camp?

"Nou malad," she retorted. "We are sick. At least they say we're sick, but look at how we're treated."

"I'll get back to those issues in a moment," Filppu said, "but let's return to the question of your desires to leave Guantánamo. If the opportunity were available, would you be willing to go to a refugee camp in a third country?"

She stared at him, incredulous. "Why would you send me to another camp?"

"What I'm trying to find out," he told her, "is whether you have any objection to living in another refugee camp in another country, for example, such as Venezuela or the Dominican Republic or Honduras."

"Why would you send me to another refugee camp?" she cried, temples throbbing. "It's like taking me from one concentration camp and putting me in another concentration camp!"

Filppu did not react, which only upset her more. As far as she could tell, he had absolutely no compassion; in fact, it seemed he had no emotions at all.

He needled her with more questions, this time returning to her medical condition. Have you been prescribed AZT? Do you know why it was prescribed? Have you taken it? When did you get your Depo-Provera shot? Isn't it true that a nurse told you about the side effects? Did you know you're not supposed to get pregnant if you have HIV? Did you know it could cause problems for the baby?

The baby. *Her* baby. The prison cell at Recherches Criminelles flashed through her mind. The blood on the floor.

Filppu asked another question, and yet another. Yvonne's heart raced and she began to shake. She wanted to grab his throat. She hated him. She hated his government. She hated everything they had done to her.

The pain in her temples spread to her neck and the room began to blur. She felt Rubin's hand on her wrist—gentle, protective. He began shouting at Filppu.

Woozy, eyelids growing heavy, Yvonne looked over at her lawyer, a scowl on his face, and then at Filppu, still wearing the same cold expression.

She tried to breathe but the air was too thin. It felt as if someone were standing on her chest. The room grew dark and Filppu and Rubin disappeared. There was nothing but a ringing sound, and then that faded, too, and it was silent.

Yvonne's deposition ended at ten minutes after twelve as she slumped against Rubin, unconscious.

Nine

THE SUPREME COURT

EVERY JANUARY, KOH took his civil procedure students to Washington to observe a Supreme Court argument. As disillusioned as Tory had been by her first semester of law school—before the Guantánamo case had begun—the visit still enthralled her. The courtroom itself was more intimate than she'd expected, but every bit as stately, with soaring columns, an immense mahogany bench, and marble friezes representing Truth, Justice, and the Defense of Human Rights. Filing into the gallery with her classmates, she'd felt enveloped by history, inspired by the majesty of the law.

Long before law school, Tory had imagined the Supreme Court justices themselves as larger than life, but when they emerged from behind the thick crimson curtains, she was stunned by how ordinary they appeared, swallowed up by their robes and dwarfed by the high-backed leather chairs. Justice Harry Blackmun was a wisp of a man well into his eighties, while Justice John Paul Stevens turned out to be a grandfatherly figure with a bow tie. Tory's strongest impression, though, was of the acerbic, sharp-witted Antonin Scalia, a boisterous justice with a wide, flat head and a curl to his lip that quickly twisted into a sneer. She'd cringed as Scalia, a former law professor, had cut the lawyers to ribbons, but she returned to New Haven still firm in her belief that the Supreme Court was a just, honorable institution.

The stay orders issued by the court in the Haiti case, however, had changed everything for her. She had come to see the justices as callous if not downright cruel. Now, in March of 1993, she was on her way back to face them, this time with her name on the brief, her analysis in the argument, and her clients' fate in the balance. After researching a key issue in the direct return case, she finally understood many of the litigation's subtleties. But she also recognized that the battle between the Yale team and President Clinton could be framed by a single question: Did the law allow the administration to intercept political refugees on the open ocean and force them back to their persecutors? Based on their exhaustive research, Tory and the rest of the team had concluded the answer was an unconditional no.

They had plenty of distinguished allies in the legal community. At Yale, professors had begun to drop by Koh's office, one by one, volunteering to put their names on the brief. Not long before the filing date, Dean Guido Calabresi asked Koh who had signed on. Koh told him and inquired if the dean ever put his own name on a brief. "No, Harold," Calabresi had said. "But I'll sign this one." Simpson Thacher partner Cyrus Vance, a former secretary of state, also signed the brief, and pro-refugee amicus briefs poured into the court from members of Congress, former attorneys general, the U.N. high commissioner for refugees, and many major human rights organizations.

The Yale team and its supporters agreed that the deciding principle was clearly set out in two laws: the Refugee Act of 1980 (a congressional statute), and Article 33 of the U.N. Refugee Convention, drafted after World War II. They were the same two legal provisions that had been at issue since Yale first went to court to halt the direct return order. Article 33 mandated that contracting nations not "expel or return (*'refouler'*)" refugees "in any manner whatsoever" to a place where they feared persecution. In similar terms, the Refugee Act required that the U.S. attorney general "not deport or return any alien" to such a place.

Based on this principle of non-return, or non-refoulement, the Second Circuit Court of Appeals in New York City had already ruled for the refugees; the question now was whether five of the nine Supreme Court justices would follow suit. Everyone figured that Justice Blackmun, Koh's mentor and the most liberal voice on the court, was certain to side with Yale. The team also felt optimistic about the other liberal justice, John Paul Stevens, for despite his unpredictable nature, he'd joined Blackmun in opposing both Supreme Court stays in the Haiti case. Yale would still need three more votes, possibly from the court's moderate conservatives: Sandra Day O'Connor, Anthony Kennedy, and David Souter. But for various reasons, none seemed better than a fifty-fifty shot, and that was where the archconservative Justice Scalia came in.

As the students already knew, Scalia was on a mission to change the way courts read congressional statutes. The justice believed that the dominant method—determining the congressional intent behind an act's words—invited judges to rewrite the laws. To remedy this ill, Scalia demanded that courts quit trying to divine what the members of Congress had in mind when they passed a law. Instead, he wanted the courts to focus on the language of the statute itself, relying on the words' ordinary meanings, unless the statute defined them in some special way. He often used a dictionary in writing his opinions, and according to some court insiders, he and his law clerks would sit down to interpret a statute together before oral argument, with only the words of the law and a dictionary to guide them. His approach also rejected "legislative history," the reports and debate transcripts that Congress churned out as it considered a bill, since none of that material was part of the law itself.

Critics charged that Scalia's "plain language" or "textualist" theory was just a tool to serve his right-wing agenda, for it often seemed to produce conservative results. But the theory was on the rise within the federal judiciary. Even the liberal Second Circuit in New York had relied on it when interpreting the Refugee Act—and declaring direct returns illegal. Indeed, despite Scalia's politics, his philosophy seemed in this instance to support Yale's position.

According to the plain language of the Refugee Act and Article 33, the government could not "return" the refugees. But that, Koh and the students reasoned, was precisely what Clinton was doing, and neither of the laws defined "return" in some narrow, specialized way that would have permitted the president's policy. In fact, the order issued by Bush and adopted by Clinton amounted to a written confession in Yale's view, for it directed the Coast Guard to "*return* the vessel and its passengers to the country from which it came."

The use of the French word "*refouler*" in Article 33 only seemed to reinforce the team's position. Veronique Sanchez found that the French newspaper *Le Monde* had used "*refouler*" to describe the direct return policy, and the French-English dictionary *Larousse* defined the word to mean "drive back" or "repel." That didn't quite mean "return," but it certainly seemed to cover what the president was doing.

Given what he considered to be a rock-solid position on plain language, Koh planned to direct much of his argument toward Justice Scalia. But exactly how the justice would react, no one could be sure. Everyone on the team knew politics mattered at the Supreme Court, and in a case challenging presidential authority outside U.S. borders, it would matter a great deal. As Yale saw it, Scalia would have to make a decision. If he was really committed to a principled textualist method and not merely to conservative results, then he would have to support the refugees against the government. Lisa reduced it to blunter terms: it was a choice between the rule of law and the unapologetic justification of raw executive power.

While the rest of the team would descend on Washington the night before the argument, Koh arrived three days earlier so he could prepare undisturbed. He went out to a convenience store and bought several cans of soup and some other groceries. Then he hunkered down in his dreary Capitol Hill hotel room. Surrounded by court filings and legal pads, Koh read, reread; wrote, rewrote; paced, rehearsed; replied, rebutted. He see-sawed from a firm conviction that Yale could win to utter hopelessness. His exhaustion and isolation didn't help. Neither did the hate mail he'd been receiving. "We never should have let your Chink ass in this country," began one letter. "Go home, Gook," said another, "you and all your Ivy League prima donnas." As a law clerk, Koh recalled similar vitriol flooding Blackmun's chambers, mostly over *Roe v. Wade.* "I try not to let it affect me," Blackmun had sighed. "Just remember: the law is not a popularity contest."

But the hate mail, Koh realized, was in some sense the point. Nobody cared about the Haitians; nobody gave a damn about the terrible human cost of the direct return policy. And yet somehow he had to persuade five justices to acknowledge that cost. If he didn't, he knew he couldn't win no matter how strong his legal argument was.

The almost insurmountable problem, he believed, was that most Americans saw Haitians as the ultimate "other"—more alien, perhaps, than anyone else. Nothing was at stake when people like Yvonne Pascal and Frantz Guerrier suffered because so few people identified with them. Even another minority group—Korean Americans, in fact—had asked him why he was spending all of his time helping "those Haitians instead of us." "They *are* us," Koh had said angrily, pointing to the internment camps of World War II and other abuses suffered by Asian Americans.

But if the connection to the Haitians wasn't apparent to his fellow Koreans, it remained painfully clear in his own mind. Under the policy of direct return, they could all have been sent back to Korea if they'd fled by boat after the 1961 coup in Seoul. Indeed, when Koh finally made his case to the Supreme Court, he would be arguing for the very principles that had saved his parents and made his own life in America possible.

———

The Solicitor General's Office kept a close eye on the direct return case after Clinton's election, and no lawyer followed the developments more keenly than Maureen Mahoney. A former law clerk to Chief Justice William H. Rehnquist, Mahoney was one of Solicitor General Kenneth Starr's top assistants during the Bush administration, and he had entrusted her with day-to-day responsibility for the direct return suit. Had the case gone to the Supreme Court while Starr was still with the government, he would have argued it himself. But with the changeover in administrations, Starr was now gone, and since Clinton's disorganized transition team had not yet named a new solicitor general, the task of arguing the case fell to her.

Mahoney believed Clinton had done the right thing by continuing the direct return policy, which she saw as an imperfect solution to a tragic problem. Then again, she didn't think her personal views on the policy mattered. That was the president's business. Her duty as a lawyer was to zealously protect the power of the Oval Office. She would therefore argue, as Starr had at the Second Circuit, that the principle of non-return had no force on the high seas.

According to the Refugee Act, the government could not "deport or return" refugees. But as Mahoney read that phrase, "return" was a special legal term that didn't have its ordinary English meaning. She believed that it applied strictly to aliens *on American soil* who didn't technically qualify for "deportation" proceedings. That, she reasoned, was why Congress had used the peculiar wording "deport or return" and why Article 33 had used a similar parallel phrase. By Mahoney's interpretation, then, Haitians intercepted *outside* the United States were not being "returned" to Haiti at all, at least not as forbidden under the Refugee Act.

She knew there were problems with this argument, the first being that the ordinary meaning of the word "return" obviously applied to what the Coast Guard was doing—and the presidential order itself had used the word "return." In addition, the purpose of both the Refugee Act and Article 33 was to protect refugees from persecution, and that would influence how the justices saw the case. Yet Mahoney was confident in her position. She knew, as Koh did, that the court usually deferred to the president when it came to foreign affairs. In fact, Mahoney had particular faith in Justice Scalia. Earlier in his career he'd advised the White House on legal matters, and she believed he was especially inclined to protect presidential authority.

Her biggest concern was Blackmun. She shared the conservative view that he often decided cases on "the equities"—his own views of basic fairness—rather than the law. Indeed, while admirers like Koh praised the justice's compassion, critics believed he was so focused on the hardships of specific human beings that he distorted the broader principles at issue. Mahoney's goal with Blackmun was to convince him the equities weren't one-sided. Refugees could die in the Windward Passage, she would argue, and a policy that encouraged them to stay home would save lives.

Mahoney also knew that Blackmun had a penchant for asking non-legal questions. In a suit dealing with a person in a vegetative state, the justice had asked Kenneth Starr if he'd ever seen someone in such a condition. Mahoney suspected that in this instance, Blackmun might ask her about the human rights situation in Haiti—perhaps even if she'd been there. She briefly contemplated going, but decided it was irrelevant. The White House had called on her to make a legal argument, not a fact-gathering trip to Port-au-Prince.

Her appearance before the justices, the ninth of her career, would make for a striking contradiction. A conservative Starr protégée hired under Bush, she was going to court to defend a Republican policy. But she was doing so on the orders of a new Democratic president who'd once branded that policy both illegal and immoral. The ironies of the situation did not, however, interfere with her dedication to winning the case. Mahoney was a fiercely competitive lawyer, and a 7–2 or 6–3 ruling for the president would not be enough for her. She was aiming for 9–0.

"*Manman* had to take a little trip. She'll be back soon."

That was all Thérèse told Yvonne's boys after their mother fled. She figured the less Daniel and Jacques knew, the better. She didn't want to scare them, nor did she want six-year-old Jacques babbling about where his mother had gone. The police officer involved in Yvonne's arrest was still skulking around the neighborhood. Thérèse knew that gossip about her daughter would quickly be relayed to the wrong people.

She counted the days quietly, careful to keep her worries from her grandchildren. But after two months passed without a word, Thérèse's fears about Yvonne began to mount. She stole away to the cinder block church almost every day to pray, and by the four-month mark she was clinging to the slightest of hopes. Thérèse knew her daughter. No matter the circumstances, Yvonne would have called the pawnshop or otherwise sent word by now—if she were alive. But the letters Yvonne wrote from Guantánamo never arrived, and the messages she'd left at the shop didn't get through. Slowly, Thérèse yielded to the inevitable. Her oldest child, the one who'd burned most brightly, was gone.

Two hundred miles away, on Guantánamo, Yvonne had told Koh how much she missed her family. He'd listened with a sympathetic ear, but privately assumed they'd all been killed. In fact, when Koh woke up in Washington on the day of his Supreme Court argument, Yvonne's parents and children were very much alive in Port-au-Prince, though they would not remain there for long. Paramilitary thugs would soon attack the shanty. There would be bullets and gasoline and screaming, and like Yvonne herself the year before, the family would flee Cite Soleil in search of refuge. Like Yvonne, too, they would have to decide whether to escape Haiti by boat.

The team gathered for breakfast in the Supreme Court's cramped cafeteria. Koh's wife and daughter had made the trip, sleeping in a separate hotel room as he prepared, and six-year-old Emily had a new burgundy winter coat for the occasion. The students were all in their best suits, clutching backpacks, an air of nervous optimism about them. Tory had stayed over with Sarah Cleveland, who was now clerking for a judge in Washington, and the former third year buoyed Tory's spirits with her conviction that Yale could win the case.

Every weekday, Justice Blackmun went to the cafeteria with his clerks just after eight a.m., and true to habit, he was there that morning. Worried about the appearance of impropriety, Koh had avoided him for months, and he watched from afar as Mary-Christy brought Emily over to say hello. But Koh had come to breakfast that day precisely because he wanted at least to see Blackmun, and when the two made eye contact, the justice gave him a friendly wave from across the room. Feeling reassured, Koh headed down the court's glowing marble hallway, his father's briefcase in hand. But as he entered the courtroom, the fear that had loomed for days closed in on him. Though he tried to concentrate on his notes, he could only think about the whispering and rustling behind him as observers streamed into the gallery.

Moments before the justices were expected, Michael Ratner appeared at his side. "There's a ton of people here," he murmured. "Don't look back."

Koh couldn't help it. He turned around and discovered a sea of expectant, familiar faces: his family; his students, new and old; a host of Clinton officials; many of the current Justice lawyers; Paul Cappuccio, who was now in private practice; Jesse Jackson and his entourage; Ted Olson, Koh's old boss at the Justice Department; scores of human rights activists; the press.

And yet, for all the people he knew there that day, Koh found himself gazing instead into the eyes of dozens of Haitians he'd never met. Then he turned back to face the bench, absolutely petrified.

The clock struck ten.

Tory and the rest of the gallery stood as the justices filed out from behind the curtains. As much as the last year had jaundiced her, she was still awed by the ceremony of it all. "Oyez! Oyez! Oyez!" cried the marshal of the court, using an ancient term for "Hear ye." "All persons having business before the Honorable, the Supreme Court of the United States, are admonished to draw near and give their attention, for the court is now sitting! God save the United States and this Honorable Court!"

The students settled into their seats, legal pads at the ready, and Deputy Solicitor General Maureen Mahoney approached the lectern. Tory could see only the back of her dark suit and her straight, shoulder-length blond hair, the justices arrayed in an imposing wall before her.

Mahoney had her usual courtroom jitters, but was determined to keep the argument as unemotional as possible, focused instead on abstract legal principles. She could not afford to have the justices imagining a Coast Guard cutter delivering frightened refugees to the Haitian military. Adopting a dry, dispassionate tone, she declared that the case was not about the principle of non-return but, rather, the president's emergency powers "to prevent a mass migration of aliens across the high seas."

Behind her flat delivery was the warning of an invasion of Haitian refugees. Indeed, while Mahoney believed she was sticking to the law,

Lisa Daugaard believed her argument was playing off the most base of emotions: fear. In the previous May alone, Mahoney told the justices, "more than 10,000 Haitians crowded into unseaworthy vessels and set sail for our shores." It was to stem this tide that the president had issued the executive order now before the court. "The threat of the out-migration continues," Mahoney said. As many as 100,000 Haitians were poised to flee if given the chance, compelling the recent decision by the White House to maintain the direct return policy.

To soften her position, Mahoney repeated Clinton's claim that he was resorting to a humanitarian measure to save hundreds, perhaps thousands, of lives. She did not say, however, that the people who'd been returned by the Coast Guard were safe. In fact, she conceded that a "variety of political and economic conditions" continued to drive people from the country. But she assured the court that the president had set up asylum processing procedures in Haiti itself, so those with legitimate fears of persecution could get out.

The students were not in the least surprised by Mahoney's argument. It was the court's reaction that made their hearts sink. If provoked, the justices could attack a lawyer like a pack of wolves, but that morning they showed no inclination to go after the administration's attorney. Nobody asked Mahoney to explain how the president's order squared with the principle of protecting refugees, and Justice Scalia said nothing about the interpretation of the word "return." Instead, the justices asked simple, polite questions that Tory felt she could have answered over breakfast.

Justice Stevens finally cut Mahoney off mid-sentence, giving Yale a glimmer of hope. "None of this has anything to do with the legal issue in front of us," he declared. Stevens demanded that Mahoney address an issue separate from non-return: Where did the president of the United States get the *affirmative* power to intercept political refugees on the open ocean and repatriate them against their will?

Mahoney quickly pointed to two laws on the president's authority to bar foreigners from "entry" into the United States.

But don't those laws deal only with *entering* the country? he asked. Isn't that different from giving the president the power to *return* people somewhere?

Mahoney stumbled and Stevens repeated that the laws spoke to entry, not return. Mahoney tried again. The only way for the president to stop refugees from *entering* the country, she said, was by *returning* them to Haiti.

Several students shook their heads. Before the direct return order, the Bush administration had intercepted people and taken them to Guantánamo to prevent them from reaching the United States. Now Clinton had the same option.

Seeming to echo their thoughts, Stevens asked why the president couldn't send the refugees somewhere other than Haiti.

"Well—" Mahoney started.

"That would be consistent with the statutory authority to keep everybody out of the United States," he went on.

"Uh . . ." Mahoney was struggling now, casting about for a response. The students' hopes rose. This was the best possible situation: one of the justices pressing the refugees' position himself.

But then, suddenly, Justice Stevens backed off—and gave her the answer. Maybe, he agreed, the president could not take the refugees elsewhere "as a practical matter." The only way to bar them from entering the United States was to forcibly return them to Haiti.

"That's the point," Mahoney quickly agreed. There was no other solution.

The students looked on, bewildered. What about Guantánamo? And what about the Refugee Act and Article 33? They weren't rules of convenience. They said the U.S. couldn't return refugees, *period*.

But Stevens pushed no further, leaving Mahoney in the clear. Plowing through the rest of her argument, she reiterated that as long as the Haitians were in international waters, they had no rights at all. The judges at the Second Circuit Court of Appeals had treated Kenneth Starr with scorn when he'd suggested as much. But today there was only silence from the bench, and the disconcerted group in the gallery watched as Mahoney, surprised at how smoothly the argument had gone, gathered up her papers.

"Well, before you sit down," came a soft voice, "a couple of irrelevant questions." It was Justice Blackmun.

True to Mahoney's prediction, he began by asking whether she had ever been to Haiti. "No, Your Honor, I have not," Mahoney said.

Then came a second question. "Are you," he asked, "familiar with a book called *The Comedians* by Graham Greene?"

Tory glanced around her. Other lawyers were whispering to one another, shaking their heads.

"No, Your Honor," Mahoney finally said, her voice cracking. "I'm sorry, I'm not."

"I recommend it to you," Blackmun admonished.

* * *

As Koh listened to Mahoney's mild exchanges with the justices, the situation became very clear to him. The court was on her side, and he would have to scratch and claw his way to a five-justice majority. Although he had to cast his arguments in legal terms, the message Koh wanted to send was closer to a newspaper headline: this was an abuse of presidential power with catastrophic human consequences.

Ratner whispered some last words of encouragement as Koh got to his feet. Tense, angry, he limped to the lectern, adjusted his notes—and then, looking up, had to stop himself from taking a quick step backward. He'd heard lawyers complain that the lectern was unnervingly close to the bench, but given all the time he'd spent at the Supreme Court, he'd assumed it would not throw him off.

He was wrong. As if framed in a film close-up, the justices occupied his entire field of vision, with the chief justice so close Koh could see the age spots speckling his forehead. If Rehnquist had leaned forward, the two men could almost have shaken hands. Blackmun was right beside Rehnquist, his gray hair swept back high on his forehead. Out on the wings, just within Koh's sight, were Justice Thomas, expressionless, and Justice Souter, who wore an enigmatic smile.

Koh roused himself. The clock was running. Clenching the lectern, he struggled to say the traditional salutation, "Mr. Chief Justice and may it please the Court." His voice surprised him. Amplified throughout the courtroom, it sounded strong and assured, and the fear drained away, leaving only an overwhelming sense of urgency.

Your Honors, he began, we are *not* claiming a right to enter the United States. We ask only that the Haitian refugees not be forced back to the land they are fleeing. There are seven hundred islands between Haiti and the United States. Haitians escaping persecution could go to the Bahamas, the Cayman Islands, Cuba, the Virgin Islands, or any number of other places, but they cannot because the United States government has erected a floating Berlin Wall around Haiti. If the administration's goal is to save lives, it can bring the refugees to Guantánamo. Returning Haitians to the Cedras regime is not, as the government claims, a way to rescue them. It is nothing more than aiding and abetting their persecutors.

Koh felt he'd gotten off to a good start, but he didn't expect an easy time of it. Moments later, the serious questioning began. Instead of an interrogation from the conservatives, though, he got a deceptively simple query from Justice Stevens.

I understand the non-return principle of the Refugee Act, he said to Koh. But what if the act has no force outside of the United States? Then couldn't the Coast Guard send back Haitians found at sea?

Koh listened carefully. He thought Stevens was tossing out a friendly question, giving Koh a chance to say that *of course* that couldn't be the law. He seized the moment to remind the court of the Refugee Act's purpose: to protect refugees wherever they might be found.

"Yes, I understand," the justice interrupted. But if the act *doesn't* apply at sea, couldn't the Haitians be sent back?

Koh's gut went tight. He'd been sure Stevens was on his side. "Your Honor, what we're saying is that—"

"Let me just state my question," the justice ordered, "so you understand it clearly."

Tory squirmed in her seat. She knew, as Koh had taught in class, that it was unwise to concede anything in oral argument if at all possible. But she could see that Koh's evasiveness was irritating Stevens. The justice wanted a straight answer.

Struggling to understand why his presumed ally was being so difficult, Koh finally gave in. Yes, he said. If the non-return principle doesn't apply beyond our borders, the United States would be free to repatriate the refugees.

But that couldn't be the case, Koh went on. Otherwise, America could send Jews back to Nazi Germany; Tiananmen Square democracy activists back to China; Aristide himself back to Haiti—so long as they were outside the United States. Think, Koh pleaded, of how other countries will act if we adopt this position. It amounts to saying we're bound by no law at all. We could simply gun down the refugees in open water.

An energetic voice cut him off. Since all these bad things might happen, they must be illegal. Is that your argument?

Koh's head jerked to the left. It was Justice Scalia.

You're confusing law and morality, the justice was implying. You're assuming that because something is terrible, there has to be a law against it.

"Justice Scalia, there *is* a law against it," Koh protested, starting to cite the Refugee Act.

"Well, let's talk about the law," Scalia cut in, as if he were addressing a student. He pointed to an earlier Supreme Court decision, *INS v. Stevic,* that dealt with the Refugee Act. In that case, he said, we never suggested the act had force outside the United States.

Koh paused. As respectfully as he could, he reminded the justice that the act's reach wasn't at issue in *Stevic*. The *Stevic* case was absolutely irrelevant. It had to do with the standard of proof in an asylum hearing. It didn't say a word about whether the law applied beyond American borders.

At that point, with most other justices, Koh might have returned to the purpose of the Refugee Act, which he believed was to protect refugees whether they were on the high seas or anywhere else. But he knew that if he were to have any chance of bringing Scalia to Yale's side, he had to make the plain-language argument instead, and he had to do it now.

Koh proceeded by reading the act aloud against its predecessor statute, an exercise in which every word counted. Having spent so many hours pondering the laws, he could repeat them word for word even half-asleep.

In the original 1952 formulation, Koh told Scalia, the non-return rule had obviously protected only refugees inside the United States:

> The Attorney General is authorized to *withhold deportation* of any alien *within the United States* to any country [where the alien fears persecution].

But compare that law to its successor, Koh said. In the Refugee Act of 1980, Congress had cut out the words "within the United States":

> The Attorney General *shall not deport or return* any alien [to any country where the alien fears persecution].

There was, Koh pointed out to Scalia, only one reasonable way to read that change: the Refugee Act now applied *outside* the United States as well as within it.

That wasn't all, Koh added. The 1952 law spoke only to "withholding deportation" of refugees. The 1980 law, though, ordered the attorney general not to "deport *or return*" refugees. As Yale had argued in its brief, "deportation" was a narrow, technical term in immigration law, relating only to people on American soil. But the word "return" had no special definition. According to the principles of textualism, therefore, it had to be read according to its ordinary meaning. In short, "no return" meant "no return."

Scalia's response, after all of Koh's efforts, was a shrug. Sure, the justice said. Congress added new words. But we looked at those additions in the *Stevic* case, and we said they didn't change the law's meaning. If Congress had wanted the non-return rule to apply at sea, Scalia said, surely we would have mentioned it in *Stevic*.

Koh was stunned. He'd argued as well as he could have hoped, relying on the words of a law that he and the team were certain supported the refugees. But Justice Scalia wasn't dealing with the plain language of the Refugee Act at all. Instead, he was relying on what Koh considered to be tangential comments from an irrelevant prior decision.

Things only got worse. During his debate with Koh, Scalia had also been discussing Yale's backup law, Article 33 of the U.N. Convention, the model for the Refugee Act. We also examined Article 33 in *Stevic,* Scalia announced. And we said it offered the same protections as the Refugee Act. That meant, Scalia implied, that Article 33 doesn't apply at sea, either.

No law protected the refugees.

Tory had grown steadily more discouraged as she watched the back-and-forth with Scalia unfold. For once, Koh did not appear in command of the situation. She kept expecting him to take over, similar to the moment in class when he revealed the hidden logic of the law and the jumble of words in a case suddenly became coherent. But as hard as Koh fought, that moment never came.

All the students felt that Scalia was being a hypocrite. The text of the law was right there in front of the justice, and he was dodging it in the most intellectually dishonest fashion. As dismayed as her teammates were, though, Lisa remained philosophical, even stoic. In her estimation, they had come to the Supreme Court simply to make a statement. She'd been certain Yale would lose; there was nothing Koh or anyone else could have done to prevent it. The only issue for her was whether Koh would force the justices to confront the consequences of the president's policy, and she believed he'd done that.

The exchanges with Justices Stevens and Scalia had taken just six or seven minutes. But they'd revealed that one of Yale's two presumably solid votes and the wild-card vote of Justice Scalia were both in grave doubt. The full significance of the two justices' remarks would only become clear months later, though, and as the brass clock high above the bench swept toward eleven, Koh fought to dislodge the impression that an armada of refugees was headed for America.

Just 10,000 Haitians had been screened into the United States during the nine months before Bush had issued the direct return order, Koh said. That was a modest figure next to the streams of refugees from other countries welcomed by the United States in the past. One of the amicus briefs had the data: 900,000 Cubans since Castro had taken power; 250,000 Soviet Jews from 1975 to 1991; 135,000 Vietnamese in 1975 alone; and on and on.

All we're asking for here, Koh said, is temporary safe haven for the refugees outside of Haiti. It doesn't even have to be in the United States. "This is not a polite, bloodless process," he added, mentioning Frantz Guerrier and another refugee who'd been repatriated. "Our clients, our named plaintiffs, were interdicted on the high seas. Their boats were destroyed by the U.S. Coast Guard. They were taken to Guantánamo and held behind barbed wire in U.S. captivity for months. And then, when they asked for lawyers before they had an asylum hearing, they were forced back to Haiti. Mr. Guerrier was driven off the boat with fire hoses. He was fingerprinted, identified by the Haitian military. That night, he was beaten, his left arm was fractured, and he went into hiding." But refugees in Guerrier's position, Koh said, could no longer flee for safety. They were trapped in Haiti.

Yet for all of Koh's passion, the justices merely sat, silent, a few of them rocking in their chairs. There were almost no questions. Experienced observers in the gallery took this as a sign that most members of the court had already made up their minds about the case. But Koh had spent days pondering his conclusion, struggling to come up with something that would reach the justices on a personal level. As the small warning light flashed to tell him the argument was almost over, he leaned forward, clutching the podium.

"Your Honors," he pleaded, "ours is a nation of refugees. Most of our ancestors came here by boat. If they could do this to the Haitians, they could do this to any of us."

The justices, however, were already setting aside the briefs, and the businesslike chief justice cut Koh off with a perfunctory thank-you. Rehnquist gave Maureen Mahoney two minutes of rebuttal time, then brusquely announced that the case was submitted.

Precisely one minute later, as everyone filed out of the courtroom, the justices had moved on to a case between South Dakota and the Cheyenne River Sioux tribe over hunting and fishing rights.

* * *

Now they could only wait. It was Tuesday, and the court would meet for conference on Friday to discuss the case and vote. Unless it was close and a justice needed persuading one way or another by a draft opinion, the decision would be made before conference was over. But then it would likely take three months before the court's opinion was completed and the decision announced to the outside world.

Koh pressed the refugees' cause to the media the rest of the day, ending with an appearance on the PBS *NewsHour*. Sandy Berger, Clinton's deputy national security adviser, refused to debate him in person. Berger made the president's case in a taped segment, his tie cinched tight around his neck and a grimace on his face. During Koh's live studio interview, the anchor asked why Clinton shouldn't have the authority to do whatever he deemed was necessary in a foreign policy crisis.

"I think the real question," Koh responded, "is whether a president who is sworn to uphold the rule of law can just disregard it because of supposedly exceptional circumstances."

By the time Koh was headed to the airport, sprawled out in a cab, the students had already traveled a few hundred miles up I-95 toward New Haven. They had to get back to work on the Guantánamo trial, now only five days away. Joe Tringali, Mike Wishnie, and others were so busy preparing for court that they they'd barely made it to Washington, and they needed a lot of help. Within minutes of arriving at Yale, many students were once again downing coffee in the Lowenstein office.

———

Yvonne was carried to the clinic on a stretcher after collapsing during Lauri Filppu's interrogation. Her vital signs were normal, but she was badly dehydrated again. She sipped a glass of water, then shuffled back to the soccer field. Having committed so publicly to the strike, she felt she couldn't just stop, but she was discouraged. Many others had quit and she could tell the soldiers weren't as worried as they'd been earlier. That was not what she wanted. The point was to exert constant pressure on her captors, and that included the INS lawyers—particularly her new enemy, Lauri Filppu.

Hoping to reenergize the rest of the camp—and send Filppu a message—she joined several others in calling for a unified demonstration. The hunger strike may have faltered, but momentum for a protest gathered quickly. The story of Yvonne's deposition had spread, and others who'd been through the process had their own bitter tales about the government attorneys. For the first time in many months, they would hold a campwide march.

At dusk, all but the sickest gathered on the soccer field—about 250 people. Those who knew some English had scrawled out signs for people to carry; Yvonne held one that read, "America Don't Forget Mayflower." Everyone locked arms and set off in a slow cadence, marching along the perimeter fence. Rain began to fall in heavy droplets. Soon it was pouring. The refugees trudged through the darkness, clothes drenched, legs spattered with mud.

Veronique Sanchez was working with Robert Rubin in a nearby trailer when she heard muffled sounds, and the two hurried out into the gloom. The lines of marchers moved past, chanting. As Veronique watched them, a woman made eye contact with her and then held out a baby. Veronique was unsure whether, as a lawyer, it was appropriate to be involved in her clients' political demonstrations. But now she felt she had no choice, and she reached for the child. While Rubin might normally have maintained a more professional distance, after two weeks in the camp his reserve was gone, and he, too, joined the march.

By the time the guards moved in and ordered everyone to disperse, the damage had been done. Lieutenant Jason Dillman had witnessed two civilians from Yale protesting with the migrants, and he advised Colonel Zinser that there'd been a breakdown in security. Lauri Filppu called Rubin the next day and accused him of inciting a riot. Rubin angrily denied it, but Filppu brushed him off. There were new rules, Filppu said. Yale was now barred from the camp.

————

Lisa Daugaard and Mike Wishnie had been organizing their own demonstrations in New York City since the previous summer, aiming to publicize the camp and pressure Washington into dealing with Bulkeley. Though some students believed nobody would support their clients—as Koh had wondered, who really gave a damn about Haitians with AIDS?—Lisa had a very different take. In her mind, the many burdens the refugees faced meant she could appeal to a wide array of groups: Haitians, human rights organizations, African Americans, the public health community, and AIDS activists.

But bringing everyone together would be no easy task, as Mike Wishnie found in meetings with several Haitian activists. So long stung by the label of AIDS carriers, they wanted no part of the HIV issue. Some even denied the real reason for the refugees' detention. The president is lying, they told Mike. No one's sick. It's a government conspiracy. This is about racism, not AIDS.

Things could not have been more different at Wishnie's first meeting with ACT UP—the AIDS Coalition to Unleash Power—in Greenwich Village, a raucous gathering of white men wearing short haircuts and leather. At ACT UP, AIDS was not a badge of shame. It was a word to be screamed at drug company shareholder meetings and "die-ins" on downtown streets until everyone understood that something had to be done to save lives—and it had to be done now. In minutes, Mike had a roster of energetic volunteers for Guantánamo protests, along with a thorny new problem. Since many Haitians would barely utter the word "AIDS" aloud, how could they possibly work alongside ACT UP?

Tense meetings followed, and some Haitian groups ultimately walked away, but the majority joined a collective statement that "many" refugees in Bulkeley had HIV or AIDS. The result was the Emergency Coalition to Shut Down Guantánamo, uniting two dozen New York groups that, listed together, sounded like a pop festival lineup: WHAM!, BAM!, *Ti Legliz,* the 10th Department, and the Red Balloon Collective.

Early protests were small, but as the trial in Brooklyn approached, the numbers grew. ACT UP members went after President Clinton, waiting in rope lines to meet him at public events, then refusing to let go when he shook hands with them. "Free the Guantánamo Haitians!" would ring out as the Secret Service hustled away one demonstrator after another. In Philadelphia, they interrupted the president as he tried to speak about the economy, hoisting a huge banner that read "Abolish AIDS Concentration Camps." Clinton grew testy, calling on the demonstrators to round up their own crowd, but that only brought louder chanting. The next day, some newspapers devoted more space to the demonstration than the president's economic speech.

Activism also reached a new intensity on Yale's campus, with students launching a weeklong hunger strike the day after Koh argued at the Supreme Court. The fasters, largely separate from the litigation team, built a miniature Camp Bulkeley out of chicken wire in the law school's main hallway, then imprisoned themselves inside, night and day, on a rotating basis. A line of votive candles on the tile floor led from the law school entrance to their little prison—a candle for each refugee in the camp. The students lit them one by one as the strike progressed.

Steve Roos considered the whole thing the height of silliness, an adolescent gesture that wouldn't accomplish a thing. When Tory, who was immersed in trial preparation, decided to join the strike, he told her she was being absurd. "You've got too much to do to mess around with this," he said. Tory went ahead anyway, but as she quickly discovered, even a brief hunger strike was not easy for someone so sleep-deprived. Her mind went foggy on the second day, the words falling out of focus whenever she tried to read. It seemed inconceivable to her that Yvonne, who had AIDS, no less, had been striking for more than a month. Sheepishly, Tory started eating again—and went back to work.

The rest of the strikers made it through the week on apple juice and V8, and despite Steve's skepticism, there was no denying the media's interest. It began with the Yale student newspaper, then the *New Haven Register* and a local television station, and soon major papers were calling about the story. The protest leaders also hit on a method to make sure the strike remained in the news. They would pass the fasting along to other schools, week to week, keeping the heat on the president.

Their own strike over, the Yale students dismantled their chicken-wire Bulkeley and drove up to Harvard, where the structure, now dubbed "Camp Clinton," was reassembled in the law school dining hall. The *New York Times* and the *Boston Globe* covered the protest's relocation, and Yale strike leader Van Jones addressed students and journalists on the steps of the main campus library, calling on "William Jefferson Herbert Walker Clinton" to shut down Guantánamo. Within weeks, the strike had spread around the nation, with students wearing red armbands and fasting at Brown, Michigan, Case Western Reserve, Maine, Howard, Columbia, Berkeley, San Francisco State, Penn State, Georgetown, CUNY Law School—where the dean joined in—and many other institutions. Churches staged hunger strikes as well, and even an NBA basketball player from Haiti went on a fast, bringing the Haitians' cause to the sports pages. There were conference calls with students from a dozen campuses, all clamoring to do more. "Get your parents to call and write letters to the president," Lisa told them. White House operators soon found themselves inundated.

Yet for all the protest, the administration wouldn't budge on Guantánamo, and the Justice Department did not encourage the president to rethink the issue. No one knew what position the new nominee for attorney general, Janet Reno, might take on the refugees, but until she was confirmed, the man effectively in charge at Justice was still Webster Hubbell. White House Counsel Bernard Nussbaum told Hubbell in so many words to maintain the status quo on Camp Bulkeley, and Hubbell, following orders, did so.

Thanks to Veronique Sanchez's deposition work on Guantánamo, the Yale team now had Yvonne's testimony on record for the Brooklyn trial. But for the sake of drama, Joe Tringali also wanted Judge Johnson to hear from the refugees in person. That would mean relying on the people who'd been flown out of Bulkeley for emergency care. Several students took the subway out to immigrant neighborhoods in Brooklyn and Queens to hunt for newly settled refugees who might be willing to testify. But most were too ill or traumatized, and everyone was nervous about publicly revealing that they had AIDS.

Finally, Tory and others found two volunteers. Fritznel Camy was a small, reserved man released due to an eye infection; Yanick Mondesir, a twenty-two-year-old firebrand flown to the United States to give birth and now living with her baby in a home run by Catholic nuns. Mondesir was furious that her husband remained on Guantánamo, and at her pre-trial deposition, she took it out on Assistant U.S. Attorney Bob Begleiter. Despite having little knowledge of the American legal system, she quickly learned how to tie Begleiter up using the interpreter, repeatedly forcing him to rephrase questions and define even the simplest terms. When she wanted to tell Begleiter something, she gave a long-winded speech; when she didn't, he had to extract it from her word by word.

But Begleiter was a savvy, experienced lawyer, and after several hours, he exposed Mondesir's weak spots. While she claimed to be a victim of persecution, she knew nothing about Haitian politics, and the story of her father's arrest didn't sound credible. Then there was her medical history. Although her records showed she'd been treated for multiple problems at Bulkeley, Mondesir stared the government attorney down, declaring that she'd received no care.

In a long meeting at Simpson, the trial team fretted over whether to put her on the witness stand. Were Mondesir to react on cross-examination as she had during the deposition, it could be disastrous. The last thing Yale needed was a witness who convinced Judge Johnson that the people in Bulkeley were liars. But among the possible refugee witnesses in the United States, Camy and Mondesir were the only realistic options, and Camy simply didn't have Mondesir's fire. If the team wanted drama, Mondesir would no doubt provide it, but at a risk. Lucas Guttentag, the ACLU lawyer who would question Mondesir on the stand, did his best to explain the situation to her. He reminded her several times: All you have to do is tell the truth.

With the depositions nearly done, Mike Wishnie secured Tringali's agreement that the students could handle some of the direct examinations in court—a plan made possible by an Eastern District rule allowing law student appearances. From the start, Mike had operated on the philosophy that they were capable of doing most any task in the case, and over the past year, he and the other students had made a believer out of Tringali as well. There were still some duties that Tringali felt the lawyers had to be responsible for themselves, including the delicate work of cross-examining government officials. But if the students wanted to question some of Yale's own witnesses on the stand, he was sure they could meet the challenge.

Adam Gutride was thrilled about the prospect of appearing in court and didn't hesitate to volunteer. Tory had a very different view. Her confidence had never been higher, but even after working on the Supreme Court brief, she still drew a sharp line between client support work and "real" law. It didn't matter that she had briefed Jesse Jackson in front of a hostile U.S. military official. That wasn't the same as standing up in court, and she feared she might falter before Judge Johnson. She wasn't about to use the refugees' best shot at freedom as a chance to develop her legal skills. Adam and Mike went ahead with their witnesses, leaving Tory to worry about the consequences.

The question for Lisa was whether she'd be at trial at all. Her fellowship had not gone well all year. Despite several warnings, she'd continued to shirk her duties in her non-Haiti cases, and things finally came to a head shortly before the trial was to start. Lisa was reviewing deposition transcripts at the ACLU when the office litigation director ordered her to come see him. He demanded that Lisa drop Haiti that instant and he reassigned her to work exclusively on abortion rights cases, with a focus on a complex lawsuit in Idaho.

"That's totally irresponsible," Lisa retorted. "And I won't do it."

Moments later, she had no desk, no fellowship, and no paycheck. She stomped off to Lucas Guttentag's office on the seventh floor, where the ACLU's immigration section was quartered. He wasn't around but she finally tracked him down by telephone.

He hired Lisa on the spot, but could only pay her a pittance—well below what she needed to cover even her modest rent. Pale and shaky from a bout of food poisoning, she caught a train to New Haven and pleaded for help from a student group that funded public interest projects with Yale alumni cash. The students sent her home to Manhattan with a check for fifteen thousand dollars. She was at work with Guttentag the next day.

The last pieces of the trial puzzle were the documents and other materials from the government. It had been a fight, but by now, the Justice Department had turned over to Yale almost everything related to the suit—though Lauri Filppu had still not produced the Bulkeley surveillance videos that Tringali had demanded six months earlier. What the team had obtained was a disorganized mass of Coast Guard reports, Guantánamo flight manifests, Joint Task Force directives, and interagency memoranda—sixty thousand pages in total, jammed into cardboard boxes and stacked to the ceiling in the Lowenstein Clinic office.

For months, Steve Roos had been leading the effort to review it all. His team went over every last piece of paper, sorting and summarizing along the way, and Steve became obsessed with the story behind the documents, opening each new box as if it were a birthday gift. Earlier in the case, he'd focused on the Guantánamo interview process. But with the new aim of freeing everyone, Steve was now searching for documents on camp conditions and medical care. Though most of the material was only vaguely useful, now and again he'd find something that made his heart race.

Especially damning was the evidence about medical treatment. He'd discovered Coast Guard and military documents that expressed grave concerns about Guantánamo's capacity to provide the refugees proper care and pressed higher-level officials to address the problem. The media had already reported that authorities on Guantánamo wanted the sickest Haitians flown off the base, and in pretrial depositions, the Camp Bulkeley doctors said they'd warned the INS to evacuate everyone with full-blown AIDS. Guantánamo, they explained, had no tertiary care facility to treat some of the most dangerous infections that could strike those with compromised immune systems.

All this information ran counter to what the government had told both Judge Johnson and the Haitians themselves. According to the minutes from an August 1992 meeting on Guantánamo—another document Steve had dug up—Brigadier General Richard Neal had advised the refugees, "You are receiving the best care that you would receive anywhere." Several months before that, Brigadier General George Walls had testified in court that the physicians' care at Bulkeley "was to U.S. standards." And in a contentious pretrial hearing, Filppu advised the judge that the military was providing "great medical care for the migrants right there on site."

As Joe Tringali considered the evidence, he began to believe the government had boxed itself into a corner. Though the time to name witnesses was over, Filppu seemed to be racing through all the doctors who'd been on Guantánamo to find someone—*anyone*—who would support his claims to the court. But the contradictory intelligence on medical care meant that something would have to give when the parties appeared before Judge Johnson.

Four days before trial, Filppu took another tack. He asked the judge to exclude the medical evidence altogether, along with any evidence on the claim against indefinite detention. The court shouldn't consider the constitutional due process claims on medical care and indefinite detention at all, he argued, because there was no legal basis for them. "I've litigated indefinite detention cases of people, aliens detained in the United States, Mariel Cuban cases," Filppu told the judge in a pretrial conference, referring to the due process cases Lisa Daugaard had been parsing for months. "Court after court rules in the government's favor to detain them forever, Your Honor." But Johnson was not deterred. He ruled that Yale could go ahead with its case in full.

On Sunday evening, less than fifteen hours before trial, the team was packed into conference rooms on Simpson's thirtieth floor. Tringali wanted to practice his opening statement, but he couldn't concentrate on it. He was overseeing a lot of people who hadn't even graduated from law school, let alone worked on a trial. The meticulous practitioner in him didn't want anything to go wrong. As lawyers and students huddled with their witnesses, he moved from group to group, listening, questioning, assuring himself everything was in order.

Lisa ticked items off on her huge chart; Tory, who would be reading from Yvonne's deposition, went over the testimony like an actor rehearsing her lines; Adam Gutride reviewed the questions for his witness, a Guantánamo translator; and Steve Roos helped recheck the final list of trial exhibits to ensure that everything was in order. Still drained from his battle with the justices, Koh sat among the students, sipping coffee and helping where he could. He was relieved and grateful that for once, the pressure didn't fall squarely on his shoulders, and he started cajoling everyone to do something he rarely did himself: finish up early and get some sleep.

Around eleven p.m., that was exactly what happened. Everyone realized, more or less at once, that there was nothing left to do. For the first time in a year, there would be no last-second copying, no sprinting for the train, no handwritten affidavits faxed from Florida at three a.m. They were ready. Lawyers and students got up from their chairs, arranged their papers, and then headed for the elevator bank together. The mood was one of confidence. The justices in Washington may have gone easy on Maureen Mahoney, but the Yale team knew Judge Johnson would not be so lenient with Lauri Filppu. The next morning, when the students poured into Brooklyn, the Haitian refugees detained on Guantánamo would have their day in court.

Ten
THE TRIAL

THE GALLERY BUZZED as Fritznel Camy walked solemnly to the witness stand. Guided by an interpreter, he placed his hand on a Bible and then swore, in Creole, to tell the truth. *That's right,* someone hollered from the back.

Judge Johnson's courtroom, where Koh had argued the first TRO hearing for Yale a year earlier, could not have struck a greater contrast with the Supreme Court. In place of the majestic chamber of marble and mahogany was the familiar, low-ceilinged room with institutional furniture and fluorescent lighting. The gallery in Washington had remained hushed from the moment the justices appeared, but the protesters on hand this early March morning bordered on rowdy. And while the students had been relegated to the back benches at the Supreme Court, today they were shuttling from the gallery to counsel's table beside Tringali, Koh, and the other lawyers, preparing for their court appearances.

At ten o'clock, with little ceremony, Judge Johnson lumbered into the courtroom, eased himself into his chair, and, after some initial rulings and a request to the court clerk to turn up the heat, invited plaintiffs' counsel to the podium.

Tringali rose, a grave look on his face, and paused for a long moment. Despite the importance of it all, Lisa couldn't suppress a smile. It was just like a movie, she thought: Tringali with his immaculate suit and perfectly knotted tie; the dour faces of the "gray men" from the Justice Department; the reporters squeezed into the jury box, poised with their notebooks; even a courtroom artist sketching the scene.

"Almost one year ago, we first came before Your Honor," Tringali began. "At the time, defendants urged the court to be deaf, dumb, and blind to the suffering of the Haitians on Guantánamo. They invited you to give them unfettered discretion to hold the Haitians however long and in whatever conditions they saw fit. Undaunted, defendants continue to act as if they are above the law. They wage a war of endurance against people who have never been charged with any crime."

Tringali preferred a straightforward manner for his court arguments, but he knew his audience for this particular trial included the press and public, so he'd opted for a more florid style. Though he kept his delivery restrained, the spectators joined in with angry murmurs, creating the call and response of an evangelical church service.

"There's much shame here," Tringali told the judge, as heads nodded along in the gallery. "Defendants will urge you not to see the sadness in the eyes of the imprisoned Haitians . . ."

That's right.

". . . not to hear the desperation in their voices . . ."

Mmm-hmm.

". . . and not to be moved by the suffering they must endure."

Lord Jesus!

By the time Fritznel Camy headed to the stand, the gallery was at a fever pitch, and people cried out their support, some of them in Creole, as he entered the witness box. For all the legal proceedings of the past year in Brooklyn, Manhattan, and Washington, Camy was the first Guantánamo refugee to appear in federal court. Tringali believed he was making just the right impression. Despite the government's vague warnings, Camy did not look like a menace to the nation's safety. He was just a small, earnest man lost in a dress shirt that was too large for him.

Under questioning from Tringali, Camy testified through an interpreter that he'd been detained on Guantánamo for months with no hint of when he might be freed. Women and children were imprisoned there as well, he said, and everyone lived in leaky huts without toilets or running water. All told, Camy charged, Bulkeley was "a park for pigs," evidently meaning a pigsty. His testimony only incited the gallery more, and Johnson announced he would remove those who couldn't keep quiet. But even after another demand for silence moments later, he did not force anyone to leave. To the evident dismay of the government lawyers, it seemed the Greek chorus at the back of the courtroom, clad in pro-Aristide sweatshirts and leather jackets, was there to stay.

Even with the gallery's encouragement, however, Camy remained subdued in his testimony. There were no passionate speeches about injustice or abuse—and that was exactly as Tringali intended it. He knew the more ground he allowed Camy to cover, the more difficult the refugee's cross-examination by the government would be. Lauri Filppu would have little to ask if the refugee simply said he'd been confined to a crude shack and denied access to a lawyer. So scarcely twenty minutes after Camy had taken the stand, Tringali sat down, smoothed his pants and waited, poised to object if he felt Filppu's cross went over the line.

The gallery hummed with hostility as Filppu—"the grayest of the gray men," Lisa called him—approached Camy. He first pushed the refugee to admit he was free to move about *within* Bulkeley despite being locked up. When that distinction got lost in translation, he asked Camy to concede that regular windows weren't necessary in the camp "houses" because it didn't rain that often. Instead, Camy replied that it did indeed rain—very hard, in fact, flooding the floors. Losing steam, Filppu then tried to make him admit he'd intended to sneak into the United States rather than simply to flee tyranny in Haiti. But Camy stood firm. By the time it was over, Tringali felt Filppu had only hurt the government. Indeed, while the students had hoped for a more dramatic start to the trial, Tringali thought it was going as well as could be hoped.

And then came Yanick Mondesir. Heavily made up and wearing a bright dress, she had brought her two-month-old baby with her, and she laid the infant in another woman's arms before striding to the witness stand. "I greet you all," she said proudly. "My name is Yanick Mondesir." With ACLU lawyer Lucas Guttentag asking the questions and the gallery encouraging her, Mondesir claimed the INS had used intimidation tactics during her asylum hearing on Guantánamo. She also testified that military doctors had drawn her blood without her consent and had then publicly announced the HIV status of a number of refugees, herself included. Mondesir said she'd been so humiliated by the event that she had contemplated suicide.

Guttentag had all the testimony he wanted and tried to sit down. But the judge's interest had been piqued and he cut in to ask his own questions. To Guttentag's dismay, Mondesir was soon expounding on her supposed political activities and persecution in Haiti. Given her disastrous deposition, Guttentag had deliberately avoided those issues, but now they would be fair game on cross-examination. On edge, he yielded the floor to Assistant U.S. Attorney Bob Begleiter, Mondesir's opponent at the deposition.

She raised her chin defiantly as Begleiter approached her, but she was in trouble from the moment he began probing her medical history. What treatment, he asked, had she had on Guantánamo? She replied that doctors had examined her unborn baby's heartbeat and she'd once gone to the hospital because her pregnancy had made eating difficult.

Nothing more? Begleiter asked.

No, she said.

"Ms. Mondesir," he scolded, "what you've told us about your medical care is untrue, isn't it?"

No, she repeated.

"In fact, you sought medical care more than twenty times?"

"No."

"In fact, you sought medical care more than thirty times?"

"No!"

In response, Begleiter dragged her through her Bulkeley medical records in excruciating detail, including her treatment for anemia, syphilis, and numerous other conditions. But Mondesir simply glared at him, head held high, and denied every illness, every clinic visit, every prescription.

Tringali sat beside Guttentag, face blank, praying: Let it be over, let it be over, let it be over. Tringali had expected to score all the points in the early rounds of the trial. But as he watched Mondesir go on, he could feel the momentum slipping away.

Begleiter was now going after Mondesir's sketchy story of political persecution. In her deposition, she had claimed to be the head of the FNCD—the party that had supported Aristide—in the major city of Cap-Haïtien in 1991. It was, Begleiter knew, an outlandish story, and he swiftly led her into repeating it on the stand. Then he finished her off.

"Do you know," he asked, "who Evan Paul was or is?"

"Evan Paul?"

"E-v-a-n P-a-u-l."

Mondesir hesitated. "I don't understand what you are telling me."

"Do you know who he is? Do you recognize the name?"

Guttentag cut in. It was "Evans" with an *s*, he said softly.

"Do you know him?" Judge Johnson asked Mondesir.

"Do you know of him?" Begleiter repeated.

Mondesir paused again. "Yes," she finally said.

"Who is he?"

"He worked at the same place where I worked."

"In Cap-Haïtien?"

"Yes."

The gallery had fallen silent except for the whimpering of Mondesir's baby. Every other Haitian in court that day knew that Evans Paul was the ousted mayor of Port-au-Prince and the leader of KID. After President Aristide himself, Paul was one of the better-known politicians in the country, but Mondesir clearly didn't even recognize his name.

The students looked on in despair. False answers about her medical condition were one thing. A sympathetic judge might have understood a desperate, if misguided, attempt to preserve some shred of personal privacy. But there was no such defense for her make-believe story of political persecution. Worse still, Mondesir was not on the witness stand just for herself. She symbolized the entire camp. She spoke for all of them, and she had now cast doubt on an assertion at the core of the case—that the Haitians on Guantánamo were bona fide political refugees.

When the examination was finally over, Lisa Daugaard lifted her head from her hands and watched as Mondesir, shoulders still thrown back, returned to the gallery to gather up her baby. Guttentag had stayed quiet to get the refugee off the stand as quickly as possible, but Lisa now wondered if it might have been better to shield her with a spate of objections. The woman had been the target of a humiliating public attack, Lisa reasoned, and she'd just been trying to protect herself. During the next break in the proceedings, Mondesir slipped out with her child, and Lisa never saw her again.

The next witness, a former Justice Department employee on Guantánamo named Ellen Powers, was Adam Gutride's responsibility. It was his first appearance in federal court, and he found himself with the unexpected task of having to regain the upper hand for Yale. Despite years of college debate experience, Adam was shaking as he got up before the judge to examine Powers, who had volunteered to testify for Yale about camp conditions. Adam was about to pose the first question from his carefully constructed outline when a short, dark-haired woman beside Filppu jumped to her feet.

It was Ellen Sue Shapiro, an OIL attorney who'd clashed with a junior Simpson lawyer during one of the pretrial depositions. The lawyer had warned that Shapiro was very aggressive, and in a sharp tone, Shapiro now accused Adam's witness of a violation of procedure: sitting in court during the testimony of prior witnesses. Before Adam could say anything, the two women were sniping at each other.

Even more unsure of himself now, Adam finally managed to blurt out his name to the judge and then, one eye on his government opponent, he struggled to question Powers. His first topic was the government's mishandling of the HIV-testing process, and specifically, the way Frantz Guerrier—whom Powers had met on Guantánamo—had been left in the dark about his test results. While Adam had practiced his examination at Simpson Thacher, he quickly found that working in court against another lawyer was far more difficult, especially one who seemed as hostile as Shapiro. She objected several times in rapid succession to his questions, and each time, he became more distracted and confused.

Based on the objections, the judge could have barred Powers from testifying about Guerrier, leaving Adam no choice but to move on to another topic. But Johnson was plainly interested in hearing what Powers had to say. He told the government lawyer she had a "continuing objection" to the testimony—meaning she should quit interrupting—and motioned for Adam to keep going.

Unimpeded now, Powers described Guerrier's futile attempt to figure out his medical status. Trying to be helpful, Powers had ultimately checked Guerrier's records herself, and discovered his positive test. But she had decided it wasn't her place to tell him such devastating news. She had no idea whether he'd ever learned the test results. Mike Wishnie looked on from the gallery with a queasy stomach. He wondered where Guerrier might be. Was he safe? Had he seen a doctor?

Adam then asked Powers if she had witnessed the government informing any other refugees of their HIV status. Yes, Powers said. In one instance, the military had corralled one hundred people into the McCalla hangar, lined them up, and tried to tell them one by one.

"There was a lot of screaming, crying," Powers explained. "It was just very chaotic."

"And what happened next?"

"And then the military riot gear people showed up."

"What do you mean by the riot gear people?"

"People dressed up in riot wear, with shields on their faces, arm shields, and billy clubs."

"Do you know what happened to the group of refugees subsequently?"

"They were eventually sent to Camp Bulkeley."

Powers also described Camp VII, the barb-wire punishment compound later dismantled by Colonel Kinder. People were there for all kinds of reasons, she testified. At least one fifteen-year-old had been confined to Camp VII for cutting off his ID bracelet; another child had been handcuffed to a chair in the sun for the same offense.

Adam collapsed in his seat, both exhilarated and relieved, but he now had to defend Powers on cross-examination—and his adversary would be Ellen Sue Shapiro. Even before Adam had gotten settled, she was pummeling Powers with questions about her work with children on Guantánamo, trying to show that Powers had a bias against the government. As Shapiro bore down on her, Tringali started hissing to Adam: *"Object! Object!"*

Adam's mind raced. He'd studied all the objections, but Shapiro and Powers were talking too fast; he couldn't think of which one to make. Tringali whispered more urgently, and Adam jerked out of his chair.

"Sustained," Johnson said, ruling for Yale before Adam had even opened his mouth. "It's argumentative."

That's it, Adam thought: argumentative, argumentative. But Shapiro kept pressing and this time, Tringali practically pushed Adam to his feet.

"I will sustain that," Johnson said, again playing Adam's role for him. *"You've got to protect your witness!"* Tringali whispered. Adam started to flush.

But a few minutes later, the judge beat Adam to the punch yet again, and when Shapiro challenged the ruling, Adam jumped up—too late.

"I'm arguing to the *judge,"* Shapiro instructed. "There's nothing objectionable before the court at the moment."

Adam shrank back into his chair, wishing he'd yielded to Tringali or some other lawyer in the first place. Shapiro, Powers, Judge Johnson, the noise from the gallery—he couldn't process it all. He normally had great faith in his ability to think on his feet, and he'd always dreamed of being a trial lawyer. But this was a nightmare.

As Shapiro sparred with the judge, though, Adam began to see that she was the one frustrating Johnson. When she pressed the witness about the handcuffed child, the judge grew downright annoyed. Shapiro wanted Powers, a former Peace Corps volunteer, to admit she'd seen children treated more harshly in Haiti than on Guantánamo. But Adam instantly recognized that Shapiro's question was beyond the scope of his own examination. Finally, he got it right.

"Objection!" he cried.

"I will sustain that," Johnson said. "Irrelevant. Confine it to the events that occurred on Guantánamo Bay on direct."

Shapiro complained, but Johnson wouldn't budge.

"All I know," the judge declared, "is what she testified to on this stand right here." When Shapiro tried to press the point one more time, the judge cut her off. Minutes later, Powers was done, and Adam, ebullient, had earned the hint of a smile from Tringali.

In the one area where the government had raised real questions that day—the legitimacy of Yanick Mondesir's claim to political asylum—the team hoped that Tory Clawson and an interpreter named Margaret Pierre would now provide the answers. Pierre, a Haitian American, took the stand to read aloud from Yvonne's deposition on Guantánamo two weeks earlier, and Tory stood to pose the questions that Veronique Sanchez had asked her. Such testimony was usually offered into evidence in transcript form, but Tringali had secured the judge's approval to present it in court, and Yvonne's words seemed tailor-made to address any doubts left behind by Mondesir's earlier meltdown.

"Miss Pascal," Tory read, holding the transcript, "why did you leave Haiti?"

"I left Haiti because I had political problems."

"What kind of political problems?"

"The problem that I had was that I was a member of KID, which works with Evans Paul in FNCD."

What, Tory asked, was Yvonne's specific role?

"In those organizations, I used to type papers for KID. After the coup, Aristide's coup, my husband, whose name is Antenor Joseph, he was still a spokesperson for KID. After they arrested Evans following the coup, my husband went into hiding at a place called Carrefour-Feuilles."

Tory and Margaret then went through Yvonne's account of her torture at Recherches Criminelles, accompanied by gasps from the gallery, and Tringali knew that Yale was now back in charge. Had the government allowed Yvonne into court to speak for herself, Filppu could have cross-examined her—though Tringali doubted there was much he could have accomplished. But since she remained on Guantánamo, Filppu's only option was to ask that other parts of her deposition be read to Johnson. This the government did briefly and to little effect, except for the curious sight of Ellen Sue Shapiro playing the part of Yvonne.

* * *

Back at Simpson Thacher that evening, the team rehashed the situation over take-out Japanese food. In Tringali's view, the government's cross-examinations had all missed the big picture. They didn't undermine any of Yale's major claims in the case—the camp conditions, the mistreatment of people with HIV, the indefinite incarceration. They were simply trying to cut little holes in Yale's arguments. And while Johnson had remained poker-faced throughout the day, Tringali pointed out that the judge wasn't interested in technicalities. Whatever objections the government made, he usually allowed the witnesses to talk. There would be no playing around with the rules to prevent the court from hearing something. "The games of hide-and-seek," Tringali said, "are over."

Starting the next morning, Yale's case moved forward on a smooth, steady course, as one expert after another spoke about the abuses suffered by the Bulkeley refugees. Following testimony from immigration law specialists, Tringali turned to the issue Filppu had fought so hard to conceal: medical treatment. Yale already had deposition testimony from military physicians who'd voiced serious concerns about the care on Guantánamo, so only three medical witnesses took the stand.

The first was Dr. Robert Cohen, an AIDS expert from a major Manhattan hospital. He furnished a ghastly account of the things that could happen to people who, like Yvonne Pascal, were at an advanced stage of HIV infection: multiple strains of pneumonia, rare cancers, and severe neurological syndromes such as toxoplasmosis and cryptococcal meningitis, resulting in high fevers, seizures, and delirium.

Access to sophisticated emergency care was critical for treating patients susceptible to these conditions, Cohen said. When the symptoms of certain brain diseases appeared, immediate CAT scans were necessary to make a diagnosis. And for eye infections resulting from AIDS, he recommended treatment by an ophthalmologist within a day, if not earlier. Tardy treatment, he warned, could lead to blindness. Cohen also discussed the psychological impact of AIDS. He said he took as long as an hour in a quiet, confidential environment to counsel someone who'd tested positive. The majority of his ongoing patients, he added, were in therapy to cope with the depression, stigma, and physical pain that accompanied the disease.

With that baseline established, Dr. Douglas Shenson then took the stand to describe the military doctors' struggle to treat AIDS on Guantánamo. The facilities were inadequate, Shenson reported, because there was no CAT scanner and an ophthalmologist was on hand only intermittently. He said the atmosphere of mistrust in Bulkeley made a doctor-patient relationship functionally impossible, resulting in widespread refusal by the refugees to take their medications. And he believed the camp itself posed a serious threat of disease due to inadequate sanitation. The ensuing cross-examination lasted all of five minutes—only slightly longer than it had for Dr. Cohen. Evidently, the government lawyers wanted the two men out of the courtroom as fast as possible.

On Wednesday morning, just forty-eight hours after trial had begun, Yale was on its last witness, a public health specialist named Dr. Jonathan Mann. Lisa had found him several months earlier amid a flurry of telephone calls to public health experts. Mann already knew about the case and was eager to help. After a long conversation, they'd finally agreed he would be of the greatest use in combating the government's most recent—and, the team felt, heinous—argument: that the Guantánamo Haitians would spread AIDS if they were allowed into the United States.

Lisa could not, however, conduct Mann's examination in court because she was stuck in professional limbo. Since she still hadn't graduated or taken the bar, she wasn't a lawyer and was not allowed to practice. And though the federal court in Brooklyn permitted court appearances by law students, she didn't qualify as one of those now, either. In the end, the expert's examination had gone to Michael Ratner.

Mann made a striking impression as he took the stand—an elegant figure with thick, silvery hair and a bow tie, both scholarly and well-groomed—and Ratner began with a painstaking investigation of the doctor's credentials. He wanted it crystal clear in Judge Johnson's mind that there was no bigger expert in the world on the spread of AIDS. A professor of epidemiology and international health at Harvard, Mann held an endowed chair and served as director of the university's International AIDS Center. He'd also led the World Health Organization's AIDS program, overseeing a staff of 250 people to develop a global strategy against the disease, and had focused his own research on AIDS for nearly a decade.

"Okay," Judge Johnson said to Mann with a smile, "you are an expert."

Ratner then asked the doctor for his views on allowing the Guantánamo refugees into the United States. Mann advised that the 215 HIV-positive people in Camp Bulkeley did not pose a significant risk to the country's public health. Over one million people in the United States were already HIV positive, he said, and somewhere between 40,000 and 80,000 more were becoming infected each year in the United States. In fact, the U.S. decision to bar immigrants with HIV had only hurt the effort to combat the disease, for it made Americans mistakenly think of AIDS as a foreign threat.

The truth of the matter, Mann said, was that the Bulkeley refugees would pose a lower risk of transmission than most people with AIDS in the United States, because unlike the majority of HIV-positive Americans, they knew they were infected. And he believed that any refugees in denial about their condition would likely accept a diagnosis once they were released. Experience, Mann testified, showed that patients had to actively participate in their education on AIDS—an impossibility in Guantánamo's prisonlike environment. Given all the facts, Mann advised that the refugees should be released.

The OIL lawyer who cross-examined the doctor asked a few random questions but challenged none of his analysis or conclusions, and an hour later, Yale was done with its case in chief. Under Tringali's disciplined guidance, the team had trimmed everything down to just two and a half days of testimony, a model of focus and efficiency.

Almost too focused and efficient, in fact, for the students, who headed to the diner across the street feeling a little let down. Despite all their anticipation, there'd been few fireworks. With a sense of disappointment hanging over them, they ate sandwiches and sipped Cokes, discussing what to expect from the government lawyers. Lauri Filppu and his co-counsel would now make the administration's case that there was nothing illegal going on in Camp Bulkeley.

———

On Guantánamo, the *militan* had agreed that it was pointless to wait for the mysterious proceedings in Brooklyn, and they'd quietly been talking about a breakout. Some wanted to steal one of the motorboats they'd seen during a beach trip under Colonel Kinder. A few thought they could sneak through the fence to Cuba, though that meant crossing minefields and risking a bullet. Yvonne considered the schemes impractical but supported them anyway. She figured an escape attempt would increase pressure on the military, and with nothing else working and her body wasting away, she had grown desperate. Eleven men finally agreed to a plan, and

Yvonne would have joined them had she not been so weak. On her bad days, even the walk to the latrines and water faucets was now a chore.

The men waited until dark, then shimmied under a razor-wire barrier and sprinted away from the glare of the spotlights—except for Bacon, who hop-skipped through the dust on his crutches. They hiked all night along empty roads and by sunrise had made their way to the Fisherman's Point ferry landing in the main area of Guantánamo. The refugees managed to blend in with Jamaican service workers taking the early-morning boat to the leeward side of the base, but their scheme unraveled after they reached the airfield. The personnel there quickly figured out they didn't belong, and minutes later, military police stormed in with batons and dogs.

Several miles away, in Camp Bulkeley, Air Force colonel Bud Paulson's first day as the new commander was not going well. His superiors, evidently displeased with the recent protest march involving Veronique Sanchez and Robert Rubin, had sent him to Guantánamo to reestablish order. But eleven refugees were missing from the morning headcount, and guards were now combing the brush outside the camp without success. Paulson demanded that the other Haitians tell him where to find the escapees. They refused and a shouting match followed.

After the MPs finally captured the eleven men near the airfield, they escorted them across the bay in a speedboat and threw them in the Navy brig, a warehouse close to the base hospital. When Paulson rejected Vilsaint Michel's request to free them, a mob in Bulkeley charged the command post. They rocked fences, smashed truck windows—and changed Colonel Paulson's mind. Soon afterward, the released prisoners arrived back at the camp as heroes, arms raised high, vowing to break out again.

"If Clinton won't accept us, then maybe Castro will," one refugee told Yale's new base representative, a Washington, D.C., lawyer named Allan Ebert. Ebert's brief tenure on the base had started out on a good note, for he'd managed to talk his way around the new rule barring Yale from Bulkeley. Now that he was in the camp, however, he had a lot of angry refugees on his hands. Appealing for calm, he reminded them that the trial for their freedom was under way, and going well. If they tried to escape again, he warned, they could be injured or even killed. Base security forces had authorization to shoot people who didn't identify themselves.

But the next evening there was another protest. More refugees ran for the fences, and guards chased after them in the darkness. For Colonel

Paulson, it was the last straw. By midnight, hundreds of soldiers had assembled around the camp.

———

The morning after Dr. Jonathan Mann testified for Yale, Assistant U.S. Attorney Bob Begleiter arrived at the courthouse for the first day of the administration's case, joined by a pack of other government lawyers in dark suits and long coats, carrying heavy briefcases. Pro-refugee demonstrators were circling the sidewalk, chanting. The lawyers avoided eye contact with them, filing into the building and then heading down the linoleum hallway to Johnson's courtroom.

Begleiter had conflicting feelings. He generally took great pride in representing the United States of America. "I'm on the side of the angels," he liked to say. But the Guantánamo case was different. Though he wasn't convinced that all of the Bulkeley Haitians were bona fide political refugees, he believed they'd left their homeland looking for a better life, and their situation troubled him. Clinton's victory in November had come as a relief to Begleiter, for he'd fully expected the president-elect to release the refugees. It had come as a shock, then, when a Justice official called to say they were going ahead with trial. After Begleiter hinted he'd rather not be involved, the official turned icy. "We just had a Saturday meeting at the Pentagon on this case," he said, "with Colin Powell and the acting AG. And if they're adopting this position, you're going to court."

The trial team included four OIL attorneys from Washington led by Lauri Filppu, along with Begleiter and Scott Dunn from the U.S. Attorney's Office in Brooklyn. While Begleiter took a workmanlike approach to the case, the OIL group still seemed zealous about winning. Begleiter was less certain about how the White House saw things. Clinton had obviously approved sending them to court, but there were no top Justice Department people involved as there had been under Bush—nobody even at the level of Paul Cappuccio, let alone Kenneth Starr. The defense team in Brooklyn was a collection of career government attorneys—loyal public servants—and they were largely on their own.

Begleiter also had doubts about the way the team was preparing. They had battled to the end to keep the court from hearing evidence about medical care and camp conditions, but now that it was coming in, they had no clear backup plan. It all felt too compartmentalized to him. Every lawyer was working with his own witnesses; there was no coordination about what they were trying to prove or how to go about doing it. Begleiter began to wonder whether the OIL lawyers were meeting about the case in private. If there was any purpose to all the harried efforts around him, it seemed to be to cover as many issues and facts as possible, creating a lot of material for the Justice Department to raise on appeal.

It was now just after ten a.m., and with everyone settled and Judge Johnson back in the courtroom, Lauri Filppu presented the government's opening statement. His tone struck Tory, who was back in the gallery, as a cross between a whine and a bureaucratic drone.

Under the law, Filppu told Judge Johnson, HIV was a legitimate ground for barring the Bulkeley "migrants" from the United States, and with nowhere else for them to go, the camp had been "evolving towards a more permanent-type facility involving long-term care."

The courtroom activists were muttering.

"You will learn," he continued, "that the migrants at Guantánamo have received outstanding medical care." He assured the judge that they were "not prisoners on Guantánamo" and that the military had "not tolerated abuses of the migrants." Indeed, Filppu promised, "you will find that we have a first-rate facility."

Johnson broke in. "You mention you want to look at Guantánamo not as a temporary holding facility, but as a permanent holding facility. How long is permanent?"

"I didn't say permanent, Your Honor. We don't know at the moment. We don't know whether the migrants will remain at Guantánamo for a long period of time or a short period of time."

"I know you are not in a position to speak about presidential policy," Johnson replied, "but I just wanted to have an idea if you knew."

"I do not, Your Honor."

From the start of the government's case, the compartmentalization Begleiter had worried about was a problem. On the first day, five different lawyers questioned five witnesses from the INS, the State Department, and the Coast Guard. They covered a dizzying array of topics, from Coast Guard rescue procedures to the 1980 Mariel boatlift. There was almost nothing about Guantánamo. The students were soon convinced that the government had no plan at all. It was more than that, Tringali said, but not by much. "They're just throwing everything out there to see what sticks," he shrugged.

The judge had other matters to attend to the next day, Friday, and the team, feeling optimistic and in control, returned to Simpson's conference rooms. While the news from Allan Ebert about the Bulkeley breakout had caused concern, everyone agreed there was only one thing to do: move trial along. Koh, recovered from the Supreme Court battle, had taken responsibility for an upcoming State Department witness, and was now preparing to conduct the first cross-examination of his life. Tory, Steve, and others were compiling evidence that supported the team's many legal claims, clipping snippets of text from transcripts and exhibits and taping them onto posters labeled with the various theories—Due Process-Medical; Due Process-Indefinite Detention; APA-Abuse of Discretion. Fueled by Simpson's Italian lemon sodas, Lisa typed it all into the computer for the proposed decision they would be submitting to Johnson. Tringali, meanwhile, was getting ready to depose yet another government doctor. Depositions rarely took place during trial, but Filppu kept producing witnesses, apparently still hunting for someone to defend the medical situation in the camp.

The next night, a fierce storm hit New York, blanketing Manhattan with almost a foot of snow. By Sunday morning, the city was at a standstill. A few members of the team trudged through the drifts, heading for the subway or looking for a cab to get them to Simpson. But no one had reached the offices when Allan Ebert's frantic call came in from Guantánamo.

"Leve! Leve! Leve!" Get up! Get up!

Yvonne shook herself awake. Bacon, the one-legged refugee, was hovering over her.

"They're coming!" he yelled.

"Who?"

"The military!"

She thought Bacon was kidding, but then she heard the tinny crackle of a megaphone. Moments later, the goalpost shelter rattled. She bolted upright. Soldiers bulled their way in, batons in hand, and Yvonne stumbled outside with a cry. It was still dark but the horizon had turned a grayish pink, and as her eyes adjusted to the faint light, a wall of soldiers came into focus.

She broke into a hobbling jog—the fastest she could go—and headed for the command post. Nobody was there. She veered back toward the main camp. Soldiers were pounding on the *kay yo*, and bewildered people streamed outside, dragging along their crying children. Interpreters were issuing orders through their bullhorns, but Yvonne couldn't understand them over all the shouting.

A *kay* suddenly burst into flames, followed by a second and then a third. The *militan* had stolen gasoline again. A dozen buildings were soon on fire, the air thick with smoke. The sun had eased above the horizon now, enveloping the camp in an orange haze—burning wooden barracks, dark bodies in T-shirts and flip-flops running in every direction.

The troops pressed forward. Something flew past Yvonne's head. She ducked. Refugees were slinging rocks and anything else they could find at the soldiers. A rock struck her shin. She dropped to the ground, clutching her leg. Pain sharpened her fear into anger, then rage. She just wanted the soldiers to go away, wanted, for once, to be free from the uniforms and the bullhorns and the barriers. Yvonne clawed at the dirt, manic, and dislodged a rock, throwing it as hard as she could at the advancing line of shields. It fell short, but she grabbed another, and then another, and another, her face twisted into a snarl, screaming at the camouflaged figures bearing down on her.

Two of them tackled Yvonne, and she crumpled like paper. The world was now tilted at an angle, soldiers towering above her. They yanked her arms behind her back and she felt plastic cuffs digging into her wrists. All around her there was kicking, shoving, shouting. Soldiers barked directions to each other in the *rrr rrr rrr* of English. More bodies crashed to the ground, followed by violent cursing in Creole. But as the rest of the refugees were herded off to the mess pavilion, the noise gradually subsided, until there was no sound except for her own breathing and the fire engine sirens wailing in the distance.

More than three dozen refugees lay on the ground in the morning sunshine, arms bound in flexcuffs, surrounded by soldiers. Siliette Theophile, seven months pregnant, was searched while her one-year-old daughter whimpered beside her. Theophile had fallen during her arrest and blood was trickling down her leg. Nernil Pierre, bedridden with pneumonia and a T-cell count of just 127, had collapsed and was arrested for failing to get to his feet. His wife sat beside him, pleading for the soldiers to let him go. One by one, the *militan* were dragged to a stifling underground bunker, sometimes with a baton shoved under each arm, their feet scraping through the dust.

Later that morning, Allan Ebert and two Yale translators drove into camp, expecting to meet with their clients as they had for the past several days. It took them a moment to absorb what had happened. Translator Ninaj Raoul hurried out of the car to check people for injuries, offering them water from her oversized McDonald's cup. She pressed the guards to return Nernil Pierre to bed, but they refused, and after an aborted attempt to photograph the scene, Raoul and the rest of the Yale group were ordered to leave. Joint Task Force guards then hauled Yvonne to the Navy brig, marched her to a cell, and slammed the door. It was March 13, 1993, and she was now in solitary confinement, exactly ten months and one day after she had fled Haiti in search of refuge.

Allan Ebert finally reached Lisa on the telephone at Simpson Thacher, and her pencil hurried across the page as he rattled off the details. Thirty-one people in the brig, including kids. Refugees possibly beaten. Allegations of vaginal searches. Numerous huts burned down. Ebert's access to both the camp and the brig denied for his "own protection," per Colonel Paulson. Alleged purpose of the operation: to conduct a headcount to see if anyone had escaped since the initial breakout.

Mike Wishnie, Lucas Guttentag, and others on the team had made it through the snow to Simpson, and during a late-afternoon meeting, they discussed the impact of the new developments on trial strategy. The Bulkeley headcount provided striking evidence to support one of the team's legal claims—that the military was not following constitutionally acceptable procedures when it disciplined the refugees. But Tringali saw a bigger purpose for what the team now dubbed the "predawn raid."

From the start, he'd wanted to be sure that the judge had all the most disturbing facts about Guantánamo before him. Stories about the arrests of pregnant women and the incarceration of dozens of others in the brig were just what Joe had in mind. He was determined to tell the judge about the predawn raid.

But the rules of evidence were going to make it very difficult for Tringali to get the information into court. Neither Ebert nor Ninaj Raoul had witnessed the raid itself, only the aftermath. They knew little more than what the refugees had told them, so their own testimony would be based on secondhand information. They would be hindered on the witness stand just the way Mike Wishnie had been a year ago as he tried to relate what he'd learned from Frantz Guerrier. While Judge Johnson had been liberal about admitting hearsay during the trial, Tringali didn't want to rely on such flimsy—and technically inadmissible—evidence for allegations of this magnitude.

The only other potential witnesses were military personnel. Not only would they be hostile, but it was unlikely anyone from the current Guantánamo Joint Task Force would be coming to the mainland for trial. When the government needed a witness from the armed services, he magically appeared—in one instance, even flying in from Korea. But when Yale wanted someone, a pressing conflict had a way of arising. Tringali had fought bitterly just to schedule Colonel Stephen Kinder's deposition by telephone. Kinder's testimony supported the refugees, and to no one's surprise, he wasn't available for trial. In the end, the group at Simpson agreed with frustration that the predawn raid would have to remain on the back burner—at least until someone could come up with a better source of evidence.

The New York streets were a slushy mess the next day, but the Emergency Coalition, led by ACT UP's Bro Broberg, went forward with a lunch-hour demonstration near St. Patrick's Cathedral to keep the media's attention on the case. After the morning trial session in Brooklyn, Lisa, Tory, and others took the subway into Midtown. A temporary stage had been set up on the sidewalk, with a seven-foot Statue of Liberty surrounded by barbwire. Police officers were everywhere. Bro had orchestrated the protest for maximum news coverage, with speeches by film director Jonathan Demme, the New York City AIDS czar, a former Yale hunger striker, and, of course, Jesse Jackson. But the defining moment was supplied by Yvonne.

She'd written a letter to her mother and children after starting the hunger strike, explaining that she might not see them again. While Yvonne had little hope that it would ever reach Cite Soleil, Cathy Powell had brought a copy of the letter back from Guantánamo, and Michael Ratner had managed to get it to Susan Sarandon. Bundled in a winter coat and scarf, Sarandon now read it aloud to a silent crowd. "Take care of my children so that they can be strong to continue the struggle," Yvonne had written to Thérèse. "Realize that you do not have a bad mother," she pleaded with her sons, "only that life took me away."

The protesters then joined arms to block traffic on Fifth Avenue. In seconds, taxi drivers were honking and swearing at them, and as the news cameras rolled, the police handcuffed everyone and guided them into paddy wagons.

Lisa left the demonstration more than a little put off. She preferred grassroots efforts to glitzy media stunts, and this protest felt particularly staged to her. The officers were even asking Sarandon for her autograph as they hauled her away. Despite everything Bro had done for the cause over the past several months, Lisa concluded he was essentially a pompous ass, with his megaphone and black baseball cap. When she'd asked him to hold something for a moment, he'd replied, "Not now. I have to get Jonathan Demme arrested." She went back to Brooklyn hoping that she'd never have to deal with him again—and Bro was happy to see her go. As far as he was concerned, Lisa was just one more useless lawyer, all caution and inaction.

In the end, though, Lisa grudgingly had to give Bro credit, for the protest drew heavy media coverage. The result was more journalists asking more questions. At a White House press briefing the next day, presidential aide George Stephanopoulos was trying to focus on Clinton's new efforts to restore democracy to Haiti. But reporters kept raising another issue:

"What are the president's feelings about the situation on Guantánamo?" one asked. "Is he comfortable with the fact that the people are there and the way they're being treated?"

"Well, obviously it's a matter of great concern," Stephanopoulos said. "We're going to do what we can to make sure they're treated as well as they can be treated on Guantánamo and to make sure the conditions are secure and safe and healthy. And we're going to continue to do what we can to ensure that."

"Well, if it's a matter of great concern, how come so far you've simply been saying that it's under review?"

"It is under review," Stephanopoulos repeated, "and we're searching for solutions."

An hour after Broberg's protest was over, the government was finally set to present its own medical testimony at the courthouse in Brooklyn. But before an OIL attorney called the first of them to the stand, Assistant U.S. Attorney Bob Begleiter made a highly unusual move, rising to address the judge. Johnson gazed at him curiously. Begleiter looked uneasy, and very much alone.

In his many years of practice, he had never found himself in so difficult a position. Until a few days earlier, he'd assumed that come the end of trial, his team would ask Johnson to maintain the status quo, leaving the refugees on Guantánamo and letting the Clinton administration handle the matter. Begleiter had felt comfortable with that decision since, as Filppu had told the judge, the refugees were receiving outstanding medical care. That's exactly what Filppu had said: "outstanding medical care."

But then an OIL attorney had pulled Begleiter aside to explain a problem. Yale had established that Guantánamo's care was at best deficient, and despite Filppu's search, no military doctor was willing to say otherwise. As an attorney who regularly appeared in Johnson's courtroom, Begleiter now felt his own integrity was at stake. The OIL lawyer told him to calm down. They would deal with whatever came out on cross-examination, but no one was about to volunteer this information to the court or to Yale. Unsatisfied, Begleiter called INS higher-ups in Washington. They told him to keep his mouth shut. After a sleepless night, he decided to go straight to the man in charge at Justice. Webb Hubbell picked up the telephone himself, and Begleiter explained the problem. Rather than ask for Hubbell's permission, he simply told the Justice official what he planned to do.

"Well," Hubbell said in his easy drawl, "go ahead."

Standing alone before Judge Johnson now, his stomach roiling, Begleiter said, "There's a point I want to make clear to the court. Today, you will begin hearing government doctors. These doctors will testify that persons with a T-cell count of two hundred or less come within the definition of persons having AIDS, as that definition was recently revised by the Centers for Disease Control and Prevention. These doctors will also testify that the medical facilities at Guantánamo are not presently sufficient to provide treatment for such AIDS patients under the medical care standard applicable within the United States itself."

There was a long pause.

"You're saying," Johnson asked, "people who have T cells under two hundred, they cannot receive adequate treatment at Guantánamo?"

"I'm saying that doctors will testify and say that presently, they could not receive sufficient treatment at Guantánamo Bay Naval Base."

Johnson cocked his head. "Is that the same thing plaintiffs are saying?"

Tringali, unsure of what Begleiter was doing, got to his feet. "Yes, Your Honor," he said. "It is."

"With regard to that group, I think the current number is nineteen out of the 215," Begleiter went on. "We're talking about a subset, not the entire group. We intend to offer no evidence to the contrary. That's my statement, Your Honor."

Filppu remained in his chair, expressionless. The courtroom was silent.

Everyone else on the base, Begleiter quickly added, was getting medical care that met U.S. standards.

There was another pause, and then Johnson finally asked, "With respect to the fifteen or twenty you say cannot receive adequate care at Guantánamo, are you saying that you are prepared to send those fifteen or twenty to the United States?"

"Let me be precise," Begleiter said, looking ill. "What I'm saying, in answer to your question, I do not have the authority to do that. And the government does not intend, at this point, to do that."

Stunned, Tringali tried to process what Begleiter had just said, then finally got up to respond. As soon as trial ended, Tringali announced, Yale would ask for the medical evacuation of everyone on Guantánamo who wasn't receiving proper care. He glanced at Filppu and Begleiter. "If they had any decent feelings about this entire case," Tringali told the judge, "they would have done something a long time ago."

"I will address that issue when I come to it," Johnson said evenly. "And Mr. Begleiter is representing his client as best he can under the circumstances." He gave the assistant U.S. attorney an understanding nod.

"I hope," Begleiter replied, "Your Honor appreciates the candor of the government and the respect we have for this court."

"I do," Johnson replied.

Begleiter slumped into his chair. None of the OIL lawyers said a word to him.

U.S. NAVAL BRIG
U.S. NAVAL STATION
GUANTANAMO BAY, CUBA

YOU ARE NOW LEGALLY CONFINED IN THE U.S. NAVAL STATION BRIG, GUANTANAMO BAY, CUBA. YOU ARE HERE AS A RESULT OF COURT-MARTIAL OR NON-JUDICIAL PUNISHMENT OR

DETAINED TO AWAIT LEGAL ACTION. UPON INITIAL CONFINE-
MENT, YOU HAVE BEEN PLACED IN MAXIMUM CUSTODY AND
WILL REMAIN IN THIS CELL UNTIL YOUR CONDUCT WARRANTS
YOUR CUSTODY CLASSIFICATION BEING CHANGED.

For two days after her arrest, Yvonne dozed on the hard floor. She
wasn't sure how much weight she'd lost, but it was a lot, and with her
bones protruding, she couldn't find a comfortable way to lie down. A
guard finally brought her a cot on her third day, though her sleep remained fitful. She was suffering from severe headaches, and the light in
her cell never went out.

About twenty refugees had been released, but eighteen others remained
in the brig with her, and she talked with them through the walls. Petit
Pierre, Yanick Mondesir's husband, was there. So was Pierre Charles, the
man who'd been handcuffed on Yvonne's Coast Guard cutter, though he'd
gone silent and everyone was beginning to worry about him.

One by one, they had all been escorted before Colonel Paulson, who
interrogated them about throwing rocks and burning down the *kay yo*.
Some denied the charges; others, like Elma Verdieu, defiantly swore that
yes, they had set the fires. In response, Paulson meted out sentences of
up to three months' incarceration.

When it was her turn, Yvonne refused to say anything in her own defense. She gazed at Paulson, at the other American military officials in the
room, at their desks, their papers.

"You are the judge. You are the lawyer. You are everything," she told
him quietly. "What am I supposed to do?"

—

"What recreational activities were available for the Haitians?" asked Bob
Begleiter's subordinate, Scott Dunn.

"We had checkers, dominoes, and cards. They played a lot of soccer.
They had Frisbee. We had recreational movies every night."

Colonel Joe Trimble of the U.S. Army, a former commander at Camp
Bulkeley, sat in the witness box, awards and decorations pinned to his
chest. One of several commanders Dunn questioned at great length about
the conditions on Guantánamo, Trimble dutifully described the *kay yo*,
known in the military as Southeast Asia or SEA huts; the showers; the latrines; the food service; the laundry facilities; and the Camp VII "segrega-

tion area." As he'd done with Trimble's colleagues, Dunn covered every possible mitigating detail about the camp. Colonel Peter Stenner had taught everyone the Pledge of Allegiance; Trimble had offered English lessons and trips to the beach.

Dunn was evidently trying to persuade Judge Johnson that things down in Bulkeley were fine. But the hours of redundant testimony were frustrating the judge, and the parade of witnesses gave Yale a shot at a half-dozen more cross-examinations. The documents Steve Roos had spent so many months reviewing became the key to destroying Dunn's efforts.

Tringali was on his feet now, interrogating Colonel Trimble. After forcing him to admit that the military guards enjoyed mattresses and flush toilets, Tringali reached for a document.

"During the summer of 1992, sir," he asked the colonel, "the military was concerned that a penal environment was being created at Camp Bulkeley. Is that correct?"

Trimble eyed Tringali. "Not that I'm aware of."

"I believe you have Plaintiffs' Exhibit Sixty-five in front of you, sir," Tringali said, referring to a three-page communication from the U.S. Atlantic Command to the Joint Chiefs of Staff in Washington. "Could you turn to the last page of the document under item number two?"

"Yes, sir," Trimble said.

Back in the gallery, Steve couldn't help but grin. He knew this document well. It had been hidden near the end of all the material the government had sent to Yale—pages 50,624 through 50,626, to be precise. He'd grabbed the pages as if he'd just found a winning lottery ticket.

Tringali now read from page 50,626: "Creation of a 'penal' environment within the camp presents the opportunity for heavy criticism from migrant support and humanitarian organizations. We have reached the point where such an environment stretches the margin of the interpretation of our humanitarian mission."

When Dunn tried to object, the judge waved him off. Trimble protested that he'd never seen the document before. It was between two generals high above his rank, he explained. But the hisses in the gallery had already begun, and Tringali moved on, forcing the colonel to explain other embarrassing memos and communications. The military had warned Washington a year earlier that medical care in Bulkeley was inadequate; the INS had shown "no apparent concern"; a big perimeter fence had been built around the camp because Americans on the base were afraid of the Haitians.

Tringali then turned to a new subject. On direct examination, Trimble had gone on at length about the fire-hose riot involving the *militan* the previous July. This was one of the events the Joint Task Force had video-taped, as Lauri Filppu had admitted to Tringali the summer before. But after eight months of requests from Yale, Filppu had still not produced the tapes. With so much else to do for trial, Tringali had chosen not to waste any more time fighting for them, for he believed he already had a strong case. But Trimble's appearance in court gave him a new opportunity, and he seized it.

Tringali asked the colonel if video footage of the camp was taken at the time of the fire-hose incident.

"Yes," said Trimble, "there was."

Tringali looked at the judge, then repeated his question.

"There was a video taken of what the military did?"

"Yes."

The students were trading glances in the gallery.

"That video," Tringali asked one more time, "would be accurate to show what the military did?"

"Yes, I'm sure it would," Trimble said, looking a little nervous. "I would have to see it. I'm sure we're about to."

"Actually, we're not about to," Tringali said slowly. He turned toward Lauri Filppu. "But we will."

During a court recess, Tringali made a beeline for Filppu. Whatever tapes there were, Tringali said, he wanted them. He wanted them all. And he wanted them now.

Filppu reluctantly conceded that yes, there were tapes, including tapes of the "headcount" by Colonel Paulson the week before. He said, as he had eight months ago, that he'd look into getting them to Tringali. But he couldn't be sure when they'd be ready.

That was enough for Tringali. He was going back to the judge. But then Filppu sprang another surprise on him. The government had decided to call a military witness, Lieutenant Jason Dillman, to testify about Paulson's headcount. It was a late-breaking move that normally wouldn't have been allowed. But Filppu had put Dillman on a pretrial witness list for other reasons and would now seek to expand the scope of his testimony.

Tringali was incensed. Filppu wanted his own witness, Lieutenant Dillman, to tell the judge what had happened the morning Yvonne was arrested. But he wouldn't let any refugees off Guantánamo to offer a competing account, and he wouldn't supply the videotape before Dillman took the stand.

The next day in court, Tringali laid out the story for the judge. Johnson's eyes narrowed. When, he demanded of Filppu, were the tapes coming?

Filppu said it would take five days.

"That's not playing on a level field," Johnson snapped. "You are asking your witness to testify to these events, the plaintiffs want to cross-examine, and you are precluding them from an effective cross-examination without these videotapes."

Filppu started in on the number of tapes and the problems involved in copying them. There were just two military flights a week off Guantánamo, he protested.

Tringali shook his head: Federal Express flew from the base almost every day, and there were also commercial passenger flights.

The judge fixed his eyes on Filppu. "Call the commanding general," he ordered, "and tell him it's important to your case to have the videotapes here by *tomorrow.*"

It was the evening before the last day of testimony, and the team had gathered again at Simpson for one more take-out dinner and trial prep session. Simpson's support staff had wheeled a big television into one of the conference rooms, and the students and lawyers squeezed around the screen. Filppu had not yet produced the headcount tapes, but he'd turned over two dozen others.

There were too many to review in their entirety before the next morning, so the team studied a few of them on fast-forward. They showed uneventful black-and-white footage of people eating at the mess pavilion and milling about the *kay* area. The students poked through the rest of the tapes, looking for something more interesting. One tape had a handwritten label that read, "Recapture of Camp Bulkeley 18 July 1992 Running Time 33:25." Somebody popped it into the VCR.

At various times, the refugees had charged that the soldiers were abusing them when nobody from the Yale team was around. The accusations ranged from guards spitting in the food to physical assaults. While everyone at Yale assumed the guards might have been stricter when the Haitians were alone, some questioned the accuracy of their clients' accounts. As supportive as he was of the refugees, Joe Tringali may have been the most skeptical of all.

But what the team saw on tape that evening left everyone amazed—and horrified. For Tory and many others, it proved in the starkest terms everything they had believed at the outset of the case. For Koh, who would see it the next day, it was a final vindication for pressing on with the lawsuit rather than joining the administration. And for Tringali, it verified even the most extreme of the refugees' charges. The Bulkeley situation was far worse than he had ever imagined.

The next afternoon in Brooklyn, eleven days after trial had begun, Lieutenant Jason Dillman strode to the stand in uniform. He was a tall, chiseled soldier—like a military recruiting poster, Joe Tringali thought—and he wore a scowl. Since Filppu had suddenly decided not to call Dillman as a witness, Tringali had done so instead.

Under questioning, Dillman growled that he was an infantry officer in the United States Army and that he'd been on Guantánamo since January 26—just under two months.

Tringali quickly got down to business. "Did the military," he asked, "make a predawn raid on Camp Bulkeley early Saturday morning?"

Dillman stiffened. "No. It wasn't a 'predawn raid.'"

"Did the military show up at Camp Bulkeley in the early-morning hours of Saturday?"

"They arrived at a staging area outside the front gate. It was actually late Friday night, around eleven."

"What time did they proceed into Camp Bulkeley?"

"I think we went inside the fence around five-thirty."

"A.m.?"

"Yes."

"How many soldiers?"

"A few hundred, three hundred to four hundred may be the total."

And at the time the military entered the camp, Tringali asked, was it quiet?

"Yes, it was."

"Were there any fires?"

"No. Not at the time."

"Any rock throwing?"

"No."

"Any violence?"

"No."

"The Haitians were sleeping?"

"I think most of them were, yes."

Tringali asked whether the military had "rounded up" people on the soccer field.

"We didn't 'round up' anyone," said Dillman.

"You went to the people sleeping on the soccer field and told them to get up?"

"What happened was the linguists had bullhorns. They announced that everyone was to start moving to the migrant chow hall."

"As far as you know, camp president Vilsaint Michel was not consulted by the military before they arrived at five-thirty a.m.?"

"I don't know if he was or not."

"How was the military dressed, sir?"

"We were wearing flight vests, gloves, helmets. Some people carried shields. Some people carried batons and some people had face shields."

Tringali walked over to a waiting video monitor. "Your Honor," he said, "I'm going to show Lieutenant Dillman Plaintiffs' Exhibit 105, which is a tape that was produced to us by the government, entitled 'Recapture of Camp Bulkeley 18 July 1992.'" Tringali had decided there was no need to wait for the headcount video. The July tape was enough.

Filppu jumped to his feet. Dillman wasn't there at the time, he told the judge. What was the relevance?

But Judge Johnson was already waiting for the tape to roll. "*I'm* the trier of facts," he declared, and Tringali pushed the button.

The entire Yale team watched Judge Johnson. He was out of his chair and leaning over the bench, eyes focused intently on the screen.

Camouflage-clad soldiers in helmets and face shields marched toward Bulkeley in long columns. There were hundreds of them, most brandishing big wooden batons. Some carried M-16s; others guided panting police dogs. The soldiers broke into a jog and took position around the camp. A crane raised two soldiers armed with M-16s to a building rooftop. The refugees, clad in shorts and flip-flops, leaned against the *kay yo,* waiting, watching nervously. The camera paused on a sign that one of them had made: "We not military. We need only freedom because freedom is life."

A military jet screamed overhead in a low flyby, shaking the camera. Some of the Haitians cowered. Others gestured in defiance. A heavy bulldozer, spouting fumes, rumbled in and crushed the camp gate. The soldiers wrestled with the razor wire, trying to cut an opening. Then they spilled into the camp and surrounded the refugees, driving them into razor-wire pens. Women clutched screaming babies. The loudspeakers blared orders in Creole over the shouts and cries.

The camera followed as the soldiers marched into the empty huts. They ripped apart cots, throwing the metal tubes into piles. They tore down the sheets hanging from the ceiling and kicked over chairs. Then they trudged out, leaving behind the wreckage. One soldier carried off an accordion, the ragged instrument groaning as he walked away.

The video then cut to two soldiers grasping the arms of a stone-faced Haitian woman in a skirt. The soldiers wore surgical gloves and the woman's wrists were bound with flexcuffs. They led her to a white police van, then pushed her inside. A small Haitian man in a turquoise shirt, also bound and escorted by two soldiers, followed. He, too, was shoved into the van. The process was repeated with a dozen more refugees, some of them bent over at the waist, tripping along between the two soldiers holding their arms. Then the vans drove off.

The operation went on for more than half an hour, and the judge would only see the full tape later. But Tringali waited long enough in the courtroom for Johnson to understand the situation; long enough for the gallery to respond with cries of *shame, shame*; long enough for Lieutenant Dillman's face to tighten into a look of profound discomfort.

Then, finally, Tringali approached the television screen. He pointed to one of the soldiers on the tape. The soldier wore a flight vest, helmet, and face mask. He looked ready for combat.

"Lieutenant Dillman," Tringali demanded, "is this how you were dressed?"

"More or less, yes," Dillman said softly.

"The batons you referred to are what the people are carrying here?"

"Yes."

"And the shields were the same as what you see in the pictures?"

"Yes."

"And the helmets with the face masks?"

"Yes."

"There were approximately this number of soldiers?"

"I don't know how many soldiers there were."

Judge Johnson cut in with a reprimanding tone. "You said three hundred or four hundred?"

"Yes."

Tringali dragged Dillman through the rest of the "predawn raid." The flexcuffing of young children. The arrest of pregnant women. The use of an underground bunker to hold people headed for the brig. But by now both he, and evidently the lieutenant, knew the game was over. Judge Johnson had seen the government's "first-rate facility" for himself, and the rest of the direct examination, Filppu's feeble cross, and Tringali's own redirect were nothing more than formalities.

If there was anything left to say, Tringali wanted it to come from the mouth of INS spokesman Duke Austin, who now took the stand. Austin, who apparently knew why he'd been called into court, wore the expression of a man who was about to be hanged. Tringali quietly asked him if he had, in fact, told the press that there was no point in flying the sickest Haitians off Guantánamo because "they were going to die anyway." Austin protested that his quote had been taken out of context. Tringali invited him to explain. Austin tried, stumbled, tried again. Three torturous minutes later, the judge excused him from the stand and Yale was done.

The judge looked at Filppu. "Is the government going to act on this themselves," he asked, "or do you want me to make a final decision?"

"Well, Your Honor," Filppu said, "I think you heard earlier that the issue is pending consideration within INS and the Justice Department."

"Mr. Tringali tells me that it was pending since June of last year."

"May, Your Honor," Tringali corrected.

"I know about INS and the bureaucracies," Johnson said in a hard voice. "And many times they do not move or respond unless you put their feet to the fire. You say it's pending. When will a decision be made?"

"I don't have the answer to that question, Your Honor," Filppu said. He asked the judge to hear him out. Tringali, he argued, was wrongly trying to cast the case as a dispute about medical treatment. It wasn't, Filppu said. The question was not where the "best treatment" might be for the refugees, but whether it was appropriate to allow them into the United States under the immigration laws. Those laws, Filppu went on, were designed not to protect aliens abroad but the American public.

"What's going to happen," he asked, "in terms of the American citizen who gets infected with the HIV virus from those migrants?"

"One of the problems *I* have," the judge replied, "notwithstanding the fact that *you* have an immigration policy: Does that policy permit the United States government to take, kidnap, or abscond, whatever you want to call it, take a group of people and put them into a compound, whether you call it a humanitarian camp or a prison, keep them there indefinitely while there has been no charge leveled against them and there is no light at the end of the tunnel?"

Tringali was up now. "Your Honor," he said, "Mr. Filppu has zero evidence in this record on the risk of spreading AIDS. Let's not deal with prejudice; let's deal with the facts and the law. You heard a hundred times there is no HIV bar to parole and no HIV bar to asylum. They have conceded that they are not providing adequate medical care. Mr. Filppu would like to change it and say, 'We can't give them the *best* possible care.' That's not what the doctors said. They said, 'We cannot provide *adequate* care.'"

Tringali's voice rose, his words coming faster, and the gallery went from murmurs to cries for justice.

"We do not ask Your Honor to order these people into the United States," he said. "We ask Your Honor to order the defendants to provide adequate medical care anyplace but Haiti. If they want to do it on Guantánamo, let them do it. If they want to do it in the United States, let them do it. You could be convicted of murder, Your Honor, on death row, and you have to be given adequate medical care. But if you're a Haitian and HIV positive, and found by the Immigration and Naturalization Service to have a well-founded fear of persecution, you're entitled to die."

A week after closing arguments, the fax arrived at Simpson Thacher, where the team was crowded into a conference room finishing up final post-trial matters. The judge's decision, termed an "Interim Order," was only a few paragraphs long. Johnson had given the Clinton administration two options. It could release all the refugees with a clinical definition of AIDS to a place where they could obtain adequate medical care. Or it could provide them that care on Guantánamo. The one thing the administration could not do, Johnson declared, was send anyone back to Haiti. The judge was still considering the case as a whole, he said, but was acting immediately to prevent the loss of life.

There was a collective shout, much clapping, and high-pitched cries from Tory, who ended up standing on a chair. Koh threw both arms in the air like a prizefighter, and Mike Wishnie doled out high fives. Joe Tringali broke into the broadest grin Steve Roos had ever seen from him.

But the jubilation in New York quickly became concern. Would the government try to appeal? Was that even permissible? Certain trial court orders could not be reviewed by higher courts. Did this unusual ruling fall into that category? Several people hurried to the Simpson Thacher library to research the possibilities.

Mike Wishnie had other concerns. As Koh was fond of joking with him, "We'll get them out, you get them in." The point was that if Yale managed to free the refugees, Mike, as the resettlement guru, would have to find them food, shelter, clothing, and medical care. In the past, Wishnie and Bro Broberg at the Coalition for the Homeless in New York had handled only three or four paroled refugees at a time. Johnson's interim order would present a huge task in comparison. Begleiter had said that nineteen refugees had the clinical definition of AIDS. But the number ballooned after Dr. Shenson and others returned to Guantánamo and persuaded most of the Haitians to take another blood test. All told, more than fifty refugees would be arriving in the United States within days. Mike and Bro put everyone in the social service network they had developed on high alert.

Tringali, meanwhile, told the team that Johnson had made a very cagey decision. His bold initial order granting Yale access to Guantánamo the year before had resulted in a stay by the Supreme Court. The current interim ruling was a more tentative measure, as if Johnson were testing the waters rather than directly challenging either the government or the justices.

A few days later, Filppu confirmed that the government would let the order stand, setting off celebratory, if frantic, preparations to welcome the refugees. Mike was on the telephone almost nonstop, and Broberg spent a week of his own vacation time arranging apartments, contacting relatives, and lining up financial support. But the press, so long an ally, suddenly became a problem. The ad hoc settlement system that Broberg and his colleagues had set up depended on the good graces of well-meaning public officials. How would they react after they saw the latest headline from the *New York Post*? HAITI'S AIDS REFUGEES ARE HEADING FOR N.Y.

Yvonne walked out of the brig and shielded her eyes against the glare, dazed, still uncertain whether to believe the news. A van was waiting to take her back to Bulkeley, where she would prepare for her departure. She already felt stronger. After learning of Judge Johnson's order, she had broken her fast—first sipping water mixed with sugar, then moving on to crackers and rice, though in small amounts. Her stomach was unable to hold more than a little food at a time.

People crowded around her when she returned, welcoming her, asking about the others still in the brig. It had been a difficult three weeks in the main camp. Colonel Paulson had surrounded the *kay* area with a new, tight ring of razor wire, telling the media that "we had to enforce order." Guards kept close watch and no one from Yale was allowed access. With the permission of Clinton's national security adviser, Jesse Jackson had visited briefly, alone, and Koh and Ratner had met with some of the refugees in the hangar. But spirits had fallen the moment they'd left.

Johnson's ruling produced more anxiety than celebration. Those with higher T-cell counts had watched another milestone pass with no change, except that they would now have to say good-bye to others in the camp. Some began to think that making themselves sicker would be the only way to get out. Yvonne's old *kay*-mate, Christa Micles, was especially down. Yvonne sat with her, held her, promised she would do everything she could to get her out, but Christa was not easily comforted.

The flight was scheduled for very early in the morning on Thursday, April 8, and guards rapped on the *kay* door at four a.m. to bring Yvonne to the airfield. She went to the dingy cement washroom and let the water run over her body, cleansing away the dirt of the camp, then toweled off and brushed her hair, which was growing out again. Wide awake despite the hour, she slipped into her new clothes, gifts from a military translator: a silky blouse with flowers, black slacks, black dress shoes. Then she used a pair of nail scissors to snip through her plastic ID wristband and threw it away. She felt better than she had in a year.

The translator had also given her a Bible, and she placed it carefully in her backpack and then left her *kay*. Christa, Armelle, and many others had risen to see Yvonne's group off, and they all walked down to the gate together. It was still dark but security lights illuminated the camp and

Yvonne could see the fading spray-painted messages on the buildings—the pleas for President Bush to free them, the lists of T-cell counts, the references to Haitian forefathers.

There were kisses, tears, and promises, and then the chosen refugees boarded the school bus, among them Yvonne; Gertil Cadet, who needed immediate throat surgery; and Jeanine Auguste and her husband and eight-week-old baby. They rode to the ferry landing and crossed the water to the airfield, where a military transport plane was waiting for them. Yvonne had never flown before, and she trembled as she followed the others inside. Someone showed her how to belt herself in against the wall with a four-point restraint. The ramp closed with a metallic moan and the propellers jumped to life. Salson Joseph, not quite two years old, began to howl, but the thunder of the engines drowned him out.

They hurtled down the runway. Yvonne clutched her belt with both hands, body rattling with the plane, convinced the enormous machine would never make it off the ground. But then the vibration fell away, replaced by a low hum and the curious feeling of suspension. She had finally left Guantánamo.

Eleven

VICTORY AND LOSS

R EPORTERS AND CAMERAMEN were clustered in the arrivals area of Miami International Airport, searching for some sign of the Haitians. Mike Wishnie appeared from behind a security door. I'm sorry, he announced, but the refugees are exhausted and might not be able to talk right now. Reporters called after him but he whisked back through the door, flashing his special INS pass. He now had a game of hide-and-seek on his hands.

Working with Bro Broberg and the resettlement team, Wishnie slipped the first group of Haitians out of the airport and sent them on their way to relatives in Miami's Little Haiti quarter. But about twenty other refugees, including Yvonne, were still in the terminal, waiting for a flight to New York City, and Mike feared they would be impossible to conceal. Sure enough, several journalists were soon onto the secret of the next American Airlines flight to LaGuardia. To Mike's dismay, they managed to buy tickets and make it on board just in time.

Moments after the jet had reached cruising altitude, the reporters were hovering over the Haitians, notebooks and Dictaphones in hand. Mike and Bro tried to run interference but they couldn't cover everyone. To their relief, a flight attendant finally asked the captain to illuminate the seat belt sign, and the scowling reporters were forced to sit down.

Yvonne missed everything. She was asleep, exhausted from the initial military flight off Guantánamo. She'd spent much of it in the crude restroom, throwing up, and by the time they'd landed in Miami, her new blouse was soaked with sweat. Her first hour in the United States had been a blur: Ronald Aubourg welcoming her with a broad smile; an INS officer with questions and forms to fill out; a band of vaguely familiar people from Yale leading her one way and then another through the astonishing airport terminal.

She'd heard people talk about Miami her whole life, but had never imagined quite how it would look. Where did all the money come from? She gaped at the long, gleaming corridors, the brightly lit gift shops, the peculiar mix of people—white, brown, black, and so many of them fat. Just before she boarded the commercial flight north, somebody from the resettlement team handed her a winter jacket. "You're going to New York," she was told. "It's colder up there."

Yvonne opened her eyes as they touched down at LaGuardia Airport, the evening before Good Friday. It was dark, and she gazed out at the eerie landscape of concrete and blinking lights. When they reached the gate, the flight attendants cleared the rest of the plane, sending the reporters away empty-handed. Bro then directed everyone to the tarmac, where yet another bus was waiting. He'd arranged a police escort, and as the reporters waited in vain at the end of the Jetway, the Haitians were whisked off to the Marine Air Terminal, a small complex a mile from the rest of the airport.

The bus came to a stop. We're here, Aubourg said to Yvonne. It's over.

She got up, unsteady from so much travel but awake and alert, and stepped off the bus into the chilly wind. Ahead of her, beyond the darkness, was a glowing doorway. She hurried toward it, Aubourg and the others right behind. She was the first inside, the first to see Koh, Ratner, and all the students, cheering, and she bounded toward them, arms outspread, unable to form any words, only joyous cries.

Mèsi, she finally managed, Koh hugging her. Mèsi, mèsi, mèsi. Thank you. We are free.

Lisa stood apart from the celebration, struggling to feel happy as she watched Yvonne emerge from the darkness and embrace Tory and Veronique. A wave of loneliness washed over her. For all the time she'd spent over the last year fighting to free the people coming off the plane, her only trip to Guantánamo had been six months earlier. To the dazed people arriving that evening, she was just another one of many smiling white faces.

There was food and Haitian music and people gave speeches in Creole and French and English. Koh spoke; Yvonne spoke; everyone raised plastic glasses of Coke and juice. But none of it lifted Lisa's mood, for she could sense the inevitable: the case was nearing its end. She expected that Judge Johnson would soon order everyone released. The fight would be over, the cause gone, the team dissolved. The lawyers and students who'd been her daily companions would never be together again—not the whole group, anyway, and certainly not with the same purpose. That very evening, she'd sensed their collective drive beginning to wane, everyone resorting to small talk while they waited for the plane. In the coming weeks, Lisa knew, there would be less and less to do, and it only made her feel emptier. All the emergencies that had galvanized them would give way to minor tasks of no particular urgency, and eventually the Haiti case would disappear into the stream of other obligations and worries.

We *succeeded,* she reminded herself. At least for these refugees, right here, right now, we won. And yet she almost felt like crying.

Mike and Bro were weaving through the crowd now, pressing apartment keys and spending money into their clients' hands. With help from Aubourg and the other translators, they ushered everyone outside. Watching Bro as he moved from refugee to refugee—explaining, gesturing, listening—Lisa realized she'd misjudged him. He was as committed to the cause as she was, willing to do even the most menial work, for long hours, to help.

The team had assembled a group of vans just beyond the reach of the streetlights. Urgent discussions about addresses and directions ensued, the sounds of honking taxis and rumbling jet engines in the background. Working in the darkness, students tucked the refugees and their military-issue duffel bags into one vehicle after another. Lisa stood on and watched, a forlorn smile on her face, as one by one, the vans jumped to life and their red taillights merged into the traffic snaking out of the airport.

Yvonne awoke on Good Friday, sore and bewildered, in her cousin Nicole's apartment in Brooklyn. A pregnant refugee had slept on the only extra bed, and Yvonne had taken the floor. She'd finally drifted off despite a bad headache and the vibrations of a washing machine thudding in the room below her.

When she remembered where she was, she sprang to her feet, heart fluttering. She had only one thing on her mind and she waited, impatiently, as Nicole helped her dial the pawnshop in Cite Soleil. The line hissed and popped, and then, faintly, there was a ring. The stunned owner told her to call again in a few minutes, giving him time to send someone to her shanty. She paced the apartment, counting the seconds.

When she called back, the voice of home, a voice she had not heard in a year, came to her over the line.

"*Alo?*"

"*Manman?*"

". . . *Yvonne?*"

"*Manman!*"

"*Mèsi Bondye!*" Thérèse cried.

"*Manman! Manman, Manman! Pitit senesòf? Pitit senesòf?*"

"*Wi, wi, wi.*" Yes, yes, her mother assured her. The kids are okay. We've got food. We're cooking for Good Friday.

Yvonne closed her eyes, exhaling in relief.

She tried Antenor next, calling the office that KID had quietly maintained since the coup. Somebody would get a message to him, she was told. A couple of days later, she at last spoke to her husband. He gave a shout when he heard her voice, begged to know how she was. Are you safe? Where are you? What happened?

She grasped the phone with both hands, tripping over her words, struggling to connect with him again. There was too much to tell: the camp, the military, the strike, the lawyers, the brig, New York. She loved him, she missed him so much. Was he all right? Was he still in Carrefour-Feuilles?

He was okay, he promised.

He had to leave, she said. They had to save the children and get the family out of Haiti as soon as possible. She knew some lawyers in New York now. She could find help to make it happen.

Antenor paused. Everyone else, he agreed, should leave. It was too dangerous to stay. But he could not seek political asylum in America. Even if he was able to visit Yvonne, he said, he had to return to Haiti to fight Cedras. No matter what.

"Why go back?" she cried. "Why?"

"I have to," he repeated.

Yvonne pressed her palm to her forehead and took a slow breath. He hadn't changed. Her husband was still the same single-minded activist, the man she'd first admired, years earlier, for his dedication and intensity. He remained focused on the political struggle to the exclusion of everything else—her, the children, the possibility of a new life. Over the course of several more calls, she tried to reason with him, listening patiently to his concerns, hoping to change his mind. But as much as he said he loved her, as much as he worried about the family, he could not pull himself away from Haitian politics. During one conversation, he talked mostly about how they had to return Evans Paul to his position as mayor. Another time, he was fastened on buying a photocopier to produce political leaflets. Could she send him money to help buy one?

He was trying to do the impossible, she said bitterly. He was fighting for something that would never, ever happen. They'd hardly seen each other since the coup, and after all this time, all their sacrifices, nothing had changed in Haiti. She was in exile; he was living like a hunted animal; the children were left with their grandparents. What was the point anymore? She hung up feeling abandoned, even more alone than she had felt on Guantánamo.

Frustrated and hurt, her hopes of reuniting the family fading, Yvonne found purpose in the fight to close down Bulkeley. Just days after arriving in the United States, she became a spokesperson for the National Coalition for Haitian Refugees, or NCHR. Relying on Ronald Aubourg to interpret, she met with reporters, delivered speeches, even appeared on the *Phil Donahue Show* with Susan Sarandon and Jesse Jackson. Most of the other refugees dealt with their trauma privately, but Yvonne found it cathartic to speak out, especially with so many people eager to hear her story. After months of being ordered to do this, do that, stay here, go there, she felt important and respected, and the busy schedule was a distraction from her crushing anxiety about the children and Antenor.

NCHR had found an ideal representative to press the refugees' cause—a beautiful, articulate, charismatic woman—and Yvonne enjoyed a brief moment of celebrity in human rights circles. Only a few weeks out of the Guantánamo brig, she had regained much of her weight and lost her ashen pallor. On television, with her hair professionally done and her bright eyes and high cheekbones, she looked more like a film star than a woman who had just been freed from a detention camp.

In return for her efforts, the refugee organization helped pay for meals, bought her clothes, introduced her to important people. But the real value for her lay somewhere else: NCHR had promised to try to get her family out of Haiti. The process, however, would take time. How long? Months, she was told.

The first refugee to die was Joel Saintil, just three weeks after arriving in the United States. His liver gave out on a Tuesday evening at a hospital in

Homestead, Florida, a poor community south of Miami where Saintil's father had lived for some time. The doctor who treated Saintil told reporters he might have survived longer had he received proper medical care on Guantánamo. Protesters held a funeral procession for him in Miami, marching past the regional INS headquarters.

At Yale, the students grew anxious as the weeks passed without a final decision from Judge Johnson. Tory saw every day of delay as precious hours lost for people with only a short time to live, and Joel Saintil's death only reinforced that conviction. Indeed, watching Yvonne's group arrive at LaGuardia, Tory hadn't been able to suppress the thought that they weren't coming to the United States to start a new life, but simply to die with some measure of dignity. And yet she wasn't sure Yale was providing even that. During her trip to Brooklyn and Queens to track down witnesses for trial, she'd been shocked by her clients' dismal housing conditions. Fritznel Camy kept his little room neat, but he was quartered in a grimy tenement located in a dangerous neighborhood. Is this, Tory wondered, what we've fought so hard to get for our clients?

May came and went. Tory and her classmates finished off their courses, went through finals, left campus for summer jobs. The Emergency Coalition continued its protests against Clinton through the spring, and earlier, at the Academy Awards, Susan Sarandon and Tim Robbins had used their presentation duties to demand that the president shut down the camp. "The whole world knows!" Tory had cried to Koh on the telephone, her face a foot away from the screen. And much of the world did seem to know, with the Clinton administration facing bitter criticism over Guantánamo at the Ninth International AIDS Conference in Berlin in early June.

Still, there was no word from Judge Johnson.

Down on Guantánamo, the atmosphere was degenerating into panic. Most Haitians had quit taking their medication out of defiance or, in some cases, in hopes that they might lower their T-cell count enough to get them out of the camp. Some launched a new hunger strike. When that failed, the *militan* began discussing a mass suicide pact. They'd seen reports on CNN of armed cult members in Waco, Texas, who'd burned down their compound rather than surrender to the FBI. Nearly eighty people had died. The refugees now talked of torching the whole camp and provoking the guards into opening fire.

Finally, on the morning of June 8, Judge Johnson's law clerk called Joe

Tringali to let him know that a final order would be signed within the hour. Tringali reached Mike Wishnie, who dashed to the courthouse. Heart pounding, he met the clerk in the courtroom. Her face was blank as she handed Mike the opinion. He walked out as calmly as he could, clutching the freshly printed copy of *Haitian Centers Council v. Sale*—the case name had changed, for Gene McNary was no longer the head of the INS. Out in the hallway, Mike madly flipped through the decision. Judge Johnson had issued a fifty-three-page ruling, and true to the form of most legal opinions, Wishnie had to turn almost to the end—page fifty-one—to find out what the judge had decided.

There was a bank of telephone booths nearby and he jumped inside one, slammed the door, and dug through his pockets for change.

At that moment, Koh was stuck in traffic, driving to New York. Lisa was on vacation in Seattle. Tory and Veronique were at their summer jobs in Washington, D.C. And Steve Roos, Laura Ho, and several other team members were in San Francisco, just waking up for work. So Mike called back to Simpson Thacher, hammering at the numbers on the dial pad, and waiting, endlessly it seemed, for Tringali to pick up his line.

"Joe! Joe! Joe!"

"Mike?"

"He's releasing them all! We won! We won! We won!"

Wishnie hurried from page to page, scanning the headings, reporting the rulings.

"Yes on due process! . . . Yes on medical care! . . . Yes on illegal punishment procedures! . . . Yes on indefinite detention! Yes on . . . *everything!*"

By the time Mike had reached Simpson to celebrate with Tringali and Lucas Guttentag, he'd reviewed almost the entire decision. It was a total victory, from all the points of legal analysis down to Johnson's tone of moral outrage.

The judge had ordered the government to free everyone immediately. His decision was based on the firm conclusion, tentatively stated in his earlier rulings, that the Constitution's due process clause applied on Guantánamo. The government had seized the refugees on the ocean and taken them to territory controlled exclusively by the United States, he emphasized. In those circumstances, American authorities were unquestionably constrained by U.S. law. Yet they had been deliberately indifferent to the refugees' medical needs and had locked them up indefinitely for no legitimate reason. The judge declared it all "totally unacceptable."

"The detained Haitians," Johnson wrote, "are neither criminals nor national security risks. Some are pregnant mothers and others are children. Simply put, they are merely the unfortunate victims of a fatal disease. The Government has failed to demonstrate to this Court's satisfaction that the detainees' illness warrants the kind of indefinite detention usually reserved for spies and murderers."

When Tory learned of the decision later that day, she was at her desk in a private law firm, where she'd decided, against her better instincts, to spend a month as a summer associate. Unable to contain her glee, she bounced from office to office, interrupting her senior colleagues with the news: "We just freed the Haitians!" They responded with tepid smiles— "Isn't that nice?" "Good for *you*."—and turned back to their work. Their indifference didn't dampen Tory's spirits. She wasn't going to be there more than a few weeks anyway. If the firm didn't understand that she'd just helped win one of the biggest human rights cases of the decade, so what? After that summer, she was never going to set foot in a law firm again.

Lisa cheered the victory from Seattle, taking special vindication in the opinion's legal arguments. All her research on due process and several other complex theories, her fights with Koh, her fierce insistence that no matter what the conventional wisdom, the law favored Yale—it had all paid off. A year earlier, the others had been content to push for the refugees' right to counsel during their Guantánamo asylum hearings. But she'd insisted that the team demand their freedom, and now the judge had ordered precisely that. She smiled to herself and thought: I was *right*.

Back at Simpson it was early afternoon, and Koh barged in, all shouts and grins, and practically squeezed the air out of Wishnie with a bear hug. But after a short celebration, the skeleton team, including Ratner, had to sit down for yet another strategy session.

The sobering question now was how the White House would respond. Koh's great fear was that Clinton would follow the strategy of the former Bush administration, going to the Second Circuit and even the Supreme Court, if necessary, to seek a stay of Johnson's order. A stay, everyone knew, would be disastrous. If a higher court put a temporary freeze on Johnson's decision, the refugees would all remain in Bulkeley while the case languished for months at the appellate level. No matter who won the appeal, it would then seem destined for a full hearing at the

Supreme Court many months after that. A year might pass before everything was resolved, perhaps longer, and there was plenty of reason to fear that in the end, the Supreme Court would rule against the refugees. Despite Judge Johnson's favorable opinion, the application of the Constitution on Guantánamo was by no means a settled issue. And his decision would have zero impact on how the Supreme Court decided the case.

By the next morning, the conference room was once again a cluttered mess. Mike Wishnie and others had stayed up most of the night, tearing through research to fight the anticipated stay request, but they were dragging now. In hopes of pressuring the White House, Michael Ratner and Joe Tringali were spinning the decision to the media as both legally and morally correct, and Koh was again calling his contacts in the administration, including Walter Dellinger, pleading with them to let the decision stand. You don't have to do anything at all, he kept saying, hunched over the phone, voice growing hoarse.

But the Clinton officials were noncommittal, and then word came from Washington that a number of senators and representatives had called on the president to challenge Judge Johnson's ruling. Michael Ratner paced the room, a sense of doom settling over him. Every time we win, he thought to himself, we end up getting kicked in the face. It's happened over and over, with both Supreme Court stays and then Clinton's betrayal. How's this going to be any different?

And then the telephone rang. It was Webb Hubbell.

Koh waved his arms, hushing everyone, then put the Justice official on speakerphone. Hubbell's easygoing drawl filled the room. "I'm calling to let you know," he said, "that we're not going to appeal the decision. The Haitians are going to be released."

Koh traded looks with Mike Wishnie, who'd gone bug-eyed, staring at the telephone. What was the catch? The trade-off? Everyone waited another moment, but Hubbell was done speaking. Shaky, Koh groped for some words of thanks. Hubbell replied that Yale would be getting another call from Justice about the logistics. Koh thanked him again. Then Hubbell wished everyone good luck and said good-bye.

Koh was on his feet now, and he pounded the speaker button several times, wildly, the telephone rattling on the conference table. He wanted to be absolutely certain no one was there.

"Hello? Hello?"

The line was dead. Hubbell was gone. The case was over.

Down the hallway, several Simpson lawyers looked up as a roar shook the team's conference room.

After issuing his decision, the judge got a check in the mail, made out to him for five dollars. "Go buy yourself some rubber gloves," said an accompanying letter, "so you can shake hands with those AIDS carriers when they come into our country."

Judge Sterling Johnson Jr. had been dubious of the government's case from the first day. Paul Cappuccio's argument that the Haitians had no rights at all struck him as preposterous, and he was disgusted by the "Just trust us, Judge" attitude that he'd heard from the government all the way along. "They had this high-handed, bullying way—'We're going to do whatever we want to these people, and no one's going to stop us,'" he recalled. "That's where the judiciary has to step in. We're the last line of defense when the executive goes too far."

He shook his head with a little belly laugh. "*Humanitarian camp*—that's what those government lawyers called it. Come on. I was born at night, but I wasn't born *last* night."

Some weeks following the trial, the judge was invited to a Rose Garden event at the White House. It was a beautiful summer day, and after the president spoke, Johnson waited in a rope line to meet him. When Clinton grasped Johnson's hand, White House Counsel Bernard Nussbaum told the president he was talking with the judge in the Guantánamo case. Clinton's face lit up. "Is that so?" he asked. Long after the White House photographer had snapped the requisite picture, Clinton was still pumping Johnson's hand, eyes twinkling, talking to the judge as if they were old buddies. But he never said a word about the case itself.

The president's staff would later admit they had struggled with how to handle Bulkeley from the outset. "It was an agonizing issue," said Sandy Berger, the former deputy national security adviser. "No one felt good about leaving the refugees on Guantánamo." But, Berger added, there was pressure from Capitol Hill—particularly from Senator Jesse Helms and certain other Republicans—not to release the Haitians. Eric Schwartz, one of Berger's subordinates, said the White House was worried about "the specter" of bringing in the Bulkeley refugees, all the more so because it would have been among the new administration's first immigration decisions.

Another factor at play, Schwartz added, was what he called "government noise." "Guantánamo just didn't get that much attention because we were dealing with a million other crises," he said, mentioning Bosnia, Somalia, and North Korea. "It's just like life—that critically important piece of paper at the bottom of your file—you're dealing with so many important things that not every issue gets the care and feeding it deserves." The White House had ultimately just let the issue play itself out at trial.

There was, however, little question about how the Clinton administration wanted the judge to rule. "A lot of people were happy when we lost," Sandy Berger said. "The president was glad. I was glad." After Judge Johnson's decision came down, the White House took less than forty-eight hours to announce it would release the refugees. "We didn't have to take any affirmative action anymore," Eric Schwartz explained. "In a political world it's very different to make an affirmative decision than to say you're complying with a court order." Judge Johnson had concluded early on in the trial that the White House had just such an outcome in mind. "They needed me for political cover," he said.

Nevertheless, a number of House Republicans were infuriated that Clinton had given up the legal battle over the Haitian refugees, and they called a news conference outside the Capitol Building in protest. "We have an immigration policy that is totally out of control in this country," raged Tom DeLay of Texas. "And for the Democrat party to refuse the American people the protection of keeping those that have AIDS and HIV out of this country is absolutely horrendous."

The Department of Justice began releasing the remaining refugees six days after the judge issued his decision. One of the last groups landed at Kennedy Airport a week later, on June 21, the first day of summer. Koh left New Haven mid-morning in his old silver Subaru and headed to New York to welcome the new arrivals.

The Supreme Court's decision had still not been issued, and each day after ten o'clock, when new rulings were announced, he'd waited to hear something. That day, after an hour on the road to New York, he stopped at a gas station and used a pay phone to call his office voice mail. He pressed the receiver to his head and plugged his other ear to block out the roar of traffic. A half-dozen new messages were waiting for him. The first was from a reporter, seeking comment about the justices' decision. A bolt of adrenaline shot through him, and he hung up the phone before the message was over. He didn't want to hear anything more. He had a gut feeling and it wasn't good.

In one of his recent dreams, Yale had won 9–0, and he'd told Mike Wishnie about it with a big grin. But when he reached Kennedy Airport that morning, he said nothing to the team about the reporter's message. An official gave Koh and Ratner special passes to go out on the tarmac, and Koh, in his usual khakis and oxford shirt, limped down the stairs onto the oil-stained concrete. He shielded his eyes and scanned the horizon, spotting a huge C-130 transport buzzing in. The plane touched down and taxied toward them, its enormous propellers whirring, then eased to a stop.

The Supreme Court decision is abstract, Koh struggled to tell himself. This is the real victory.

One by one, the refugees hiked down the ramp, their clothes billowing in the wind. Vilsaint Michel waved, sunglasses hiding his bloodshot eyes. Behind Michel were the final few children. Wadson Fortune was there, a year older now, gaping up at the plane. The *militan* followed, bags slung over their shoulders, and they pumped their fists in the air when they saw their lawyers.

Koh pounded Ratner on the back, his older colleague staring in wonder at their clients, almost unable to believe his eyes.

"We made an American military aircraft do this!" Koh shouted over the roar of the government's colossal machine, its engines still churning. "Law made this happen!"

But when Koh finally read the Supreme Court opinion later that day, he was crushed. As lopsided as Johnson's ruling had been in the Yale team's favor, the high court's decision was just as sharply against it. The justices ruled eight to one in favor of the president's power to return fleeing refugees directly to Haiti, with Harry Blackmun as the lone dissenter. Even Justice Stevens had sided with the government—in fact, he had written the decision, adopting Deputy Solicitor General Maureen Mahoney's argument on almost every point.

The crux of the matter, Stevens wrote for the court, was that neither the Refugee Act of 1980 nor Article 33 applied at sea. The bar against "return" of refugees in each of those laws applied only to people who were already in the United States. The president could deal with the Haitians however he saw fit if he found them out on the ocean. Beyond American borders, at least when it came to foreigners fleeing persecution, he was bound by no law at all.

And yet, as Koh saw it, Stevens was not comfortable with the decision. Near the end of his opinion, the justice observed that the U.N. treaty's drafters "may not have contemplated that any nation would gather fleeing refugees and return them to the one country they had desperately sought to escape; such actions may even violate the spirit of Article 33." But the spirit of the law wasn't enough to save the Haitians, the justice said, because the precise language of the disputed provision could not "reasonably be read" to have force outside the United States. "This case," Stevens concluded, "presents a painfully common situation in which desperate people, convinced that they can no longer remain in their homeland, take desperate measures to escape. Although the human crisis is compelling, there is no solution to be found in a judicial remedy."

In dissent, Justice Blackmun protested that the court was ignoring the plain words and the purpose of the Refugee Act and Article 33. "The refugees attempting to escape from Haiti," Blackmun wrote, "do not claim a right of admission to this country. . . . They demand only that the United States, land of refugees and guardian of freedom, cease forcibly driving them back to detention, abuse, and death. That is a modest plea, vindicated by the treaty and the statute. We should not close our ears to it."

Blackmun had faced an impossible situation when the justices met for conference to decide the case, as his notes from the meeting would later reveal. Justice David Souter had conceded that the Refugee Act was "literally" in the refugees' favor; Justice Sandra Day O'Connor said much the same thing. But they were evidently nervous about interfering with presidential authority and had hunted for other ways to get around the wording of the statute. Blackmun had also debated the scope of the Refugee Act at length with Justice Stevens. Stevens's evident conclusion, set out in Blackmun's personal notes, was that a ruling for the refugees "places a limit on the power of the president. Not good."

Koh spent the rest of the day handling calls from the media. He'd already thought out his comments in the event that Yale lost.

"I think it's a sad day for anyone whose ancestors came to this country by boat," he told one reporter after another.

"That's most of us," asked one of them. "Right?"

Alone, rereading the decision, he brooded. The law had been *clear.* It wasn't even close. But if he'd hoped for any clue as to Justice Scalia's thinking, he wasn't going to get it. While the justice had a penchant for issuing separate opinions, this time around he had joined the majority decision without adding a word of his own. And when Blackmun's notes were released many years later, they revealed almost nothing about what Scalia might have said at the justices' conference.

As the weeks went by, Koh struggled to take a more detached view of the case. The outcome, he told himself, was inevitable. Two presidents, one Republican and one Democratic, had both taken the position that they could return the refugees, and the court itself had already issued two stays in the government's favor. In those circumstances, the justices were never going to rule against the White House. Indeed, that was what his own scholarship had predicted: the president would take the initiative, and no matter how unlawful his policy might be, the courts would tolerate it. And nothing—not the plain language of a law, not the purpose behind it, not the human cost of the president's action—was going to change things. Based on the team's Supreme Court brief, Koh wrote an academic article that summer assailing "the Rehnquist Court's disturbing pattern of reflexive deference to presidential power in foreign affairs and hostility toward both aliens and international law."

National security official Eric Schwartz later explained why the Clinton administration had defended the Bush direct return order at the Supreme Court. Since the decision had already been made to keep the policy in place, White House officials felt they had no choice but to seek a legal basis to support it. "We could always do the right thing," Schwartz explained, meaning allow the refugees to flee their country. "But the thinking was, let's have the law in place to have a greater degree of flexibility. It's a rare senior executive official who will surrender that flexibility."

In the end, the students were shocked only by the Supreme Court's vote. Most had thought that at least Stevens would have joined Blackmun, and there was a widespread conviction that Scalia had ignored his own plain language principles. "It's hard to believe there's *any* consistent judicial philosophy," one of Tory's friends on the team said. "It's usually driven by politics. It's so naive to think otherwise, and we fell into this trap of believing the law can be decided on the merits without political issues coming into play." But Lisa felt that for Koh, it was more than that. "Harold always thought by working harder and caring more, we could win," she said. "The Supreme Court was where that ended, where working harder, caring so much, being right—none of it was enough."

The team glumly accepted that President Clinton was now free to keep the direct return policy in place as long as he wished. That left Haitians who wanted to leave their country only one realistic option: apply for asylum at the American consulate or one of the other U.S. processing centers in Haiti. But as one Justice Department official would later concede, "The program's driven by the predisposition to reject claims, and we've gotten quite good at it." As of the beginning of June 1993, Haitians had filed 18,348 applications for asylum. American officials had rejected almost 5,000 of them, while most of the others were still pending. Only 380—or two percent—had been approved. The numbers were not good for someone hoping to get her relatives out of the country.

With help from the Yale resettlement team, Yvonne moved into a small apartment in Queens. She figured out how to use the bus, take the subway, and manage a bank account. She struggled to learn English. And despite holding on to a fragment of hope, she was prepared for the worst when she went to a clinic that had agreed to treat some of the Bulkeley refugees. She left with more AZT, resolved to stay healthy as long as she could.

But NCHR had not been able to get her family out of Haiti yet, and in early July, three months after arriving in New York, Yvonne received a tape cassette in the mail from her mother. In a common Haitian practice, Thérèse had taped herself on a borrowed machine and sent the *kasèt* to the United States. Her voice was quivering. *Attachés,* she said, had sprayed their home with gunfire and poured gasoline on the walls. Then they'd dragged the family dog behind a truck until it was a heap of bloody fur and bones. We've got to get the kids out of here, Thérèse said. The tape ended with a plea for help.

Yvonne dialed the pawnshop as fast as she could.

"Your mother's gone," someone told her. "The whole family left. We think they went to Jacmel." There were no more details.

She buried her head in her hands. Thérèse had a brother in Jacmel, on Haiti's southern coast, but there was no way to reach anyone there. She picked the phone up again and left a message for Antenor, but when they finally spoke, he knew nothing more than she did. He assured her he would find out what had happened. And then, not long afterward, he, too, vanished.

Beside herself, Yvonne begged for help from the people at the KID office. Someone *had* to know what was going on. But the woman who answered the phone there only made Yvonne more upset. She didn't know where Antenor had gone, wasn't sure when he'd be back. Another time, she said he was in the hospital and needed money for treatment. Yvonne scrounged up some cash, kept calling, kept asking questions. Her fears multiplied. The KID people were now making elliptical remarks—something very bad had happened, someone would tell her—but she couldn't get any straight answers. Finally, NCHR representative Pierre Esperance, who was heading to Haiti to monitor human rights conditions, promised to investigate and report back to her from Port-au-Prince.

A few days later, at dinnertime, Yvonne's phone rang. It was Ronald Aubourg. Something felt wrong to her right away. They'd been working at the NCHR office together an hour earlier and had just said good-bye.

"Why are you calling me?" she demanded.

There was a pause. "The thing you think is true—is true," Aubourg finally said. "Antenor is dead."

She slumped against the wall.

"Yvonne? Yvonne?"

"Thank you," she finally whispered. She let go of the receiver and dropped to the floor. She was still there an hour later when someone tapped on the door. It was Wadson Fortune. He lived nearby with his uncle, who'd also been in Bulkeley, and Yvonne wondered, in a moment of clarity, if Aubourg had sent him over. The boy brought her a glass of water and then busied himself making tea. She sat staring at nothing, images of her husband flashing through her mind.

There he was in Cite Soleil, dancing with her the night of Aristide's victory, arms swaying and head bobbing to the music. And there, striding into the courtyard, to warn everyone of the coup. And there, holding her, after she'd lost the baby.

Wadson came in with the tea and sat with her. In a flat voice, she asked him about his new school, his friends, his uncle. She hardly heard the answers.

Yvonne was still in a daze when she thanked Wadson and sent him home, and she lay in the darkness, staring at nothing, unable to sleep, unable to think, unable even to cry.

She tried for weeks to find out how Antenor had died. Someone said he'd been poisoned in the Artibonite Valley, in the central part of the country, many miles from Port-au-Prince. Another person told her he'd been killed on the way to the airport. Nobody knew for sure—or at least would say anything. There was no funeral, no way for her to say good-bye. All she had was a letter he'd written to her along with a small photograph, a picture of him in jeans and a cream-colored shirt, standing beside a jeep, with his familiar, confident smile.

Yvonne drifted through the days in a stupor. While she continued to speak publicly—her new target was the coup leaders—her energy and passion were gone; her remarks, bitter. "God," she told the *New York Times,* "should just erase Haiti from the face of the earth and create another world." All she wanted now was word from her mother and children. But for weeks, she heard nothing.

Then, as the weather grew cold, her fortunes turned. She called the pawnshop once again, and purely by chance, her sister, Yoleine, was in the neighborhood.

"Where have you been?" Yvonne cried.

They'd fled after the attack, Yoleine said. She'd returned from Jacmel to borrow money for the family but was planning to go back immediately. Things were as bad as the first weeks of the coup. It was FRAPH, she said: a new paramilitary group aligned with General Cedras. They were terrorizing everyone.

Yvonne knew all too well. The Haitian papers in New York were packed with stories about it.

"We have to leave Haiti," Yoleine told her sister.

"That's what I've been trying to arrange," Yvonne said, "but you vanished!"

"We've been thinking of taking a boat."

"NO!" Yvonne shrieked.

She ordered her sister to get everyone back from Jacmel and then track down Anne Fuller, an American NCHR representative who worked in the Pacot district of Port-au-Prince. Fuller already understood the family's situation, Yvonne said. She was waiting to help them file papers to leave the country.

With thousands of Haitians seeking asylum through the American consulate, Fuller's involvement made all the difference. She understood how to prepare the complicated forms, and she knew the people who processed them for the consulate, ensuring that Yvonne's family would not get lost in the shuffle. It was the sort of assistance most Haitians could never hope to receive, and within weeks, Yvonne's children, parents, brother, and sister were all slated to leave the country. The clinching fact in their applications was Yvonne's own activism in the U.S. It had been so widely reported in the American media, Fuller said, that even military authorities in Port-au-Prince had gotten wind of it.

There was now one last hurdle to getting everyone out: the test for communicable diseases that Yvonne knew only too well. The family was sent to a U.S.-designated physician for medical examinations, and to Yvonne's immense relief, everyone proved to be HIV negative. But the doctor discovered a spot on Thérèse's X-ray that made him suspect tuberculosis. While he cleared the rest of the family to enter the United States, she would have to wait behind for several months.

On a freezing day in January 1994, Ronald Aubourg and Johnny McCalla drove Yvonne to LaGuardia Airport. It had now been almost two years since she'd slipped away from the shanty in Cite Soleil, leaving her parents and children behind. At the gate, Yvonne peered down the Jetway, straining for a glimpse of Daniel or Jacques. And then, as if by magic, a boy, now seven years old, raced toward her, legs churning, eyes wide, seeing no one else in the world. She knelt and reached out and he hurled himself into her arms. She pressed him to her breast, kissed the top of his head, her tears spilling into his hair, murmuring her thanks to *Bondye*. Twelve-year-old Daniel followed, and she gathered him up, clutching both children now, and promised she would never, ever leave them again, they were safe now, everything was okay.

When Yvonne finally allowed herself to let go and look at them, she was amazed at how much they had grown. Jacques's face had broadened and his cheekbones were developing the same high, wide curve of her own. Daniel was taller, his frame beginning to fill out, and a hint of peach fuzz covered his upper lip. She embraced her father and sister, and had to stop herself from laughing at her brother, Jean, who liked to act tough but looked miserable from airsickness.

They drove back to Yvonne's small apartment, everyone marveling as she once had at the highways and the traffic and the buildings, and she served them a hearty meal of rice, beans, pork, and greens. Her father took the couch and the rest of the family all squeezed into Yvonne's bed, stunned by the frigid temperature but ecstatic to be free of the violence in Cite Soleil. Several months later, the doctor in Port-au-Prince determined that Thérèse did not have tuberculosis, and the family returned to the airport to welcome her. She arrived on a warm spring day in May 1994, with New York City in full bloom, and for the first time since before the coup that ousted Aristide, Yvonne felt almost whole.

———

In early August 1993, the Justice Department reversed course and appealed Judge Johnson's decision. The move had no impact on the Bulkeley refugees, all of whom were safely in the United States by late June of that year. It was about the law. Judge Johnson's ruling that the Constitution's due process clause applied on Guantánamo was a precedent that even the Clinton White House didn't want on the books. According to a former presidential adviser, the reasoning was much the same as it had been in defending the direct return order: administration officials wanted "maximum flexibility" on Guantánamo, "confident that they would do the right thing but not wanting to be forced by the law to have to do so."

The move by the Justice Department was a bitter pill for Koh and everyone else at Yale, for Judge Johnson's decision was the last ruling left in favor of the refugees. When the Supreme Court issued its decision in the direct return case, it had also made a separate ruling that got no attention from the media. On the Clinton administration's request, the high court had thrown out the landmark due process decision issued by the Second Circuit Court of Appeals the year before. It was the exact result Cappuccio had sought at the settlement meeting with Koh and Ratner the prior October.

And now the Clinton White House wanted an appellate court to reverse Judge Johnson's decision, effectively wiping away the last trace of the Guantánamo litigation. It was late summer and no students were around, so Koh met with Ratner, Tringali, and Guttentag to discuss the situation. Koh was adamant that they try to preserve Judge Johnson's opinion. They had to prevent Guantánamo from returning to the status of a law-free zone, a place where rights did not exist. "We've killed ourselves on this case," he said. "We want them to close Guantánamo and never open it again."

But if he was going to persuade the government to drop the appeal, Koh had only one bargaining chip to use—money. Having won the trial, Yale was entitled to attorneys' fees and court costs under a law called the Equal Access to Justice Act. The amount would be considerable, though not from the federal government's perspective. Koh started with the fact that he alone had spent about three thousand hours on the case. Four other lawyers had also invested a massive effort: Ratner, Tringali, Guttentag, and Robert Rubin. Then there were all the law students—Lisa Daugaard, Tory Clawson, Mike Wishnie, Veronique Sanchez, Steve Roos, Adam Gutride, Graham Boyd, Sarah Cleveland, Ray Brescia, Michael Barr, Paul Sonn, and dozens of others, totaling over one hundred people. Some, including Lisa, Tory, and Mike, had put in almost as many hours as Koh. There was also the work of a half-dozen other attorneys and numerous translators and expert witnesses. It all added up to about 20,000 hours, and even after charging only a small amount for the students' time, the total bill came to $3.5 million.

Koh told the Justice Department lawyers that Yale would cut the fee demand if the government dropped the appeal and let Judge Johnson's decision stand. Justice came back with a counteroffer: There would be no appeal and the government would pay part of Yale's bill if Koh joined in asking that the judge's final opinion be vacated, meaning that it would not exist as legal precedent.

A debate among the Yale lawyers followed. On the one hand, fighting the appeal would mean another year of work, maybe more, and if the case ended up at the Supreme Court, Koh was now certain they would lose. Money was also an issue, though far less important. In addition to lawyers' fees, the litigation team had run up over one hundred thousand dollars in expenses—and the government was prepared to cover those costs and much more.

Still, no one liked the idea of another vacated opinion, especially after all the work that had gone into obtaining it. Somebody played devil's advocate: At the end of the day, did the precedent really matter? Even if the opinion were vacated, lawyers in future cases could bring it to a court's attention based on its "persuasive authority"—the power of its reasoning. Some federal courts had rules against citing vacated opinions, but others were willing to examine them, and though the case wouldn't have the force of law, how much did that matter? Judge Johnson was only a district judge, the lowest rung on the federal ladder, so no higher court had to follow his decision. Perhaps vacating the opinion didn't matter that much.

Koh was mulling over the situation when a Justice attorney called. He gave Koh a one-week deadline to agree on the settlement, then hung up. The call left Koh mystified. What, he wondered, was the sudden rush? And why that particular date?

The next day, a school librarian dropped by his office. She was giving away the temporary paperbound editions of certain court decisions because the final hardbound volumes had arrived. As Koh flipped through the cases, a thought grabbed him. He called a representative at West Publishing, the mammoth legal publisher that printed most federal court opinions.

"The paperbound version of volume 823 of the Federal Supplement is out," Koh said, referring to the volume with Johnson's decision in it. "But what's the due date for changes to the hardbound version?"

The rep checked. It was the same day as the deadline set by Justice.

"So what happens," Koh asked, "if a decision in the paperbound reporter is vacated by agreement of the parties?"

"It won't be in the hardbound reporter."

"Not even listed as vacated?"

"Nope."

"Will it be on Westlaw?" This was West Publishing's computer database.

"No. It'll be like the case never happened."

Koh went back to the rest of the team and hashed out the situation. Everyone finally agreed they should take the settlement offer and Koh reluctantly called Justice—but two days *after* the deadline. A number of weeks later, West Publishing issued volume 823 of the Federal Supplement, a heavy, dark-beige book with gold, red, and black trim. Judge Johnson's opinion in *Haitian Centers Council v. Sale* appeared on page 1028. And though the case could only be cited in future briefs as a vacated decision, Koh gleefully discovered that the final order to vacate was nowhere to be found in the volume itself.

After Judge Johnson approved the deal, the government cut a check to Yale, Simpson Thacher, and the other lawyers for $634,100. A big chunk of the money went to cover plane tickets, Express Mail packages, printing, photocopying, telephone bills, and so forth. Koh paid off the team charges that he had put on his own credit cards, including a fee of $7,500 for one of Jesse Jackson's chartered jets to Guantánamo, then gave the rest of Yale's portion to the Lowenstein Clinic. Michael Ratner had his own bills to pay and allotted the balance to his organization, the Center for Constitutional Rights.

Simpson Thacher donated its portion of the money to several nonprofit groups, including Bro Broberg's employer, the Coalition for the Homeless, to help resettle the refugees. Joe Tringali then did the requisite internal paperwork for his firm, and the matter was officially closed out at Simpson. In a prominent place in his office, above stacks of litigation documents and his antique toys, he hung a framed courtroom artist's sketch of him questioning his first witness at the trial, refugee Fritznel Camy. Tringali was again submerged in his antitrust practice, shuttling back and forth to Paris for an arbitration involving Fiat and Ford Motor Company. The years passed, clients came and went. But well over a decade later, his hair gently receding and the crinkles around his eyes deepening, Tringali still considered the trial for the Guantánamo Haitians the biggest victory of his career.

In December 1993, two months before Yale received the check from the government, President Clinton's top human rights official at the State Department, John Shattuck, visited Haiti to assess the human rights situation. The administration's negotiations to remove Cedras from power had led nowhere. Political violence was worse than ever. Repatriated refugees were being arrested and American refugee-processing centers were overrun by military thugs. Deeply troubled, Shattuck called for a review of Clinton's direct return policy.

Shattuck was rebuked in the media by a State Department higher-up, but momentum for a change began to gather. The Congressional Black Caucus stepped up pressure on the White House, and in the spring, anti-apartheid activist Randall Robinson launched a highly publicized hunger strike against the repatriations. In early May, three days after Robinson was hospitalized, Clinton announced he would abandon the policy of direct returns. National Security Adviser Anthony Lake later said he had already changed his own mind about the policy, but when asked if Robinson's hunger strike had any impact on him, he said, "Of course. I was worried Randall might die."

With violence in Haiti still widespread and the embargo continuing, Haitians began fleeing in huge numbers. In late June 1994, the administration reopened Guantánamo, cramming thousands onto the McCalla tarmac once again. Koh was dismayed. Now that the decisions by Judge Johnson and the Second Circuit were gone, Guantánamo was again a lawless zone, and he feared that executive abuse would inevitably follow.

But the refugee exodus put Haiti back in the news and spurred support for U.S. intervention to restore democracy and stem the tide of fleeing Haitians. An unlikely coalition of pro-Haitian groups and anti-immigrant interests pressed for Cedras's ouster, galvanizing a president who'd once asked his adviser Sandy Berger, "If we can't restore democracy to that tiny country a few hundred miles from the U.S., what kind of superpower are we?" In September 1994, despite a divided Congress, Clinton authorized a military invasion to return Aristide to power. Cedras only stepped down when he learned U.S. paratroopers were already heading for Port-au-Prince.

Along with several hundred other official U.S. guests, an elated Michael Ratner flew to Haiti for Aristide's restoration. Thousands of U.S. troops were waiting in formation at the airport, and Ratner's delegation inched its way through the city streets amid throngs of cheering Haitians. As it had been for Aristide's inauguration, Port-au-Prince was once again swept clean, everything painted in the national colors of red and blue. At the National Palace, Ratner watched as a helicopter touched down on the sweeping lawn. Aristide emerged wearing the gold-fringed presidential sash, released a white dove, and then addressed his delirious fellow citizens. "Never, never, never, never again will one more drop of blood flow," he called in Creole. He promised security, justice, economic opportunity, a new beginning for the country. Today, he said, "affirms the strength of solidarity, the fortitude of conviction, the power of dreams."

More idealistic and committed than ever, Lisa Daugaard nursed ambitions of launching a new struggle for social justice on a grand scale. She still didn't have her law degree, but managed to win the job of legal director at the Coalition for the Homeless in Manhattan. Soon she was orchestrating class action suits against the New York City Police Department, with bigger plans in the works. No one shared her zeal for political discussion more than Bro Broberg, her former antagonist and now coworker. The two became inseparable friends and then, to their astonishment, fell in love. Neither could explain it, and Bro felt he was betraying the gay community, but they moved in together. He finally insisted Lisa finish law school in 1995, all but shutting her in her room to write her final four papers. She graduated, took the bar, and more than three years after leaving Yale, officially became a lawyer.

Along with her degree, though, Lisa acquired a growing sense of disillusionment. Her work wasn't adding up to the "incipient revolution" she'd imagined. Even after organizing a massive shutdown of Manhattan's bridges and tunnels to publicize homelessness and AIDS, she awoke the next morning to find the world very much the same place it had been the day before. It didn't matter how committed to the cause she was; she would never be able to undo the radically unfair structure of modern American society.

Persuaded that her efforts were best spent on a local level, Lisa moved back with Bro to her hometown of Seattle and took a job as a public defender. She still retained her modest faith in the law—a faith she had developed during the Guantánamo suit. Statutes, codes, and precedents might usually favor the powerful, but she believed she could *always* find some provision to throw a wrench in the government machine, slowing it down, buying time for more litigation, or a political argument, or a street protest—whatever it took to keep fighting.

Yet she remained ambivalent about the broader meaning of Yale's case for the Haitian refugees. In pessimistic hours, she would say that the team had been battling against a tide of presidential power and bureaucratic indifference that could only be held back for a brief moment. "We can't put thousands of hours into fighting every injustice," she sighed, cradling her newborn baby. "We don't have the resources. And Guantánamo was just one instance, a battle for this small group of people."

Then, however, the energy would return to her voice. "If you're collectively ambitious enough," she'd challenge, "what can you accomplish? The Haiti case set the standard. We started out with the law against us and everyone thought we would fail. It was, 'Who the hell do they think they are?' But we inspired each other. We worked all the time. Day and night. We simply would not take no for an answer. People—my friends— did unbelievable things. And we won. If you're serious about something, you'll act."

Mike Wishnie stuck with his Haitian clients long after his classmates had moved on. In the weeks following Judge Johnson's final order in 1993, he spent all his waking hours on the resettlement effort, stopping only for a frantic two-week cram session to prepare for the bar exam. He then set to work on asylum applications for the refugees, for Judge Johnson's decision wasn't the end of the matter. After the Haitians entered the United

States, the INS refused to honor the results of the final asylum hearings it had held on Guantánamo the year before. Still more paperwork had to be filed; every Bulkeley refugee had to prove a "well-founded fear of persecution" to avoid being deported.

A few years later, following a clerkship with Justice Harry Blackmun, Mike joined the faculty at the New York University School of Law and co-founded an immigrants' rights clinic. The Haiti case had confirmed for him that big, ambitious lawsuits had their value alongside smaller cases to help individual clients, and Wishnie and his students went on to file major class action cases for immigrant laborers, as well as fight the deportation of foreigners jailed in INS detention centers. He earned tenure and helped win a key Supreme Court case against the INS.

The Haiti case, nevertheless, remained a landmark in his life. "I'll always extend my legal career back to my years in law school so that I can say I helped shut down the HIV camp on Guantánamo," he said, sitting in his office off Sixth Avenue. "When I'm seventy-five years old, I'll still have that. But I hope that it isn't the top. I hope I don't look back and think, This is the best thing I ever did."

"It had this dangerous lesson," he added. "It gave us a sense of invincibility: 'We're going to outsmart them and outfight them, and we're going to make this happen!' But it's not true. It doesn't always work out that way. Going on in life, I've seen it. Sometimes you lose. And we did lose a big piece of our case, of course, at the Supreme Court. And we lost some of our clients in Haiti—like Frantz Guerrier. I can still see him, still see his eyes. He's the face of Guantánamo."

Tory spent her third year at Yale living like a normal law student. She spoke up in class without fear. She found a boyfriend. She went out to dinner with her roommates and lazed around at home watching the winter Olympics. Many of the Bulkeley refugees were living just two hours away, struggling to find jobs and deal with their illness, and she felt guilty for not keeping up with them. But she was worn out by Haiti. She wanted to move on, and was again hearing the call of Nepal. After clerking for a judge, she took up the struggle for social justice in the small mountain country that was her first love.

Back in Kathmandu, she became an advocate against the use of child labor in Nepalese carpet factories, ultimately leaving the law. She was tired of the adversarial process, the two clashing fists Koh had made on the first day of class. The factory owners, she discovered, were not beyond redemption. She decided her objectives were best served by developing a positive program with the owners rather than simply pressuring them not to use children. Compromise and engagement fit her personality better anyway, she realized. The world still needed damn-the-torpedoes human rights lawyers. But that just wasn't her role in life.

She married a Canadian, started a family, and joined the Nepalese office of Save the Children—the group she'd first learned about from the television ad she'd seen as a twelve-year-old. Now a decade out of law school, Tory was shocked to realize that she was almost the age Koh had been when they'd filed the litigation. He'd seemed so *grown-up,* she mused. And so different from the lawyer he had become. "Harold thinks the Haiti case changed all of us," Tory said, her face turning serious, knowing. "Made us into better lawyers, human rights people, all of that. But that's what I already wanted to do—the human rights part, anyway. If I dare say it, we changed his outlook more than he did ours. We opened up a new world for him."

In mid-1998, Koh received a call from a former student, Jim O'Brien, who was an aide to Secretary of State Madeleine Albright. The assistant secretary for democracy, human rights, and labor, John Shattuck, was stepping down, O'Brien said. Shattuck and others at State thought Koh might make a good replacement.

Koh was stunned. "But I've spent all this time suing the government," he said.

"That's a plus," O'Brien answered. "You're nobody's yes-man."

After Haiti, Koh and a new group of students had sued the Clinton administration again, this time to free Cubans held on Guantánamo. He'd also continued the Lowenstein Clinic cases, suing dictators for human rights crimes, and had publicly castigated the White House for failing to stop human rights abuses around the world. His reputation at Yale had changed so dramatically that even before Tory had graduated, she'd heard first years express surprise that Koh taught international business transactions. "I thought," one conservative student sniffed, "that he was just some human rights guy."

Shattuck, the current assistant secretary, warned Koh the job would not be easy. The State Department was a grinding bureaucracy with a mass of different bureaus fighting for influence. The human rights bureau wielded little power, with a paltry budget and an agenda often discounted by others in the organization. But despite his lingering feelings of betrayal over the direct return order, Koh decided to seek the post. He was convinced he could do as much good working within the administration as he had in fighting it.

After his Senate confirmation, Koh resumed the hectic schedule of the Haiti litigation—one hundred hours a week, sometimes more. He traveled the world, investigating ethnic cleansing in Kosovo, attacks on refugees fleeing East Timor, abuses against the Kurdish minority in Turkey. He promised the United Nations that America was "unalterably committed to a world without torture." And he issued the official State Department reports on human rights in every country around the world, sometimes ruffling feathers. He wanted the reports to tell the blunt truth, especially after the way he felt the Bush administration had whitewashed the situation in Haiti.

Among more than 150 foreign trips, he flew to Port-au-Prince in 1999 to meet with Jean-Bertrand Aristide, hoping to revive what had become a failing democracy. The two already knew each other, for Aristide, while still in exile, had come to speak at Yale Law School not long after the Haiti litigation ended. "My dear brother," he'd called Koh. But the speech itself had been oddly wandering and self-absorbed. Tory Clawson and the other students were deeply disappointed—*This* was the man for whom Yvonne Pascal had sacrificed so much?—and Koh would later see that awkward day as a harbinger.

Aristide's 1994 restoration by the United States had not turned out as Koh or many others had hoped. The president continued to be a popular hero to many, abolishing the army and, with the heavy assistance of U.S. and U.N. troops, largely halting the widespread human rights abuses of the Cedras era. But the international community failed to commit the aid necessary to reverse the devastation of the coup and the embargo, and most Haitians remained in misery. Struggling to navigate between World Bank officials demanding harsh reforms and a citizenry desperate to survive, the president avoided difficult economic decisions—and lost much of his foreign support. The Lavalas political movement splintered, with various factions battling for power, and some former allies began to accuse Aristide of authoritarian tendencies. Though he left office in 1996 (the Haitian constitution barred the president from serving consecutive terms), he remained the central figure in Haitian politics and few doubted that he still controlled the country.

Koh had once seen Aristide as Haiti's savior, but by the time he sat down with him in his home outside Port-au-Prince in 1999, he'd grown disillusioned with the former president. "Are you going to be the man who changes Haitian politics," Koh implored, "or just another Haitian politician?" Aristide won the presidency in another landslide in 2000, but his party was accused of tampering with the parliamentary elections in a bid, some said, to take over the entire government. Aid groups cut off funds to Haiti, punishing the poorest in much the way the embargo had. Aristide and his *boujwazi*-backed opponents plunged into a bitter fight for control of the country, and armed pro-Aristide gangs reminiscent of the *attachés* from the Cedras years roamed the streets of Port-au-Prince. Dismayed, some democracy activists walked away from politics altogether, and one especially popular Lavalas militant killed himself, leaving behind a note that said, "I am exiting the stinking sewage."

When Koh left the State Department at the end of Clinton's presidency, he received high marks from the human rights community. But one country he'd been able to do little for was Haiti. "The U.S.," he sighed, "simply gave up on it."

Koh returned to Yale in January 2001, resuming his oversight of the Lowenstein Clinic. On his first day back, he shuffled into class with his battered briefcase and overstuffed Lands' End canvas bag. An eager group of students was waiting, some liberal, some moderate, even a few conservatives. They knew about Koh, knew that he'd been at the State Department. A few were vaguely aware of a case he'd filed about Guantánamo many years earlier.

"Hi, everybody," he said with a tired grin. "I'm Harold Koh." He had no grand choreographed presentation planned. He'd given up that method of teaching, believing he'd been too focused on cramming information into his students' heads. His goal now was to help them think critically about the legal system.

He gave a brief introduction to the clinic and told a few war stories from the State Department, his voice in the guttural buzz that past students at Yale knew so well. Then he turned serious, describing the lawsuits the clinic would try to file. "This course," he concluded, "is about saving people. And not just the people you'll be helping, but all of *you*."

Several students shot him a doubtful look.

After the Haiti case, five more years of human rights litigation, and two years fighting the detention, torture, and murder of innocent people around the world, Koh was on a mission. As he now saw it, the talented student body around him had an obligation to serve the least privileged in society. Nobody needed the best and the brightest as desperately as people like the Haitian refugees—and torture victims in Turkey, and religious refugees from Tibet—because the odds were so stacked against them. Koh didn't want Yale to be just another professional school, training hired guns. He envisioned a community of higher moral purpose, learning for the sake of service.

After Koh's comments, several students gathered up their papers and backpacks and walked out. He didn't care. If the rest of the class stuck with him, that would be enough. They had work to do.

Epilogue
THE AFTERMATH

IN THE WAKE of the September 11, 2001, terrorist attacks on New York City and Washington, D.C., the United States invaded Afghanistan. American troops waged a military campaign against the governing Taliban regime and the al-Qaeda terrorist network harbored by it, capturing scores of terrorist suspects. Shortly thereafter, President George W. Bush concluded that they were not entitled to prisoner-of-war status under the Geneva Conventions. In late December, Secretary of Defense Donald Rumsfeld announced that the government was transporting the prisoners to Guantánamo Bay for detention and interrogation.

The first detainees arrived in Cuba by military transport plane in January 2002. By mid-2003, the United States was holding over six hundred terrorist suspects from over forty countries at Guantánamo in a maximum-security facility known as Camp Delta. Members of the Joint Task Force assigned to guard them were quartered in new, air-conditioned barracks in nearby Camp Bulkeley.

The Bush administration declared that the detainees were the "worst of the worst" and claimed it had the power to hold them indefinitely. No formal charges were filed against them, and they were denied access to counsel and all communication with the outside world.

In February 2002, a team of lawyers including Michael Ratner of the Center for Constitutional Rights filed suit against the Bush administration in federal court in Washington, D.C., challenging the legality of the detainees' confinement. The case, *Rasul v. Bush*, asserted that holding the detainees indefinitely on Guantánamo violated the Constitution's due process clause and other laws. In support of this argument, the detainees' lawyers relied in part on the decision in *Haitian Centers Council v. Sale*.

The government, in response, claimed that no U.S. law applied on Guantánamo, that the detainees had no enforceable rights, and that the court itself had no jurisdiction—that is, authority—to hear the case. The federal district court dismissed the lawsuit. The appellate court upheld the dismissal, refusing to follow *Haitian Centers Council* on the grounds that it had been vacated and was, in any event, wrongly decided.

In November 2003, over the government's objection, the Supreme Court agreed to review *Rasul v. Bush*. Guantánamo was by now the subject of intense criticism, both international and domestic, and a number of foreign governments were calling on the United States to release nationals of their respective countries. Dozens of amicus briefs were filed in support of the detainees, including one co-authored by Professor Harold Hongju Koh of Yale Law School and the students of the Lowenstein International Human Rights Clinic, and another co-authored by Professor Michael Wishnie of the New York University School of Law.

The justices heard oral argument in *Rasul v. Bush* in April 2004. Solicitor General Ted Olson presented the case for the Bush administration, repeating the claims that the Constitution had no force on Guantánamo and that the courts had no authority to hear the case. Olson's written brief to the Supreme Court stated that the detainees were being treated "humanely." The brief also referred to a White House press release assuring that they would "not be subjected to physical or mental abuse or cruel treatment."

Days after the argument, the media reported that American soldiers had been torturing detainees at the Abu Ghraib prison in Iraq. Allegations of abuse on Guantánamo soon followed. In a letter to the *New York Times*, Michael Ratner charged that two Guantánamo detainees represented by his organization had been left in solitary confinement for up to three months and interrogated for twelve hours at a time while shackled to the floor. They were ultimately released with no charges having been filed against them.

On June 28, 2004, the Supreme Court issued its decision in *Rasul v. Bush*. In broad terms, the court rejected the government's argument and ruled that the federal courts had the authority to hear the Guantánamo detainees' claims. The vote was 6–3, and Justice John Paul Stevens wrote the majority opinion. While Stevens did not mention *Haitian Centers Council* by name, he stated that if—as claimed—the detainees were not involved in terrorism, then holding them for two years on the naval base without access to a lawyer "unquestionably" violated the "Constitution or laws or treaties of the United States."

Justice Anthony Kennedy wrote a separate opinion to explain why he had sided with the majority. "What matters," he said, "is the unchallenged and indefinite control that the United States has long exercised over Guantanamo Bay. From a practical perspective, the indefinite lease of Guantanamo Bay has produced a place that belongs to the United States, extending the 'implied protection' of the United States to it."

Justice Antonin Scalia dissented, joined by Chief Justice William H. Rehnquist and Justice Clarence Thomas. "Today," Justice Scalia wrote, "the Court springs a trap on the Executive, subjecting Guantanamo Bay to the oversight of the federal courts even though it has never before been thought to be within their jurisdiction." Scalia described the majority decision as "monstrous."

Despite the significance of its ruling, the court in *Rasul v. Bush* did not make a final determination about the fate of the Guantánamo detainees. Instead, having set forth the basic principle that the president is constrained in his use of the naval base as a detention facility, the court left it to the lower courts to review the detainees' claims and determine the exact scope of their rights. Litigation then resumed in federal district court in Washington, D.C., with the Bush administration struggling to downplay the requirements of the *Rasul* ruling.

Advocates for the detainees considered the Supreme Court's decision a landmark victory for human rights. Although further proceedings were still necessary, a six-justice majority had made it clear that the government could not hold anyone on Guantánamo indefinitely without answering to a federal court. Indeed, the lawyers and law students of the *Haitian Centers Council* case read *Rasul* as the final word on a claim they had first made in 1992: Guantánamo is a land governed by the laws of the United States of America.

THE CHARACTERS*

THE YALE LAW SCHOOL LITIGATION TEAM

Harold Hongju Koh, *professor of law*
Michael Ratner, *visiting clinical professor of law and attorney,
Center for Constitutional Rights, New York City*

Law Students

Michelle Anderson, Michael Barr, Graham Boyd, Ray Brescia, Tory Clawson, Chris Coons, Sarah Cleveland, Lisa Daugaard, Adam Gutride, Laura Ho, Christy Lopez, Steve Roos, Veronique Sanchez, Paul Sonn, Mike Wishnie

Outside Attorneys

Lucas Guttentag, *director, Immigrants' Rights Project,
American Civil Liberties Union*
Jennifer Klein, *associate, Simpson Thacher & Bartlett*
Robert Rubin, *attorney, San Francisco Lawyers' Committee for Civil Rights*
Joseph Tringali, *partner, Simpson Thacher & Bartlett*

Advocates, Translators, Guantánamo Representatives, and Others

Ronald Aubourg, *staff member, National Coalition for Haitian Refugees*
William ("Bro") Broberg, *crisis intervention director, Coalition for the Homeless*
Allan Ebert, *private attorney, Washington, D.C.*
Evelyne Longchamp, *board chair, Haitian Women's Program, and registered nurse*
Johnny McCalla, *executive director, National Coalition for Haitian Refugees*
Cathy Powell, *postgraduate fellow, Harvard Law School*
Ninaj Raoul, *director, Haitian Women for Haitian Refugees*
Elliot Schrage, *consultant, Lawyers Committee for Human Rights*
Betty Williams, *volunteer, Coalition for the Homeless*

*Titles and organization names pertain to the period 1991–1993.

Physicians and Medical Experts
Dr. Robert Cohen, *attending physician, AIDS Center, St. Vincent's Hospital*
Dr. Jonathan Mann, *professor, Harvard School of Public Health*
Dr. Douglas Shenson, *board of directors, Doctors of the World*

THE HAITIANS

The Refugees Detained on Guantánamo Bay
Fritznel Camy, Pierre Charles, Wilson Edouard, Wadson Fortune, Frantz Guerrier, Harold Michel, Vilsaint Michel, Christa Micles, Yanick Mondesir, Armelle Nelson, Yvonne Pascal, Joel Saintil

The Government and Military in Haiti
Jean-Bertrand Aristide, *president*
Raoul Cedras, *brigadier general and commander, armed forces*

Activists and Others
Antenor Joseph, *spokesperson for KID (Confederation for Democratic Unity)
    and husband of Yvonne Pascal*
Thérèse Pascal, *mother of Yvonne Pascal*
Jacques and Daniel, *children of Yvonne Pascal*
Evans Paul, *leader of KID and mayor of Port-au-Prince*
Claudel Pierre, *refugee*
Decoste Veillard, *refugee*

THE UNITED STATES GOVERNMENT

The Bush Administration (1991–1992)
James Baker, *secretary of state*
George H. W. Bush, *president of the United States*
Dick Cheney, *secretary of defense*

The Bush Department of Justice (1991–1992)
William Barr, *attorney general*
Paul Cappuccio, *associate deputy attorney general*
Maureen Mahoney, *deputy solicitor general*
Kenneth Starr, *solicitor general*
Steven Valentine, *deputy assistant attorney general, Civil Division*

The Clinton Administration (1993)
Sandy Berger, *deputy national security adviser*
Bill Clinton, *president*

Hillary Rodham Clinton, *first lady*
Walter Dellinger, *transition official and attorney, White House Counsel's Office*
Anthony Lake, *national security adviser*
Bernard Nussbaum, *White House counsel*
Eric Schwartz, *national security council official*

The Clinton Department of Justice (1993)
Michael Cardozo, *transition official*
Webster Hubbell, *transition official and associate attorney general*
Maureen Mahoney, *deputy solicitor general (Bush holdover)*

Immigration and Naturalization Service
Duke Austin, *special assistant to the director of congressional and public affairs*
Gene McNary, *commissioner*
Grover Joseph Rees, *general counsel (Bush holdover)*

Office of Immigration Litigation
Lauri Filppu, *deputy director*
Allen Hausman, *staff attorney*
Ellen Sue Shapiro, *staff attorney*

United States Attorney's Office for the Eastern District of New York
Robert Begleiter, *assistant United States attorney and chief, Civil Division*
Scott Dunn, *assistant United States attorney*

United States Department of Defense Joint Task Force
Jason Dillman, *lieutenant, United States Army*
Stephen Kinder, *colonel, United States Army*
Bud Paulson, *colonel, United States Air Force*
George Walls Jr., *brigadier general, United States Marines*
Larry Zinser, *colonel, United States Marines*

United States Coast Guard
James Carlson, *combat information center officer*

Centers for Disease Control and Prevention
Paul Effler, *physician, Epidemic Intelligence Service,*
    Division of Sexually Transmitted Diseases

American Embassy, Port-au-Prince, Haiti
Dudley Sipprelle, *consul general*

THE UNITED STATES JUDICIARY

United States District Court for the Eastern District of New York
Sterling Johnson Jr., *district court judge*
Eugene H. Nickerson, *district court judge*
Jack B. Weinstein, *district court judge*

United States Court of Appeals for the Second Circuit
George Pratt, *circuit court judge*

United States Supreme Court
Harry Blackmun, *associate justice*
William H. Rehnquist, *chief justice*
Antonin Scalia, *associate justice*
John Paul Stevens, *associate justice*
Clarence Thomas, *associate justice*

OTHER CHARACTERS

Advocates for the Refugees
The Reverend Jesse Jackson
Susan Sarandon

The *Baker* Litigation Team
Ira Kurzban, *partner, Kurzban, Kurzban & Weinger, P.A.*
Cheryl Little, *attorney, Haitian Refugee Center*

Georgetown Law School
David Cole, *professor*

Yale Law School
Guido Calabresi, *dean*
Jay Pottenger, *clinical professor*

Harold Hongju Koh's Family
Kwang Lim Koh, *Harold Hongju Koh's father*
Mary-Christy Fisher, *Harold Hongju Koh's wife*

United States Congress
Lamar Smith, *congressman (R-Texas)*

LIST OF TERMS

A PREFATORY NOTE: immigration law is a technical field in which many common words have very specific, complex meanings. For instance, "refugee," "admit," "asylum," "deport," "enter," "expel," and "remove" all have legal definitions that differ from their everyday meanings. This book uses these words as a layperson would, except for a few instances indicated in the text. In particular, the word "refugee" is used, as it was in most media reports, to describe all Haitians fleeing Haiti during the relevant time period. However, as noted in the text, the legal term "refugee" is restricted to those fleeing their country because they have a "well-founded fear of persecution" based on their political opinions or certain other factors (as explained below in the definitions of Article 33 and the Refugee Act of 1980). The legal term "refugee" does not include people leaving their homeland in search of greater economic opportunity.

AG: The attorney general of the United States.

Article 33: Article 33 of the 1951 United Nations Convention Relating to the Status of Refugees mandates that "No Contracting State shall expel or return ('*refouler*') a refugee in any manner whatsoever to the frontiers of territories where his life or freedom would be threatened on account of his race, religion, nationality, membership of a particular social group or political opinion." The U.N. Refugee Convention is the key international legal treaty that defines the rights of refugees and the legal duties owed to them by contracting states. The United States became a party to the U.N. Refugee Convention in 1968.

Asylum hearing: An administrative proceeding to determine whether an applicant has a "well-founded fear of persecution" and is thus entitled to asylum in the United States. The hearing takes place before an INS (see below) asylum officer, and the applicant has the right to counsel, though not at government expense. If the application for asylum is denied, the applicant may renew the claim before an immigration law judge, and if necessary, may appeal to a federal court. *Note:* Under INS regulations, the asylum hearing is technically known as an "interview." But it is sometimes referred to as an "asylum hearing," and the text uses that latter phrase to avoid confusion with the "screening interviews" that took place on Guantánamo.

Baker: *Haitian Refugee Center v. Baker.* The lawsuit filed against the federal government in November 1991 in Miami by Ira Kurzban and other immigration experts. *Baker* sought more thorough INS screening interviews of Haitians fleeing their homeland after the September 1991 coup ousting President Jean-Bertrand Aristide.

Direct return order: The executive order issued by President George H.W. Bush in May 1992, authorizing the Coast Guard to intercept all Haitians fleeing their homeland and return them directly to Haiti, regardless of any claim they might have to asylum in the United States.

DOJ: U.S. Department of Justice.

Due process: The Fifth Amendment of the Constitution provides in part that "No person shall . . . be deprived of life, liberty, or property, without due process of law. . . ." This open-ended provision served as the basis for the Yale team's argument that the Haitians detained on Guantánamo had the right to counsel and to adequate medical care, and the right not to be detained indefinitely.

Eastern District: The United States District Court for the Eastern District of New York, located in Brooklyn, where Judge Sterling Johnson Jr. began his service in 1991. The Eastern District is a trial court, the first tier in the federal court hierarchy. Decisions by the district, or trial, courts, are reviewed by the circuit courts (see Second Circuit, below). Decisions by the circuit courts are reviewed by the U.S. Supreme Court.

HIV ban: An informal term for the regulation issued by the Department of Health and Human Services barring the entry of HIV-positive foreigners into the United States.

INA: Immigration and Nationality Act. The congressional statute that addresses most all immigration matters, including the authority to grant asylum.

INS: U.S. Immigration and Naturalization Service. The INS was part of the Department of Justice during the time period covered by the book.

(In 2003, Congress abolished the INS and assigned its functions to the new Department of Homeland Security.)

McNary: *Haitian Centers Council v. McNary.* The lawsuit filed by the Yale team against the federal government in March 1992, demanding access to the Haitian refugees on Guantánamo and a halt to the INS screening process and Coast Guard repatriations. *McNary* essentially became two cases, each with the same name, when the Yale team returned to Judge Johnson in May 1992 to challenge President Bush's direct return order. The cases were officially separated ("bifurcated," in legal terminology) by the judge in November 1992. Both cases were renamed *Haitian Centers Council v. Sale* in early 1993, when Gene McNary stepped down as commissioner of the INS and Chris Sale became acting commissioner.

OIL: Office of Immigration Litigation. OIL, part of the Department of Justice, is responsible for representing the United States in immigration litigation across the country.

Refugee Act of 1980: At the time of the *McNary* case, the Refugee Act of 1980 included the U.S. equivalent of Article 33 (the rule against sending refugees back to a place where they might be persecuted). The key provision of the Refugee Act stated that the "Attorney General shall not deport or return any alien . . . to a country if the Attorney General determines that such alien's life or freedom would be threatened in such country on account of race, religion, nationality, membership in a particular social group, or political opinion." The Yale team argued at the Supreme Court that this mandate not to "return" refugees to possible persecution extended to Haitians intercepted by the Coast Guard on the open ocean. The Supreme Court disagreed, holding in June 1993 that neither the Refugee Act nor Article 33 protected anyone beyond U.S. borders—thus leaving the Coast Guard free to return fleeing Haitians directly to Haiti. (Congress replaced the relevant provision of the Refugee Act in 1996, deleting the "shall not deport or return" language. The new provision still only has force within U.S. borders, consistent with the Supreme Court's 1993 decision.)

Res judicata: A legal doctrine, res judicata prevents a plaintiff from bringing the same legal claim against the same defendant twice.

Screening interview: The preliminary process the INS used to separate Haitians who might qualify for asylum from those who clearly did not. Screening interviews were conducted on Guantánamo from November 1991 through May 1992 (after which all Haitians were directly returned to Haiti without screening). Haitians who demonstrated a "credible fear of persecution" in their screening interviews were flown to the United States to file for asylum—with the exception of those who were HIV positive and thus held indefinitely on Guantánamo. Haitians who failed the screening interview were returned to Port-au-Prince.

Second Circuit: The United States Court of Appeals for the Second Circuit, located in New York City. The Second Circuit reviews decisions by all the federal district courts in New York, among other states. All appeals of decisions by Judge Sterling Johnson Jr. of the Eastern District thus go to the Second Circuit.

SG: The solicitor general of the United States, whose primary responsibility is to represent the federal government before the U.S. Supreme Court.

Stay: A court order temporarily halting judicial proceedings. In the case of *McNary,* stays were issued by the Supreme Court to prevent orders by Judge Johnson and by the Second Circuit from taking effect.

TRO: Temporary restraining order. A TRO is an emergency court order issued in exceptional situations to prevent irreparable harm.

NOTES AND SOURCES

THIS IS A work of nonfiction. The events and individuals in the book are real, and the narrative is based in large part on hundreds of hours of personal interviews I conducted with those directly involved in the litigation. I also relied on thousands of pages of court filings; hearing, trial, and deposition transcripts; judicial opinions; government documents produced to the Yale team during the litigation; and other documents from the files of the Lowenstein International Human Rights Clinic at Yale and the law firm of Simpson Thacher & Bartlett. In addition, I consulted scholarly and journalistic accounts of the events depicted; videotapes of events at Camp Bulkeley and of Coast Guard interdictions of Haitian refugee boats; and books, articles, and professional experts on various subjects that figure prominently in the story (such as Haitian studies and the treatment of AIDS).

Between March 1999 and February 2005, I interviewed most of the people listed in the Characters section at the back of the book, as well as many other participants, observers, and experts, totaling over two hundred people. The interviews included, among others, government lawyers* and executive branch officials, government representatives on Guantánamo, and individuals in the U.S. military services and the Coast Guard. (In a few instances, the interviews were off the record or on background.) Most central to the book, however, were interviews with Yale team members and interviews with the Haitian refugees held on Guantánamo.

I conducted multiple in-person and telephone interviews with members of the Yale team, with a particular focus on Professor Harold

*Several attorneys then with the Office of Immigration Litigation, most notably Lauri Filppu, declined my requests to interview them.

Hongju Koh (twenty-seven interviews), attorney Michael Ratner (seventeen), and almost two dozen of the more than one hundred law students who worked on the litigation—most frequently, Lisa Daugaard (thirty-five), Tory Clawson (twenty-four), and Michael Wishnie (twenty-one).* In addition, I conducted multiple interviews with all of the other Yale team members identified in the Characters section.

I also interviewed more than a dozen Haitians who were detained on Guantánamo, including most of those listed in the Characters section, with a special emphasis on Yvonne Pascal (thirty-four times). Most of the Haitians' interviews were conducted in English, but Ronald Aubourg served as a Creole and French translator for my early interviews with Pascal. After April 2002, Pascal and I communicated directly in English. (At their request, I have used pseudonyms for several Haitians, most notably Yvonne Pascal, because they wish to keep their medical condition private. I have also used pseudonyms for Pascal's children.)

Relying on the evidence from these and other interviews as well as the documents and other sources noted, I have tried to re-create events from multiple perspectives. Of course, no two people experience or recall an event in precisely the same way, and the same individual may, over time, have different perceptions and memories of the same event. When several individuals' descriptions of events diverged or a single individual's memories varied over a series of interviews, I tried to provide the account that seemed to be the most internally consistent and the most consistent with others' recollections, whenever available. (I should also note that the narrative deviates at a few points from some published descriptions because it relies primarily on the accounts of those who participated in or observed the events at issue.)

Where possible, dialogue is taken directly from court and deposition transcripts, newspaper articles, television broadcast transcripts, and other printed sources. On occasion, I have removed extraneous words from the quotations for the sake of clarity and brevity. The rest of the dialogue, as well as people's interior thoughts, comes from interviews with the participants.

---

*I knew a number of the people depicted in this book before I began my research, including several of the law students, two of the lawyers, and most particularly Harold Hongju Koh, who was one of my professors at Yale Law School during the early events described in the book. I also witnessed firsthand a few incidents in the narrative as a third-year law student and attended one early team strategy session. However, I never worked on the litigation for the Haitian refugees.

Direct sources for the narrative are cited in the Notes section, except that interviews with members of the Yale team and the Haitian refugees are generally not cited. Multiple interviews form the basis for most scenes involving people from those groups, making individual references impracticable. Whenever Yale team members or Haitian refugees are involved in a scene, it is my interviews with them that form the basis for that scene, in addition to any other sources cited in the notes to that section.

Many of the documents cited in the notes are readily available on Westlaw or Lexis. A number of the pleadings filed by the parties and other documents and materials, including the videotapes mentioned in the text and notes, are not. Those documents and materials were lent to me by the Lowenstein Clinic at Yale and the law firm of Simpson Thacher & Bartlett, and will ultimately be archived at Yale.

The lawsuit that is the focus of this story, *Haitian Centers Council v. McNary,* filed in March 1992 in the United States District Court for the Eastern District of New York, is abbreviated in the notes as *HCC v. McNary.* Where the notes cite documents submitted to the court, they are listed by both title and exhibit number. There are separate exhibit numbers for documents submitted prior to trial, designated "Pl. Ex." or "Def. Ex.," and documents submitted at trial, designated "Pl. Tr. Ex." or "Def. Tr. Ex."

Chapter One

1   Antenor Joseph swept into KID headquarters: For two accounts of the military coup in Haiti on September 29, 1991, see Paul Farmer, *The Uses of Haiti,* 2d ed. (Monroe, ME: Common Courage Press, 2003), pp. 150–55; and Mark Danner, "The Fall of the Prophet," *New York Review of Books,* Dec. 2, 1993, pp. 44, 52–53.

3   But KID's headquarters had been: Americas Watch et al., *Return to the Darkest Days: Human Rights in Haiti Since the Coup* (New York: Human Rights Watch, 1991), pp. 6–7; Karen Payne, "Haitian Dissident Deserves Our Help," *Atlanta Journal and Constitution,* Nov. 28, 1991, p. H1.

4   A sturdy Asian man: The author witnessed this event firsthand.

5   The idea had seized her: Sanjoy Hazarika, "Army in Nepal Opens Fire, Killing Demonstrators," *New York Times,* Apr. 7, 1990, sec. 1, p. 11; Sanjoy Hazarika, "Nepal's King Lifts Ban on Politicking," *New York Times,* Apr. 9, 1990, p. A1.

6   "Each of you thinks": Interview with Victoria ("Tory") Clawson, July 24, 2000.

9   Lisa finally found: Frances Dinkelspiel, "Portrait of Two Protesters," *Post-Standard* (Syracuse), May 3, 1987, p. C1.

10   Bearded, bald, and fond: *Inmates of Attica Correctional Facility v. Rockefeller,* 477 F.2d 375 (2d Cir. 1973); *Sanchez-Espinoza v. Reagan,* 770 F.2d 202 (D.C. Cir. 1985).

10   Along with his colleagues: *Conyers v. Reagan,* 765 F.2d 1124 (D.C. Cir. 1985); *Dellums v. Bush,* 752 F. Supp. 1141 (D.D.C. 1990).

11   In early October: Associated Press, "Haiti's Military Assumes Power After Troops Arrest the President," *New York Times,* Oct. 1, 1991, p. A1.

11   Almost two hundred years earlier: Farmer, *The Uses of Haiti,* pp. 53–107; Amy Wilentz, *The Rainy Season: Haiti Since Duvalier* (New York: Simon and Schuster, 1989), pp. 74–78; William G. O'Neill, "The Roots of Human Rights Violations in Haiti," 7 *Georgetown Immigration Law Journal* 87 (1993), pp. 87–94.

12   But in December 1990: Danner, "The Fall of the Prophet," p. 48; Bella Stumbo, "From Horror to Hope," *Los Angeles Times Magazine,* Apr. 21, 1991, p. 8.

12   From the start: Danner, "The Fall of the Prophet," pp. 49–52.

12   After nightfall, soldiers: Danner, "The Fall of the Prophet," p. 53; Farmer, *The Uses of Haiti,* p. 152.

12   In the weeks that followed: Farmer, *The Uses of Haiti,* pp. 153–55; Irwin P. Stotzky, *Silencing the Guns in Haiti: The Promise of Deliberative Democracy* (Chicago: University of Chicago Press, 1997), pp. 29, 221 n. 54; Amnesty International, *Haiti: The Human Rights Tragedy—Human Rights Violations Since the Coup* (New York: Amnesty International, 1992), pp. 1–2.

13   A trade embargo: Howard W. French, "Land and Health Also Erode in Haiti," *New York Times,* Jan. 28, 1992, p. A3.

13   She saw Washington's other: Karen De Witt, "Bush Reassures Haiti's Ousted Chief," *New York Times,* Oct. 5, 1991, sec. 1, p. 4.

13   Haiti was poverty-stricken: Stumbo, "From Horror to Hope"; Stotzky, *Silencing the Guns,* pp. 45, 242 n. 38. U.S. officials also accused Aristide of encouraging mob violence. Stotzky, *Silencing the Guns,* p. 242 n. 38.

13   Around Halloween, the U.S. Coast Guard: Harold Maass and Karen Branch, "Haitians Caught in Legal Limbo," *Miami Herald,* Nov. 5, 1991, p. 1A.

13   Still, the boats kept coming: Lizette Alvarez, "Haitian Repatriations Halted," *Miami Herald,* Nov. 20, 1991, p. 1A.

13   Reports of vessels lost at sea: See, e.g., Lee Hockstader, "Haitians' Boat Sinks," *Washington Post,* Nov. 22, 1991, p. A35.

13   Human rights groups: Paul Anderson, "3 Latin Nations Will Shelter Haiti Refugees," *Miami Herald,* Nov. 15, 1991, p. 1A; Paul Anderson, "Protected Status Urged for Haitians," *Miami Herald,* Oct. 18, 1991, p. 4B; Paul Anderson, "Dade Officials Urge Better Treatment of Haitians," *Miami Herald,* Oct. 17, 1991, p. 3B.

13   Coast Guard spokesmen made no effort: Howard W. French, "U.S. Is Holding 200 Haitians on 2 Ships," *New York Times,* Nov. 8, 1991, p. A3.

13   Yvonne stopped typing to listen: Some details in this scene are based on the deposition of Yvonne Pascal, Feb. 21–22, 1993. (All depositions cited are from *HCC v. McNary* unless otherwise noted.)

14   They threw her to the floor: Yvonne Pascal's torture in Haiti and detention on Guantánamo are recounted by Paul Farmer, who interviewed her in 1993.

See Farmer, *The Uses of Haiti*, pp. 217–43; and Paul Farmer, *Pathologies of Power: Health, Human Rights, and the New War on the Poor* (Berkeley, CA: University of California Press, 2005), pp. 51–69.

17 He'd helped send over two dozen: Interview with Harold Koh, June 19, 2004.

17 So, under orders from the White House: Howard W. French, "U.S. Starts to Return Haitians," *New York Times,* Nov. 19, 1991, p. A1.

17 Convinced innocent people: Interviews with Ira Kurzban, June 1, 2001; and Cheryl Little, Jan. 11, 2001; *Haitian Refugee Center v. Baker,* 789 F. Supp. 1552, 1557 (S.D. Fla. 1991). (The case is referred to as *HRC v. Baker* or *Baker* in subsequent notes.)

18 It turned out that the Coast Guard: Agreement Effected by Exchange of Notes, U.S.-Republic of Haiti, Sept. 23, 1981, 33 U.S.T. 3559. Several days after the United States entered into the interdiction agreement with Haiti, the president authorized the Coast Guard to begin intercepting Haitian vessels. Executive Order No. 12,324, 46 *Federal Register* 48,109 (1981).

18 The United States had no such agreement: Cheryl Little, "United States Haitian Policy: A History of Discrimination," 10 *New York Law School Journal of Human Rights* 269 (1993), pp. 295–96; Presidential Proclamation 4,865, 46 *Federal Register* 48,107 (1981).

18 But the deal had a critical exception: Executive Order No. 12,324, § 2(c)(3).

18 Under both American: Section 243(h)(1) of the Immigration and Nationality Act (INA), as amended by the Refugee Act of 1980, 8 U.S.C. § 1253(h)(1) (1992); Article 33 of the 1951 U.N. Convention Relating to the Status of Refugees, July 28, 1951, 19 U.S.T. 6259. The United States did not ratify the Refugee Convention but acceded to the U.N. Protocol Relating to the Status of Refugees, Jan. 31, 1967, 19 U.S.T. 6223, which incorporated the provisions of the Refugee Convention. The origins of the non-refoulement principle date back to the post–World War I era. Guy S. Goodwin-Gill, *The Refugee in International Law,* 2d ed. (Oxford: Oxford University Press, 1996), p. 118.

18 Over one hundred nations: The Lowenstein International Human Rights Clinic, "Aliens and the Duty of Nonrefoulement: *Haitian Centers Council v. McNary*," 6 *Harvard Human Rights Journal* 1 (1993), p. 14.

18 To ensure that no political: Arthur C. Helton, "The United States Government Program of Intercepting and Forcibly Returning Haitian Boat People to Haiti: Policy Implications and Prospects," 10 *New York Law School Journal of Human Rights* 325 (1993), pp. 329–30; interview with Ira Kurzban, June 1, 2001.

18 The INS statistics on Haitian refugees: Helton, "Forcibly Returning Haitian Boat People," p. 330.

18 During the same time: Immigration and Naturalization Service (INS), *1991 Statistical Yearbook of the Immigration and Naturalization Service* (Washington, DC: U.S. Government Printing Office, 1992), pp. 81, 84.

19 The INS simply declared: "Stop Haitian Interdiction!," *Miami Herald*, Nov. 20, 1991, p. 18A.

19   They called for a more careful: Victoria Clawson, Elizabeth Detweiler, and Laura Ho, "Litigating as Law Students: An Inside Look at *Haitian Centers Council,*" 103 *Yale Law Journal* 2337 (1994), pp. 2340–41.

19   After a lot of procedural wrangling: *Baker,* 789 F. Supp. at 1557–58.

19   The court order preventing: Al Kamen, "Refugees Taken to Guantánamo," *Washington Post,* Nov. 27, 1991, p. A14.

19   The administration did not want: Paul Anderson and Lizette Alvarez, "Bush Defends Policy on Haitians," *Miami Herald,* Nov. 21, 1991, p. 1A; Anderson, "3 Latin Nations."

19   Nobody considered that: Interview with anonymous INS official, Feb. 22, 2002.

19   As the clock ticked: Deposition of Lloyd Allen Jr., *HRC v. Baker,* Feb. 3, 1992, p. 15; interview with Grover Joseph Rees, Mar. 17, 2005.

19   The naval base at Guantánamo: Tom Miller, "Castro, a Reluctant Landlord, Won't Cash the Rent Check," *New York Times,* June 16, 1993, p. A25; Ann Banks, "Inside Gitmo," *New York Times,* Mar. 31, 1991, sec. 6, p. 27; Mark Falcoff, *Cuba the Morning After: Confronting Castro's Legacy* (Washington, DC: AEI Press, 2003), pp. 106–08; Jane Franklin, *Cuba and the United States: A Chronological History* (New York: Ocean Press, 1997), pp. 57–59; Lynn Darrell Bender, *The Politics of Hostility: Castro's Revolution and United States Policy* (Hato Rey, Puerto Rico: Inter American University Press, 1975), pp. 110–17; Agreement for the Lease to the United States of Lands in Cuba for Coaling and Naval Stations, U.S.-Cuba, Feb. 23, 1903, T.S. No. 418; Treaty Between the United States of America and Cuba Defining Their Relations, May 29, 1934, T.S. No. 866 (continuing 1903 agreement).

20   The government had little precedent: David Binder, "101 Haitian Refugees Pose Painful Problem for U.S.," *New York Times,* Sept. 1, 1977, p. 3; "97 Who Fled to U.S. Base in Cuba Are Flown Back Home to Haiti," *New York Times,* Sept. 7, 1977, p. 6.

20   Now, though, officials from: Interviews with Paul Cappuccio, Feb. 21, 2000, and Feb. 25, 2005; Grover Joseph Rees, Feb. 22, 2002, and Mar. 17, 2005; and anonymous government official, Jan. 10, 2004; Michael Ratner, "How We Closed the Guantánamo HIV Camp: The Intersection of Politics and Litigation," 11 *Harvard Human Rights Journal* 187 (1998), pp. 191–92.

20   Defense officials didn't like: Kamen, "Refugees Taken to Guantánamo"; Susan Beck, "Cast Away," *American Lawyer,* Oct. 1992, p. 51.

20   Castro had cut off: Bender, *The Politics of Hostility,* p. 112.

20   In a last-ditch argument: Kamen, "Refugees Taken to Guantánamo."

20   Two days before Thanksgiving: Art Pine and Melissa Healy, "U.S. in Uncharted Waters in Move to Shelter Haiti Refugees at Cuba Base," *Los Angeles Times,* Nov. 27, 1991, p. A8; Associated Press, "U.S. Beefs Up Capacity for Haitian Refugees," *Miami Herald,* Dec. 3, 1991, p. 13A.

21   Soon, more than six thousand: "Haitians' Fate May Rest with U.S. Appeals Court," *Washington Post,* Dec. 24, 1991, p. A7.

21   The results made Kurzban seethe: Interview with Ira Kurzban, June 1, 2001;

Karen Branch, "Haitian Advocates Back from Guantánamo Visit," *Miami Herald,* Dec. 2, 1991, p. 11A.

21   Their efforts paid off: *Baker,* 789 F. Supp. at 1578.

21   The media, meanwhile: Lizette Alvarez, "Haitians Score Legal Victory," *Miami Herald,* Dec. 4, 1991, p. 1A; Little, "United States Haitian Policy," pp. 300, 301 & n. 134.

21   But the government quickly appealed: The contradictory rulings are described in *HRC v. Baker,* 953 F.2d 1498, 1503–05 (11th Cir. 1992); Lizette Alvarez, "Judge Preserves Ban on Sending Haitians Home from Guantánamo," *Miami Herald*, Dec. 24, 1991, p. 5A.

21   To the students' disappointment: *Baker*, 953 F.2d at 1515.

24   It had sputtered out: *HRC v. Baker,* 502 U.S. 1122 (1992).

24   Koh read Blackmun's dissent aloud: Ibid. (Blackmun, J., dissenting).

24   "It's like *Gideon versus Wainwright,* right?": *Gideon v. Wainwright,* 372 U.S. 335 (1963) (addressing the right to counsel in a criminal prosecution).

24   The court had to stay involved: Harold Hongju Koh, *The National Security Constitution: Sharing Power After the Iran-Contra Affair* (New Haven, CT: Yale University Press, 1990), p. 227.

26   While President Bush was the clear: Thomas B. Edsall et al., "Tsongas Wins Maryland, Clinton Georgia; Buchanan Again Gets Large Protest Vote," *Washington Post,* Mar. 4, 1992, p. A1; John Aloysius Farrell, "Open Doors/Closing Minds," *Boston Globe,* Feb. 23, 1992, p. 61.

Chapter Two

28   Months before Hitler's tanks: Gordon Thomas and Max Morgan Witts, *Voyage of the Damned* (New York: Stein and Day, 1974).

29   In November 1989, the president had hailed: Valerie Strauss, "Hong Kong Expulsions to Continue," *Washington Post*, Dec. 13, 1989, p. A27; "U.S. Aides Critical of Britain's Move," *New York Times*, Dec. 13, 1989, p. A11.

29   Graham, under the guidance: *Savage v. Aronson,* 571 A.2d 696 (Conn. 1990).

30   At the age of thirty-six: Interview with Harold Koh, Mar. 22, 1999.

30   After years of dictatorship: Gregory Henderson, *Korea: The Politics of the Vortex* (Cambridge, MA: Harvard University Press, 1968), pp. 182–85; Howard Kyongju Koh, ed., *Koh Kwang Lim: Essays in Honor of His Hwegap: 1980* (New Haven, CT: East Rock Press, 1982), pp. 21–23.

32   He was directed to work: Harold Hongju Koh, "An Uncommon Lawyer," 42 *Harvard International Law Journal* 7 (2001), p. 8; Case Concerning Military and Paramilitary Activities in and against Nicaragua (*Nicaragua v. U.S.*), 1986 I.C.J. 14 (June 27); 8 Opinions of the Office of Legal Counsel of the United States Department of Justice 271 (1984); interview with Harold Koh, July 26, 1999.

37   Over the last several days: On res judicata, see Jack H. Friedenthal, Mary Kay Kane, and Arthur R. Miller, *Civil Procedure* (St. Paul, MN: West, 1985), §§ 14.1–.8, pp. 606–57.

37 Lawyers had a right to communicate: *Flower v. United States,* 407 U.S. 197 (1972).

38 She faced a seemingly impossible task: Laurence H. Tribe, *American Constitutional Law,* 2d ed. (Mineola, NY: Foundation Press, 1988), pp. 355, 358; *Fiallo v. Bell,* 430 U.S. 787 (1977); *Chae Chan Ping v. United States (The Chinese Exclusion Case),* 130 U.S. 581 (1889).

42 He used litigation like a spotlight: Ratner, "How We Closed the Guantánamo HIV Camp," p. 193.

42 With the courts and the media: Little, "United States Haitian Policy," pp. 300, 301 & nn. 133–34. The higher screen-in rate may also have been due to INS officials providing asylum officers with better information about conditions in Haiti. Interview with Scott Busby, Oct. 30, 2000; Beck, "Cast Away."

45 "I've been at this for a long, long time": This scene is based on interviews with Ira Kurzban, June 1, 2001; Cheryl Little, Jan. 11, 2001; Irwin Stotzky, Jan. 10, 2001 (all of the *Baker* team); Graham Boyd, Sept. 20, 2000; Lisa Daugaard, Oct. 9, 2000; Harold Koh, Jan. 20, 2000; and Robert Rubin, Oct. 3, 2003; and on Cheryl Little, "InterGroup Coalitions and Immigration Politics: The Haitian Experience in Florida," 53 *University of Miami Law Review* 717 (1999), pp. 724–25.

45 The Justice Department had been nothing: Application to Stay the Mandates of the U.S. Court of Appeals for the Eleventh Circuit, *HRC v. Baker,* Feb. 10, 1992, pp. 31–41; Little, "United States Haitian Policy," pp. 306–07 & nn. 153–63; Little, "InterGroup Coalitions and Immigration Politics," pp. 724–25.

46 The Eleventh Circuit, he pointed out: The case is *Jean v. Nelson,* 727 F.2d 957 (11th Cir. 1984) (en banc), which the *Baker* majority never mentioned. See *Baker,* 953 F.2d at 1516 (Hatchett, J., dissenting).

47 More than half black and Latino: U.S. Census Bureau, *1990 Census of Population: Social and Economic Characteristics* (Washington, DC: U.S. Government Printing Office, 1993), p. 348.

47 Famous for handling: Peter H. Schuck, *Agent Orange on Trial: Mass Toxic Disasters in the Courts* (Cambridge, MA: Belknap Press of Harvard University Press, 1986), p. 111.

48 If the Yale team went in: Rule 50.5 of the United States District Courts for the Southern and Eastern Districts of New York (Miscellaneous Judge); Rule 4 of the United States District Courts for the Southern and Eastern Districts of New York (Civil Actions or Proceedings [Filing and Assignment]).

48 But Weinstein was slated: Interviews with Harold Koh, July 26, 1999; and Michael Ratner, July 7, 1999.

49 We have government contacts: Interviews with Lisa Daugaard, July 15, 2001; and Michael Ratner, Oct. 5, 2000.

49 According to the treaty: U.S.-Cuba Lease Agreement, T.S. No. 418.

50 But the big news: Letter from Father Jacques Fabré to Johnny McCalla, Mar. 2, 1992 (Pl. Ex. 8).

50   Under the rule of "administrative exhaustion": Richard J. Pierce Jr., *Administrative Law Treatise*, 4th ed. (New York: Aspen Law and Business, 2002), vol. 2, § 15.2, pp. 967–78.

50   One of the first: *Paul v. Avril,* 901 F. Supp. 330 (S.D. Fla. 1994).

51   The next morning: Letter from Harold Koh to Gene McNary, Mar. 11, 1992 (Pl. Ex. 7).

55   From early November 1991 through: Complaint, *HCC v. McNary*, Mar. 18, 1992, pp. 5–7. For news reports with similar figures, see, e.g., David G. Savage, "Court Rejects Haitians' Bid for U.S. Asylum," *Los Angeles Times,* Feb. 25, 1992, p. A1.

55   According to a United Nations: Information on the screening process comes from an interview with Cheryl Little, Jan. 11, 2001; and affidavits of Cheryl Little, Mar. 13, 1992, p. 3 (Pl. Ex. 6); and Jennie Smith, Feb. 10, 1992, p. 3 (Pl. Ex. 24).

55   Screen-in rates varied: Information on pressure from State Department officials is based on an interview with Cheryl Little, Jan. 11, 2001; and on Little, "United States Haitian Policy," p. 301 n. 134.

56   What Rubin had sent was a memo from Grover Joseph Rees: Memorandum from Grover Joseph Rees to John Cummings [INS official on Guantánamo], Feb. 29, 1992 (Pl. Ex. 1). The Rees memo was initially obtained by Arthur Helton and then faxed to Rubin. Interview with Robert Rubin, Oct. 3, 2003.

56   Years earlier, the federal Centers: The section on Haitians and AIDS is based on Paul Farmer, *AIDS and Accusation: Haiti and the Geography of Blame* (Berkeley, CA: University of California Press, 1992), pp. 210–20, 260; Associated Press, "Haitians Removed from AIDS Risk List," *New York Times,* Apr. 10, 1985, p. A13; and Lawrence K. Altman, "Debate Grows on U.S. Listing of Haitians in AIDS Category," *New York Times,* July 31, 1983, sec. 1, part 1, p. 1.

57   Until that point, the screened-in refugees: Clawson, Detweiler, and Ho, "Litigating as Law Students," p. 2353 (citing Brief for the Respondents in Opposition to Certiorari, *Baker v. HRC,* Feb. 1992); 8 U.S.C. § 1158(a) (1992); 8 C.F.R. §§ 208.9, 208.18(b) (1992). Technically, an applicant was not allowed to "appeal" the denial of an asylum application, but instead was permitted to "renew" the application before an immigration judge in exclusion or deportation proceedings. 8 C.F.R. § 208.18(b).

57   Government statistics showed: General Accounting Office, *Asylum: Approval Rates for Selected Applicants* (Washington, DC: General Accounting Office, 1987), pp. 2–3.

58   For years, Rabinovitz: Under the INA, any alien with a "communicable disease of public health significance" was not allowed into the United States. 8 U.S.C. § 1182(a)(1)(A)(i) (1992). HIV was designated as such a disease by a Department of Health and Human Services (HHS) regulation. 42 C.F.R. § 34.2(b)(4) (1992). The HIV ban was formerly required by statute, the result of an amendment introduced by Jesse Helms in 1987, but later legisla-

tion gave HHS the discretion to revoke the ban. Bowing to political pressure, HHS failed to revoke it. Elizabeth Mary McCormick, "HIV-Infected Haitian Refugees: An Argument Against Exclusion," 7 *Georgetown Immigration Law Journal* 149 (1993), pp. 157–62.

58 But support for the: Malcolm Gladwell, "Reversal of AIDS Exclusion Is Said to Be Shelved," *Washington Post,* May 25, 1991, p. A6.

58 Given the volatile history: Ratner, "How We Closed the Guantánamo HIV Camp," p. 197; interview with Michael Ratner, Aug. 11, 1999.

Chapter Three

60 Michael Ratner hurried into: This scene is based on interviews with Michael Ratner, July 7, 1999, and Oct. 6, 2000; Robert Begleiter, Apr. 18, 2001; and Scott Dunn, Nov. 27 and 29, 2000.

62 In fact, his landmark: *Filartiga v. Pena-Irala,* 577 F. Supp. 860 (E.D.N.Y. 1984).

62 The deputy court clerk eyed Koh: This scene is based on interviews with Harold Koh, July 26, 1999, and Oct. 19, 2000; Michael Ratner, Oct. 6, 2000; Lisa Daugaard, July 21, 1999, and Mar. 5, 2000; Sarah Cleveland, Aug. 6, 1999, and Jan. 6, 2001; Robert Begleiter, Apr. 18, 2001; Scott Dunn, Nov. 29, 2000; and Peter Choharis (law clerk to Judge Nickerson), Sept. 23, 2000. Since no transcript was available for the court proceedings on the first day of the case—initially before Judge Nickerson and later before Judge Johnson—the citations include all interviews that served as sources for quotations from the two judges and the lawyers in court.

65 Lisa leaned against the wall: This scene is based on the interviews set forth immediately above (with the exception of Choharis).

66 They had been on the ocean: This scene is based in part on interviews with Randy Beardsworth, Dec. 14, 2000; James Carlson, Oct. 12, 2000; and Greg Saniel, Apr. 10, 1999; Beardsworth's personal journal; Carlson's photographs and personal notes; William Booth, "The Haitians' Emotional Wake," *Washington Post,* June 19, 1992, p. A1; and John H. Cushman Jr., "Haitians Face Perils of Sea to Reach U.S.," *New York Times,* Feb. 11, 1992, p. A7.

68 He was a Bush appointee: "Today's News," *New York Law Journal,* Sept. 5, 1991, p. 1.

69 The Eastern District was undergoing: This scene is based on interviews with Judge Sterling Johnson Jr., Dec. 29, 2003, and Jan. 5, 2004; Tawana Davis (law clerk to Judge Johnson), Sept. 26, 2000; and the interviews with Koh et al. (with the exception of Choharis) set forth above for the Judge Nickerson court scene.

71 Also, the INS was: Koh is referring to the "changed circumstances" exception to the doctrine of res judicata, under which the doctrine will not apply if the legal claim at issue did not exist at the time of the earlier litigation. The Rees memorandum was issued five days *after* the Supreme Court declined to review the *Baker* case, so Yale was arguing that any claim based on the legality of the Rees memorandum could not have been barred. Among the cases

the Yale team relied on for its argument on this point are *Prime Management v. Steinegger,* 904 F.2d 811, 816 (2d Cir. 1990), and *National Labor Relations Board v. United Technologies,* 706 F.2d 1254, 1260 (2d Cir. 1983).

73   Pierre told them: Affirmation of Michelle Anderson on Behalf of Anonymous Haitian Refugee, Mar. 17, 1992 (Pl. Ex. 10); interviews with Michelle Anderson, Dec. 10, 2000; and Tory Clawson, July 17, 2000.

76   When Johnson resumed the hearing: Quotations in court are from the Hearing Transcript, *HCC v. McNary,* Mar. 18, 1992.

78   Several times that morning: This scene is based in part on the interviews with Beardsworth et al.; the documents of Beardsworth and Carlson; Booth, "Emotional Wake"; and Cushman, "Haitians Face Perils of Sea," set forth above for the boat interdiction scene.

81   According to the Justice Department: Defendants' Motion for Sanctions, *HCC v. McNary,* Mar. 20, 1992.

83   Along with the sanctions motion: Defendants' Memorandum in Opposition to Plaintiffs' Motion for Temporary Restraining Order, *HCC v. McNary,* Mar. 20, 1992, pp. 78, 81.

85   To make matters worse: Interview with Jay Pottenger, Jan. 11, 2005.

85   As it turned out: Harold Hongju Koh, "Reflections on Refoulement and *Haitian Centers Council,*" 35 *Harvard International Law Journal* 1 (1994), p. 5.

86   With the brief out of the way: This scene is based on interviews with Harold Koh, July 26, 1999, Jan. 20, 2000, and Jan. 15, 2005; and Ray Brescia, July 9, 1999.

87   Later that day: This scene is based on interviews with Harold Koh, July 26, 1999, and Jan. 20, 2000.

88   The call finally came: The author witnessed part of this event firsthand.

88   Ratner raced through the opinion: *HCC v. McNary,* 789 F. Supp. 541 (E.D.N.Y. 1992).

Chapter Four

90   On the March morning: This scene is based on interviews with Robert Begleiter, Jan. 24, 2002; Paul Cappuccio, Feb. 21, 2000, and Apr. 8, 2001; and Steven Valentine, Oct. 25, 2001; and on Paul M. Barrett, "Rising Star: How a Young Lawyer Is Making His Mark at a Washington Firm," *Wall Street Journal,* Feb. 15, 1995, p. A1; and Edward Lazarus, *Closed Chambers: The First Eyewitness Account of the Epic Struggles Inside the Supreme Court* (New York: Times Books, 1998), p. 315.

91   Cappuccio allegedly wielded: Lazarus, *Closed Chambers,* pp. 266, 314–22.

93   Under the law, that required: As explained later in the chapter, the Yale team was seeking a preliminary injunction. The standard the team had to meet is set forth in *Resolution Trust Corp. v. Elman,* 949 F.2d 624, 626 (2d Cir. 1991).

95   "This is a military base": Interview with Michael Wishnie, Nov. 10, 1999. Other quotations from government lawyers in this scene are based on interviews with Michael Wishnie, Nov. 10–11, 1999; and Robert Rubin, Aug. 16, 1999.

96   *MRs lawyers, We say:* Letter from Frantz Guerrier, Martin Chéry, and Soinel Joseph to counsel, Mar. 30, 1992 (Pl. Ex. 41).

97   Mike didn't understand: Interview with Jean-Louis Dallard, Feb. 17, 2001.

98   A dentist from Port-au-Prince: Declaration of Frantz Guerrier, Mar. 31, 1992 (Pl. Ex. 45).

99   They, too, described threats: Affirmation of Examine Pierre, Mar. 31, 1992, pp. 4–5 (Pl. Ex. 58); Declaration of Martin Chéry, Mar. 31, 1992, pp. 4–5 (Pl. Ex. 59).

100 The Bush administration had: Barbara Crossette, "White House Presses a Ban on Haitians," *New York Times,* Feb. 15, 1992, sec. 1, p. 3; "Safety of Returned Haitians Not Being Monitored," *Nightline,* ABC, Feb. 24, 1992, available on Lexis (ABC News Transcripts database).

100 Though journalists and human rights: Amnesty International, *The Human Rights Tragedy,* pp. 26–28; Linda Diebel, "Rendezvous with Terror," *Toronto Star,* Mar. 22, 1992, p. F1.

101 If Veillard's account was: Affidavit of Michel Augustine, Mar. 30, 1992 (Pl. Ex. 48); interviews with Michelle Anderson, Dec. 10, 2000; and Tory Clawson, July 24, 2000.

101 Zette, he said, had been returned: Affidavit of Marcus Antoine, undated (Pl. Ex. 52).

101 From a makeshift facility: John Lancaster, "Growing Desperation Marks Haitian Camp," *Washington Post,* May 23, 1992, p. A1.

102 One morning, finally: This scene is based in part on interviews with Scott Busby, Oct. 30, 2000; and Ninaj Raoul, Dec. 13, 2000; the deposition of Scott Busby, May 6, 1992; and Beck, "Cast Away."

103 Like his colleagues: Beck, "Cast Away"; interview with anonymous INS official, Feb. 22, 2002.

105 Yale now had proof: Quotations in court are from the Hearing Transcript, *HCC v. McNary,* Apr. 1, 1992.

105 The interview records: Deposition of Irma Rios, Mar. 31, 1992.

106 Cappuccio had grave doubts: Interview with Paul Cappuccio, Feb. 9, 2002.

108 The last straw for her: *Bertrand v. Sava,* 684 F.2d 204, 212 n. 12 (2d Cir. 1982).

108 It involved *enemy* aliens: *Johnson v. Eisentrager,* 339 U.S. 763 (1950).

108 It was based on the Fourth: *United States v. Verdugo-Urquidez,* 494 U.S. 259 (1990).

110 Five days after the hearing: *HCC v. McNary,* No. 92 CV 1258, 1992 WL 155853 (E.D.N.Y. Apr. 6, 1992), at *6–*10.

111 Paul Cappuccio had appealed: The stay process is described in Charles Alan Wright, Arthur R. Miller, and Mary Kay Kane, *Federal Practice and Procedure,* 2d ed. (St. Paul, MN: West, 1995), Ch. 8, § 2908 (discussing Rule 62 of the Federal Rules of Civil Procedure).

112 Yvonne didn't know: Inadequacies in the HIV testing and counseling process are described in the deposition of Dr. Paul Effler, June 10, 1992.

114 Court TV was providing: Quotations in court are from the Court TV broadcast, Apr. 14, 1992.

115 The government had again: Government's Emergency Application for a Stay Pending Appeal, *HCC v. McNary,* Apr. 21, 1992, pp. 12–13.

115 Included with the brief: Declaration of Donna Hrinak, Apr. 20, 1992, p. 1 (incorporated in Government's Stay Appendix, p. 190).

115 Judge Johnson had already rejected: *HCC v. McNary,* 1992 WL 155853, at *4.

115 But according to the Kurzban team: Application to Stay the Mandates of the U.S. Court of Appeals for the Eleventh Circuit, *HRC v. Baker,* Feb. 10, 1992, pp. 31–41; Little, "United States Haitian Policy," pp. 306–07 & nn. 153–63; Little, "InterGroup Coalitions and Immigration Politics," pp. 724–25.

116 The Hrinak declaration, they argued: Letter from Harold Koh to Francis Lorson, Chief Deputy Clerk, U.S. Supreme Court, Apr. 22, 1992, p. 2.

116 That evening, the Supreme Court: *McNary v. HCC,* 503 U.S. 1000 (1992).

116 The ruling came during: Telephone Conference Call Transcript, *HCC v. McNary,* Apr. 22, 1992.

116 The next day: Interview with Robert Rubin, Aug. 16, 1999; Clawson, Detweiler, and Ho, "Litigating as Law Students," pp. 2358–59.

116 "We push him any further": Ultimately, the team did decide to have Michael Ratner seek a new temporary restraining order, but Judge Johnson never ruled on the request. Telephone Conference Call Transcript, *HCC v. McNary,* Apr. 24, 1992.

117 *"They're escorting eighty-nine"*: Interview with Robert Rubin, Aug. 16, 1999; Clawson, Detweiler, and Ho, "Litigating as Law Students," p. 2358.

118 "Look," he said: Interviews with Harold Koh, Oct. 31, 1999, and Jan. 15, 2005.

Chapter Five

119 At six a.m. on April 23: This scene is based on the deposition of Scott Busby, May 6, 1992; Beck, "Cast Away"; interviews with Scott Busby, Oct. 30, 2000; and Ronald Aubourg, Dec. 15, 2000, and Jan. 30, 2003; and the Trial Transcript, *HCC v. McNary,* Mar. 16, 1993 (testimony of Brigadier General George H. Walls Jr.).

119 "The haste was just unseemly": Beck, "Cast Away."

120 The only way off: The attorney general had the power to "parole" HIV-positive aliens into the United States for "emergent reasons," 8 U.S.C. § 1182(d)(5)(A) (1992), and the power to waive the HIV exclusion on an individual basis "for humanitarian purposes." 8 U.S.C. § 1157(c)(3) (1992). INS General Counsel Grover Joseph Rees testified that the Justice Department would not use either legal mechanism to bring the HIV-positive refugees to the United States. Deposition of Grover Joseph Rees, Mar. 31, 1992.

120 For some time, he'd been: Memorandum from Peter R. Stenner, Director, Operations, to Commanding General, Mar. 3, 1992, p. 2 (Pl. Tr. Ex. 61).

120 "We could," the operations director: Ibid.

120 After rising through the chain of command: Marlene Cimons and Melissa Healy, "Public Health Threat Cited in Isolation of Ill Haitians," *Los Angeles Times,* Apr. 25, 1992, p. A1.

120 After a stint supervising: Memorandum from Paul Effler to Charles Mc-Cance, Director, Division of Quarantine, Centers for Disease Control, Mar. 1, 1992, p. 1 (Pl. Tr. Ex. 23); Cimons and Healy, "Public Health Threat"; interview with Dr. Paul Effler, Dec. 12, 2001.

121 After finally reviewing: *HCC v. McNary,* 969 F.2d 1326, 1341–46 (2d Cir. 1992).

121 Since the Second Circuit had only: Interview with Paul Cappuccio, Feb. 21, 2000.

122 The main area of Bulkeley: Numerous news reports describe Camp Bulkeley. See, e.g., Andres Viglucci, "Haitians Fled Repression, But Now Are HIV Prisoners," *Miami Herald,* Dec. 12, 1992, p. 1A. Among the most detailed written accounts of the camp is in an unpublished manuscript by Dr. Douglas Shenson, who visited Bulkeley in March and April 1993 (provided to the author, Nov. 11, 2001). The description in the text also relies on the testimony of Colonel Larry Zinser, Trial Transcript, *HCC v. McNary,* Mar. 18, 1993; and Colonel Frederick George Fox III, Trial Transcript, *HCC v. McNary,* Mar. 15, 1993; interviews with Colonel Stephen Kinder (retired), June 3, 2004; and members of the Yale team and the Haitian refugees; and the personal photographs of Kinder.

123 She had a T-cell count of 235: Camp Bulkeley Battalion Aid Station medical records of Yvonne Pascal, July 7, 1992, p. 26; testimony of Dr. Joseph Malone, Trial Transcript, *HCC v. McNary,* Mar. 15, 1993.

123 The actual prognosis was more dire: Kenneth G. Castro et al., "1993 Revised Classification System for HIV Infection and Expanded Surveillance Case Definition for AIDS Among Adolescents and Adults," 41 (RR-17) *Morbidity and Mortality Weekly Report,* Dec. 18, 1992, p. 1; Anthony S. Fauci and H. Clifford Lane, "Human Immunodeficiency Virus (HIV) Disease: AIDS and Related Disorders," in *Harrison's Principles of Internal Medicine,* 15th ed., eds. Eugene Braunwald et al. (New York: McGraw-Hill, 2001), pp. 1852–1913; Gina Kolata, "After 5 Years of Use, Doubt Still Clouds Leading AIDS Drug," *New York Times,* June 2, 1992, p. C3.

124 "I'm trying to track down": Interview with Harold Koh, Feb. 18, 2002.

125 Michelle soon had: Four affirmations of anonymous Haitian refugees prepared by Michelle Anderson, Apr. 17, 1992, and attached to a letter from Harold Koh to the Honorable Sterling Johnson Jr., Apr. 21, 1992 (Pl. Ex. 74–77).

125 As Koh had feared: Letter from Paul Cappuccio to the Honorable Sterling Johnson Jr., Apr. 20, 1992, p. 3.

125 The woman's full name: Declaration of Dudley G. Sipprelle, Apr. 21, 1992, pp. 1–2 (Def. Ex. 146).

125 Zette *had* been killed: Letter from Harold Koh to the Honorable Sterling Johnson Jr., Apr. 21, 1992, p. 3.

126 To Mike Wishnie's astonishment: Some details in this scene are from a draft affidavit of Frantz Guerrier, Aug. 14, 1992, prepared in anticipation of Guerrier seeking asylum through the U.S. consulate in Port-au-Prince.

126 The Coast Guard had broken: Telecommunication from U.S. Coast Guard Cutter *Tampa* to Commander, Task Unit 44.7.4, Apr. 29, 1992 (Pl. Tr. Ex. 34).

126 Nor, despite U.S. government: Bill Frelick, "Haitian Boat Interdiction and Return: First Asylum and First Principles of Refugee Protection," 26 *Cornell International Law Journal* 675 (1993), pp. 684–85 (according to the U.S. Committee for Refugees, as of March 1992, the Dominican government had accepted no Haitians fleeing the coup as political refugees and had treated the few who had filed formal asylum applications with open hostility).

126 "I've met a lot of people": Interview with Elliot Schrage, Dec. 19, 2002.

127 Using Schrage's notes: Declaration of Elliot Schrage, May 11, 1992 (Pl. Ex. 85).

127 By mid-May, more than twelve thousand: John Lancaster, "Growing Desperation Marks Haitian Camp," *Washington Post,* May 23, 1992, p. A1; Lee Hockstader, "Sanctions on Haiti Tightened," *Washington Post,* May 18, 1992, p. A1.

127 But some in the Bush administration: Howard W. French, "Americans Approve Forceful Steps to Restore Ousted Haitian Leader," *New York Times,* May 18, 1992, p. A1.

128 Food prices had doubled: Lizette Alvarez, "Embargo Choking Haiti's Poorest," *Miami Herald,* May 17, 1992, p. 1A.

128 As Deputy Secretary: Hockstader, "Sanctions on Haiti Tightened." The State Department argued that the INS was contributing to the refugee exodus by supposedly screening in too many refugees (ibid). Other Bush officials believed the Coast Guard was also part of the problem because its cutters had crept too close to Haitian shores, encouraging people to flee. Interview with Paul Cappuccio, Feb. 21, 2000.

128 The administration considered building: Lizette Alvarez, "U.S.: No Room at Tent City," *Miami Herald,* May 22, 1992, p. 1A.

128 But the Pentagon was adamantly: Clifford Krauss, "U.S. Uncertain on How to Deal with Haitian Exodus," *New York Times,* May 23, 1992, sec. 1, p. 2.

129 Hours earlier, President Bush: Ann Devroy, "U.S. to Halt Haitians on High Seas," *Washington Post,* May 25, 1992, p. A1; Executive Order No. 12,807, 57 *Federal Register* 23,133 (May 24, 1992).

129 Refugee boats were not: Press release, Office of the Press Secretary, The White House, May 24, 1992, p. 1 (reprinted in Joint Appendix, *McNary v. HCC,* 509 U.S. 155 (1993) (No. 92–344), pp. 327–28).

129 But as human rights monitors: Declaration of William G. O'Neill, May 26, 1992, p. 2 (Pl. Ex. 86).

130 Article 33 of the U.N.: Article 33, U.N. Refugee Convention, 19 U.S.T. 6259.

130 Most striking of all to her: Deposition of Scott Busby, May 6, 1992.

132 "I do not see Bulkeley": Minutes of Camp Bulkeley Meeting, July 10, 1992, p. 1.

133 Several days later, the refugees: Some details in this scene are from a Joint Task Force videotape of Camp Bulkeley, July 13, 1992.

134 Human rights groups denounced: Thomas L. Friedman, "Haitians Returned Under New Policy," *New York Times,* May 27, 1992, p. A1; Barbara Crossette, "U.N. Official Rebukes U.S. on Haitians," *New York Times,* May 28, 1992, p. A3.

134 But the State Department: Howard W. French, "Haitians Expected to Snub U.S. Rules," *New York Times,* May 26, 1992, p. A5.

134 Compared with other refugee crises: Michael Wines, "Switching Policy, U.S. Will Return Refugees to Haiti," *New York Times,* May 25, 1992, sec. 1, p. 1.

134 The U.S. itself, in fact: INS, *1991 Statistical Yearbook*, pp. 27, 81.

134 But Haitian refugee boats: Christopher Marquis, "Bush Fears a Haitian Mariel," *Miami Herald,* May 27, 1992, p. 1A.

134 Out on the campaign trail: "U.N. Aide Assails Haiti Repatriation," *San Francisco Chronicle,* May 28, 1992, p. A14.

134 "I am convinced the people": James Gerstenzang, "President Angrily Defends Haiti Repatriation Order," *Los Angeles Times,* May 28, 1992, p. A4; Crossette, "U.N. Official Rebukes U.S."

135 "I am appalled": Statement by Governor Clinton on Haitian Refugees, U.S. Newswire, May 27, 1992.

135 He called the White House: Ibid.; "Clinton Urges Temporary Asylum in U.S. for the Haitian Boat People," *Los Angeles Times,* May 27, 1992, p. A8.

135 In fact, he suggested: Interview with Harold Koh, Oct. 19, 2000.

136 Congress had adopted: Section 243(h)(1) of the INA, as amended by the Refugee Act of 1980, 8 U.S.C. § 1253(h)(1) (1992).

136 Often described as gracious and courtly: Tony Mauro, "Devotion to Duty Has Long Propelled Starr," *USA Today*, Aug. 17, 1988, p. 4A; Kim I. Eisler, "Rising Starr?," *Washingtonian Magazine*, Jan. 1995, p. 35; Lazarus, *Closed Chambers*, pp. 437–38.

137 Koh hammered home: Quotations in court are from the Hearing Transcript, *HCC v. McNary*, May 29, 1992.

137 Just two days before: Howard W. French, "16 Haitians Slain in Week of Strife," *New York Times,* May 28, 1992, p. A3.

139 But when Judge Johnson issued: *HCC v. McNary*, No. 92 CV 1258, 1992 U.S. Dist. LEXIS 8452 (E.D.N.Y. June 5, 1992). Judge Johnson held that Article 33 did not apply because under an earlier Second Circuit ruling, the U.N. Refugee Convention was not "self-executing," meaning that it had no force without special implementing legislation. Johnson also held, with minimal analysis, that the Refugee Act of 1980 had no force outside U.S. borders.

140 Days after President Bush's order: French, "16 Haitians Slain"; "Haitian Detained Despite Efforts of 3 Diplomats," *Washington Post,* May 28, 1992, p. A24.

140 By the end of June: Eric Schmitt, "Haitian Exodus Has Slowed to a Trickle, U.S. Says," *New York Times,* July 2, 1992, p. A9.

140 With no new arrivals: Barbara Crossette, "U.S. to Close Refugee Camp at Guantánamo to Haitians," *New York Times,* May 29, 1992, p. A2.

140 On the first of July: Schmitt, "Haitian Exodus Has Slowed to a Trickle."

140 Amid the crush of bodies: Some details in this scene are from a Joint Task Force videotape of Camp Bulkeley, July 17, 1992.

141 One refugee kicked a soldier: Trial Transcript, *HCC v. McNary,* Mar. 17, 1993 (testimony of Colonel Joe Trimble).

143 We can do whatever we want: Audiotape of oral argument before the Second Circuit Court of Appeals, *HCC v. McNary,* June 26, 1992.

143 In late July, the court issued: *HCC v. McNary,* 969 F.2d 1350, 1367 (2d Cir. 1992).

143 "The Court of Appeals made the right": Clinton Statement on Appeals Court Ruling on Haitian Repatriation, U.S. Newswire, July 29, 1992.

143 Just seventy-two hours after: *McNary v. HCC,* 505 U.S. 1234 (1992).

144 There'd been protests, she confirmed: Memorandum from Graham Boyd and Michael Wishnie to Harold Koh, Sept. 2, 1992, p. 1.

144 It was August 29: Minutes of Camp Bulkeley Meeting, Aug. 29, 1992, pp. 2–3; Memorandum from Colonel Joe W. Trimble to Joint Task Force Re: Standard Operating Procedures for Camp VII [Segregation Camp] Operations, Aug. 31, 1992.

144 "I won't talk about Camp VII": Quotations are from the Aug. 29, 1992, Minutes of Camp Bulkeley Meeting, pp. 2–3.

145 Over twenty guards: Trial Transcript, *HCC v. McNary,* Mar. 17, 1993 (testimony of Colonel Joe Trimble).

145 When the rest of the Haitians: Some details in this scene are from an appendix to the Aug. 29 Minutes of Camp Bulkeley Meeting entitled "Sequence of Events—29 August 1992."

Chapter Six

148 There'd even been features: Anthony Lewis, "Mockery of Justice," *New York Times,* May 21, 1992, p. A29.

149 Democratic candidate Bill Clinton: "Clinton Still Holds a Strong Lead in Polls," Live Report, CNN, Sept. 3, 1992, Tr. #158-1, available on Lexis (CNN Transcripts database).

149 In early September: Governor Clinton Reaffirms Opposition to Administration Policy on Haiti, U.S. Newswire, Sept. 9, 1992.

149 Clinton also announced: Bill Clinton and Al Gore, *Putting People First: How We Can All Change America* (New York: Times Books, 1992), pp. 41, 120.

150 People in government custody: See, e.g., *City of Revere v. Massachusetts General Hospital,* 463 U.S. 239, 244 (1983).

150 It was a restricted right: See, e.g., *O'Connor v. Donaldson,* 422 U.S. 563, 575–76 (1975); *Doherty v. Thornburgh,* 943 F.2d 204, 209 (2d Cir. 1991).

150 But a few paid: See, e.g., *Doherty,* 943 F.2d at 209.

151 In mid-September: This scene is based in part on the deposition of Colonel Stephen Kinder, Feb. 26, 1993; interviews with Kinder, June 3 and 29, 2004; and e-mail correspondence with Kinder in November 2004.

154 Whenever she went, the staff: Deposition of Yvonne Pascal, Feb. 21, 1993.

154 Mistakenly believing it was: Ibid.; Camp Bulkeley Battalion Aid Station medical records of Yvonne Pascal, Sept. 29, 1992, p. 20.

154 She didn't really: Camp Bulkeley Battalion Aid Station medical records of Yvonne Pascal, Oct. 22, 1992, p. 18.

155 As a colleague later recalled: Interview with Lory Rosenberg, Feb. 21, 2005.

155 "The case simply is not ready": Quotations in court are from the Hearing Transcript, *HCC v. McNary,* Sept. 22, 1992.

156 In one recent letter: Letter from Lauri Filppu to Joseph Tringali, Sept. 18, 1992, p. 4.

157 Politics aside, he thought: Interview with Paul Cappuccio, Feb. 16, 2003.

157 The Justice Department, he said: Ibid.; interview with Michael Ratner, Jan. 24, 2003.

158 The refugees who won: The attorney general had the power to waive the HIV exclusion on an individual basis "for humanitarian purposes." 8 U.S.C. § 1157(c)(3) (1992).

159 Under the ethics of the legal profession: Professional legal ethics require that a settlement offer be communicated to the client. American Bar Association, Model Rules of Professional Conduct, Rule 1.4 & comments (2002).

160 As Tory's eyes: Some details in this scene are from Clawson, Detweiler, and Ho, "Litigating as Law Students," pp. 2364–68.

166 Days earlier, Ratner had: Effler Memorandum, Mar. 1, 1992, p. 2 (Pl. Tr. Ex. 23).

167 "What's going on?": Interview with Lisa Daugaard, June 25, 2003.

170 "We're closed, sir": Interview with Harold Koh, Mar. 22, 1999.

172 Back home, Koh and Ratner: Ratner, "How We Closed the Guantánamo HIV Camp," p. 202.

173 After a baby born: Clawson, Detweiler, and Ho, "Litigating as Law Students," pp. 2361–62.

173 An official told Mike: Interview with Michael Wishnie, Nov. 30, 2004.

174 A strident, self-described: Sara Miles, "He Kissed a Girl," *Out Magazine* (1999), pp. 51–52.

174 It was an arduous process: Interview with Betty Williams, Mar. 8, 2002; and William Broberg, Nov. 9, 2003.

174 In addition to the deal for: Ratner, "How We Closed the Guantánamo HIV Camp," p. 205.

175 She already knew: Interview with Harold Koh, Apr. 3, 2003.

176 "With polls closed in thirty-nine states": "Dems Break Republican Hold on

South," Live Report, CNN, Nov. 3, 1992, Tr. #85-18, available on Lexis (CNN Transcripts database).

176 Finally, at 10:48 p.m: "Ohio Puts Clinton Over the Top for the Presidency," Live Report, CNN, Nov. 3, 1992, Tr. #85-32, available on Lexis (CNN Transcripts database).

176 "My fellow Americans": "'Together, We Can Do It,' Says President-Elect Clinton," Live Report, CNN, Nov. 4, 1992, Tr. #86-11, available on Lexis (CNN Transcripts database).

Chapter Seven

178 Walter Dellinger, a respected constitutional: Interviews with Walter Dellinger, Apr. 4, 2005; and Harold Koh, June 10, 2003.

178 Just two months earlier: Gary Lee and Molly Sinclair, "Refugees Policy Protested," *Washington Post,* Sept. 10, 1992, p. A9.

179 Drew Days, a Yale professor: Al Kamen, "For Espy, A Strong Show of Support from Major Environmental Groups," *Washington Post,* Dec. 16, 1992, p. A25.

179 Koh's friend Kathleen Sullivan: Al Kamen and Tom Kenworthy, "Liberals Hold Sway on Agency Audit Teams," *Washington Post,* Dec. 7, 1992, p. A13.

179 While Starr had wanted: Interview with Harold Koh, June 10, 2003.

179 The team also had access: Ratner, "How We Closed the Guantánamo HIV Camp," p. 207 n. 65.

179 The administration's new AIDS policy: Ibid., p. 207; interviews with Michael Ratner, July 17, 2003; and Johnny McCalla, July 2, 2003.

179 Proposals for shutting down: Interview with Michael Ratner, July 7, 1999.

179 The immigration cluster even: Interview with Lucas Guttentag, Dec. 18, 2003.

179 Then, in the midst: Interview with Harold Koh, Apr. 6, 2003.

180 Cappuccio seemed more willing: Andres Viglucci, "Legal Morass Claims Haitians with HIV," *Miami Herald,* Dec. 20, 1992, p. 1B.

180 In any event: Interview with Paul Cappuccio, Feb. 16, 2003.

180 During the campaign: Thomas B. Edsall, "3 Democrats Now Willing to Support Death Penalty," *Washington Post,* Jan. 23, 1992, p. A14.

180 Rector was so confused: Sharon LaFraniere, "Governor's Camp Feels His Record on Crime Can Stand the Heat," *Washington Post,* Oct. 5, 1992, p. A6.

180 Cappuccio warned Ratner: Interview with Michael Ratner, Jan. 24, 2003.

180 Dear Mr. President: Letter from Vilsaint Michel et al. to President-elect Bill Clinton, Nov. 17, 1992.

181 Two weeks after Clinton's victory: Trial Transcript, *HCC v. McNary,* Mar. 10, 1993 (reading of deposition testimony of Colonel Stephen Kinder); "Haitians in HIV Prison Camp Attempt Suicide," Lowenstein Clinic press release, Nov. 18, 1992.

181 As their hopes for freedom: Interviews with Jean-Louis Dallard, Mar. 8, 2003; and Oneza Lafontant, Feb. 16, 2005; Charles Arthur et al., "Popular Religion and Culture," in *Libète: A Haiti Anthology,* eds. Charles Arthur and

Michael Dash (Princeton, NJ: Markus Wiener, 1999), pp. 255–74; Selden Rodman and Carole Cleaver, *Spirits of the Night: The Vaudun Gods of Haiti* (Dallas: Spring Publications, 1992).

183 The next day, the story: "Report: Guantánamo Haitians in 'HIV Prison Camp,'" Associated Press, Dec. 2, 1992.

183 Barred from the base: Emily Barker, "Big Suits—Pro Bono/Public Interest," *American Lawyer,* Jan./Feb. 1993, p. 105.

184 Colonel Kinder, too: Richard Cole, "'HIV Concentration Camp' Remains Despite Complaints by Feds, Military," Associated Press, Dec. 12, 1992.

184 "We have no policy": Ibid.

184 "I did say it, yes": Philip J. Hilts, "U.S. Denies Appeal for 4 Ill Haitians," *New York Times,* Dec. 13, 1992, sec. 1, p. 9.

184 A *USA Today* columnist: DeWayne Wickham, "U.S. 'Leper Colony' a Disgrace," *USA Today,* Dec. 14, 1992, p. 12A.

184 And at the center: Cole, "'HIV Concentration Camp' Remains."

184 As a last gesture: Some details in this scene are from a Joint Task Force videotape, apparently from Dec. 15, 1992, in the possession of Haitian refugee Pierre Charles.

185 He left the next morning: Interview with Stephen Kinder, Jan. 29, 2005.

187 A few days after: "I Intend to Look Beyond Partisanship," *Washington Post,* Nov. 13, 1992, p. A10 (excerpts from Clinton press conference).

187 Some transition officials: Interview with Harold Koh, June 10, 2003.

187 An NAACP lobbyist: Ratner, "How We Closed the Guantánamo HIV Camp," p. 207.

188 General Cedras remained firmly in power: Christopher Marquis, "Haitian Exodus May Loom," *Miami Herald,* Nov. 14, 1992, p. 1A.

188 While touring the Haitian coast: Michael Norton, "U.S. Congressman Talks to Haitian Boat-Builders, Warns of 'Human Tidal Wave,'" Associated Press, Nov. 16, 1992; Christopher Marquis, "No Halt to Repatriations," *Miami Herald,* Jan. 15, 1993, p. 1A (Cheney quotation).

188 The U.S. Coast Guard advised: Marquis, "Haitian Exodus May Loom"; Lizette Alvarez, "Haitian Exodus Is No Sure Thing," *Miami Herald,* Nov. 22, 1992, p. 1A.

188 State officials prepared to: Peggy Rogers and Harold Maass, "Dade Braces for Influx of Haitians," *Miami Herald,* Jan. 10, 1993, p. 1B.

188 The Pentagon assured: Paul Anderson and Christopher Marquis, "Pentagon Devises Haiti Plan," *Miami Herald,* Jan. 12, 1993, p. 1A.

190 "Three people are on": Interview with Harold Koh, Apr. 6, 2003.

191 And while most: Interview with Michael Ratner, July 7, 1999.

191 He'd never forgotten: Harold Hongju Koh, "A Tribute to Justice Harry A. Blackmun," 108 *Harvard Law Review* 20 (1994), p. 20.

192 "*Nou pa wè chenn sa?!*": Interview with Ronald Aubourg, June 9, 2003.

193 It now seemed obvious: See, e.g., deposition of Gunther Wagner, May 5, 1992.

193 And when he joined: Interview with Carol Wolchok, July 11, 2003.

193 "Democracy cannot succeed": Interview with Harold Koh, June 10, 2003.

195 "The big news out of": "Clinton Rethinks Position on Haitian Refugees," Live Report, CNN, Jan. 14, 1993, Tr. #257-2, available on Lexis (CNN Transcripts database).

197 "Our greatest strength": "This Is Our Time. Let Us Embrace It." (text of President Clinton's Inaugural Address), *Washington Post,* Jan. 21, 1993, p. A26.

197 At least seventeen cutters: Andres Viglucci, "U.S. Barricading Haiti Flotilla of Boats," *Miami Herald,* Jan. 16, 1993, p. 1A.

197 The Florida Marine Patrol: Andres Viglucci, "Marine Patrol on Standby," *Miami Herald,* Jan. 20, 1993, p. 3B.

197 Whatever the cause: Don Bohning, "Inauguration Day Brings No Haiti Exodus," *Miami Herald,* Jan. 21, 1993, p. 17A.

Chapter Eight

199 As it turned out: Interview with Samuel ("Sandy") Berger, Feb. 12, 2004.

199 Years later: Ibid.

200 Back in 1980, then-Governor: David Maraniss, *First in His Class* (New York: Touchstone, 1995), pp. 376–81, 387–88.

200 There were now just: Associated Press, "Haitians Weak from Hunger Strike," *Miami Herald,* Feb. 9, 1993, p. 6A.

201 Like Kenneth Starr: Interview with Paul Cappuccio, Apr. 18, 2001; Barrett, "Rising Star."

201 No one at the Justice Department: Interview with Michael Ratner, Oct. 5, 2000.

202 Back in Port-au-Prince: Farmer, *The Uses of Haiti,* p. 115.

202 "It's time to head back": Interviews with Yvonne Pascal, Apr. 8, 2002, and Dec. 7, 2002; and Jean-Louis Dallard, Apr. 30, 2001.

203 In a panic: Some details in this scene are from Clawson, Detweiler, and Ho, "Litigating as Law Students," pp. 2374–76.

203 Hurried research by: Charles H. Halsted, "Malnutrition and Nutritional Assessment," in *Harrison's Principles of Internal Medicine,* pp. 455–61.

204 In a stroke of good fortune: This scene is based in part on Cathy Powell, "'Life' at Guantánamo: The Wrongful Detention of Haitian Refugees," 2(2) *Reconstruction* 58 (1993).

204 *You said you are my lawyer:* Ibid., p. 61.

206 At the time, he was already: Bob Liff, "Jackson Presses Clinton on Haiti," *Newsday,* Jan. 26, 1993, p. 79.

207 "We met with Secretary Warren Christopher": Powell, "'Life' at Guantánamo," p. 67.

208 *"My brothers and sisters":* Ibid.

208 The *Boston Globe* devoted: Derrick Z. Jackson, "Ready to Be a Martyr," *Boston Globe,* Feb. 14, 1993, p. A7.

209 Colonel Zinser also vented: Lynne Duke, "Haitians Hope Strike Will Open Safe Haven," *Washington Post,* Feb. 11, 1993, p. A4.

209 Even if many people: Trial Transcript, *HCC v. McNary,* Mar. 18, 1993 (testimony of Colonel Larry Zinser).

209 "You can stop this": Interview with Yvonne Pascal, Dec. 7, 2002.

209 As Shenson understood it: Personal communication with Douglas Shenson, Nov. 11, 2001.

209 After examining the hard-core: Statement by Douglas Shenson, MD, MPH, Regarding the Condition of HIV-Infected Haitian Refugees at Guantánamo Naval Station (Doctors of the World press release), Feb. 9, 1993, p. 2.

209 Bulkeley, Shenson reported: Mike Clary, "Haitians in Camp May Die, Doctors Warn," *Los Angeles Times,* Feb. 11, 1993, p. A30.

211 "I am working for your release": Interviews with Tory Clawson, July 24, 2000; Jean-Louis Dallard, Feb. 17, 2001; and James Dieudonne, Oct. 31, 2001.

211 Some had been on: Transcript of Hearing, *HCC v. McNary,* Sept. 22, 1992.

212 "Is Jesse Jackson coming in today?": White House press briefing by Dee Dee Myers, U.S. Newswire, Feb. 15, 1993.

212 Bringing in the Bulkeley Haitians: "Politically Inconvenient," *Nation,* Mar. 8, 1993, p. 289; "Hunger Strike Threatened," *Washington Post,* Feb. 16, 1993, p. E3.

212 Smith wanted no part: *Sonya Live,* CNN, Feb. 19, 1993, Tr. #241, available on Lexis (CNN Transcripts database).

212 Smith was leaving out: Deborah Sontag, "White House Again Defends Bush's Policy on Haitians," *New York Times,* Mar. 9, 1993, p. A16; Philip J. Hilts, "U.S. Still Holds Haitians with HIV in Cuba," *New York Times,* Dec. 10, 1992, p. A13; Christine Gorman, "Opening the Border to AIDS," *Time,* Feb. 22, 1993, p. 45; Senate Floor Debate, 139 *Congressional Record* S1761-04 (daily ed. Feb. 18, 1993) (statement of Senator Feinstein).

213 The Public Health Service: Gorman, "Opening the Border to AIDS."

213 But fear of AIDS: Clifford Krauss, "Senate Opposes Immigration of People with AIDS Virus," *New York Times,* Feb. 19, 1993, p. A11.

213 Jackson's deadline for the president: National Institutes of Health Revitalization Act of 1993, Pub. L. No. 103-43, § 2007, 107 Stat. 122, 210 (June 10, 1993) (amendment to § 212(a)(1)(A)(i) of the INA, 8 U.S.C. § 1182(a)(1)(A)(i)); "NIH Act Highlights," 51(12) *Congressional Quarterly Weekly Report,* Mar. 20, 1993, p. 670.

213 His first choice: Ruth Marcus and David S. Broder, "President Takes Blame for Rushing Baird Selection," *Washington Post,* Jan. 23, 1993, p. A1.

214 Mike Wishnie joined: Stuart Gerson was the acting attorney general at the time, but he was a Bush holdover, and Hubbell, who had no official title yet, had the power of the White House behind him. Michael Isikoff and Sharon LaFraniere, "Urgent Hunt Launched for an Attorney General," *Washington Post,* Jan. 23, 1993, p. A10.

214 Before Koh had finished: Interview with Michael Wishnie, June 9, 2003.

214 "In the view of those close": Interviews with Michael Ratner, Oct. 5, 2000;

and Harold Koh, Apr. 6, 2003. Almost identical language appears in Ratner, "How We Closed the Guantánamo HIV Camp," p. 210.

215 "We just wanted to let you know": Interview with Harold Koh, Apr. 6, 2003.

220 Answering through an interpreter: Deposition of Yvonne Pascal, Feb. 21, 1993.

221 Back in the trailer: All quotations are from the deposition of Yvonne Pascal (continued), Feb. 22, 1993.

Chapter Nine

224 "No, Harold," Calabresi had said: Interview with Harold Koh, Jan. 15, 2005.

224 Article 33 mandated that: Article 33, U.N. Refugee Convention, 19 U.S.T. 6259.

224 In similar terms: 8 U.S.C. § 1253(h)(1) (1992).

224 As the students already knew: William N. Eskridge Jr., "The New Textualism," 37 *UCLA Law Review* 621 (1990). For examples of Scalia's position, see *INS v. Cardozo-Fonseca,* 480 U.S. 421, 445–53 (1987) (Scalia, J., concurring in the judgment) and the cases collected by Eskridge, "The New Textualism," p. 651 n. 116.

225 He often used a dictionary: Interview with William N. Eskridge Jr., Oct. 26, 2004.

225 Critics charged that Scalia's: Eskridge, "The New Textualism," p. 668.

225 Even the liberal Second: *HCC v. McNary,* 969 F.2d at 1361.

225 In fact, the order: Executive Order No. 12,807, 57 *Federal Register* 23,133 (May 24, 1992) (emphasis added).

225 Veronique Sanchez found that: "Le bourbier haïtien," *Le Monde,* June 1, 1992 ("Les États-Unis ont décidé de *refouler* directement les réfugiés recueillis par la garde côtière."); *Dictionnaire Larousse* (Paris: Larousse, 1981), p. 631.

226 "We never should have": Hate-mail quotations and quotation from Justice Blackmun are from an interview with Harold Koh, June 10, 2003.

226 Even another minority group: Ibid.

227 The Solicitor General's Office: This scene is based on an interview with Maureen Mahoney, Nov. 21, 2003; Brief for the Petitioners, *McNary v. HCC,* available on Westlaw, 1992 WL 541276; and Lyle Denniston, "Dress Rehearsal for Civil Rights Battle," *American Lawyer,* Sept. 1988, p. 129.

227 But as Mahoney read: Brief for the Petitioners, 1992 WL 541276, at *51–*52.

228 Indeed, while admirers: Koh, "Tribute to Justice Blackmun," pp. 21–22; Jeffrey Rosen, "Sentimental Journey," *New Republic,* May 2, 1994, p. 13.

228 "*Manman* had to take a little trip": Interviews with Thérèse Dume, Dec. 9, 2002; and Yvon Dume, June 8, 2003.

229 Every weekday, Justice Blackmun: Interview with Harold Koh, Jan. 24, 2004; Lazarus, *Closed Chambers,* p. 38.

230 "Oyez! Oyez! Oyez!": Lazarus, *Closed Chambers,* p. 29.

230 Mahoney had her usual: Interview with Maureen Mahoney, Nov. 21, 2003.

230 Adopting a dry, dispassionate: All quotations in court are from the Oral Argument Transcript, *Sale v. HCC,* Mar. 2, 1993, available on Westlaw, 1993

WL 754941. (The case name changed because INS Commissioner Gene McNary resigned when President Clinton took office and was replaced temporarily by Acting Commissioner Chris Sale.)

231 Mahoney quickly pointed to: Sections 212(f) and 215(a) of the INA, 8 U.S.C. §§ 1182(f), 1185(a) (1992).

234 He pointed to an earlier: *INS v. Stevic,* 467 U.S. 407 (1984).

235 In the original 1952 formulation: INA, Pub. L. No. 82-414, § 243(h), 66 Stat. 163, 214 (1952) (emphasis added).

235 In the Refugee Act of 1980: 8 U.S.C. § 1253(h)(1) (1992) (emphasis added).

237 One of the amicus briefs: Brief of Amici Curiae American Jewish Committee and Anti-Defamation League in Support of Respondents, *McNary v. HCC,* pp. 13, 19.

237 Precisely one minute later: *South Dakota v. Bourland,* 508 U.S. 679 (1993).

238 Koh pressed the refugees' cause: *The MacNeil/Lehrer NewsHour,* PBS, Mar. 2, 1993, Tr. #4575, available on Lexis (*NewsHour* database). Description of Sandy Berger is based on a videotape of the broadcast.

238 Sandy Berger, Clinton's deputy: Interview with Harold Koh, June 10, 2003.

238 Her vital signs: Camp Bulkeley Battalion Aid Station medical records of Yvonne Pascal, Feb. 22, 1993, p. 5.

239 Those who knew some English: Some details in this scene are based on photographs in the possession of Yvonne Pascal and Betty Williams.

239 Lieutenant Jason Dillman: Government Witness Summary for Lieutenant Jason T. Dillman, Mar. 3, 1993; Hearing Transcript, *HCC v. McNary,* Mar. 4, 1993; interview with Robert Rubin, Jan. 29, 2002.

239 Lauri Filppu called Rubin: Interview with Robert Rubin, Jan. 29, 2002.

239 But bringing everyone together: Ratner, "How We Closed the Guantánamo HIV Camp," p. 212; interview with Michael Wishnie, Apr. 1, 2003.

240 Tense meetings followed: Ratner, "How We Closed the Guantánamo HIV Camp," pp. 212–13 & nn. 80, 82.

240 "Free the Guantánamo Haitians!": Interview with Betty Williams, Oct. 30, 2001.

240 In Philadelphia, they interrupted: Craigg Hines, "AIDS Protest Irks Clinton," *Houston Chronicle,* May 29, 1993, p. A4; Frank J. Murray, "AIDS Activists Annoy Clinton," *Washington Times,* May 29, 1993, p. A5.

241 It began with the Yale student newspaper: Jennifer Sherinsky, "Students Rally for Haitians," *Yale Daily News,* Mar. 4, 1993, p. 1; Fred Laberge, "Students Share Haitians' Hunger Strike," *New Haven Register,* Mar. 9, 1993, p. 1.

241 The *New York Times* and the: Nadine Brozan, "Chronicle," *New York Times,* Mar. 12, 1993, p. B6; "Rally for Haitian Refugees," *Boston Globe,* Mar. 11, 1993, p. 34.

241 Within weeks, the strike: Clawson, Detweiler, and Ho, "Litigating as Law Students," p. 2378 n. 152; Ratner, "How We Closed the Guantánamo HIV Camp," p. 215.

241 Churches staged hunger strikes: "Polynice Joins Fast to Protest Policy," *New York Times,* Feb. 18, 1993, p. B17.

242 White House Counsel Bernard Nussbaum: Interview with Webster Hubbell, Jan. 13, 2004.

242 Mondesir was furious: Deposition of Yanick Mondesir, Feb. 24, 1993.

243 He demanded that Lisa: Interview with Lisa Daugaard, Sept. 11, 2003.

244 What the team had obtained: Clawson, Detweiler, and Ho, "Litigating as Law Students," p. 2382.

244 He'd discovered Coast Guard and military documents: Coast Guard Communiqué, June 23, 1992 (Pl. Tr. Ex. 41); Stenner Memorandum, Mar. 3, 1992, p. 2 (Pl. Tr. Ex. 61).

244 The media had already reported: Lynne Duke, "Haitians Hope Strike Will Open Safe Haven," *Washington Post,* Feb. 11, 1993, p. A4; Andres Viglucci, "Marooned at Guantánamo by HIV," *Miami Herald,* Feb. 11, 1993, p. 1A; deposition of James Wesley Myers, Mar. 1, 1993.

244 Guantánamo, they explained: Myers deposition.

245 According to the minutes: Camp Bulkeley Meeting Minutes, Aug. 11, 1992, p. 1 (Pl. Tr. Ex. 45).

245 Several months before: Hearing Transcript, *HCC v. McNary,* Apr. 1, 1992 (testimony of Brigadier General George H. Walls Jr.).

245 And in a contentious: Hearing Transcript, *HCC v. McNary,* Mar. 4, 1993.

245 "I've litigated indefinite detention": Ibid.

Chapter Ten

247 "Almost one year ago": Quotations in court are from the Trial Transcript, *HCC v. McNary,* Mar. 8, 1993.

248 Though he kept his delivery: Interviews with Lisa Daugaard, Nov. 9, 2003; Harold Koh, Jan. 24, 2004; and Michael Ratner, Feb. 3, 2001 (all describing the response from the gallery).

250 In her deposition: Deposition of Yanick Mondesir, Feb. 24, 1993.

255 Starting the next morning: The summary of testimony from Robert Cohen and Douglas Shenson is from the Trial Transcript, *HCC v. McNary,* Mar. 9, 1993. The summary of trial testimony from Jonathan Mann is from the Trial Transcript, *HCC v. McNary,* Mar. 10, 1993.

258 The men waited until dark: This scene is based in part on an interview with Allan Ebert, Jan. 19, 2002; a memorandum from Allan Ebert to the Yale legal team, Mar. 11, 1993, pp. 1–4; and David Kidwell, "Violence Erupts at Guantánamo Refugee Camp," *Miami Herald,* Mar. 15, 1993, p. 1A.

258 His superiors, evidently displeased with: Andres Viglucci, "Soldiers Crack Down on Restive Haitians," *Miami Herald,* Mar. 21, 1993, p. 8A.

259 By midnight, hundreds of soldiers: Testimony of Lieutenant Jason T. Dillman, Trial Transcript, *HCC v. McNary,* Mar. 19, 1993.

259 Begleiter had conflicting feelings: This scene is based on interviews with Robert Begleiter, Jan. 24, 2002, and Nov. 25, 2003.

260 Under the law: Quotations in court are from the Trial Transcript, *HCC v. McNary,* Mar. 11, 1993.

261 The next night, a fierce storm: Russell Ben-Ali, "Whiteout '93," *Newsday,*
     Mar. 15, 1993, p. 19.

261 *"Leve! Leve! Leve!":* This scene is based in part on the declaration of Yvonne
     Pascal, Mar. 19, 1993; a memorandum from Allan Ebert to the Yale legal
     team, Mar. 16, 1993; undated statements of fourteen refugees prepared by
     Allan Ebert; interviews with Allan Ebert, Jan. 19, 2002; and Ninaj Raoul,
     Aug. 26, 2004; and notes on the medical conditions of various refugees taken
     by Harold Koh in March 1993.

263 Allan Ebert finally reached: Notes of Lisa Daugaard from the Lowenstein
     Clinic files, undated; interview with Allan Ebert, Jan. 19, 2002; affidavit of
     Allan Ebert, Mar. 13, 1993, pp. 2, 4.

264 When the government needed: Testimony of Colonel Frederick George Fox
     III, Trial Transcript, *HCC v. McNary,* Mar. 15, 1993.

264 She'd written a letter: Letter from Yvonne Pascal to her family, Feb. 3, 1993
     (Ex. 1 to the deposition of Yvonne Pascal, Feb. 21, 1993).

265 In the end, though, Lisa grudgingly: "Jackson Arrested at Protest," *New
     York Times,* Mar. 16, 1993, p. B2; "Jesse Jackson is Arrested at Refugee
     Rally," *Los Angeles Times,* Mar. 16, 1993, p. A5.

265 At a White House press briefing: White House Briefing, Federal News Ser-
     vice, Mar. 16, 1993, available on Lexis (FedNewsServ database).

265 An hour after Broberg's: This scene is based in part on interviews with
     Robert Begleiter, Nov. 25, 2003, Jan. 24, 2003, and Apr. 18, 2001; and Web-
     ster Hubbell, Jan. 13, 2004.

266 That's exactly what Filppu had said: Trial Transcript, *HCC v. McNary,* Mar.
     11, 1993.

266 Standing alone before: Quotations in court are from the Trial Transcript,
     HCC v. McNary, Mar. 15, 1993.

267 **U.S. NAVAL BRIG**: Brig Rules and Regulations, undated, provided to Allan
     Ebert by Lt. Colonel Peter Kleff, approx. Mar. 14, 1993.

268 For two days after her arrest: Declaration of Yvonne Pascal, Mar. 19, 1993,
     pp. 1–3.

268 About twenty refugees: Memorandum from Harold Koh to Joe Tringali,
     Mar. 20, 1993, p. 1.

268 Some denied the charges: Declaration of Elma Verdieu, Mar. 19, 1993,
     p. 1.

268 In response, Paulson meted: Koh Memorandum, p. 1.

268 "What recreational activities": Quotations in court are from the Trial Tran-
     script, *HCC v. McNary,* Mar. 17, 1993.

269 Tringali now read from: Telecommunication from U.S. Commander-in-
     Chief, Atlantic, to Joint Chiefs of Staff, Washington, D.C., July 18, 1992, p. 3
     (Pl. Tr. Ex. 65).

270 During a court recess: Interview with Joe Tringali, Nov. 3, 2004.

271 The next day in court: Quotations in court are from the Trial Transcript,
     HCC v. McNary, Mar. 18, 1993.

272 The next afternoon: Quotations in court are from the Trial Transcript, *HCC v. McNary,* Mar. 19, 1993.

273 "Your Honor," he said: Joint Task Force videotape of Camp Bulkeley, July 18, 1992 (Pl. Tr. Ex. 105).

275 The judge looked at Filppu: Quotations in court are from the Trial Transcript, *HCC v. McNary,* Mar. 19, 1993.

276 The judge's decision: *HCC v. Sale,* 817 F. Supp. 336 (E.D.N.Y. 1993).

277 But the number ballooned: Personal communication with Douglas Shenson, Nov. 11, 2001.

277 How would they react: Ransdell Pierson, "Haiti's AIDS Refugees Are Heading for N.Y.," *New York Post,* Apr. 6, 1993, p. 15.

278 Colonel Paulson had surrounded: Viglucci, "Soldiers Crack Down."

278 With the permission of: Interviews with Harold Koh, Mar. 22, 1999, and Jan. 24, 2004.

278 The flight was scheduled: Joint Task Force flight manifest, Apr. 8, 1993.

279 There were kisses, tears: Memorandum from Margaret Hennessy and Oneza ("Cassignol") Lafontant to the Yale legal team, Mar. 18, 1993, p. 6 (detailing Gertil Cadet's medical condition).

Chapter Eleven

284 Relying on Ronald Aubourg: Anna Quindlen, "A Death Watch," *New York Times,* May 30, 1993, sec. 4, p. 11; *Phil Donahue Show,* syndicated feature, Apr. 1993.

284 The first refugee to die: David Hancock, "Haitian Detainee with AIDS Dies in Homestead," *Miami Herald,* Apr. 29, 1993, p. 3B (article reports incorrectly how long Saintil was alive in the U.S.).

285 The doctor who treated: Andres Viglucci, "Guantánamo a Place of Listless Despair," *Miami Herald,* May 27, 1993, p. 1A.

285 The Emergency Coalition: William Grimes, "Eastwood Western Takes Top 2 Prizes in 65th Oscar Show," *New York Times,* Mar. 30, 1993, p. C15.

285 And much of the world: Dolores Kong, "AIDS Outlook Grim," *Boston Globe,* June 8, 1993, p. 4.

285 Most Haitians had quit: Viglucci, "Guantánamo a Place of Listless Despair"; interview with William Broberg, Aug. 20, 1999.

285 When that failed: Clawson, Detweiler, and Ho, "Litigating as Law Students," p. 2375.

286 Judge Johnson had issued: *HCC v. Sale,* 823 F. Supp. 1028, 1045 (E.D.N.Y. 1991).

287 All her research on due process: The Yale team had also continued to press the equal protection claim in a modified form, arguing that by treating Haitians differently from other aliens seeking asylum, the government had violated a statute known as the Administrative Procedure Act (APA). The strategy was essentially to disguise a difficult constitutional argument as a statutory claim instead, an idea based in part on an article Lisa Daugaard had

read by Hiroshi Motomura, "Immigration Law After a Century of Plenary Power: Phantom Constitutional Norms and Statutory Interpretation," 100 *Yale Law Journal* 545 (1990). Judge Johnson ruled for Yale on the APA claim. *Sale,* 823 F. Supp. at 1045–49.

288 But the Clinton officials: Larry Rohter, "Long Exodus Nears End for HIV-Infected Refugees from Haiti," *New York Times,* June 13, 1993, sec. 1, p. 24; Lisa Ocker and William E. Gibson, "U.S. to Accept HIV Haitians," *Sun-Sentinel* (Fort Lauderdale), June 10, 1993, p.1A; Greg McDonald, "Clinton Will Abide by Haitians Ruling," *Houston Chronicle*, June 10, 1993, p. A1.

288 "I'm calling to let you know": Interview with Harold Koh, June 10, 2003.

289 After issuing his decision: Interviews with Judge Sterling Johnson Jr., Dec. 29, 2003, and Nov. 12, 2004.

289 The president's staff: Interviews with Sandy Berger, Feb. 12, 2004; and Eric Schwartz, Sept. 13, 2004.

290 After Judge Johnson's decision came down: Lynne Duke, "White House to Obey Order to Admit HIV-Infected Haitians," *Washington Post,* June 10, 1993, p. A30.

290 "We didn't have to take": Interview with Eric Schwartz, Sept. 13, 2004.

290 Judge Johnson had concluded: Interview with Judge Sterling Johnson Jr., Dec. 29, 2003.

290 Nevertheless, a number of House Republicans: Republican House Members News Conference, "Admission of HIV-Infected Haitians into the United States," Majority Leader Special Transcript, Federal News Service, June 24, 1993, available on Lexis (FedNewsServ database).

290 The Department of Justice began releasing: Larry Rohter, "Haitians with HIV Leave Cuba Base for Lives in U.S.," *New York Times,* June 15, 1993, p. A20.

291 The justices ruled: *Sale v. HCC,* 509 U.S. 155, 177–88 (1993). For the sake of brevity and accessibility, the narrative does not address the dispute between Yale and the government over the lengthy and ambiguous negotiating history of Article 33 of the U.N. Refugee Convention. The main point of disagreement involved the interpretation of statements by the Dutch and Swiss representatives that the bar against "return" of refugees was limited to people physically within a country's territory. See *McNary*, 969 F.2d at 1365–66. The government took these comments as evidence that Article 33 did not apply on the high seas; Yale, in response, argued that the Dutch and Swiss position expressed a minority view not adopted by the treaty itself. The Second Circuit sided with Yale on the negotiating history, while the Supreme Court took the government's position. See ibid.; *Sale*, 509 U.S. at 184–87. The Yale team had assumed it would enjoy an advantage on this issue before the Supreme Court because Justice Scalia, as part of his textualist philosophy, did not condone reliance on negotiating history. But Scalia ultimately joined the opinion by Justice Stevens, which drew on Article 33's negotiating history to rule for the government. (The narrative also does not discuss the legislative history of

the Refugee Act of 1980, which provides little guidance on whether the act was meant to apply beyond U.S. borders. The Supreme Court favored the government's interpretation of that history. See *Sale*, 509 U.S. at 174–76. Justice Blackmun sharply criticized the court's reasoning in his dissent. See ibid., at 202–05.)

292 Near the end of his opinion: *Sale,* 509 U.S. at 183.

292 "This case," Stevens concluded: Ibid., at 188 (quoting *Haitian Refugee Center v. Gracey,* 809 F.2d 794, 841 (D.C. Cir. 1987) (Edwards, J., concurring in part and dissenting in part)) (quotation marks omitted).

292 In dissent, Justice Blackmun: *Sale,* 509 U.S. at 208.

292 Blackmun had faced: Personal notes of Justice Harry A. Blackmun at Supreme Court conference, Mar. 5, 1993, for *McNary v. HCC* (*Sale v. HCC*), available in Box 623 of the Papers of Justice Harry A. Blackmun, Manuscript Division, Library of Congress, Washington, D.C.

292 "That's most of us": Interview with Harold Koh, June 19, 2004.

293 Based on the team's Supreme Court brief: Koh, "Reflections on Refoulement," p. 2.

293 National security official Eric Schwartz: Interview with Eric Schwartz, Sept. 13, 2004.

293 "It's hard to believe": Interview with Jessica Weisel, Oct. 26, 2004.

294 But as one Justice: Michael Kramer, "The Political Interest: Putting People Second," *Time,* Nov. 1, 1993, p. 29.

294 As of the beginning: Andres Viglucci and Paul Anderson, "Returning of Haitians is Upheld," *Miami Herald*, June 22, 1993, p. 1A.

295 Someone said he'd been poisoned: Ian Fisher, "Haitians Living in New York Are Digesting New Letdown," *New York Times,* Nov. 1, 1993, p. B1.

296 "God," she told the *New York Times*: Ibid.

296 It was FRAPH, she said: The formation of FRAPH (Front for the Advancement and Progress of Haiti) is described in Stotzky, *Silencing the Guns,* pp. 34–35.

296 With thousands of Haitians: Interviews with Anne Fuller, Dec. 5, 2003, and Mar. 22, 2005.

298 According to a former presidential adviser: Anonymous interview, Jan. 4, 2005.

298 Having won the trial: 28 U.S.C. § 2412(d)(1)(A) (1993).

299 It all added up to about: Harold Hongju Koh, "Democracy and Human Rights in the United States Foreign Policy? Lessons from the Haitian Crisis," 48 *Southern Methodist University Law Review* 189 (1994), p. 191.

299 Koh told the Justice Department lawyers: Interview with Harold Koh, June 10, 2003.

299 Even if the opinion: See, e.g., *McKenzie v. Day,* 57 F.3d 1493, 1494 (9th Cir. 1995).

300 The rep checked: Interview with Harold Koh, June 10, 2003.

300 After Judge Johnson: Settlement Agreement, *HCC v. Sale,* Oct. 21, 1993; Stipulated Order Approving Class Action Settlement, *HCC v. Meissner,* Feb. 22,

1994 (Doris Meissner was appointed commissioner of the INS in the fall of 1993, leading to another change in the name of the case); letter from Michael Jay Singer to Joseph Tringali re: final payment of claim, Feb. 24, 1994.

301 In December 1993: John Shattuck, *Freedom on Fire: Human Rights Wars and America's Response* (Cambridge, MA: Harvard University Press, 2003), pp. 77–112; interview with John Shattuck, Dec. 13, 2004.

301 Shattuck was rebuked: Steven A. Holmes, "Rebuking Aide, U.S. Says Haiti Policy Stands," *New York Times,* Dec. 16, 1993, p. A6.

301 In early May: Richard J. Norton, "Haiti," in *Case Studies in Policy Making and Implementation,* 6th ed., ed. David A. Williams (Newport, RI: Naval War College, 2002), pp. 32, 42, 43.

301 National Security Adviser Anthony Lake: Interview with Anthony Lake, May 26, 2004.

301 "Of course. I was worried": Norton, "Haiti," p. 42.

301 In late June 1994: Ann Devroy and Daniel Williams, "Haiti Refugee Center Reopened in Cuba," *Washington Post,* June 29, 1994, p. A1.

302 An unlikely coalition: Interview with Sandy Berger, Feb. 12, 2004.

302 In September 1994: Norton, "Haiti," pp. 47–48.

302 As it had been for Aristide's inauguration: Stotzky, *Silencing the Guns,* pp. 4–6.

303 After the Haitians entered the United States: Interview with Michael Wishnie, Apr. 12, 2005. An INS official later agreed to award asylum to some Bulkeley refugees without the filing of another asylum application. Ibid.

305 In mid-1998, Koh received: Interview with Harold Koh, June 19, 2004.

305 After Haiti, Koh: *Cuban American Bar Association v. Christopher,* 43 F.3d 1412 (11th Cir. 1995).

305 He'd also continued the Lowenstein Clinic: Paul Anderson and Christopher Marquis, "Graham and Mack Deliver Plea on Haiti," *Miami Herald,* May 14, 1994, p. 1A; Jonathan Schell, "Missing in Action: The Constitution," *Newsday*, Sept. 25, 1994, p. A49.

305 Shattuck, the current assistant secretary: Interview with John Shattuck, Dec. 13, 2004.

306 He traveled the world: Details of Koh's experience in the State Department are based in part on Harold Hongju Koh, "A United States Human Rights Policy for the 21st Century," 46 *Saint Louis University Law Journal* 293 (2002).

306 He promised the United Nations: Edward Alden, "US Interrogation Debate," *Financial Times,* June 10, 2004, p. 7.

306 The two already knew each other: Robert S. Capers, "Aristide Hits 'Sham Embargo,'" *Hartford Courant,* Apr. 26, 1994, p. D12; interview with Harold Koh, Jan. 15, 2004.

306 Aristide's 1994 restoration by the United States: Robert Fatton Jr., *Haiti's Predatory Republic: The Unending Transition to Democracy* (Boulder, CO: Lynne Rienner Publishers, 2002), pp. 107–14; interview with Robert Maguire, June 24, 2003; interview with Alex Dupuy, May 21, 2005; Douglas

Farah, "A First in Haiti: Democratic Succession," *Washington Post*, Feb. 8, 1996, p.A1.

307 Aristide won the presidency: Fatton, *Haiti's Predatory Republic,* pp. xiii, 141–56; interview with Robert Maguire, June 24, 2003.

307 Dismayed, some democracy activists: In February 2004, soldiers allied with the 1991 coup leaders forced Aristide from power once again. Kevin Sullivan and Scott Wilson, "Aristide Resigns, Flies into Exile," *Washington Post,* Mar. 1, 2004, p. A1.

307 When Koh left the State Department: Interview with John Shattuck, Dec. 13, 2004.

Epilogue

309 Shortly thereafter, President George W. Bush: Scott Higham, Joe Stephens, and Margot Williams, "A Holding Cell in War on Terror," *Washington Post,* May 2, 2004, p. A1; White House Statement on Guantánamo Bay Detainees, U.S. Newswire, Feb. 7, 2002, available on Westlaw, 2002 WL 191074.

309 The first detainees arrived: Higham, Stephens, and Williams, "Holding Cell"; Neil A. Lewis, "U.S. Erecting a Solid Prison at Guantánamo for Long Term," *New York Times,* Oct. 22, 2003, p. A20.

309 Members of the Joint Task Force: http://www.globalsecurity.org/military/facility/guantanamo-bay_delta.htm (compiling and summarizing media reports and official government sources).

309 The Bush administration declared: Sue Anne Pressley, "Preparing for Role in War on Terror," *Washington Post,* Jan. 10, 2002, p. A12; John Mintz, "Extended Detention in Cuba Mulled," *Washington Post,* Feb. 13, 2002, p. A16.

309 The case, *Rasul v. Bush*, asserted: *Rasul v. Bush*, 215 F. Supp. 2d 55, 62, 72–73 (D.D.C. 2002).

310 The appellate court: *Al Odah v. United States*, 321 F.3d 1134, 1143, 1145 (D.C. Cir. 2003).

310 Dozens of amicus briefs: Brief of Amici Curiae Former U.S. Government Officials in Support of Petitioners, *Rasul v. Bush,* Jan. 14, 2004 (Koh brief), available on Westlaw, 2004 WL 96757; Brief of Amici Curiae Legal Historians Listed Herein in Support of the Petitioners, *Rasul v. Bush,* Jan. 14, 2004 (Wishnie brief), available on Westlaw, 2004 WL 96756.

310 The justices heard oral argument: Oral argument Transcript, *Rasul v. Bush*, Apr. 20, 2004, available on Westlaw, 2004 WL 943637.

310 Olson's written brief: Brief for the Respondents, *Rasul v. Bush*, Mar. 3, 2004, p. *7, available on Westlaw, 2004 WL 425739.

310 The brief also referred: Ibid. (citing White House press release available at http://www.whitehouse.gov/news/releases/2002/02/20020207–13.html).

310 Days after the argument: James Risen, "G.I.'s Are Accused of Abusing Iraqi Captives," *New York Times*, Apr. 29, 2004, p. A15.

310 In a letter to the *New York Times*: Letter from Michael Ratner, *New York Times,* May 19, 2004, p. A24.

310   On June 28, 2004: *Rasul v. Bush*, 542 U.S. 466 (2004).

310   While Stevens did not: Ibid., at 483 n. 15 (quoting 28 U.S.C. § 2241(c)(3)) (quotation marks omitted).

311   Justice Anthony Kennedy: Ibid., at 487 (quoting *Johnson v. Eisentrager*, 339 U.S. 763, 777–78 (1950)) (Kennedy, J., concurring in the judgment).

311   Justice Antonin Scalia dissented: Ibid., at 497–98, 506 (Scalia, J., dissenting).

311   Litigation then resumed: See, e.g., *In re Guantánamo Detainee Cases*, 355 F. Supp. 2d 443 (D.D.C. 2005); *Khalid v. Bush*, 355 F. Supp. 2d 311 (D.D.C. 2005).

311   Advocates for the detainees: Interview with Michael Ratner, Jan. 20, 2005.

ACKNOWLEDGMENTS

A BOOK LIKE this is a collaborative project. It depends upon the recollections and goodwill of the hundreds of people who were involved in the events depicted in the story. While it would be redundant to list here all those individuals I interviewed who appear in the text or the notes, I wish to express my extraordinary gratitude to them.

I owe a special debt to several people at the center of the story. Over the course of six years of interviews, Harold Hongju Koh of Yale Law School gave generously not only of his time but of himself, answering endless questions about almost every aspect of his life. I owe a great debt, too, to Yvonne Pascal, who has shown the courage to revisit her painful past with me again and again, even as she works a full-time job, cares for her family, and fights to maintain her health. I also wish to express my deep appreciation to the former Yale law students—in particular, Lisa Daugaard, Tory Clawson, Mike Wishnie, and Steve Roos—and the other key lawyers on the Yale team—Lucas Guttentag, Michael Ratner, Robert Rubin, and Joe Tringali—who all racked their memories time and time again to help reconstruct the story. Finally, I wish to thank Judge Sterling Johnson Jr. for granting me several in-depth interviews.

This book cuts across a number of subjects; to enrich my understanding about each, I relied on the generosity of many people. On the topics of Haiti and Haitian refugees, I am especially grateful to Ronald Aubourg, who introduced me to Yvonne Pascal, served as an interpreter, and advised me in countless ways, and to Ninaj Raoul, who helped me meet several of the Camp Bulkeley refugees and educated me about the Haitian community in New York. I also wish to thank James Dieudonne, Emmanuel Dostaly, Dallard Jean-Louis (who died in 2003), and Johnny McCalla, as well as Patricia Benoit, Pierre Esperance, Henry Frank, Leopold Joseph, Gabrielle Kersaint, Oneza Lafontant, Daniel Michaud, Jean-Baptiste Mondesir,

Daniel Morel, Murat Noelsaint, Dr. Marie Carmel Pierre-Louis, Vaval Pierre, Marie M. B. Racine, Jane Regan, and Betty Williams, among others. I am grateful to Yvonne Pascal's family for welcoming me into their lives.

On the subjects of Haitian politics and society, I learned much from Robert Maguire, Alex Dupuy, and Jenna Ben-Yahuda, while Jeanne Butterfield and Carol Wolchok provided valuable information on conditions in Haiti after the 1991 coup. For insight into the history of litigation on behalf of Haitian refugees, I am grateful to Robert Juceam, Ira Kurzban, Cheryl Little, and Irwin Stotzky, as well as Sharon Ginter.

In the areas of human rights law and immigration law, I benefited from discussions with Ignatius Bau, Susan Benesch, Lenni Benson, Erin Corcoran, Lucas Guttentag, Carrol Lucht, Kenneth Roth, and Michael Wishnie. I developed a better understanding of other legal issues relating to the case through conversations with David Gelfand, Jack Gerstein, William Eskridge, and Andrew Schapiro.

For their recollections of various events on Guantánamo, I wish to thank Leslie Chace, Dan Coughlin, Margaret Hennessy, and Kim Ives. Jonathan Hansen provided valuable background on the history of the naval base.

I learned much about the United States Coast Guard from Randy Beardsworth, James Carlson, and Greg Saniel, as well as from a visit to the United States Coast Guard Historian's Office.

In addition to those people mentioned in the text, a number of former executive officials, congressional staff members, and other government employees provided information on U.S. Haitian refugee policy and many other topics. Among these generous people are Robert Begland, Bennett Freeman, Anita Cavallino, Peter Corsell, Tawana Davis, James Dobbins, Brad Glassman, Vicki Huddleston, Janice O'Connell, Jeremy Rosner, Paul Virtue, and Edwin Williamson.

Several physicians provided explanations about the medical aspects of the story, including Dr. Stephen Migueles, Dr. Jack Billi, Dr. Paul Effler, Dr. Amita Gupta, Dr. Brent Lee, and Dr. Fred Lee Jr.

Students on the Yale team who discussed the case with me but whose names do not appear in the narrative include Elizabeth Detweiler, Song Richardson, Todd Thomas, and Jessica Weisel, among others. I also benefited from the recollections of many other former students, including Felipe Arroyo, Brian Casey, Peter Choharis, Willis Chou, Hampton Dellinger, Bill Dodge, Chris Gilkerson, Mercer Givhan, Steve Koh, Eric Nelson, Kurt Petersen, Steve Vladeck, and Ursula Werner.

I received invaluable assistance from Yale Law School, where I was an associate in research from 1999 to 2001. I wish to thank former dean Anthony Kronman for welcoming me back to the law school, as well as Paul Gewirtz, Carroll Lucht, and Bob Solomon for their advice and insights. The computer, library, and registrar's office staff were of great help, as were Renee DeMatteo, Georganne Rogers, and Kris Kavanaugh. I am also grateful to the Lowenstein International Human Rights Clinic at Yale and to Simpson Thacher & Bartlett for furnishing access to their files on the lawsuit. Betty Walrond at Simpson Thacher helped me deal with all the documents, and Susan Sawyer, a former lawyer there, provided me with her recollections of the case.

While working on this project, I enjoyed much support from the law firm of Cleary, Gottlieb, Steen & Hamilton and the law firm of Ross, Dixon & Bell. At Cleary, Gottlieb, I am grateful to, among many others, Brian Byrne, Paul Marquardt, Mark Nelson, Michael Lazerwitz, Janice Roebuck, and especially Eugene Marans. At Ross Dixon, my thanks to Terri Carnahan, Gary Dixon, Chuck Hadden, Merril Hirsh, Stu Ross, Mary Ellen Ash, Judy Sebold, and many others. A warm thank-you to Sol Wisenberg as well.

I benefited from the fine research assistance of Danielle Morris, Jessica Lawrence, Marla Goodman, and Joseph Masters, and the help of librarians Susan Burroughs, Mary Maguire, and especially Lynn Hartke.

During the writing process, I enjoyed the help of many insightful readers. I would like to thank in particular Susan Benesch, Lincoln Caplan, Kevin Heller, and Curtis Runyan for their comments on various drafts, as well as Michelle Burnett, Marie Burke, Ona Ferguson, Julie Hilden, Dahlia Lithwick, Sarah Ludington, William O'Neill, Stephen Pomper, David Segal, Peter Spiro, and Rebekah Tosado.

At Scribner, my editor, Sarah McGrath, provided sharp insight, excellent advice, and much common sense. Her assistant, Samantha Martin, showed endless patience and solved problems with efficiency and good humor. Many thanks to Jane Herman for fine copyediting, Laura Wise for overseeing production while I kept coming in past deadline, Veronica Jordan for conducting a meticulous legal review, and to Suzanne Balaban, who in concert with Lynn Goldberg and Angela Hayes of Goldberg McDuffie developed the great publicity plan. A special thanks to Nan Graham, whose enthusiasm for the project fueled my own.

My agent, Henry Dunow, saw the promise of this story from the start and provided a steady hand on the tiller and much wise counsel over the years. I owe him more than I can say. Sylvie Rabineau and Michael Seitzman provided an enormous boost from the West Coast.

My family gave me extraordinary support as this project dragged on, my spirits flagged, and my bank account ran low. Special gratitude goes to my mother, Jone Rymer, who read every word four or five times and provided outstanding editing and so much encouragement; to my father, Irwin Goldstein, whose boundless faith and enthusiasm—and extraordinary example—kept me going; and to my brother and fellow traveler, Garth Goldstein, who understood perhaps better than anyone what the struggle was about. I am also indebted to Martha Mayo for her generosity and fine editing eye, and to Doug Kevorkian, Joanne Jaffin, David Sharken, Renee Rymer, Tony Clementino, Mira Hinman, Todd McDermott, and especially Rick Erickson.

I am deeply grateful to several extraordinary people in my life who helped me see this project through. A special, loving thank-you goes to Elissa Austria, whose passion for language is reflected in these pages and whose companionship, wisdom, and generous spirit kept me whole. John Pollack, Rodger Citron, and William Ingle were the best of friends in the most trying of hours. Peter Lurie, Peter Jacobson, Liz Katkin, Dahlia Lithwick, Matt Klam, and Felipe Arroyo all provided good cheer and much-needed perspective—time and time again. Finally, I wish to acknowledge two extraordinary mentors, Judge Harry T. Edwards and Dr. Amitai Etzioni.

Many other friends and colleagues assisted in ways large and small, among them: Jennifer Balch, Gadi Ben-Yahuda, Allison Binder, David Brock, Teresa Byrne, Margaret Clancy, Andy Cohen, Lara Cox, Anja Dalgaard-Nielsen, Tammy Daub, Nicole Devero, Tom Doyle and the Jam Crew (Z., Jamie, Michael, Jay), Kevin Downey, Aaron Fein, Jock Friedly and Deborah Gist, Pauline Gerson, Melissa Goldstein, Jolle Greenleaf, Sheryl Grossman, Phil and Sarah Guire, Mitch Herr, Jennifer Jenkins, Jed• Hakken, Kristin Karmon, Tovah LaDier, Edward Lazarus, Jamie Levitt, Michael Lippman, Julie Lynn, Joanne Mariner, Fergus McCormick, Brad Meltzer, Steve Nemeth, Michael O'Connor, Paul Oetken, Rusty O'Kelley, Wendy Patten, Andrew Patzman and Michele Rivard, Hank Pollack, Judy Rabinovitz, Ellen Ratner, Alan Rautbort, Heidi Ruffler, Deborah Schneider, Tamar Schoenberg, Whitney Scott, Jeff Shesol, David Solomon, Rudi Stern, Jan Vulevich, Liza Wachter, Julie Warner, Rich Waryn, Steve Waters, Joe Weisberg, Alcaz', Jerry, Michael, Mike, Peter, and Bill. Thank you all.

INDEX

Constitution, U.S.:
  Article III of, 7–8
  First Amendment of, 37–38, 39, 46,
    58–59, 70–71, 76–77, 83, 84, 99, 104,
    107–8, 110–11, 112, 121, 158–59
  Fifth Amendment of, 111
  immigration and refugee rights under,
    38, 107, 108
  jury trials and, 217
contras, Nicaraguan, 28
Coons, Chris, 55
Cornell University, South Africa
  divestment struggles at, 9–10
Cuba:
  Haitian refugees and, 114, 257, 258
  refugees from, 200, 213, 237
  see also Guantánamo Bay

Daniel (Pascal's son), 2, 3, 15, 22, 189,
  203, 228, 297
Daugaard, Lisa, 9–13, 27–28, 127, 128,
  143–44, 185, 199, 281–82, 302–3
  at ACLU, 127, 150, 164, 170, 243–44
  activism of, 9–11, 29, 30, 33, 170, 183,
    184
  Baker and, 17, 18, 19
  and Bulkeley hunger strike, 201, 204,
    206–7, 208, 209
  Haitian Centers Council and, 28, 29,
    32–35, 38–39, 40, 41, 42, 46, 48–49,
    50, 53–55, 56, 57–59, 62, 65, 70, 72,
    75–76, 80–81, 82, 88, 108, 114, 116,
    117, 118, 126, 127, 130–31, 143,
    150–51, 158, 188–89, 194, 217–18,
    226, 231, 236, 243–44, 245–46, 251,
    256, 261, 286, 287, 299, 303
  and pro-refugee demonstrations,
    239–40, 264–65
  Ratner and, 10–11
  refugee interviews conducted by, 162,
    164–66, 167, 169–70, 171–72, 201, 281
Days, Drew, 179
DeLay, Tom, 290
Dellinger, Walter, 178, 190, 288
Demme, Jonathan, 264, 265
Democratic party, election of 1992 and,
  135, 143, 149, 163, 172, 175–77

Dillman, Jason, 239, 270–71
direct return order (1992), 129–31,
  134–36, 143, 187, 188
  and Article 33 and Refugee Act (1980),
    130, 134, 136, 138–39, 143, 224, 225,
    227, 233–37
  as campaign issue (1992), 134–35, 143,
    149, 163, 188, 195, 215
  Clinton and, 179, 180, 185, 187, 194,
    195–97, 198, 199–200, 224, 227, 228,
    293–94, 298
  as floating Berlin Wall, 136, 233
  refugees as potential victims of,
    226–27
  see also Haitian Centers Council v. Mc-
    Nary (Sale); Haitian refugees, forced
    repatriation of
District Court, U.S., for Eastern District
  of New York:
  Haitian Centers Council and, 47–48, 55,
    61, 63–64, 65, 66, 68, 69, 71–72, 75,
    77, 90, 104, 109, 242, 249–51, 259,
    260, 265–67, 268–69
  random selection of judges in, 48, 63,
    64–66, 68
District Court, U.S., for Northern District of California, 47
District Court, U.S., for Southern District of New York, 48
Doctors of the World, 209
Dominican Republic, Haitian refugees in,
  126, 138, 149, 190
due process, 121, 150–51, 158, 217, 245,
  286, 287, 298
Duke, Lynne, 144
Dunn, Scott, 60–61, 63–64, 65, 66, 68,
  69, 71–72, 75, 77, 90, 104, 259,
  268–69
Duvalier, "Baby Doc," 18
Duvalier, François, regime of, 11

Eagleburger, Lawrence, 128
Ebert, Allan, 258, 261, 263
Edney, Leon, 120
Edouard, Wilson, 132–33, 159, 162, 163
Effler, Paul, 120, 166
election of 1992, Haitian refugee issue in,

AUTHOR Q AND A

Since the publication of *Storming the Court,* I have spoken across the country about both the lawsuit to free the Haitian refugees and how it relates to the current situation at Guantánamo Bay. The book seems to have touched a nerve, especially with students and with Americans concerned about our government's use of Guantánamo to detain terrorist suspects after September 11. But—as I had always hoped—readers also seem taken with the story itself and often want to know more about the people portrayed in the book. And whether the subject is the fate of the characters or a bigger-picture issue, such as what the United States should do about Guantánamo today, I've found that audiences tend to ask many of the same questions. In hopes of initiating further discussion, I've tried to address several of the most common of those questions here.*

What happened to Yvonne Pascal?

Yvonne Pascal lives outside of New York City and works full time as an aide at a nursing home. It is a difficult job, with a long commute and late hours. But along with her small paycheck, she receives medical insurance to pay for the antiretroviral therapy that keeps her in relatively good health. Though Yvonne still has fears about her condition, she prays for strength and tells herself there is much to live for: some years ago, she met an older Haitian American man who works at an auto-supply company, and they now have a healthy six-year-old girl—the light of Yvonne's life.

Yvonne's two sons, Daniel and Jacques, both graduated from public high school in Queens. Fluent in English and immersed in American cul-

---

* For additional information about *Storming the Court* and a schedule of speaking engagements, please visit www.stormingthecourt.com.

ture, the two children from Cite Soleil now look and sound like native New Yorkers. Jacques, the younger son and a talented basketball player, recently finished his freshman year at a community college not far from Manhattan. Daniel, to the dismay of his mother, enlisted in the Marines in 2002. His family was inconsolable when he left for Iraq in early 2005, but he completed his tour of duty unharmed and returned to civilian life after an honorable discharge in the summer of 2006.

Despite her many worries, Yvonne feels more secure in the United States than she did in Haiti. But her life here has been a constant struggle, in large part due to the INS, now known as Citizenship and Immigration Services, or CIS. Though her lawyer, former Yale student Ray Brescia, submitted endless filings for her, she never technically received asylum, and in 2003, a full decade after her arrival in New York, Yvonne was still not a legal permanent resident. Ray finally asked the office of Senator Charles Schumer to intervene at CIS on her behalf, yet even then, it took immigration officials two more years to resolve her status. She finally became a legal permanent resident in February 2005, and in 2010 she will be eligible to apply for U.S. citizenship.

While Yvonne no longer fears that CIS will force her to leave the country, her efforts to support her family and manage her illness continue to take their toll. In addition to ongoing bouts of depression, she suffered a minor stroke in early 2006, which her doctors attributed in part to extreme stress. On good days, she dreams of becoming a nurse, but while her English is now quite good, she has no time to take the preparatory courses for nursing school. And more than fifteen years after the triumph of President Aristide's first election, Yvonne's youthful idealism is long gone. She never thinks about Haitian politics now, and when President Aristide was ousted for a second time in the coup of February 2004, she simply shrugged, convinced that her former hero was not the savior she'd once believed him to be.

What about the other Haitians held on Guantánamo?

Although no single refugee advocacy group knows the location and health status of all the Guantánamo Haitians, most of the surviving refugees reside in either the New York City or Miami metropolitan area. They work as taxi drivers, construction workers, caterers, nursing home aides, and, in one or two cases, musicians. Some are college graduates, and most have become legal permanent residents. Almost all want to remain anonymous, in part because they wish to keep their medical condition private. Those faring the best, not surprisingly, seem to be the children, most of whom are HIV negative and recall Guantánamo with far less clarity or bitterness than the adults.

Advocates in the Haitian community estimate that as of mid-2006, about half of the Bulkeley refugees had died of AIDS. This group includes two of the refugees whom I interviewed at length for the book, Vilsaint Michel, the former camp president at Bulkeley, and Dallard Jean-Louis, whose name does not appear in the text. In 2003, Vilsaint succumbed to kidney-related complications in Miami, where he had founded a small nonprofit organization that resettles Haitian refugees. Dallard died of cryptococcal meningitis in July 2004 in Brooklyn. A slight man with an easy smile, he spoke excellent English and was instrumental in helping me locate several other Bulkeley Haitians in New York City.

And the members of the Yale team?
A majority of the Yale students most deeply involved in the Haitian case today work in the public interest or academia. Tory Clawson and her husband and two sons stayed in Nepal even after the king seized power from the democratic government in February 2005, and she continues her efforts there on behalf of Save the Children. Lisa Daugaard and Bro Broberg remain in Seattle with their young daughter, Lucy; Lisa is still with the public defender's office in Seattle, and Bro is a criminal appeals attorney. Mike Wishnie recently accepted an offer to move from NYU back to Yale Law School, where he will be a clinical professor of law, focusing on the rights of immigrants and workers.

Ray Brescia directs a community development project at the Urban Justice Center in Manhattan and teaches legal ethics at New York Law School. Michelle Anderson was recently named dean of CUNY Law School in Flushing, New York, and specializes in sexual-assault law. Michael Barr is a law professor at the University of Michigan, where his research includes efforts to improve financial services for low-income households. Graham Boyd runs the ACLU's Drug Law Reform Project in Santa Cruz, California, and has argued a case before the United States Supreme Court.

Sarah Cleveland, an international law professor at the University of Texas, will be a visiting professor at Harvard in the fall of 2006. Paul Sonn, an attorney at the Brennan Center for Justice at New York University, is a leader in the campaign to establish higher minimum-wage laws. Steve Roos is a partner at a private law firm in Seattle, where he works on land-use and real estate matters. Laura Ho is a partner at a private firm in Oakland, California, that specializes in civil rights and employment-discrimination litigation. Adam Gutride founded a two-person law firm that focuses on false-advertising cases; he also works for a group that promotes peace and respect between Israelis and Palestinians.

Harold Koh became dean of Yale Law School in 2004. Although his focus remains human rights, he still teaches civil procedure to first-year students. He continues to speak out against Guantánamo, often appearing in the media to urge that the current Bush administration shut down its detention facility there.

What significance does the Haitian case have for Guantánamo today?

As the Epilogue suggests, the lawsuit to free the Haitians anticipated by a decade the current debate over the use of Guantánamo as an extralegal prison in the "War on Terror." Indeed, the Haitian case can be seen as a cautionary tale about Guantánamo—a tale that the current Bush administration has ignored at great cost to the nation. According to this view, what the Haitian litigation should have taught us is that when the White House runs an extralegal prison camp beyond American borders, in secret and without accountability, the consequences can be disastrous. Innocent people may suffer. We undermine our most fundamental values, from individual freedom to the rule of law. And we compromise the moral leadership that is so critical to our foreign policy.

Many people now believe, of course, that the Bush administration's handling of the terrorist suspects on Guantánamo has led to all those problems and more. True, it might be said that this charge ignores a key difference between the Haitians and the current detainees: the Haitians were not hell-bent on killing Americans. Yet there now turns out to be little incriminating evidence against many post-9/11 detainees, and the U.S. government has openly admitted that some of those held on Guantánamo have done nothing wrong. Factor in the abuse and possible torture of prisoners (as well as three detainee suicides), and the record looks worse—much worse, in fact—than it did in 1992 and 1993. The detention facility at Guantánamo has alienated even the closest of U.S. allies, become a rallying cry for jihadists, and put American troops at further risk wherever they are captured. In short, rather than making Americans safer in the "War on Terror," Guantánamo seems to have done just the opposite. Even President Bush now says he wants to see it closed down.

Why, then, has the current White House paid so little heed to the Haitian case? The short answer is that it didn't have to because the case wasn't binding legal authority. As described in Chapter 11, Judge Johnson's 1993 decision applying due process to Guantánamo was vacated, or wiped off the books, as part of Yale's final settlement with the Clinton administration. In December 2001, Bush administration lawyers relied on that fact when they advised the White House that terrorist suspects could be held on Guantánamo indefinitely and without access to the courts.* Moreover, Judge Johnson serves on a district court—the lowest rung of the federal court system—so no higher court would have been bound by his decision even if it were still good law. (Indeed, while lawyers for the current detainees decided to mention Johnson's vacated decision in some of their arguments, the federal appellate courts essentially ignored it.)

Yet, as the Epilogue emphasizes, when the question of the post-9/11 detainees' right to challenge their indefinite confinement finally reached the Supreme Court in the 2004 case of *Rasul v. Bush,* the court seemed to agree with Judge Johnson that United States law does indeed apply to foreigners on Guantánamo. And while there are important legal differences between the Haitian case and the *Rasul* case, the essence of *Rasul*—that no president can lock people away on Guantánamo without answering to a federal court—is very much in keeping with Judge Johnson's decision.

That, however, is not the end of the story. The litigation over Guantánamo continues, and as of this printing, there have been two critical new developments.

First, in the fall of 2005, Congress passed the Detainee Treatment Act, and despite his initial opposition, President Bush signed it into law. Enacted largely due to the efforts of Senator John McCain—who was a prisoner of war for over five years in Vietnam—the law bans cruel and degrading treatment of detainees in United States custody at Guantánamo

---

*The Justice Department's December 2001 legal memorandum about Guantánamo is widely available on the Internet, including at www.stormingthecourt.com under "Special Features." The memo's coauthor was former Justice Department attorney John Yoo, who also helped draft the so-called torture memo of August 2002. Yoo, ironically, was a Harold Koh protégé and member of the Yale Law School class of 1992, which also included Michael Barr, Graham Boyd, Ray Brescia, Sarah Cleveland, Lisa Daugaard (though she technically graduated later), Paul Sonn, and the author.

Bay and elsewhere around the world. But buried in the act was a p
that seemed to take away what the Supreme Court's *Rasul* decisio
earlier affirmed: the power of the federal courts to hear the deta
claims that they were illegally imprisoned. Human rights groups fe
that the Bush Justice Department would rely on this so-called jurisdicti
stripping provision to demand that the courts dismiss the nearly two hu
dred cases filed by Guantánamo detainees. Weeks after the law wa
passed, that is exactly what the Justice Department did.

This brings us to the second key development. In June 2006, the
Supreme Court again weighed in against the Bush administration, ruling
in *Hamdan v. Rumsfeld* that the Detainee Treatment Act did *not* foreclose
the court challenges filed by the detainees. The specific challenge by the
prisoner in *Hamdan* was directed not at the legality of his confinement,
but at the draconian military tribunals set up by the Bush administration
to try terrorist suspects at Guantánamo. The court struck down the tribunals and echoed Senator McCain's efforts by declaring that Common
Article 3 of the Geneva Conventions, which prohibits torture and cruel
and degrading treatment, protected all Guantánamo detainees—including
members of al Qaeda. In the *New York Times,* Harold Koh called the ruling "a stunning rejection" of President Bush's antiterror strategy, and
Michael Ratner, who had endured hate mail and even death threats for
helping to file the first post-9/11 Guantánamo case, added, "It doesn't get
any better."

Some observers believed the Supreme Court's *Hamdan* ruling would
hasten the day when the Bush administration closes the detention facility
at Guantánamo for good. But while hundreds of detainees have been
sent to their home countries in the last two years, the White House has
announced no plan to shut Guantánamo down. While the prisoners who
are still held there may now proceed to challenge their detention, the
Supreme Court has pointedly left undecided the ultimate question—
whether the government may indeed detain them at Guantánamo Bay
until the conclusion of a "War on Terror" that may never end. And so,
more than fourteen years after Yale first went to court on behalf of the
Haitian refugees held at Camp Bulkeley, the legal battle over Guantánamo drags on.